Laureate Dong's *Story of the Western Wing*

Laureate Dong's *Story of the Western Wing*

Passion and Desire in a Temple for Universal Salvation

Stephen H. West

OXFORD
UNIVERSITY PRESS

OXFORD
UNIVERSITY PRESS

Oxford University Press is a department of the University of Oxford.
It furthers the University's objective of excellence in research, scholarship,
and education by publishing worldwide. Oxford is a registered trade mark of
Oxford University Press in the UK and in certain other countries.

Published in the United States of America by Oxford University Press
198 Madison Avenue, New York, NY 10016, United States of America.

Library of Congress Control Number is on file at the Library of Congress.

ISBN 978-0-19-758359-3

Printed by Sheridan Books, Inc., United States of America.

The manufacturer's authorised representative in the EU for product safety is
Oxford University Press España S.A. of El Parque Empresarial San Fernando de
Henares, Avenida de Castilla, 2 – 28830 Madrid (www.oup.es/en or
product.safety@oup.com). OUP España S.A. also acts as importer into
Spain of products made by the manufacturer.

Contents

Acknowledgments

I would like to thank those who have aided me through the preparation of this book. First, a heavy debt of gratitude to my wife, Joanne Tsao, for her critical eye, her help in solving problems in the text, her support while writing, and her presence in my life. I would also like to thank He Yuming, Robert Ashmore, Ling Xiaoqiao, and particularly Wilt L. Idema. They have been a critical and thoughtful presence during the compilation of this book

Secondly, I would like to express my appreciation for the extraordinarily patient and helpful guidance of the members of the Hsu-Tang editorial team: Stefan Vranka, Wiebke Denecke, Lucas Klein, and Eleanor Goodman for their editorial insights, and Isabella Furth for careful reading of and suggestions for changes to the draft manuscript.

Stephen H. West
Tempe, AZ
December 30, 2024

Table of Dynasties

SHANG ca. 1300–1046 BCE

ZHOU ca. 1046–256 BCE
   Western Zhou ca. 1046–771 BCE
   Eastern Zhou 770–256 BCE
   Spring and Autumn 770–481 BCE
   Warring States 481–221 BCE

QIN 221–207 BCE

HAN 206 BCE–220 CE
   Western Han 206 BCE–8 CE
   Eastern Han 25–220

THREE KINGDOMS
   Wei 220–266
   Shu-Han 221–263
   Wu 222–280

WESTERN JIN 266–316

EASTERN JIN 317–420

NORTHERN AND SOUTHERN DYNASTIES 420–589

SUI 581–618

TANG 618–907

FIVE DYNASTIES 907–960

SONG 960–1279
   Northern Song 960–1127
   Southern Song 1127–1279

LIAO 916–1125

JIN 1115–1234

YUAN 1271–1368

MING 1368–1644

QING 1636–1911

Introduction

Laureate Dong's Story of the Western Wing (*Dong Jieyuan Xixiang ji zhu-gongdiao* 董解元西廂記諸宮調; DJY) is a musical ballad that first appeared in the Jin Dynasty in the twelfth century in the Northern part of what is now called China. While in the west, we use only two musical modes (major and minor), the ballad uses fourteen different modes by which to arrange some 130 individual song titles for the 454 songs of its 195 suites. By virtue of this musical panoply, Laureate Dong took his place in a line of authors and in the development of texts that spanned a nearly five-hundred year period from an original Tang dynasty short story, "The Tale of Oriole" ("Yingying zhuan" 鶯鶯傳), to the late Yuan or early Ming twenty-act play, *Story of the Western Wing*.[1] In his "Critical Introduction" to S. I. Hsiung's translation of this play, the late Professor C. T. Hsia (1921–2013) described the play's direct source, *Laureate Dong's Story of the Western Wing*, as "without doubt the greatest narrative poem in the Chinese language. . . . Certainly, no previous Chinese author has ever caught the changeable states of a young man in love, by turns enraptured and dejected, tender and silly, with as much precision in such a copious volume of impassioned verse."[2]

This young man in love, Zhang Junrui 張君瑞, originally sets out on a journey to find an appropriate teacher to help him in his studies for the imperial civil service examination, held triennially in the Tang capital of Chang'an. He leaves the capital for a short journey along a postal road that runs along the Wei River to the east, crosses that river to the north, and then heads west, only to cross again into Henan. We enter the story when he has reached the first major city (called "a prefecture" in the text) after crossing the bridge over the Yellow River. Bored in his inn in Puzhou 蒲州, he asks about beautiful sights to see, and the innkeeper guides him to the Monastery of Universal Salvation (Pujiu si 普救寺), several miles away.

---

1 Also known as "Story of Meeting a True Goddess" ("Huizhen ji" 會真記), written by the Tang author Yuan Zhen 元稹 (779–831).

2 Hsia 1968.

Here, in the fictive space of a Buddhist monastery, unfolds one of the most beloved love stories in Chinese literature. The twenty-two-year-old[3] Zhang sees a girl six years his junior emerge from a courtyard's vermilion doors, and he is smitten by desire at first sight of Oriole 鶯鶯 whom he will pursue, win, and finally marry over roughly a three-year period set during 801 to 803. They are surrounded by a cast of others including the girl's overbearing mother, the rather cold and calculating Madam Zheng 鄭夫人, wife of the deceased Prime Minister Cui 崔相國 (hence referred to throughout as Madam Cui); the Grand Master and abbot of the Monastery of Universal Salvation, Dharma Source 法本; a fierce acolyte named Dharma Wit 法聰 who befriends the young student; a bandit called Flying Tiger Sun 孫飛虎; and Du Que 杜確, the valiant White Horse General who not only relieves the bandits' siege of the monastery, but also makes the marriage possible by forcing the death of an ugly and boorish rival for Oriole's hand, her maternal cousin, Zheng Heng 鄭恆.

Zhang pursues Oriole by writing her poetry and by playing his zither late into the night. Its plaintive strings arouse within Oriole a deep compassion for his failing body, afflicted as it is with lovesickness,[4] as well as instilling in her a sense that the springtime of her own life is quickly passing by. The desire, the lovesickness, and the match of a brilliant poet to a graceful and beautiful young girl are recognizable as one of the earlier extended iterations of the stories of "talented young men and beautiful women" (*caizi jiaren* 才子佳人) that populate the canonical texts of the colloquial tradition in the early modern through late imperial periods of Chinese literary history.

This long ballad is one of three, possibly four, song-ballads that are still extant. The earliest example is the *The Story of Liu Zhiyuan in All-Keys-and-Modes* (*Liu Zhiyuan zhugongdiao* 劉知遠諸宮調). A partial remnant of the ballad was unearthed in an early twentieth-century archeological excavation in the ancient city of Khara-Khoto in Gansu. What was left of the ballad was, along with other block prints originally from Shanxi, discovered by the Russian explorer Pytor Kuz'mich Kozlov (1863–1935). The text of that all-keys-and-modes unfortunately is only partially preserved,[5] but it is clearly one of the sources for the later drama,

---

3   I am using Western counts for years of age; Chinese culture begins the age count at birth.

4   Lovesickness is called "an illness of yearning" (*xiangsi bing* 相思病); it is also called a "ghostly illness" (*guibing* 鬼病) because the afflicted, unable to nourish or medicate himself or herself, grows more haggard every day.

5   There are twelve complete or partial chapters left; see Anon. 2005. It has been translated as *Ballad of the Hidden Dragon*; see Doleželová-Velingerová and Crump 1971.

The White Rabbit (*Baitu ji* 白兔記), about the rise of Liu Zhiyuan from a farmer to become the First Emperor (Han Gaozu 漢高祖) of the Later Han dynasty (947–951).[6] There are indications that this text was printed sometime before 1137.[7]

A second all-keys-and-modes is called *The Affairs of the Tianbao Reign in All-Keys-and-Modes* (*Tianbao yishi zhugongdiao* 天寶遺事諸宮調), and has been reassembled in various ways by various scholars from individual suites or songs preserved in a variety of music formularies published in the mid- and late Ming.[8] The ballad is based on a late Tang work, *The Affairs of the Tianbao Reign,* that chronicles the story of the aging Tang emperor Li Longji 李隆基 (685–762), better known to history as Emperor Xuanzong 唐玄宗 (r. 711–756), and his favorite consort, Yang Guifei 楊貴妃.[9] The story was beloved in the Song-Yuan era, the period in which *The Affairs of the Tianbao Reign in All-Keys-and-Modes* was performed. Yang Guifei's execution, the emperor's love, and his last years of despair after turning over his throne to his son have remained popular until the current moment, even making their way into modern television dramas. Two famous plays, *The Autumn Nights of the Lustrous Emperor: Rain on the Wutong Trees* (*Tang Minghuang qiuye wutong yu* 唐明皇秋夜梧桐雨) by the eminent Yuan dynasty writer Bai Pu 白樸 (byname Renfu 仁甫, 1226–post 1327) and *The Palace of Long Life* (*Changsheng dian* 長生殿) by the early Qing dynasty writer Hong Sheng 洪昇 (byname Fangsi 昉思, 1645–1704), have long captured the minds of readers.[10] These dramas, like the ballad, draw much of their inspiration from the themes and characterization in another Tang literary source, Bai Juyi's (白居易, byname Letian 樂天, 772–846) long poem "Song of Everlasting Regret" 長恨歌

A third all-keys-and-modes self-identifies itself as such: its short text is found in a prologue to the earliest known Chinese drama, *Top Scholar*

6   The other major source for the drama is a chapter on the Later Han Dynasty in *The History of the Five Dynasties in Plain Language* (*Wudai shi pinghua* 五代史平話). See Idema and West 2016, xviii–xix; Lu Shihua 2009, 93–102.

7   For instance, there are no sets of arias called "beguiling songs" (*zhuanci* 賺詞) in the *Liu Zhiyuan All-Keys-and-Mode*s. The "beguiling song" is noted as being created in 1137 and it becomes a staple suite in *Laureate Dong's Story of the Western Wing*; see Appendix 3.

8   For detailed information, see Fan Ben Chen 1990–1992, 2006; Liu Xiaomei 2018; and Wu Runting 2023.

9   Yang Guifei 楊貴妃 means "Valued Consort Yang." Her actual name was Yang Yuhuan 楊玉環 (719–756). She was a young consort whom the aging monarch had purloined from his younger son. For a translation of *The Autumn Nights of the Lustrous Emperor: Rain on the Wutong Trees,* see West and Idema 2010, 105–183.

10 See Hong Sheng 1975 for the Chinese text. For two very loose translations into English see: Hong Sheng 1983; and Hong Sheng 2012.

Zhang Xie (*Zhang Xie zhuangyuan* 張協狀元). A translation of this very short all-keys-and-modes is found in Appendix Four. While this may simply be a parody of an all-keys-and-modes, it still holds interest because of its use of the metrical structure and format of the all-keys-and-modes.

Laureate Dong, the Author of *The Story of the Western Wing in All-Keys-and-Modes*

Little is known about the author of the fourth text, translated here. Even his name provides no more than a surname, Dong (董), and a form of address, *jieyuan* (解元), that literally meant the top graduate in a provincial examination, which I have taken the liberty of translating as "laureate." Implicit in the term, perhaps, is the idea of a person who has performed well in the examinations centered on the classics and *belles lettres* for recruitment into the civil bureaucracy, but only to the provincial level, perhaps one who did not sit for or did not pass the highest examination, the "advanced scholar" held triennially in the capital.

What little information we have for Dong Jieyuan comes from two records. In his *Register of Ghosts*, Zhong Sicheng 鍾嗣成 (ca.1279–1360, byname Jixian 繼先) lists Dong first in the first section, "Those Deceased Famous Writers of Previous Generations Who Have Musical Verses Circulating in the World." There, he simply remarks, "A man of the time of Emperor Zhang of the Jin (r. 1190–1208). Since he was the one who began it all, I have therefore listed him at the head."[11] The same approximate dates for Dong Jieyuan are also given in Tao Zongyi's 陶宗儀 (1322–1403, byname Jiucheng 九成) *Nancun's Records from a Break in Plowing*, (*Nancun Chuogeng lu* 南村輟耕錄): "The *Story of the Western Wing* was compiled by Laureate Dong not long in the past, still there are now rarely those who can understand it."[12]

Information is a little more fleshed out in a later preface to Zhong's work by Jia Zhongming 賈仲明 (1343–1422), written to accompany his own supplement:

> My interest spurred by a rain-spattered window, I began to look over the *Register of Ghosts* by the former high talent of Yimen [Kaifeng], Mr. Zhong Sicheng. . .who compiled into his register some 150 personages beginning with Mister Laureate Dong at the beginning of the Jin and Guan Hanqing at the early Yuan. Before

---

11   Wang Gang 1991, 5. The *Register* bears a preface dated December 31, 1330.
12   Tao Zongyi 1958, 332, preface to this record is dated to 1366.

Zhong's time, people like Laureate Dong, some forty-four personages, were all. . .[high officials].[13]

Little more is known about Dong Jieyuan, but his ballad marked a new era in the development of the all-keys-and-modes and of performance literature in general. It certainly set the stage musically for the structure of Yuan drama, which retained the musical suites first found in the ballad, along with a single singer for one play. As Li Xiusheng remarks:

> Chinese popular literature developed rapidly until it reached the Song dynasty, and in the last years of the Song and in the Jin, popular literature became the new master of the literary covenant. The one representative work that signals their advent is the *All-Keys-and-Modes Ballad of the Story of the Western Wing* by Dong Jieyuan . . . who was the creator of "popular songs" [*sanqu*散曲] as northern songs [*beiqu* 北曲].[14]

The fourth narrative ballad and the substance of this book, *Laureate Dong's Story of the Western Wing*, is ascribed to this Dong Jieyuan. It directly adapts a good portion of its story and much near-verbatim wording from the classical language "Tale of Oriole," which was written by the ninth-century author Yuan Zhen 元稹 (779–831, byname Weizhi 微之).[15] The story is adapted in the ballad, but undergoes significant changes. For instance, while the lovers part from each other in the tale, they wind up together in the ballad. This kind of adaptation was not unusual, since the story was rewritten in many forms as early as the Song dynasty, with many of its adaptations closely tied to Su Shi 蘇軾 (1037–1101, byname Zichan 子瞻), perhaps the most eminent writer in the Song period, and his circle of younger friends.[16] Su Shi himself wrote several lyric poems (*ci* 詞) using the story of "The Tale of Oriole," including for instance "Flowers in the Rain; Slow Mode" 雨中花慢.

Somewhere, in doubled curtains in the sequestered courtyard—
    one stirred to fullness of passion
        sorrowfully facing the shifting light of nature's scene.

---

13 Wang Gang 1991, 127. This record was written around September 1, 1422.
14 Li Xiusheng 1994, 70.
15 For translations of this tale, see Hightower 1973 or Owen 1995, 540–549.
16 For his friends, see Huang Dongbo 1995.

Arising from sleep, still feeling the wine, flowers fall away,
    butterflies go wild, bees are busy as can be.
Who, tonight
    will play the mouth organ on the northern ridge[17]
        or "wait for the moon by the western wing?"
Where I look with vain regret
    is only a single red apricot tree
        its branches lying over a short wall.[18]

Here Su Shi conflates his references: to the famous lovers and musi-cians Xiao Shi and Nongyu, and more generally to a woman like Oriole, waiting for her lover in the western wing. The red apricot and short wall also refer to a famous scene found in nearly all renditions of the story in later ballad and drama, in which Student Zhang climbs over the wall for a tryst with Oriole.[19]

Su's younger colleagues also wrote several lyric poems to the tune "The Teasing Song" 調笑令, each accompanied by a classical old-style poem (古詩). These were meant to accompany a troupe dance perfor-mance. Perhaps the most famous is one by Qin Guan 秦觀 (1049–1101, byname Shaoyou 少遊), in which Oriole is listed among twelve famous beauties. His poem and song read:

The Poem:

The Cui family had a daughter by the name of Oriole,
Still unaware of spring's luster, but already full of passion.
Soldiers rebelled at the Yellow River bridge, then pressed around
    the Buddhist Temple:
Grieving for red, feeling misery for green—she spied Student
    Zhang.
As soon as he saw her his spring passion weighed, ever more
    intense—

---

17 An ancient myth about two lovers, Xiao Shi 蕭史 and Nongyu 弄玉. Xiao Shi was a master of the pipes, able to summon peacocks and cranes to the courtyard with his music. Nongyu, one of the daughters of Duke Mu of Qin 秦穆公 (?705–621 BCE; reigned 659–621 BCE), fell in love with him, and he took her as a wife. After a period of time, they flew off through the clouds with the phoenixes.

18 Su Shi 2010, vol. 9, 749–751. "Bees and butterflies" is a metaphor for the busy flights of matchmakers between young women (flowers, honey) and possible paramours.

19 See suites III.14 to III.18.

Climbing over the wall in the bright moonlight, flowers and trees
    shook.
Crimson bundled the girl to Zhang at midnight and
There deep feeling startled his soul as though it were a spring
    dream.

The Song:

A spring dream
In the grotto of divine transcendent ones.
Lacking strength he climbed the wall; flowers and trees quivered.[20]
Waiting for the moon by the western wing, who was to accompany
    her?
She was even more aware of the weight of the Jade One's passion—
In the depths of the night Crimson brought the clouds to him;[21]
Worn out, tired, hairpins lay across her phoenix headdress.[22]

In these poems one can sense a change in writers' attitudes towards
Student Zhang in particular, who is presented here as a person lacking
true feeling, bent only on sexual conquest. While this group wrote mainly
to the tune "The Teasing Song," one of Su's younger colleagues, a member of the royal Zhao family of Song, Zhao Lingzhi 趙令畤 (1064–1134,
byname Delin 德麟),[23] made an intervention into the original story,
rewriting parts of it and larding it with ten stanzas to the lyric poem
formula "Butterflies Love the Flowers" 蝶戀花. Zhao's song lyrics not
only recapitulate the main scenes of the story, but also make critical
comments on each character. It is the first time we know of that the
original story of Oriole and Student Zhang was set to an extended musical performance. It is clear to see that the way in which Zhao divided
the story also set the selection and arrangement of scenes in both the
ballad as well as in the later drama.[24] This is an important work, and
I have included his rendition of the story of Oriole, interlarded with

---

20 The scene of barely making it over the wall is part of the popular lore of the story
    of the two lovers, a humorous sketch to poke fun at the student, and at the physical
    ineptitude of scholars in general.
21 From the euphemism of "clouds and rains" for sex.
22 When she had to leave the next morning. See Qin Guan 1985, 124, and Qin Guan
    2003. 294.
23 See Zhao Lingzhi 2000, 135–148.
24 See Lan Hui 2017, Luo Xiaoqian 2008, Wang Zuoliang 2004, Xu Dajun 2023, and Yu
    Tianchi 1999.

his songs, in Appendix One. The reader is encouraged to first read this appendix and Zhao's shortened version of Yuan Zhen's tale to become familiar with the outline of the original version before continuing.

It is quite remarkable that Dong's work would be so influential, yet he would remain so unknown to the world. This is partly because popular literature lay outside the circle that highly educated classes drew around the classics, literature, religious texts, and *belles-lettres*, a domain of texts associated only with high culture. While these literati may have themselves enjoyed popular literature at the time (or even written it), they did not consider it to be "real literature," but simply a form of entertainment. This all changed as the centuries wore on: by the late Ming, the period from which our surviving editions of *Laureate Dong's Story of the Western Wing* stem, there was increasing interest in dramatic texts, culminating in annotations such as those by Tang Xianzu, and particularly by Jin Shengtan (金聖嘆1608–1661), who altered parts of the *Story of the Western Wing* (*Xixiang ji* 西廂記) and wrote a brilliant annotation to produce the most widely read edition of the Yuan play. In this sense, the reappearance of *Laureate Dong's Story of the Western Wing* during the Ming and Qing reinforces the sense that classical and classically trained scholars in the late imperial period (after about 1400) had begun seeking older ballads and plays in local vernaculars as part of more unified literary heritage.

But in bibliographical practice it was still primarily works in the classical language that were included in library catalogs, creating lineages of classical texts of various genres from the early Han period. Laureate Dong and his work were simply not appropriate: his language and genre were both associated with urban popular culture or itinerant performers. Preservation (or non-preservation) came down to accident in the pre-Ming era. But later a new consciousness of the place of colloquial literature within Chinese literature began to develop. Despite the fact that many works on performance and music were written in the Ming and Qing dynasties, not one text touched upon the history of vernacular performance literature, or even classical Chinese literature, until the late nineteenth and early twentieth centuries, when Russian and Japanese scholars wrote the first histories of Chinese literature.[25] Living in Japan at this time was the young Chinese polymath, Wang Guowei 王國維 (1877–1927), who was inspired by the Japanese histories of Chinese

---

25 See Denecke 2023, 219–220.

literature to write the first history of Chinese vernacular performance literature, *A History of Song and Yuan Drama* (*Song Yuan xiqushi* 宋元戲曲史). It was thus the first academic work to treat the all-keys-and-modes as the precursor of northern drama (called *yuanqu* 元曲 or *beiqu* 北曲) in the Yuan.[26]

We have only a few references to Laureate Dong's ballad beyond this point, scattered among works on Chinese performance literature, often simply repeating what one finds in *The Register of Ghosts*. Zhong Sicheng did mention Dong Jieyuan twice more, once giving the title of a lost play by Guan Hanqing entitled *Laureate Dong Flees the Pavilion of Willow Withes* (*Dong Jieyuan zou liusi ting* 董解元走柳絲亭), and again in the section of his *Register* entitled "Deceased Talented Ones with Whom I Was Not Acquainted," where he discusses a person called Hu Zhengchen:

> Hu Zhengchen was a man of Hangzhou and was a good friend of Zhifu and Cunfu. [27] He could sing the entirety of Dong Jieyuan's *Story of the Western Wing* from the opening lines to the very end. He knew all the old musical poems [*yuefu* 樂府], the "drawn-out musical song lyric" [*manchang ci* 慢唱詞], and Li Shuangya's [李霜涯 ca. 1250–1280] beguiling songs. He has been dead for some thirty years.[28]

This anecdote is later discussed in the *Pen Notes from the Grass Hut of Beautiful Flowers* (*Meihua caotang ji* 梅花草堂集) by the dramatist Zhang Dafu 長大復 (1544–1630):

> There has been no complete copy of Dong Jieyuan's *Western Wing* in the Wu area for the past one hundred years. Wen Peng [文彭 1489–1573, byname Shoucheng 壽承] got a complete copy from the West Mountain Wang family [西山汪氏], but it was missing the beginning and end sections. Later, He Liangjun [何良俊 1506–1573, byname Tuohu 拓湖] obtained a complete copy from Yang Xunji [楊循吉 1458–1546, byname Nanfeng 南峰] and the three afficionados from Wu each made one [full] copy. Several years

---

26 See Wang Guowei 1915, 45–65.

27 Zhifu (Chen Yiren 陳以人 (n.d.)) and Cunfu (Jin Renjie 金仁傑 (d. 1329)) were both dramatists. Jin had been a close friend of Zhong Sicheng for some twenty years, so this story must have come to Zhong from his friend.

28 Wang Gang 1991, 84–85.

later Yuan Hongdao [袁宏道 1568–1610, byname Shigong 石公] was a magistrate of Wu, and he really loved this work, calling it "a book to keep on the desk." From that point onward this work was even more famous.[29]

Performance of the All-Keys-and-Modes

Zhang Dafu goes on in his short note to discuss performance at a seventeenth century gathering, in which songs or perhaps suites in the all-keys-and-modes were performed in a round-robin:

> My father once told me, "When I was very young, I saw a performance at Minister of War Lu's house, where one person performed the ballad on strings, several others sat in a circle, each taking a section to sing in turn. This was called millwheel singing. Sire Lu was deeply involved with song and dance, but after this one episode there were no more. Zhao Changbai [趙長白 late. 16th c.) said, "It is not true that it is sung by one person."[30]

The earliest comment that we have on how this ballad was performed comes from a 1274 description of life in Hangzhou. The section devoted to "Sing-Song Girl Music" (*jinü yue* 妓女樂) describes the performance thusly:

> Singing and narrating the all-keys-and-modes: Formerly, in the [Northern Song] capital of Bianliang there was a certain Kong Sanzhuan [Three Commentaries Kong 孔三傳], who compiled romantic stories and stories of spirits and monsters, and set them in music lyric [*qu* 曲] form for recitation and singing. Currently in Hang[zhou] city there are the female performers Xiong Bao-bao and later generations of young girls who all imitate her. Their singing and recitation are also highly skilled. The performance is identical to [story recitations or music] set to clapper beats.[31]

The term used here for Kong Sanzhuan's creating the all-keys-and-modes is *biancheng* 編成, which is best understood as "to compile extant items"; that is, to adapt other kinds of musical performance and storytelling.

---

29 Zhang Dafu 1986, 3.9b–10a. Also in Jiao Xun 1959, 104.
30 Zhang Dafu 1986 and Jiao Xun 1959, 104.
31 Wu Zimu 2000, 289.

Kong was probably one of a corporate body of performers and writers that created this musical form over time, in different spaces, and in different places. Since authorial identity was usually not a concern in early performance literature—except when a (real or purloined) name was assigned to a work to give it an air of authority—perhaps we should best understand the practice as bringing a story or stories together to set them in a different generic form. Just, in fact, as Dong Jieyuan did with material floating around about Oriole and Student Zhang.

Although earlier compilers and performers all have male names, in Hangzhou, the capital of the Southern Song, the performance of all-keys-and-modes seems to be primarily linked to female performers. This indicates that they were a part of a vibrant entertainment-prostitution complex, in which the quality of a songstress's voice would ideally be matched with physical beauty. In a later text about Hangzhou, it is clear this practice continued.[32] These same female entertainers would have performed in urban spaces and, on special command, in the royal palace.

A more detailed look occurs in a passage from the fiftieth episode of the early sixteenth century novel *Water Margin* 水滸傳, which describes a performance of the all-keys-and-modes by an itinerant performer. This episode clearly depicts what the capital journals of Hangzhou intimate, but leave unspoken, namely that the ballad was performed by a single singer:

> Lei Heng . . . went off with Little Li Two to the theater. Banners with gold characters hanging over the door were the first thing to meet his eyes, and there were body-sized banderole suspended from staffs. He went into the theater and took the "black dragon head," the best seat in the house, where he sat down. Looking at the stage, he saw they were doing a funny farce skit . . . . Then, when the sound of the gong was heard, Bai Xiuying had already ascended the stage, where she greeted the entire audience . . . . She proceeded to narrate an introduction and then sang; then narrated after singing. The whole audience, standing and sitting, let out shouts of admiration . . . .When she sang to a suspenseful point in the piece, Bai Yuqiao put a damper on the audience's shouts, and said, "Although we don't have a talent sufficient to earn enough money to purchase a horse, still we would like to urge all of you talented and knowledgeable men. All your shouts of appreciation are past, so now come down for a bit, my child, for this skit is 'Filling up the Drum.'"[33]

32 See Zhou Mi 2007, 185.
33 That is, probably collecting money in an upside down drum.

These moments of suspense where texts pause also occur frequently in our all-keys-and-modes ballad; sometimes they are simple rhetorical questions, like, "And who was it? Who? It was Crimson," or the text simply inserts two characters yun_{yun} (云云) indicating a point at which the performer can ad-lib or halt the performance to take a collection. I have identified these moments of suspense in the translation and noted them in the footnotes.

Musical Features

The all-keys-and-modes ballad, Long Jianguo says,

> is an artistic whole that is an amalgam of many modal suites. And the transition between the song suites is usually comprised of spoken text. That is to say, the pitch and tonality of each mode was different, so the suites were not suitable for singing one after the other. After singing the last aria in one mode, the performer would then enact a spoken passage or perhaps intersperse a poem before singing the next aria in a different mode.[34]

"A mode," as explained succinctly by Regina Llamas, "is a musical term that indicates the pitch on which a basic scale is constructed."[35]

The number of possible modes used at any time and with any kind of music varies, but there will be at most twenty-eight possible combinations. In the case of *Laureate Dong's Story of the Western Wing*, only fourteen different modes are used. It is a general rule that the arias are interspersed with spoken text, but there are cases in which no spoken text intervenes between songs.[36]

The genre did not create new forms of music but adopted both lyrical poems that had been in use since the mid-Tang as well as then-circulating popular songs. It combined what are called "performative lyrics" (*quzi ci* 曲子詞, individual lyrics meant to be set to music) with extant metrical and musical structures, weaving these songs into a long narrative. For instance, individual songs in the all-keys-and-modes use the same metrical and tonal formulary (*cipai* 詞牌) as lyrical poetry: they are basically songs of two parallel (or closely parallel) stanzas and do not for the most part reflect the single-stanza patterns of later songs used in

34 Long Jianguo 2003b, 62.
35 Llamas 2021, 389 n. 32.
36 Long Jianguo 2003b, 68.

either northern or southern dramas. Northern and southern drama both adopted this later single-stanza form, arranging current or new songs into suites in which a single stanza could contain several tunes. Some longer suites of popular songs in *Laureate Dong's Story of the Western Wing* do represent a form of musical suite that was later adapted into drama (see below). The all-keys-and-modes appears to be a transitional genre that made free use of both literati lyric poetry of the Song and colloquial songs that were in circulation.

There are several features to note about the lyrics in this all-keys-and-modes. First, not every line of a poem will rhyme; secondly, not all end phrases of rhyme lines conclude a semantic sequence, and neither do they necessarily signify the end of a sentence, much like enjambment in English-language poetry. Chinese originally did not use punctuation, but was read in rhythmic cadence, pausing for aspiration after certain grammatical structures and rhyme lines.

While it may be impossible to capture the tonal aspect of individual words in a non-tonal language like English, in this translation, I have attempted to at least demonstrate how rhyme works by adopting the following principle: any sentence that begins flush left indicates that it is a new line in a song or one in which a preceding line has ended in a rhyme, hence, flush left sentences start a new rhyme line. Semantic meaning may carry across the line to all or part of the next rhymed line, and a new thought and sentence can also begin in the middle of a rhyme line.

In the all-keys-and-modes there are three basic suite arrangements, all of which usually include at least a designation of mode and the title of the formulary pattern. The first kind is simply a single song that does not have a coda (the coda, called a "tail" (*wei* 尾) or an "ending tail" (*shawei* 煞尾) is a song of three lines that normally ends the suite). This pattern accounts for forty-two of the 195 suites in Dong's *Story of the Western Wing*. Almost all of the lyric poem formulary patterns used in these suites are also common in lyric songs produced by literati in the Song-Yuan period.[37]

The second and most common arrangement is one song concluded by a coda. This pattern is the earliest and simplest form of suite-aria, and it accounts for ninety-four of the 195 suites. The attached coda seems to have originated with a separate musical form called the "beguiling songs," which included the "bound suite" (*chanling* 纏令) and the "bound repetition" (*chanda* 纏達). The earliest definitions of the bound suite are found in Song texts dating from the thirteenth century.[38] The coda

---

37 I am following the count of suites as given in Zhang Xuehuan 2020, 48–50.
38 See Appendix 1.

enhances the effect of the preceding song both musically and terms of the lyrics. Codas are old in Chinese music, going back to the pre-Han era, with the *Verses of Chu* (*Chuci* 楚辭), a collection of poems that includes the first long narrative poem, where the coda is called a *luan* 亂. In Tang and Song court music, the coda is simply known as an "ending" (*sha* 煞).

The beguiling suite seems to be the origin of the *wei*-coda, and it has strict stipulations about the number of lines in a song and how the clappers control the tempo of each song. There are two beguiling suites extant in a compendium of documents traced to the very end of the thirteenth century; the compendium stipulates that each coda should have three lines and that twelve beats of the clapper are used: four in the first line, five in the second, and three in the third. This three-line coda is retained in the all-keys-and-modes form, although it is sometimes doubled or trebled for effect.[39]

The third pattern is a suite of multiple songs (three or more) with a coda. There are fifty-nine bound suites in *Laureate Dong's Story of the Western Wing*, and thirty of these are clearly titled as "bound suites." All other references to the bound suite are from the thirteenth century and refer retrospectively to the bound suite and bound repetition as having been performed in the Northern Capital of the Song. The references to the bound suite from later times all refer to its "inelegant" or "lascivious nature." Shen Yifu's 沈義父 *Dispelling Doubts about Musical Literature* (*Yuefu zhimi* 樂府指迷) makes a distinction between performative lyrics and chanted lyric poems, which are no more than "classical poetry with long and short lines," that is, lacking any musical finesse:

> The sounds must be concordant with the mode. If not, then it is just classical poetry with long and short lines. In selecting words, one must be elegant; if not elegant, then it begins to resemble the nature of the bound suite. One cannot be too apparent when employing words; if too apparent it is too direct and lacks any deep and enduring flavor. One cannot be too high-flown; too high-flown, and it turns strange and eccentric and loses its gentle and tactful intent.[40]

Likewise, in his *Font of Lyric Poetry* (*Ciyuan* 詞源), Zhang Yan 張炎 (1248–1320) remarks:

---

39 The doubled codas are called either "complex endings" (*cuosha* 錯煞) or "continued endings" (*xusha* 緒煞); see for example suites IV.2 and IV.20. For an example of a trebled coda, see suite II.41.

40 Shen Yifu 1986, 277, following the notes of Cai Songyun in Shen Yifu 1981, 43.

For playing about with the moon and the wind[41] or pleasing one's emotions and feelings, the lyric poem is more tactful and gentle than classical poetry [*shi* 詩]. Its sounds emanate from the throats of orioles and tongues of swallows,[42] so it can be a little more truthful to the emotions. But if it falls into the neighborhood of the lascivious songs of Zheng and Wei, then it is no different than the bound suite.[43]

The bound repetition, the special form of a repetitive bound suite, does occur (although not labeled as such) in Dong's *Western Wing*, where there are repeats of songs, as in the long suite in which the tune "Woodpecker in the Flowers" 閒花啄木兒 is repeated eight times.[44]

The Language of the Text

There are basically three kinds of language used in the ballad translated here: vernacular, literary parallel prose, and classical poetry. The arias use a vernacular that stems from the Shanxi area and is clearly northern in nature. Its features include the use of resultative verbal compounds[45] that make verb phrases more lively, expressive of emotions, and show a clearer result of actions. This new vernacular introduced more aspect particles, more vernacular binomial expressions, and a collection of adjectives with two-word adverbial modifiers that help aestheticize emotional statements.[46]

As Zhang Haimei remarks, the audiences for all-keys-and-modes "were generally town folk, so its language had to approximate the spoken language of the people and maintain a simple and natural style; because its language was meant to be common and popular, its vernacular nature

---

41 That is, relating stories of love and seduction.

42 Here referring to courtesan-performers; that is, to the social place and level of the lyric poem's articulation as song.

43 Zheng and Wei are a reference to portions of the *Classic of Poetry* (*Shijing* 詩經) that are thought to be too direct in expressing sentiments of love or sexual congress. For the quote, see Zhang Yan 1981, 23.

44 See IV.31

45 Resultative compounds are a type of compound structure that consists of two verbs, where the second verb describes the resulting state or activity of the subject or object from the first verb's action.

46 For a binomial expression, see *"The Case of Unblemished Jade"* IV.18, for instance. For adverbial modifiers, see "Coda" in IV.4 in the accompanying Chinese text, I have left the adverbial modifiers for the most part as single words, since the repetition in English tends to make the meaning of the original seem trivial.

is very strong."[47] This northern dialect also introduced many new words into the lexicon of later colloquial text, and many of these words were retained in Yuan and Ming drama. They do not appear elsewhere in text and most of them faded from view when northern drama (*zaju* 雜劇) was supplanted by southern forms.

These dense vernacular arias are interspersed with spoken passages that are nearly verbatim quotes from the original "Tale of Oriole," citations of then-contemporary literati poetry about that tale, as well as newly composed classical poetry, colloquial dialogue, and long passages of parallel prose. Parallel prose, as the name suggests, is akin to free verse in English. It is usually made up of matching lines of four and six, or five and seven characters, usually carefully balanced by contrasting tonal pitch. This passage after the "Coda" of suite I.9 shows the characteristic form of descriptive parallel prose, in which position two and four in each line roughly contrast or match to create a distinct cadence in speech (○ ● represent level tone and oblique tone respectively):

●●●●	此寺蓋造	The construction of this monastery
○●●●	真是富貴:	was truly splendid:
●○○○●	搗椒紅泥壁,	Crushed fagara mudded the red walls,
○○○●○	雕花間玉梁;	carved flowers were spaced along jade rafters;
○○○●●	沈檀金四柱,	Aloeswood turned the four columns to gold,
●●○○○	玳瑁壓堦矼。	And tortoise shell was pressed into the stairs' treads.

Since parallel prose, like blank verse, is written in a regular meter, dictated by contrastive and complementary arrangements of tonal contours and is unrhymed, I have chosen to represent it as one would verse. For a fuller definition of parts of the text and how they are represented, see below in "Conventions."

47 Zhang Haimei 2014, 27.

Conventions

Names of Modes ARE SET IN LOWERCASE CAPITALS.
Titles of Songs *are italicized*.
Typefaces

Bold type: parts of the Chinese text marked with tailed-dots (、) in the original edition. These will often, but not always, be associated with the commentary found in the margin.

Italic type: parts of the Chinese text marked with circles (◦) in the original edition. These will often, but not always, be associated with the commentary found in the margin.

Sung text: As explained in the introduction, songs are written to a predetermined metrical pattern, and each rhymed line can be composed of one or more phrases; each of these phrases, in turn, will be written to a pre-determined tonal pattern. In the representation of songs in the text, they are written in descending order and indented, phrase by phrase, until a rhyme occurs, at which point the line placement returns to the left margin:

The traces of Junrui's weeping had stained the sleeves of his gown,
and powdery tears covered Oriole's cheeks. [rhyme]
One could not stop his long sighs,
the other could not relax her brows of kohl. [rhyme]
Junrui said, "Take care of yourself, darling,"
and Oriole replied, "Have patience on the long road." [rhyme]

Thus, a new rhymed line will always begin at flush left; the other lines are indented in order of the phrases. Since Chinese was unpunctuated, know that the symbols for commas, periods, semi-colons, and em-dashes are created and inserted by the translator. In the base text, marks are sometimes used to indicate the end of a rhymed line as a point for aspiration. The end of a rhymed line does not always reflect the end of a semantic unit, which may run into the next rhymed line. Conversely, the phrases themselves sometimes can contain an entire semantic unit (usually when asking questions).

Spoken text: there are three varieties, all set in smaller type size. The first is spoken free text, entered as a paragraph. The second is descriptive and formal writing using lines of 4 and 6 or 5 and 7 syllables in a strict tonal system of contrast or comparison, entered as blank verse, flush left and indented. The third is classical poetry, which is set flush left, and is presented as a block in the text, centered on the longest line. An example follows:

(*Free prose*:) The madam said, "Let him get on the road, it's getting dark." Oriole wept bitterly and composed another poem to give to the student. It read

> (*Poetry*)
> Cast aside now, what should I say?
> I was the one who drew close back then.
> **Take your old feelings once again**
> **And treat with sympathy the one before your**
>   **eyes.**

. . . .

(*Free prose*:) Oriole, the ill-fated, sends this letter to the desk of the talented gentleman.

(*Blank verse*:)
From autumn of last year,
I have been in a daze, as though I were lost.
Amid the noise of daily life
I could perhaps banter with others,
But night after night, when all alone,
there was never a time I would not weep.

Laureate Dong's *Story of the Western Wing*

玉茗堂批訂《董西廂》敍

[缺]。。。雷陽謫居，真不減鴟夷五湖、相如臨邛耳已。令平昌，邑在萬山中，人境僻絕。古廳無訟，衙退疏簾，捉筆了霍小玉公案。時取參觀，更覺會心，輒泚筆淋灕，快叫欲絕。何物董郎，傳神寫照，道人意中事若是。適屠長卿訪余署中，遂出相質。長卿曰：記崔張者凡五人：北則人知有王關，而不知有董；南則人知有李，而不知有陸。為子玄稱冤，並以娑羅園題評見示。且欲易余董本，余戲謂長卿：昔東坡欲以仇池石易王晉叔韓乾二駃馬，晉叔推之。

<hr>

1 Copied from an earlier 1577 edition.

2 For a short time, he held a post in Xuwen 徐聞, a town on the Leiyang Peninsula just north of Hainan Island.

3 One of the names of Fan Li 范蠡 who, after sending the beauty Xi Shi to delude Fu Chai, the King of Yue, left his post as minister in the state of Wu after feeling uneasy about such decisions by the King of Wu. He floated off on a little boat, finally reaching Shandong, where he became an entrepreneurial whiz. Here, of course, the main point is that he escaped court politics.

Preface to the Jade Camellia Hall Edition of *Laureate Dong's Story of the Western Wing*[1]

[*missing*]...when I was banished to live in Leiyang,[2] it was truly equal to the Five Lakes where Leathersack went,[3] or the equivalent of Linqiong for Sima Xiangru.[4] I acted as magistrate for Pingchang,[5] a district located among a myriad of mountains, cut off at the edge of the human world. There were no legal suits brought in the ancient halls, so I went to a quiet place after work and took up the pen to finish off the case of Huo Xiaoyu.[6] It was then I took up this book to peruse, and I felt, at that moment, that I really understood how good it was. I would often dip my pen in the ink until it was saturated, then quickly jot things down as I exclaimed in admiration. Who was this Esquire Dong, who could bring to life such characters and speak as he did of what lay in a person's mind?

Tu Long[7] was visiting me in my residence then, so I showed it to him to get his opinion. Changqing said, "There have been five people to have recorded the story of Oriole and Student Zhang: in the north there was *The Story of the Western Wing* by Wang Shifu and Guan Hanqing, but Dong was unknown. In the south people knew about Li Rihua, yet Lu Cai[8] remained unknown."

He was stating that Lu Cai had been wronged, and he took out his comments on the *Garden of the Sala Tree* to show me, and then he wanted to exchange that for my copy of Dong's all-keys-and-modes. I jokingly said to him, "Once, Su Shi wanted to exchange his rock from Qiuchi for Han Gan's painting of 'Two Loose Horses' in the possession of Wang Jinshu, but Wang would

---

4   See Book I, fn. 87.
5   Another term for Suichang 遂昌, in Zhejiang.
6   Tang Xianzu was writing the fifty-three act drama, *The Purple Hairpin* (*Zichai ji* 紫釵記), based on the love story of Huo Xiaoyu (霍小玉). See Zhenjun Zhang 2010 and Yuanfei Wang 2021.
7   屠隆 (1542–1605, byname Changqing 長卿).
8   Lu Cai (ca. 1495–1540) was written alternatively as 陸采, 陸採, or 陸彩; byname Ziyuan 子元, sobriquet Tianchi 天池.

錢穆公 欲兼取二物，蔣穎叔欲焚畫 碎石。竟成聚訟。予請
以石歸蘇，以魚 歸王。今日請以娑羅歸屠，玉茗歸湯。

乙末上巳日清遠道人纂

not agree.[9] Qian Mufu wanted to take them both away and Jiang Yingshu wanted to burn the painting and smash the rock.[10] No one could come to a final determination. I would have requested to "return the stone to Su" and "the painting to Wang."[11] So today, I will request to return *Sala Trees* to Tu Long and the *Jade Camellia* to Tang Xianzu.

> Compiled by the Daoist of the Clear and Distant on the third day of the third month of the year *yiwei*.[12]

---

9 See Xiaoshan Yang 2022, 317. The point being the incommensurability of worth between objects.
10 See Xiaoshan Yang 2022, 320. See also Li Waiyee 2022, 33.
11 That is, each would keep their own.
12 April 12, 1595.

《董解元西廂記》題辭

余於聲律之道，瞠乎未入其室也。《書》曰：「詩言志，歌永言，聲依永，律和聲。」志也者，情也。先民所謂：「發於情，止乎禮義者」是也。嗟乎，萬物之情各有其志。董以董之情而索崔、張之情於花月徘徊之間。余亦余之情索董之情於筆墨烟波之際。

Introductory Words to *Laureate Dong's Story of the Western Wing*

My relationship to the principles of scale and pitchpipe is that I have long stared at them with astonishment but remain an outsider. *The Documents* remarks, "Poetry gives expression to *zhi*,[13] singing prolongs the tone of expressive words, the scale and tonal pitch of music allows that singing to be elaborated, and scale and tonal pitch must be harmonized by the pitchpipes of various lengths.[14] Now *zhi* is *qing*,[15] what earlier people meant by "What is produced by the emotional essence of humans comes to rest in ritual propriety or right action."[16]

Ah, in the innate essence of all things there is *zhi*-ambition, volition, intent, or desire. With his emotional essence, Dong Jieyuan brought out the emotional essences of Cui Yingying and Zhang Rui from amid the fluctuations of flowers and moonlight;[17] I have also teased out Dong Jieyuan's emotional essence at the convergence of my own brush and ink and points of climax [*in the ballad*].[18]

---

13 The word *zhi* 志 can be understood as "where the heart goes" which includes one's ambition, intent, desire, volition.

14 The somewhat overelaborate translation of this quotation attempts to capture the understanding of the original passage as explained by Qu Wanli 1984, 18–19.

15 Here, *qing* 情 is understood as the emotional essence of humans, including passion, desire, sentiment. This interesting statement is difficult to translate, since English grammar calls for an absolute identity (A is B), but in Chinese the phrase (志也者 清) can represent not only complete correspondence, but also be understood as partial: "emotional essence is part of volition/intent, etc.(A is partially or completely correspondent to B).

16 Referring to a section from the "Great Preface" to the *Classic of Poetry*:
Those above transform those below by the wind [of their virtue]; those below goad those above by the wind [of their criticism]. They focus on embellishment of words to offer circumlocutive but righteous criticism. Those who speak it are without guilt. Those who hear it find it sufficient to guard against [wrong action]. So, it is called "airs." To give vent through essential feelings is the nature of the people. To stop at correct ritual and right action is the fecundity of the former kings. This is how the affairs of a state are tied to a source within a single person. This is designated as "wind" or "airs."

17 That is, the uneven progress of their romantic encounter.

18 That is, in his commentary.

董之發乎情也，鏗金戛石，可以如抗而如墜；余之發乎情
也，宴酣嘯傲，可以以翱而以翔。然則余於定律和聲處，
雖於古人未之逮焉，而至如《書》之所稱為「言為永」
者，殆庶幾其近之矣。

　　　　　　　　　　　　　　　　清遠道人書於玉茗堂。

Dong's expressions of emotional essence are "clinking metal and striking lithophones"[19] that one can resist or fall for, while my outpouring of emotional essence is the unrestrained singing and whistling of haughty satisfaction while tipsy at a banquet that one can use to soar and take flight at the moment. But as for that space in which tonal pitch is created to harmonize with the scales of music—although I have yet to match the ancients, I come close to what *The Documents* claim as the "words are prolonged."[20]

Written by the Daoist of the Clear and Distant
in the Hall of the Jade Camellia

---

19 Meaning "a beautiful and flowing text."
20 While the reference is to the *Book of Documents*, one of the five ancient classics, this is also possibly a self-deprecating pun: "I can go on forever."

董解元西廂 卷一
明 臨川湯顯祖義仍甫評

i.1 仙呂調 (醉落魄纏令) 引辭

　　吾皇德化。

　　喜遇太平多暇。

　　干戈倒載閑兵甲。

　　這世為人，

　　　白甚不歡洽。

　　秦樓謝館鴛鴦幄。

　　風流稍是有聲價。

　　教惺惺浪兒每都伏咱。

Book I

Laureate Dong's Story of the Western Wing

Commentary by Tang Xianzu, byname Yireng, of the Ming Dynasty and from Linchuan

i.1 Xianlü Diao Mode

Drunk and Down on My Luck: A Bound Suite (Introduction)[21]
Our emperor transforms all through virtue,
We happily encounter the Great Age of peace and pleasure.
Spear and lance are now carried upside down; weapons and armor
  are stored away.
To be alive in such an age—
  why not be joyous?

In mandarin-duck snugs in the lofts of Qin and pleasure halls of
  Xie,[22]
A reputation for romantic talent is what counts,
And I make all the other bright playboys[23] bow to me.

---

21 This is a typical introduction for a performance piece, making a context for the topic it will cover. In *The Drunken Man's Talk* (*Zuiweng tanlu* 醉翁談錄), a southern text that is contemporary with Dong's ballad, the author ends the first section on "small talks" (小說) with a poem:

> Small talks are many and varied, incorporating everything,
> One must rely on actual study, for that is the foundation of all.
> To open up Heaven or refer to Earth, one must have thorough knowledge of
>   the classics and histories.
> To have exhaustive knowledge of the past to understand the present, one
>   must peruse all the tales.
> Then store them away to nurture and fill one's thoughts with the wind and
>   the moon,
> For there are songs and poems to spit out conversation in ten thousand
>   chapters.
> To identify and discuss demon anomalies, there is language that is smart,
> To discriminate divine spirits and transcendent beings, there are the
>   stratagems of the learned.
> It involves cases of spear and sword, as well as iron cavalry,
> Of idle passions, sexual congress, and stolen trysts.
> There are infinite events in this world of ours—
> Go through them all, and from the start explain them subtly in detail.

See Luo Ye 1957, 5, and for a different translation of this passage, see Luo Ye 2015, 9.

22 Houses of pleasure.

23 Or layabouts.

不曾胡來，
　俏倬是生涯。

（整金冠）
　攜一壺兒酒，
　　戴一枝兒花。
　醉時歌，
　　狂時舞，
　　　醒時罷。<small>諫客</small>
　每日價。
　疏散不曾着家。
　放二四不拘束，
　　儘人團剝。

（風吹荷葉）
　打拍不知個高下。
　誰曾慣對人唱他說他。
　好弱高低且按捺。
　話兒不是，
　　朴刀桿[1]棒，
　　　長槍大馬。

（尾）
　曲兒甜，
　　腔兒雅。
　裁剪就雪月風花。
　唱一本兒倚翠偷期話。

i.2 般涉調 （哨遍）<small>斷送引辭</small>
　太皥司春，
　　春工着意，
　　　和氣生暘谷。

---

24   Lines in small capitals are notes penned at the end of various lines or between larger characters in normal lines.

25   To accompany his performance.

26   The term I have translated as "tailor" literally means to trim a piece of cloth to a pattern" or "to cut out a piece of cloth." This begins a series of metaphors that runs through the text about the creation of performance literature as combining pieces of

I never make a misstep,
> for perfect romance is my life.[vi]

Adjusting a Ritual Cap of Gold
I bring along a pot of wine
> and wear a sprig of flowers in my hair.

Drunk, I sing,
> *manic, I dance,*
>> *sober, I stop.* AN UNINHIBITED GUEST.[24]

Every day I am loose and free,
My feet never touch home.
I play, shamelessly unrestrained—
> go ahead, try and tear me down!

Wind Blows the Lotus Leaves
I strike the clappers,[25] but don't know high from low.
There is no comfort in singing and reciting in front of others.
Good or bad, high or low, just put up with it for now.
The topic today mentions nothing
> of clubs and knives, staves or sticks,
>> long spears or stout steeds.

Coda
The song is sweet,
> the melody elegant—
I'll tailor[26] a snowy moon and windblown flower
To sing a text about cuddling green and stealing a tryst.[27]

i.2 Banshe Diao Mode

Whistling Song (Completing the Introduction)
> Tai Hao[28] governs the spring
and spring's work is ever more deliberate as
> pleasant ethers arise from the Valley of Brightness.[29]

cloth into a whole garment. This continues with references to lines stitched or sewn together into beautiful patterns that are decorated, or embellished.

27 Part of a common four-character phrase to "draw near the kohl-limned eyebrows and red face." Note the relationship to willows and flowers, and their coloring in spring.

28 Another name for the mythical ruler Fuxi. In the Han period the mythical Five Emperors were each assigned to a particular season and direction. Tai Hao ruled in the eastern quadrant, where he governed through the element of wood, and where he received sacrifice as the "ruler of spring." See Lü Buwei 2000, 60, 93.

十里芳菲，
　儘東風絲絲柳搓[2]金縷。
漸次第，
　桃紅杏淺，
　　水綠山青，
　　　春漲生煙渚。
九十日光陰能幾，
　早鳴鳩呼婦。
乳燕攜雛。
亂紅滿地任風吹，
　飛絮蒙空有誰主。
春色三分，
　半入池塘，
　　半隨塵土。

滿地榆錢，
　算來難買春光住。
初夏永薰風池館，
　有藤床、冰簟、紗幬。
日轉午。
脫巾散髮，
　　沈李浮瓜，
　　　寶扇搖紈素。
着甚消磨永日。
有掃愁竹葉，
　侍寢青奴。

四詞多少留
連。有物換
星移之感。

Ten miles of rich fragrance wearies the eastern wind
    as on willows, skein after skein of withes rub their gold
       together.
Then, gradually, one after the other, peachblow reddens, apricot
    blossoms fade,
    waters turn green and mountains verdant
       as spring spates spit out misty strands of sand.

How enjoyable and well strung together these four phrases are. They have the feel of things changing and time moving on.

How many springs will there be? For
    rock dove cocks already cry their mates home,[30]
And mother swallows dote on their hatchlings.
A chaos of red fills the ground: let the wind blow
    as flying floss obscures the void: who is its master?
From full measure of spring's three months[31]
    half falls into ponds and reservoirs and
       half trails the eddying dust away.

Coins from elms now fill the ground,[32]
    count them up—never enough to stay the radiance of
       spring.
Early summer seems eternal
    as nurturing southern winds waft through the pondside
       hall
       with its rattan beds, cooling mats, and gauzy
          enclosures.
The sun turns toward noon.
Off comes the headscarf, the hair flows free—
    there are sinking plums and floating melons in cool water
       and a jeweled fan to wave its plain white gauze.
And what helps while away these eternal days?
    "Bamboo leaf"[33] **to sweep away the sorrow,**
       And a "green maid"[34] **to serve me in bed.**

29 In legend, the valley from which the sun rises every morning to bring light to the
    world.
30 They drive their mates from the nest when rain comes and summon them back when
    it clears.
31 Flowers of spring. The Chinese lunar year and spring both begin on the second new
    moon after the winter solstice.
32 The circular, rimmed, and nearly transparent seedcases of elms, with a dark seed in
    the middle, look like copper coins.
33 A fine distilled white liquor.

霎時微雨送新涼，
　些少金風退殘暑，
　　韶華早暗中歸去。

（耍孩兒）
　蕭蕭敗葉辭芳樹。
　切切寒蟬會絮。
　淅零零疏雨滴梧桐，
　　聽啞啞雁歸南浦。
　澄澄水印千江月，
　　淅淅風篩一岸蒲。
　窮秋盡，
　　千林如削，
　　萬木皆枯。

　朔風飄雪江天暮。
　似水墨工夫畫圖。
　浩然何處凍騎驢。
　多應在霸[3]陵西路。
　寒侵安道讀書舍，

春夏靡麗，寫
景易工，入人
亦淺。秋冬蕭
瑟，寫景難
工，入人亦
深。

34　A hollow wicker container plaited from strips of green bamboo. Also called a "bamboo wife," it kept the sleeper cool when they embraced it at night.

35　In the directional complements of the five elements, autumn is the element of metal and the direction of injury and death.

36　Normally referring to the refulgent splendor of spring, but here to the end of summer.

37　A particular type of small cicada, the males of which begin drumming at the end of summer and beginning of autumn. It was thought that its buzzing signaled the advent of Yin.

And then, in an instant, a light drizzle brings new coolness,
**   a metal-tinged freshet forces the end of summer to**
**   retreat;[35]**
**   and the bright flourishes[36] slip away unnoticed.**

Playing the Child
Soughing and sighing, sere leaves bid the fragrant tree adieu.
Chirping and chirring, cold cicadas chitter away in unison.[37]
Pittering and pattering and cold, scattered rain drips on the
    paulownia tree—
Listen to the honking geese as they return to southern banks.
In crystalline waters a thousand moons are imprinted in streams
*   as rustling and swishing winds winnow banks full of rushes.*
And as the last vestige of autumn is done,
*   a thousand forests look as though they were pared*
*   as ten thousand trees all wither away.*

A boreal wind tosses snow in river's dusk
Like a depiction by a master of ink-wash painting.
Where did Haoran freeze riding his donkey?
Most certainly the road west from Baling.[38]

Spring and summer are magnificently full of growth and the scene is easy to describe well. But it has minimal effect for the reader. Autumn and winter are cold and desolate, and such a scene is difficult to do well. But it has maximum effect for the reader.

---

38 A legend had it that the Tang poet Meng Haoran 孟浩然 (689–740) would go out
in late winter to find new plum blossoms, but no historical source talks about Meng
composing poetry on the Baling Bridge. This reference is a conflation of two sources
in the Song. Wang Wei, the famous Tang poet and painter, once painted a picture
entitled "A Painting of Meng Haoran Reciting Poetry on Horseback" 孟浩然馬上
吟詩圖. The late Tang writer Zheng Qi 鄭綮 (d. 899) is attributed with the line,
"poetic thoughts come while riding on the back of a donkey on Ba Bridge in the
snow" 詩思在灞橋風雪中驢子上. See Wei Qingzhi 2007, 295. But the story passed
into popular lore (see Liu and Shang 2017). Su Shi noted the model image of Meng
Haoran : "Do you not see the Vice-Governor of Luzhou [later Emperor Xuanzong
of the Tang], with eyes like lightning, / A bow hanging from his left hand, arrows
sideways across his lap? / Do you not see Meng Haoran riding a donkey in the snow, /
Eyebrows scrunched and reciting poetry, his shoulders jutting mountains?" There
are two *zaju* dramas about the topic by Ma Zhiyuan 馬致遠 (ca. 1300–1324), *Meng
Haoren in the Wind and Snow on an Ass (Fengxue qilu Meng Haoran* 風雪騎驢孟浩然)
and *Frozen, Reciting Poetry, Looking for Plum Blossoms in the Snow (Dong yinshi taxue
xunmei*凍吟詩踏雪尋梅); while both were lost, the latter was apparently the basis
for a play by Zhu Youdun 朱有敦 (1379–1439) entitled *Meng Haoran Treads through
Snow to Look for Plum Blossoms (Meng Haoran ta xue xun mei* 孟浩然踏雪尋梅). See
Zhuang Yifu 1982, 201, 207; Zhu Youdun, 2017, 469–501.

冷浸文君沽酒壚。
黃昏後，
　風清月澹，
　　竹瘦梅疏。

（太平賺）

四季相續。
光陰暗把流年度。
休慕古。
人生百歲如朝露。
莫區區。
好天良夜且追游，
　清風明月休辜負。
但落魄
　一笑人間今古。
聖朝難遇。

俺平生情性好疏狂，
　疏狂的情性難拘束。
一回家想麼，
　詩魔多愛選
　　多情曲。

比前賢[4]樂府不中聽，
　在諸宮調里卻着數。

---

39 Wang Huizhi 王輝之 (338–386) once traveled in the cold aftermath of a snowstorm to see his friend Dai Kui 戴逵 (?326–396, byname, Andao). He went there on a whim, but, finding his inspiration exhausted when he arrived, he returned without even knocking on Andao's door.

40 In popular legend Zhuo Wenjun 卓文君 (BCE 175–121), widowed at a young age, falls in love with Sima Xiangru 司馬相如 (ca. BCE 179–117), and their story provides the prototype for the so-called "scholar and beauty tales" (caizi jiaren 才子家人) of the Chinese tradition. Sima, the son of a rich family, fails in his first attempt to make a career and returns home to find the family estate in ruins. The magistrate of

Cold invades Andao's study,[39]
> chill soaks Wenjun's wine stall.[40]

After dusk
> *the wind is fresh, the moon pale*
>> *bamboos thin, and apricots widely spaced.*

Great Peace Beguiling Style
The four seasons follow one upon another,
Silently, light of day and dark of night measure out the passing
> years.
Don't be stupid or old fashioned,
For the hundred years of a man's life are but a morning's dew.[41]
Don't waste time on little things!
Pursue now the pleasures of fine days and beautiful nights,
Never forsake fresh breezes or bright moons.
Down on your luck?
> **Laugh off the past and present of the world of men,**
For an era of sagely rule like ours is seldom encountered.

My nature has always been to enjoy the unrestrained,
> and an unrestrained nature is hard to control.
A moment's reflection—
> the demon of poetry loves to pick out
>> songs full of feeling—

Linqiong, who treats him with utmost courtesy, houses him. Sima meets a certain Zhuo Wangsun (卓王孫 fl. BCE 140), and when invited by the latter to a party, he plays the zither at his host's command. Zhuo's young widowed daughter, Wenjun, overhears the music, espies the young scholar, and falls in love with him. Sima Xiangru bribes an attendant to take her a note and they elope that night. Her father cuts her off financially, and the young couple is forced to eke out a living by running a wine shop in Linqiong. The father, embarrassed, funds the couple. In the meantime, Sima Xiangru's fame spreads until the emperor enlists his services at court. In legend, Zhuo Wenjun, remaining in Linqiong and hearing that Sima had taken a concubine, writes a famous poem, "Song of White Hair" 白頭吟, in which she expresses her hope that they remain faithful to each other. He is so moved that he gives up his concubine and returns to be by her side. See Idema 1984.

41 Alluding to the famous "Short Song" 短歌行 by the late Han general and statesman Cao Cao 曹操 (155–220): "Facing ale one should sing, / How long is a human life? / Compare it to the morning dew— / I am troubled by how many days have passed already." See Cao Cao 1959, 5.

一個個

旖旎風流濟楚。

不比其餘。

（柘枝令）

敘次風流。

也不是崔韜逢雌虎。

也不是鄭子遇妖狐。

也不是井底引銀瓶，

也不是雙女奪夫。

42 Cui Tao had the misfortune of meeting a girl who had made her entrance in his life covered by a tiger pelt. He throws the pelt in a well and goes on to have a son with her. Later when he recovers the pelt, she dons it and turns into a tiger, eats both Cui and their son, and runs off into the wild. As DJY, 50 points out, among the 102 poems on paintings by the staunch Confucian Zheng Sixiao 鄭思肖 (1241–1318), several have the same titles as known performance texts, including one on Cui Tao and the tigress. There is a remarkable similarity between the titles of the paintings—all episodes that would be familiar in primers for the young (e.g., *Mengqiu* 蒙求)—and those of performance literature. While there is no extant ballad or drama on this topic, it is listed as the theme of storytellers in the late Song under the name of Cui Zhitao 崔智韜 (Luo Ye 1957, 4; Luo Ye 2015, 7). There are two variety skits noted in Zhou Mi's 周密 (1232–1298) *Old Affairs of Wulin* (武林舊事) in a section entitled "An Enumeration of Government Edition Variety Skits by Section" ("官本雜劇段數"): "Cui Zhitao Performs Moxibustion on a Tiger [Cub]" (崔智韜艾虎兒) and "Tigress: Cui Zhitao" (雌虎:崔智韜). The name of Cui is in smaller characters in the original, indicating that it was probably only one of several "tigress" skits. See Zhou Mi 2007, 247, 249. See also Hsieh 2008, 132–134 and Yenna Wu 1995, 239 n. 107 for a close summary of the tale in English; for a thorough examination in Chinese of this and the following story, see Sun Kaidi, 1985, 264–269.

43 The story of a young student named Zheng who meets a beautiful woman who later turns out to be a fox spirit; he discovers she is such, but they stay together, and she helps the young man succeed. Unfortunately, in the end, she is sniffed out by a hunting dog and killed. For a translation, see the short story, "Miss Jen." Nienhauser 1986.

44 To "pull a silver bowl from the bottom of a well" is nigh impossible. This refers to New Yuefu poem by Bai Juyi, which recounts elopement, life as a concubine instead of a wife, and the deep disappointment at being unable to free oneself from the situation. The long poem begins,

Though never the match of star poets of the past,
    still good enough to be enumerated in an all-modes medley
As one after another,
    sinuously supple, they offer up a romantic air clear and sharp
That cannot be compared to the rest!

Chinese-Mulberry Branch Song
This is not about Cui Tao encountering a tigress,[42]
Nor about Master Zheng encountering a demon fox;[43]
Neither is it about pulling a silver bottle from the bottom of
a well,[44]
    nor about two women fighting over a man.[45]

Enumerates the romantic one by one.

"Pulling a Silver Vase from the Bottom of the Well"—
    To halt elopement based on sexual attraction
Pull a silver vase from the bottom of the well,
That silver vase is about to rise when the cord of silk snaps.
Shape a jade hairpin on a rock,
And when it just about finished it snaps in the center.
Who knows what to do about a vase that sinks or a pin that snaps.
It's like parting from you this morning.

The poem then goes on to list the difficulties of her life as a concubine, her rejection by her husband's family, and her husband's emotional betrayal. The last few stanzas close with a brutal assessment of her plight:

He has ruined my hundred years of life.
I tell all you doltish girls at home,
Never lightly grant your body to another. (See Wang Rubi, 1980, 78–80.)

This, in turn was the basis for a popular play by Bai Pu 白樸 (1226–1306), entitled *From Wall's Top to Horseback* (牆頭馬上). A textual discussion can be found in Zhuang Yifu 1982, 174–75; translation of the play is found in Hsia, Li, and Gao 2014, 333–69.

45 A reference to the story of Zhao Wuniang 趙五娘 ("fifth daughter Zhao") and Cai Yong, the famous Han literatus, as performed in Gao Ming's *The Story of the Lute* (琵琶記). Zhao is left destitute when Cai is forced to take another wife. She searches for him for five years, staying alive by performing with her lute. Eventually reconciled with Cai, she becomes the paragon of wifely filial piety. See Gao and Mulligan, 1980, for a translation.

也不是離魂倩女。
也不是謁漿崔護。
也不是雙漸豫章城，
　也不是柳毅傳書。

（牆頭花）

這些兒古蹟，
　見在河中府。
即目仍存舊寺宇。
這書生是西洛名儒。
這佳麗是博陵幼女。
而想得，
　冷落了迎風戶。
唯有舊題句。
空存着待月迴廊，
　不見了吹簫伴侶。

聰明的試相度。
惺惺的試窨付。
不同熱鬧話，
　冷澹清虛最難做。
三停來是閨怨相思，
　折半來是尤雲殢雨。

閑點綴，俯仰憑弔。情生於文。

46 When a scholar leaves his wife Qiannü to take the examinations in the capital, her *hun*, or "cloud soul," departs from her body to accompany him. Meanwhile, her physical body lingers at home in a semi-comatose state. Her husband in the meantime successfully passes the examinations and then takes office. They live together for a few years before returning home. When she returns, her soul reintegrates with her body, and she rises from her bed a whole woman. For a discussion and translation of this play by Zheng Guangzu (ca.1260–1320) see *Dazed Behind the Green Lattice: Qiannü's Soul Leaves her Body*, in West and Idema 2010, 195–236.

47 Cui Hu, of uncertain historicity, wanders about during a spring festival and asks for a drink of water from a house south of Chang'an. A young girl brings him a cup of water and then silently lingers under a blossoming peach tree to express her interest. He is also interested, but having no reason to remain, he departs. Returning the next year, he finds her house bolted and shuttered. About to leave, he is accosted by the

It is not about Qiannü whose soul departed,[46]
Nor about Cui Hu seeking something to drink;[47]
Nor Shuang Jian at Yuzhang City,[48]
 nor Liu Yi transmitting a letter.[49]

Flowers on the Wall
These famous sites I sing of today
 remain yet in Hezhong Prefecture,
Where he saw that the old temple still stood.
This student was a famous scholar from Western Luo,
And that fine beauty, a young girl from Boling.

So leisurely strung together, every glance a meditation on the past. The writing creates the passion.

But what I imagine now
 is a long-deserted gate that once welcomed the breeze.
Nothing there but old inscribed lines of poetry,
And a winding corridor where he waited for the moon, but
 meaningless now—
 for his flute-playing companion has long since disappeared.[50]

You, the sharp and smart, try and take its measure,
You, the quick and clever, try to figure it out.
Unlike trite chatter of ordinary days,
 banal nothingness is the hardest to create.
For it is three parts boudoir lament or love's longing,
 and half obsession with sensual pleasure.

girl's father, who accuses him of killing his daughter, who has been lying sick for a year. Cui weeps over her unconscious body and she wakens.

48 The most popular love story of the Yuan era, this involved the triangle of Su Xiaoqing, a prostitute; Shuang Jian, who was in love with her; and a rich merchant who purchases her and takes her away. The story is complicated and exists in several versions. See Li Diankui 1989, Dolby 1997, Qi Xiaofeng 1988, Zhuang Yifu 1982, 45–46, and, for a fuller discussion, West and Idema 2025, 28–64.

49 Liu Yi 柳毅, a failed candidate in the imperial examinations, meets the young daughter of a Dragon King. He takes a letter from her to the king, is rewarded, takes her in marriage and lives happily ever after. Based on a Tang short story, "Tale of a Supernatural Marriage at Dongting" (洞庭湖靈姻), a drama titled *Liu Yi Delivers a Letter at Dongting Lake* (洞庭湖柳毅傳書) is attributed to Shang Zhongxian 尚仲賢 (ca. 1300). For the tale, see the translation by Meghan Cai in Nienhauser 2016, 1–70; for the drama see the free adaptation by David Hawkes in Shang Zhongxian 2003.

50 Alluding to Xiao Shi and Nongyu. See n. 17.

（尾）

窮綴作，

　腌對付。

怕曲兒撚到風流處。

教普天下顛不剌的浪兒每許。

此本話說，唐時這簡書生，姓張名珙，字君瑞，西洛人也。從父宦遊於長安，因而家焉。父拜禮部尚書，薨。五七載間，家業零替，緣尚書生前守官清廉，無他蓄積之所致也。珙有大志，二十三不娶。

i.3 仙呂調 （賞花時）

西洛張生多俊雅。

不在古人之下。

苦愛詩書，

　素閒琴畫。

德行文章沒包彈，

　綽有賦名詩價。

選甚嘲風詠月，

　擘阮分茶。

平日春闈較才藝，

　策名屢獲科甲。

家業零凋，

　倦客京華。

宋包拯善彈人過。譽人者因有「沒包彈之諺」。

Coda
I'll exhaust my stitching work,[51]
    to brazenly show my superficial skill.
But perhaps when the songs spin out those romantic places,
It will make all the dashing little lads of the world sigh in praise.

Our tale will speak about a student of the Tang dynasty, named Zhang
Gong, also known as Zhang Junrui, a man of Luoyang. He followed his
father's official posting to Chang'an and consequently lived there. His
father was Secretary of the Board of Rites, but he soon passed away.
In no more than five or six years, Zhang's family fortune had dwindled
to nothing. This was because his father had been an incorruptible and
pure official when alive, and he had accumulated no other savings.
Now, Zhang Gong certainly had great ambitions, but at twenty-three
he had yet to take a wife.

i.3 Xianlü Diao Mode

Time to Enjoy the Flowers
Student Zhang of Western Luo was handsome and elegant—
In no way inferior to the ancients.
He loved the *Odes* and *Documents* to excess[52]
    and was fully adept at both zither and painting.
His virtuous conduct and his literary writings beyond reproach,[53]
        he had a reputation for rhapsodies and was vaunted for his
        verse.
He could write any kind of shallow poem on love,[54]
    play the moon guitar or discern any tea.

Judge Bao of the Song was skilled at pointing out the transgressions of people. So, when praising someone, there is the saying, "beyond the criticism of Judge Bao."

Often in the springtime arena he tested his talent and art,
        and seized first place in the local examinations.
But his family fortune dwindled to nothing and
        he became a worn-out traveler in the capital precincts.

---

51 The story, first trimmed, now made into whole cloth.
52 The *Classic of Poetry* (*Shijing* 詩經) and the *Classic of Documents* (*Shujing* 書經)—
    Confucian classics—here used metonymically to denote elite education and the cur-
    riculum for the examinations.
53 Confucius on evaluating his disciples: "Those known for virtuous conduct: Yan Hui,
    Min Ziqian, and Ran Boniu; those known for cultural learning [*wenxue* 文學, a term
    that later meant literary writings]: Zi You and Zi Xia." See *Analects* 11.3.
54 A curious use of a phrase that normally is a slightly pejorative term for romantic
    poetry that lacks depth. Here, of course, the use could be ironic.

收拾琴書訪先覺。

區區四海遊學。

一年多半，
　身在天涯。

（尾）

愛寂寥，
　耽瀟灑。

身到處他便為家。

似當年未遇的狂司馬。

貞元十七年二月中旬間，生至蒲州，乃今之河中府是
也。有詩為證。詩曰：

濤濤金汁出天涯，
滾滾銀波通海窪。
九曲灣澴衝孟邑，
三門洶湧返中華。
瞿塘潋灩人虛說，
夏口喧轟旅謾誇。
傍有江湖競相接，
上連霄漢泛浮槎。

落拓有骙。

55 In popular legend Zhuo Wenjun and Sima Xiangru provide the prototype for the
so-called "scholar and beauty tales" (*caizi jiaren* 才子家人) in the Chinese tradition.
Sima, the son of a rich family, fails in his first attempt to make a career and returns
home to find the family estate in ruins. The magistrate of Linqiong, who treats him
with utmost courtesy, houses him. Sima meets a certain Zhuo Wangsun (卓王孫 fl.
BCE 140), and when invited by the latter to a party, he plays the zither at his host's
command. Zhuo's young, widowed daughter, Wenjun, overhears the music, espies
the young scholar, and falls in love with him. Sima Xiangru bribes an attendant to

Gathering his zither and books he set out to visit the finest minds.
To roam and study throughout the world
> for the better part of a year and
>> he was now at the very edge of heaven.

Coda

He loved lonely solitude,
> delighted in the free and unrestrained—
At home wherever he landed,
> **he was like a wild Sima Xiangru of long ago, who had yet to be acknowledged.**[55]

A summary of his uninhibited nature.

In the middle decade of the second month of the seventeenth year of the Zhenyuan reign,[56] the student reached Puzhou, which is now Hezhong Prefecture. There is a poem that provides evidence. It reads:

Swell upon swell, its golden liquor issues from the edge of heaven,
Rolling and riling, its silver waves connect to the very depths of the sea.
The "Nine Bends" swirl and pound the area of Meng,
At Mount Three Gates it gushes up and circles back in the Central Plain.[57]
People speak spuriously of the brimming fullness of Qutang,[58]
And travelers exaggerate the pounding thunder of Xiakou;[59]
At its side, rivers and lakes vie to receive its waters,
And at its source, it connects to the Han in the sky,[60] bearing a raft afloat.

take her a note and they elope that night. Her father cuts her off financially, and the young couple is forced to eke out a living by running a wine shop in Linqiong. The father, embarrassed, funds the couple. In the meantime, Sima Xiangru's fame spreads until the emperor enlists his services at court. In legend, Zhuo Wenjun, remaining in Linqiong and hearing that Sima had taken a concubine, writes a famous poem, "Song of White Hair" 白頭吟, in which she expresses her hope that they remain faithful to each other. He is so moved that he gives up his concubine and returns to be by her side. See Idema 1984.

56 January 28–February 6, 801.
57 Located in modern Henan.
58 One of the three gorges on the Yangzi River.
59 Modern Wuhan, near the confluence of the Yangzi and the Han Rivers.
60 The Milky Way.

這八句詩題着黃河。黃河那裏最雄。無過河中府。

i.4 仙呂調(賞花時)

芳草茸茸去路遙。
八百里地秦川春色早。
花木秀芳郊。
蒲州近也，
　景物盡堪描。

西有黃河東華嶽。
乳口敵樓沒與高。
俊雅。　　彷彿來到雲霄。
黃流滾滾，
　時復起風濤。

（尾）

東風兩岸綠楊搖。
馬頭西接着長安道。
正是黃河津要。
用寸金竹索纜着浮橋。

入得蒲州，見景物繁盛，君瑞甚喜，尋旅舍安止。

i.5 仙呂調(醉落魄)

通衢四達。
景物最堪圖畫。

This eight-line poem is entitled "The Yellow River." And where is the Yellow River most awe-inspiring? Nowhere can match right here in Hezhong Prefecture.

i.4 Xianlü Diao Mode

Time to Enjoy the Flowers
Through fragrant grass dense and fine, the road runs far away.
Spring comes early to eight hundred miles of riparian lands in Qin,
And flowers and bushes grow lush in the fragrant suburbs.
Puzhou is near and
    its sights and scenes are all worth sketching:
To the west is the Yellow River and to the east great Mount Hua—
Its crenelations and battle towers higher than anything around,[61]
Seeming to reach to the cloudy empyrean.
The Yellow River's flow roils and boils,
    stirred, from time to time, into windblown waves.

Beautiful and elegant.

Coda
In easterly winds, green willows wave on both banks.
The pier[ii] connects westerly to the road to Chang'an.
How true that "At the junction with the Yellow River—
An inch-thick hawser of bamboo and iron is used
    to tether the floating bridge."[62]

After he entered Puzhou, he saw that what lay before his eyes was splendid. Junrui was thrilled and looked for an inn in which to settle.

i.5 Xianlü Diao Mode

Drunk and Down on My Luck
The main thoroughfares ran to the four directions.
The sights and scenes were most worthy of depicting in a painting.

---

61 Mount Hua's rugged crags.
62 From Zhang Yue 張說 (667–731), "In Praise of the Bridge at Pu Crossing" (蒲津橋贊"), "There are three bridges across the Yellow River, and Pu Crossing is one. . . . Its older construction was thus: Hawsers made of plaited bamboo linked by hempen ropes were stretched across the river, connecting ten or more large vessels. Plaited hemp was used to strengthen it, and a wooden enclosure was tied together to keep [the boats] properly spaced. In the twelfth year of Kaiyuan (725), iron replaced bamboo. It was linked together to make a chain or was melted to make reclining oxen anchors." See Zhang Yue 1937, 8.87.

龍蔥瑞靄迷鴛瓦。
接屋連甍，
　五七萬人家。

六街三市通車馬。
風流人物類京華。
張生未及游州學。
策馬攜僕，
　尋得個店兒下。

　　有宋玉十分美貌，
　　懷子建七步才能，
　　如潘岳擲果之容，
　　似封驚心剛獨正。

時間尚在白衣，目下風雲未遂。張生尋得一座清幽店
舍下了。住經數日，心中似有悶倦。

i.6 黃鐘調（侍香金童）
　清河君瑞，
　　邸店權時住。
　又沒個親知為伴侶。
　欲待散心沒處去。

63 That is, the busy central areas of towns.
64 Song Yu 宋玉 (fl. 3rd century BCE) was accused by Deng Tuzi of being a lecher. In response, Song wrote the "Rhapsody on the Lecher Deng Tuzi" 登徒子好色賦, in which he describes a beautiful young girl, a neighbor to the east, to whose entreaties he has never assented. In contrast, he says, Deng Tuzi has a clutch of children by a very ugly wife. Song Yu also authored the "Rhapsody on the Gaotang Shrine" 高塘賦, in which he brings to life the archetypal image of perfectly matched lovers: the king of Chu and the mysterious beauty of Shamanka Mountain (巫山神女) who could summon the rain and clouds. This poem brings the term, "clouds and rain" (雲雨), into the literary vocabulary as a metaphor for sexual intercourse. See Xiao and Knechtges 1996, 349–350.
65 A general term for skill in poetic composition. It stems from a story of Cao Zhi 曹植 (192–232, byname Zijian 子健) and his brother, Cao Pi 曹丕 (?187–226, byname

Like a luxurious growth, auspicious mists blurred mandarin duck
   tiles,
Building upon building, roof beam connecting to roof beam—
   homes of fifty thousand people and more.
The six main streets and three markets[63] gave access to carts and
   horses,
The dashing and sophistication of the people were near those in
   the capital.
Before he set out to explore the prefectural school,
Student Zhang whipped his horse and pulled along his servant,
   looking for an inn in which to settle.

Now, he had the perfect beauty of Song Yu,[64]
Held within himself the seven-step talent of Cao Zijian;[65]
He possessed a "fruit-tossing" face like Pan Yue,[66]
And had a firm heart and unique rectitude like Feng Zhi.[iii]

He still wore plain garb and had yet to meet his time.[67] When he found
a quiet, out-of-the-way inn to settle in, he stayed there for several days.
But he seemed a bit tired and depressed.

i.6 Huangzhong Diao Mode

Golden Lad Minding Incense
Junrui from the Qinghe Zhangs[68]
   stayed for the moment in a local inn.
Alone, without a single relative or friend to accompany him.
He longed for a place to give his heart ease,

The narration here is most leisurely paced yet appears to be most detailed. Each time, it brings out those cold and desolate moments.

Zihuan 子桓), who was the founding monarch of the kingdom of Wei. Cao Zhi was
ordered to come to the court and compose a poem in the length of time it took to
take seven paces; if he failed, he would be executed. Cao Zhi responded with an
appropriate poem that shamed his elder brother. See Cao Zhi 2021, 214 and especially Cutter 2003.

66 Pan Yue 潘岳 (247–300, byname Pan Anren 潘安人), who is better known in drama
   as Pan An 潘安, was a prodigy whose hair turned gray at the age of thirty-two. As
   a youth he was so handsome that women would wait by the roadside to throw fruit
   into his chariot as he passed by in the streets of the capital at Luoyang.

67 That is, he was not yet subject to the strict sumptuary rules that identified rank and
   status in the bureaucracy by the assigned color of robes.

68 Not his home, but the ancestral site in Hebei Province of the esteemed Zhang clan
   from which he stemmed.

正疑惑之際，
　二哥推戶。
張生急問，
　道「都知聽說
　　不問賢家別事故。
聞說貴州天下沒。
有甚希奇景物。
　你須知處。」

叙詞最閑又似
最詳。每有冷
況。

（尾）

二哥不合盡說與。
開口道不勘十句。
把張君瑞送得來腌受苦。

帶敍帶描，文
人妝點如許。

被幾句雜說閑言，
送一段風流煩惱。

道甚的來。道甚的來。道「蒲州東十餘里，有寺曰：『普
救』，自則天崇浮屠教，出內府財敕建，僧藍無麗於此。
請先生一觀。」

i.7 高平調（木蘭花）

店都知，
　說一和。
道「國家修造了，
　數載餘過。
其間蓋造的非小可。
想天宮上光景，
　賽他不過。

And just as he was caught between doubt and indecision,
    the innkeeper pushed open the door.
Student Zhang immediately questioned him
    saying, "My fine innkeeper, please—
I will ask you nothing else about this place of yours, aside from
Your wonderful prefecture, which I have heard is peerless in the
    world.
What extraordinary and rare sights are there to see?
You must know of a place."

Coda
That innkeeper should never had told him anything.
But he opened his mouth and spoke just a few sentences—
Sending Zhang Junrui off to meet his bitter fate.

Both narrating and reinforcing; this is how a literatus embellishes the text.

    A whole raft of romantic headaches came
    From these few lines of chit-chat and idle chatter.

And what did the innkeeper say? What did he say?[69] He said, "Ten miles east of Puzhou is a temple called Universal Salvation. Wu Zetian[70] was enamored of Buddhism, so she had it constructed by royal fiat, using money from the imperial treasury. No other monastery is as beautiful! You should go and have a look, sir."

i.7 Gaoping Diao Mode

Magnolia Blossoms
The overseer of the inn
    explained a bit,
Saying, "For the state to finish it up
    took many years and more,
For its interior buildings were no easy thing.
I think even the resplendent vista of Heaven's Palace
    could not best it in any way.

---

69 Suspense point 1.
70 Wu Zhao 武 曌 (624–705), better known by her posthumous name of Wu Zetian 武
    則天 ruled the Tang empire from 660 to 705, first as dowager of two young emperors
    and then from 660 to 690 on her own. She was the only woman ever to rule as true
    empress.

說謊後，
　　小人圖甚麼。
普天之下，
　　更沒兩座。」
張生當時聽說破。
道「譬如閑走，與你看去則個。」

生出蒲州，隨喜普救寺，離城十餘里，須臾早到。

i.8 仙呂調（醉落魄）

綠楊影里。
君瑞正行之次。
僕人順手直東指。
道：「兀底一座山門。」
　君瑞定睛視。

見琉璃碧瓦浮金紫。
若非普救怎如此。
張生心下猶疑貳。
道「普天之下行來，
　　不曾見這區宇。」

（尾）

到跟前，
　　方知是。
覰牌額分明是敕賜。
寫着簸箕來大六個渾金字。

祥雲籠經閣，
瑞靄罩鐘[5]樓。
三身殿琉璃吻，
高接青虛；

妝成問答，口
吻似諧似謔。

淡致。

寫生奇手。

What would I gain
  by telling you lies.
For all the world over
  no one is better."
At that moment, Zhang understood what he was saying
And said, "Let's just take a leisurely walk
  and go have a look together."

The tone that embellishes the question and answer seems both playful and teasing.

The young Zhang left Puzhou to enjoy the sights of the Monastery of Universal Salvation. It was ten miles outside the city, but he was there in no time at all.

i.8 Xianlü Diao Mode

Drunk and Down on My Luck
In the shadow of green poplars
Just as Junrui was in progress,
The servant casually raised his hand and pointed due east,
Saying, "Look, the main gate of a monastery!"
    Junrui stared hard at it.

Perfectly bland.

He saw ceramic blue tiles, floating amid gold and purple.[71]
Only Universal Salvation could be like that!
But, still bewildered,
He said, "In my travels throughout the world,
    I've never seen such a monastery."

Coda
He went straight to the gate
    before he knew he was right:
He scrutinized the lintel plaque, clearly an imperial bestowal,
Upon which were written six pure gold characters, each as large as a
    winnowing tray.

A rare hand that reproduces the actual scene.

Auspicious clouds englobed the sutra gallery,
Mists of good fortune covered the bell tower.
On the Hall of the Three Bodies,[72] glazed rafter ends
rose up to meet the blue void.

71 The painted rafters, corbels, and brackets.
72 The Body of Dharma ("transcendence of form of realization of thusness"), the Body of Reward ("enjoyment of merits attained as a bodhisattva"), and the Corporeal Body ("manifested in response to the need to teach sentient beings"). See Muller 2012.

舍利塔金相輪，

直侵碧漢。

出牆有千竿君子竹，

繞寺長百株大夫松。

綠楊映一所山門，

上明書金字牌額，

簸箕來大，

顏柳真書，

寫「敕賜普救之寺。」

秀才看了寺外景早喜。入寺來謁，知客令一行童引隨喜，陡然頓豁塵俗之性。

i.9 商調（玉抱肚）

普天下佛寺，

無過普救。

有三檐經閣，

七層寶塔，

百尺鐘樓。

正堂里

幡蓋懸在畫棟，

迴廊下簾幕金鈎。

一片地

是琉璃瓦，

瑞煙浮。

千梁萬斝。

寶堦數尺是琉璃甃，

73 The nine horizontal wheels or circles at the top of a pagoda.

74 One of the four plants associated with the gentleman: bamboo, plums, thoroughwort, and chrysanthemum.

75 When the first emperor of China was descending from his sacrifices on top of Mount Tai, he stopped beneath a tree to avoid a thunderstorm. He enfeoffed the tree as "a Fifth-Order Grandee."

The golden wheels[73] of the relic pagoda
went straight into the blue sky-river.
**Rising above the wall were a thousand stalks of "gentleman's
bamboo,"[74]**
**and circling around the monastery grew hundreds of "grandee's
pines."[75]**
Green poplars concealed a main gate,
above which golden characters were written clearly on a lintel plaque,
each as big as a winnowing tray.

There, in the true style of Yan Zhenqing or Liu Gongquan,[76]
was written, "By Imperial Bestowal, the Monastery of Universal
Salvation."

Our budding scholar, already pleased as he looked at the exterior
appearance of the monastery, went inside to make his visit. The Re-
ceiver of Guests ordered an acolyte to lead Zhang around to view the
place and, **in an instant Zhang's nature expanded beyond its normal
dust-ridden commonness.**

i.9 Shang Diao Mode

Jade Enwraps the Stomach
No monastery in the whole world
        could surpass Universal Salvation:
It had a sutra gallery of triple eaves,[77]
        a seven-floor precious pagoda,
                and a hundred-foot bell tower.
A canopy and streamers were suspended from the painted rafters,
        bamboo shades and golden hooks were in the winding
                corridors.
It was all a stretch of glazed tiles,
        floating mists,
                and rafters in the thousands, corbels and brackets by the
                myriads.
The several feet of the precious steps were glazed ceramic
        brickwork—[78]

---

76 Yan Zhenqing 顔真卿 (709–785, byname Qingchen 清臣) and Liu Gongquan 柳公
    權 (778–865, byname Chengxuan 誠懸) were two extraordinary Tang calligraphers.
77 Three main stories.
78 Whence the Buddha descends.

重檐相對，
　一謎地是寶妝就。

佛前的供床金間玉，
　香煙裊裊噴瑞獸。
中心的懸壁，
　周回的畫像，
　　是吳生親手。
金剛揭帝骨相雄，
　善神菩薩相移走。
張生覰了，
　失聲的道，
　　「果然好。」
　　頻頻地稽首。
欲侍問是何年建，
　見梁文上
　　明寫着「垂拱二年修。」

描畫入睹。

（尾）
　都知說得果無謬。
　若非今日隨喜後。
　着丹青畫出來不信道有。

　　此寺蓋造
　　真是富貴：
　　搗椒紅泥壁，
　　雕花間玉梁；
　　沈檀金四柱，
　　玳瑁壓堦矼。
　　松檜交加，
　　花竹間列。
　　觀此異景奢華，
　　果是人間天上。
　　若非國力，
　　怎生蓋得。

Doubled eaves faced each other,
> the whole dazzling place was sumptuously decorated.
The offerings-table before the Buddha was gold inset with jade,
> and incense smoke coiled and curled, puffing from auspicious
> beasts.[79]

Turning back on the innkeeper's song, this carries to the full the marvelousness of this interlude.

A hanging mural in the very center
> was overspread with painted images—
> all from the very hand of Wu Daozi.[80]
Vajra and Gade had fierce bony images,[81]
> **As kind devas and bodhisattvas seemed to move one among
> the others.**
After Student Zhang had observed them all,
> **he blurted out, "They really are that fine!"**
> **And he kowtowed again and again.**

A portrayal so vivid it is as if it were right in front of one's eyes.

Just as he was about to ask when it had been built,
> *he saw clearly written in the roof beam text,[82]*
> *"Finished in the second year of Chuigong."[83]*

Coda
Indeed, the innkeeper had spoken the truth,
But if Zhang had not seen it himself that day—
Even if painted in full color
> *he would not have believed it so.*

The construction of this monastery
was truly splendid:
Crushed fagara reddened the mud walls,
carved flowers were spaced along jade rafters.
Aloeswood turned the four posts to gold,
And tortoise shell was pressed into the stairs' treads.
Pine and cypress ran hither and thither,
flowers and bamboo were set out in rows.
Observing this rare scene of sumptuous splendor—
indeed, it was heaven in the realm of men.
If this were not a state effort,
it could never have been built!

79 Incense censers.
80 A famous muralist and portrait artist (吳道子 ±680–±760).
81 Protectors of the Dharma whose statues grace the entrance to the Buddha Hall, here
    painted in what is called the "bony" style.
82 A celebratory text upon completion of construction.
83 A reign title of the Empress Wu Zetian; the second year would be 686.

i.10 雙調（文如錦）

景清幽，
　看罷絕盡塵俗意。
普救光陰，
　出塵離世。
明晃晃，
　輝金碧。
修完濟楚，
　栽接奇異。
有長松矮柏，
　名葩異卉。
時潺潺流水。
　湊着千竿翠竹，
幾塊湖石。
瑞煙微。
浮屠千丈，
　高接雲霓。

前面壯麗鋪
張祇說寶塔
鐘樓等項耳。
此卻寫竹石
花溪。非複說
也。

行者道：「先生本待觀景致。
把似這裏閑行，
　隨喜塔位。」
轉過迴廊，
　見個竹簾兒掛起。
到經藏北，
　法堂西。
廚房南面，
　鐘樓東裏。
向松亭那畔，
　花溪這壁。
粉牆掩映，
　幾間寮捨，
　　半亞朱扉。
正驚疑。
張生覷了，
　魂不逐體。

i.10 Shuang Diao Mode

Patterned Like Embroidery
The scene was fresh and secluded and, as he
    finished looking, thoughts of the vulgar dust simply
      disappeared.
The shifting moods of Universal Salvation
    rose out of the dust and left this world behind.
Glistening and glimmering,
    the gold and blue brightly shone.
To bring it all to orderly perfection
    only the marvelous and rare were planted and grafted:
There were tall pines and dwarf cedars,
    famous flowers and rare ornamental grasses.
From time to time, gurgling and bubbling, flowing water
Poured through a thousand stalks of kingfisher green bamboo
    and around a rockery made of stones from Lake Tai.
In subtle auspicious mists
    the Buddha pagoda rose a thousand rods tall,
      stretching high to join with clouds and rainbows.

The elaboration of the magnificence of the monastery in the earlier passage spoke only about such things as the precious pagoda and the bell tower. This section describes bamboo and rocks and flowers and streams. It is not redundant.

The acolyte spoke, "You said, sir, that you wanted to see the best
    sights.
And there is nothing better than to stroll here
    and enjoy the pagoda site."
They turned past a winding corridor,
    where they saw a furled and hooked bamboo blind.
They went north of the sutra library,
West of the dharma hall,
South of the kitchen and
    east of the bell tower,
Heading to a pine arbor there,
    or a flowery brook here.
Now and again, inside whitewashed walls appeared
    several lodgings,
      and in one, a leaf of a vermilion doorway stood ajar.
He was just struck with wonder—
After student Zhang looked,
    his soul no longer followed his body!

（尾）

出得神鬼。

驀然見了如風的。

有甚心情更待隨喜。

立掙了渾身森地。

當時張生卻是見甚的來。見甚的來。與那五百年前疾憎的

冤家，正打個照面兒。

一天煩惱，

當初指引為都知；

滿腹離愁，

到此發迷因行者。

一場旖旎風流事，

今日相逢在此中。

i.11 仙呂調（點絳唇纏）

樓閣參差，

瑞雲縹緲香風暖。

法堂前殿。

數處都行遍。

花木陰陰，

偶過垂楊院。

香風散。

半開朱戶，

驀見如花面。

（風吹荷葉）

寫崔處輕～
冉～，有嫣然
欲笑之意。

生得於中堪羨。

露著龐兒一半。

宮樣眉兒山勢遠。

十分可喜，

二停似菩薩，

多半是神仙。

Coda
At first sight, he suddenly became a madman.
He didn't have the heart to keep on sightseeing,
But stood dazed as his whole body turned numb.

*She comes out like
a spirit or a ghost!*

And what was it that Student Zhang saw? What did he see?[84] He ran right into that hateful sworn enemy from five hundred years before![85]

A whole heaven of headaches:
from the start he was guided here by the innkeeper.
A full belly of parting's sorrow:
after he arrived, he was led into delusion because of the acolyte.
This fine romantic affair happened
Just because they met right there exactly on that day.

i.11 Xianlü Diao Mode

Dotting Crimson Lips: A Bound Suite
Ragged rooftops of towers and galleries in
auspicious clouds dimly discernible and fragrant winds
warm.
From the front hall of the Dharma Palace where he started,
He made his tour to many places.

Through flowers and trees deep in shade,
by chance he passed a courtyard of weeping willows—
A fragrant wind wafted,
A vermilion leaf half opened in a doorway—
suddenly he saw a face like a flower.

Wind Blows the Lotus Leaves
She had been born with a natural beauty worth admiring.
She revealed but half her face:
Palace-style eyebrows—the repose of distant mountains.
So completely loveable—
two parts resembled a bodhisattva,
but more like a divine transcendent.

*The part describing
Miss Cui is light
and graceful, and
it shows the intent
of a beautiful one
on the verge of
smiling.*

84 Suspense point 2.
85 That is, his predestined love. Here, "hateful" and "sworn enemy" are ironic terms that imply the opposite (反語); in this case, both are terms of endearment for one's lover, as in someone who causes you consternation but to whom you are inextricably bound.

（醉奚婆）

　　儘人顧盼。

　　手把花枝撚。

　　瓊酥皓腕。

　　微露黃金釧。

（尾）

　　這一雙，

　　　　鶻鴒眼。

　　須看了可憎底千萬。

　　兀底般媚臉兒不曾見。<small>鶻鴒即胡伶，聰明之意。</small>

　　　手撚粉香春睡足，

　　　倚門立地怨東風。

　　　髻綰雙鬟，

　　　釵簪金鳳。

　　　眉彎遠山不翠，

　　　眼橫秋水無光。

　　　體若凝酥，

　　　腰如弱柳。

　　　指猶春筍纖長，

　　　腳似金蓮穩小。

　　正傳道：「小生二十三歲，未嘗近於女色。其心雖正，見此女子，頗動其情。」

i.12 中呂調（香風合纏令）

　　轉過荼蘼架。

　　正相逢着，

　　　　宿世那冤家。

　　一時間見了他。

Drunken Mama Xi
Unconcerned about the stares,
Her hands twirled a sprig of flowers.
Wrists white as curds of jade
Barely revealing bracelets of gold.

Coda
His pair of clever and flashing eyes
Could have looked at a million predestined lovers
And never seen a face as enchanting as this.[86] *FLASHING EYES: BRIGHT,*
CLEVER, LIVELY EYES.

Just awake from a satisfying springtime nap, her hand twirled pollen's
    fragrance,
standing firm against the door, she begrudged the eastern wind—
Her hair bound in doubled coils,
her hairpin and comb a golden phoenix.
Eyebrows arch and distant mountains lose their green.
Eyes glance to one side and autumn waters lose their glimmer.
Her body like firm curds,[87]
her waist like a tender willow.
Her fingers were springtime bamboo shoots, delicate and long,
her feet like golden lotuses,[88] steady and small.

The original story says, "The young student was twenty-three and had
never drawn close to feminine beauty. Although his heart was upright,
when he saw this girl, she really shook his emotions."

i.12 Zhonglü Diao Mode

Fragrant Winds Converge: A Bound Suite
Turning past the arbor of blackberry rose,
He ran straight into
        that resentful lover from a previous life.
He saw her only for an instant,

---

86 Another possible reading of this coda would be, "Her pair / of clever, flashing eyes— /
You could look at a million predestined lovers / And never see a face as enchanting
as this." I am following DJY, 69.
87 As in the moist and shiny luster of new yogurt, or the warm white of jade.
88 A metaphor derived from the lotus-like impressions that bound feet, which are com-
pressed together in a pucker at the arch, leave on cold tiles.

十分地慕想他。
不道措大連心，
　要退身卻把個門兒亞。
喚別人不見吵。
不見吵。

朱櫻一點襯腮霞。
斜分着個龐兒鬢似鴉。
那多情媚臉兒，
　那鶻鴒淥老兒，
　　難道不清雅。
「見人不住偷睛抹，
　被你風魔了人也嗏。
風魔了人也嗏。」

北人指眼，謂
「淥老」。

（牆頭花）
也沒首飾鉛華。
自然沒包彈，
　淡淨的衣服兒扮得如法。
天生更一段兒紅白，
　便周昉的丹青怎畫。

手托着腮兒，
　見人羞又怕。
覷舉止行處管未出嫁。
不知他姓甚名誰，
　怎得個人來問咱。

不曾舊相識，
　不曾共說話。
何須更買掛。
已見十分掉不下。

But utterly longed for her, infatuated.
No one knew what this vinegar sack[89] had in mind
     as he withdrew,[90]
          but he closed the door—
He didn't want anyone else to see her!
No one else to see her!

Her lips, a single dot of vermilion cherry, were set off by the sunset
     hue of her cheeks,
And her hair, parted across her face, was black as a raven.
With that beautiful visage so full of emotion,   *Northerners call*
     those flashing and limpid orbs,   *eyes "limpid orbs."*
          was she not pure and elegant?
"Furtively but without cease her eyes caressed me—
Oh, you drive a man mad!
You drive a man mad!"

Flowers on the Wall
No adornment in her hair, no blossom of lead on her face,[91]
So natural and flawless,
     her neat and unadorned clothes were worn just right.
That natural red and white complexion—
Could even the colors of Zhou Fang[92] have depicted it?

Hand pressed against her cheek,
     shy and timid when she saw him.
By her movements and actions, he knew she was yet unmarried.
Who knew her name, or who she was?
And whom could he ask to find out?

She was not an old acquaintance,
     he had never talked to her—
But there was no need to cast his fortune to foretell the future;
Because once he saw her, he would never be quit of her.

---

89 A pejorative term for students, who were fed preserved and pickled vegetables from   *Clustered like the*
    government stores as staple food.   *sound of singing*
90 That is, he would rather have barged right into the compound.   *and pipes on a*
91 A powder of white lead was used as makeup.   *painted pleas-*
92 Zhou Fang (周昉, byname Zhonglang 仲郎, ca. 700–800). A famous mid-Tang painter   *ure craft that*
    noted for his paintings of the Buddha, Daoist immortals, personalities, and ladies in *comes from afar,*
    waiting.   *indistinctly passes*
                                                                                         nearby and just as
                                                                                         indistinctly goes off
                                                                                         to a distant place.

兀的般標格精神，
　管相思人去也媽媽。

來如畫舫笙歌從遠地來，茫近地過，又茫遠地去。

（尾）
　「你道是
　　『可憎麼。』
　被你直羞落庭前無數花。」

　門前縱有閑桃李，
　羞對桃源洞里人。
　佳人見生，羞婉而入。

大石調（伊州袞）
　張生見了，
　　五魂肖[6]無主。
　道：「不曾見恁好女。
　普天之下，
　　更選兩個應無。」
　膽狂心醉，
　　使作得不顧危亡，
　　　便胡做。
　一向痴迷，
　　不道其間是誰住處。

　忒昏沈，
　忒粗魯。
　沒掂三，沒點三不着緊要點。
　　沒思慮。

Such deportment, such lively elegance—
oh mama! He was destroyed by love sickness.

Coda
"You say,
    'Despicable?'
Well, all the flowers in the courtyard would drop, shamed by you."

> Even if carefree peaches or plums were clustered in front of the door,
> they would be too embarrassed to face this girl from the Peach Blos-
>   som Grotto.[93]
> After the beauty saw the student,
> graceful and embarrassed, she went into her rooms.

i.13 Dashi Diao Mode

Yizhou Tremolo
After Student Zhang saw her,
    his five cloud souls[94] spun out of control,
As he cried, "I've never seen such a fine girl!
In all this world
    her match could never be found."
Gall wild and heart intoxicated,
    acting without regard to danger or death
        he did something crazy.
Completely lost in obsession,
    he gave no thought as to who might live inside.

He was so beclouded,
    so impetuous,
Weighing no consequences, <small>"LACKING FORETHOUGHT" MEANS CONSIDERING IT UNIMPORTANT.</small>

---

93 A conflation of two popular stories: that of Tao Qian's 陶潛 (365–427, byname
    Yuanming 淵明) idyllic paradise, the Peach Blossom Spring (桃花源) which was
    discovered by a fisherman from Wuling; and that of Liu Chen 柳晨 and Ruan Zhao
    阮肇 of the Han, who went up to Mount Tiantai 天台山 to pick medicinal herbs and
    stayed to share a grotto with two transcendent maidens with whom they had long
    been destined to be lovers.
94 The light, Yang (陽), spiritual or celestial souls, matched by the heavy, Yin (陰),
    material, or "earthly" souls. There are usually three cloud souls and seven earthly
    souls. See Pregadio 2008, 521–523. Performing literature, ever given to hyperbole,
    seems to prefer to use five cloud and nine earthly souls. There is also the possibility
    that "three" (三) has been mis-transcribed as "five" (五).

i.13   可來慕古。

少年[7]做事，

大抵多失心麄。

手撩衣袂，

大踏步走至根前，

欲推戶。

腦背後個人來，

「你試尋思怎照顧。」

（尾）

驀地出聰。

凜凜地身材七尺五。

一隻手把秀才捽住。

吃搭搭地拖將柳陰里去。

真所謂：「貪趁眼前人，不防身後患。」捽住張生的是
誰。是誰。乃寺僧法聰也。生驚問其故。

僧曰：「此處公不可往，請詣他所。」

生曰：「本來隨喜，何往不可。」

僧曰：「故相崔夫人宅眷，權寓於此。」

i.14 仙呂調（惜黃花）

張生心亂。

法聰頻勸。

「這裏面狼籍

又無看玩。

不是廓[8]遮攔。

解元聽分辯。

這一位也非是佛殿。

lacking any forethought,
He went wild.
Now, when youngsters act
    they never think it through—
He grabbed up his sleeves
    and with wide strides raced ahead
And was about to push open the door,
When someone came up behind him—
    "Hey, you'd better think about what you're doing!"

Coda
An awesome and forbidding frame seven-and-a-half foot tall,
Held the student tight with a single hand
And quickly dragged him into the shade of a willow.

Suddenly Dharma
Wit appears.

It's truly said, "A person lusting to take advantage of what's before his eyes never guards against troubles from behind!" And who was it who grabbed student Zhang? Who was it?[95] Well, it was that Buddhist monk, Dharma Wit. The student, startled, asked him why he did it.

The monk replied, "You, sir, cannot go into this place. Please visit somewhere else."

The student said, "I came here to sightsee, can't I go anywhere?"

The monk said, "This is the household of the wife of the former minister Cui, who is temporarily lodging here."

i.14 Xianlü Diao Mode

Cherishing the Crysanthemum
Student Zhang's mind was in turmoil,
And Dharma Wit kept on urging restraint.
"Everything is a mess inside and
    there is nothing to see.
I'm not trying to hinder you,
But, Laureate, listen to my explanation:
This area is not a Buddha Hall.

---

95 Suspense point 3.

舊來是僧院。
新來做了客館。
崔相國家屬,
　現寄居裏面。」

君瑞道:「莫胡來。
　便死也須索看。
這裏管塑蓋得希罕。

（尾）

莫推辭,
　休解勸。
你道是有人家宅眷。
我甚恰才見水月觀音現。」

僧笑曰:「子言謬矣。何觀音之有。此乃崔相幼女也。」

生曰:「家有閨女,容艷非常,何不居驛而寄居寺中。」

應曰:「夫人,鄭相女也。閨門有法。至於童僕侍婢,各有所役。間有呼召,得至簾下者,亦不敢側目。家道蕭然。惡傳舍冗雜,故寓此寺。」

生曰:「幾日見歸。」

僧曰:「近日將作水陸大會,及今歲有忌而不得葬,權置相公柩於客亭,率幼女孤子,嚴祭祀之禮。待來

In the past it was monks' quarters,
But has recently been converted to guest quarters.
Minister Cui's family
    is lodging inside."
Junrui said, "Don't be ridiculous—
    I'm going to look if it kills me!
Certainly, everything built or sculpted here is the rarest of rare.

Truly mimes the drollery of a vinegar sack!

Coda
"Don't put me off,
    don't try to calm me down.
You say it's someone's family member?
Well then, why did I just see the apparition of the Guanyin of
    moon and water?"[96]

The monk laughed and said, "You are mistaken sir, there was no Guanyin. That is the young daughter of Minister Cui."

The student replied, "If they have a virgin in the family whose looks are so gorgeous, what are they doing staying in a monastery and not in a post-house?"

"The matriarch is the daughter of Minister Zheng," he replied. "She has a rule about the inner chambers. Every serving boy or maid has an assigned duty, and those who are summoned report to the screen[97] and dare not even shift their gaze. The family is run according to strict rules. She found the confusion and disorder of the relay station to be repugnant and so lodged in this monastery."

The student said, "How many days before they leave?"

"In a few days," said the monk, "they will be doing the Water and Land Rite for the Dead. But since this year has a taboo associated with it, they cannot bury the minister right away. So, she has temporarily lodged the casket in their guest quarters and makes the young girl and orphaned son strictly observe the rituals of sacrifice. They will wait for next year,

---

96 There are thirty-three apparitions of the Bodhisattva Guanyin, known as the Goddess of Mercy. She is often portrayed with a bottle of pure water that has a willow twig inside. "Moon and water" refer to the moon (pure Yin) in heaven reflected in water (pure Yin) on earth.

歲通，方詣都營葬。今於此守服看靈而已。」

怎見得當時有如此事來。有唐李紳公垂作《鶯鶯本傳歌》為證。歌曰：

> 伯[9]勞飛遲燕飛疾，
> 垂楊綻金花笑日；
> 綠窗嬌女字鶯鶯，
> 金雀髻鬟年十七。
> 黃姑上天阿母在，
> 寂寞霜姿素蓮質；
> 門掩重關蕭寺中，
> 芳草花時不曾出。

i.15 大石調（驀山溪）

法聰頻勸，
道：「先輩休胡想。
——話行藏。
不是貧僧說謊。
是崔相國的女孩兒，
十六七，
小字喚鶯鶯，
白甚觀音像。」

張生聞語，
轉轉心勞攘。
使作得似風魔，
說了依前又問當。
顛來倒去，
全不害心煩，
貪說話，
到日齋時，
聽磬鐘響。

轉換如神。

---

97 Kept between the matriarch and ordinary household servants, particularly males.
98 A head adornment.
99 Meaning her father has passed away, but her mother is still alive.

which is auspicious, before they go to the capital to arrange the burial. Right now, they are keeping filial watch and guarding the casket."

Now, how do we know this really happened then? A poem by Li Shen, "The Song of Oriole," is proof:

Shrikes fly slow, swallows are swift,
Weeping willows reveal golden leaves on days when flowers laugh,
By the green window is a comely girl by the name of Oriole,
A golden swallow[98] in her raven locks, she is just seventeen.
The Herdboy has ascended to heaven, but the Queen Mother of the West is still here.[99]
Lonely and pure as frost, the girl has the character of a white lotus.[100]
The door is closed and double locked inside the Monastery,
And in the season of flowers and fragrant grasses she never emerges.[101]

i.15 Dashi Diao Mode

Jumping Across a Mountain Stream
Dharma Wit kept trying to conciliate,
        "Don't think wild thoughts, my good sir,
I will tell you everything,
I'm not going to lie.
That beauty who just came out
        is the daughter of Prime Minister Cui,
                sixteen or seventeen,
                    whose baby name is Oriole—
                        she's surely no image of Guanyin!"

When Student Zhang heard these words,
        his mind became ever more agitated—
He seemed utterly unhinged and
        kept repeating everything, asking the same questions—
Again and again, he kept at it,
        but it never assuaged his troubled heart—
                he was greedy to keep talking,
                    but it came time for the daily meal
                        and he heeded the ringing of the dinner bell.

A sudden change of subject as nimble as a divine spirit.

100 She is in mourning clothes.
101 Following the notes of Wang Xuanbo 1985, 129–130.

語話之間，行者至，請生會飯。生不免從行者參堂頭和尚
至德大師法本。法本見生服儒服，骨秀過群，離禪榻以釋
禮敬待。

i.16 仙呂調（戀香衾）
　　法本慌忙離禪榻。
　　連披法錦袈裟。
　　君瑞敬身，
　　　大師忙答。
　　各序尊卑對榻坐，
　　　須臾飲食如法。
　　一般般滋味，
　　　肉食難壓。

少不得插入
此數語。
　　君瑞雖然腹中餒，
　　　奈胸中鬱悶如麻。
　　待強吃些兒，
　　　咽他不下。
　　飯罷須臾卻卓几，
　　　急令行者添茶。
　　銀瓶湯注，
　　　雪浪浮花。

（尾）
　　紙窗兒明，
　　　僧房兒雅。
　　一碗松_語風_雋啜罷。
　　兩個傾心地便說知心話。

氣合道和，如宿昔交。法本請其從來。生對以：「儒學進
身，將赴詔選，遊學連郡，訪諸先覺。偶至貴寺，喜貴寺
清淨，願假一室，溫閱舊書。」

While he was talking, an acolyte arrived and invited the student to the communal meal. The student had no choice but to follow him and pay a visit to the head monk, Dharma Source, the Great Teacher of Perfected Virtue. When Dharma Source saw the student clad in Confucian dress and carrying himself in a certain way, he left his meditation couch to greet him with the proper Buddhist ritual.

i.16 Xianlü Diao Mode

Quilt with the Fragrance of Love
Hurriedly, Dharma Source left his meditation couch,
And threw on his brocaded cassock.
Junrui raised his body slightly in respectful salute,
    and the Great Master quickly responded.
And they sat, according to propriety, on facing couches
    and leisurely took drink and food as etiquette required.
Every single flavor
    surpassed any dish made with meat.

Junrui's belly was famished,
    but his heart was depressed and confused.   *These are indis-*
He tried to force himself to eat a bit,   *pensable phrases*
    but found he could not swallow.   *inserted here.*
When the meal was finished and tables were quickly removed,
    the acolyte was ordered to pour tea.
From a silver flask the tea poured out
    in snowy billows and floating flowers.[102]

Coda
The papered window was bright,
    the monk's room, elegant.
When the cup of pine wind[103] was finished THE PHRASE IS RIGHT ON THE MARK.
The two talked heart to heart as old friends.

Their spirits melded, and their Ways were in harmony, as if they had been longtime friends. Dharma Source asked about his life, and the student replied, "I am trying to succeed through Confucian study and am about to go in response to the examination's summons. Now I am roaming from place to place to learn. By chance I came to your monastery and have found a serene purity here. I would like to rent a room so I can review all that I have read."

i.17 般涉調 （夜遊宮）

君瑞從頭盡訴。

「小生是西洛貧儒。

四海遊學歷州府。

至蒲州，

因而到梵宇。

一到絕了塵慮。

欲假一室看書。

每月房錢併納與。

問吾師，

心下許不許。」

生曰：「月終聊備錢二千，充房宿之資。未知吾師允否。」

i.18 大石調 （吳音子）

張生因僧好見許，

以他辭說。

道：「比及歸去，

暫時權住兩三月。

欲把從前詩書溫閱。」

巧插閒綴。

若不與後，

而今沒這本話說。

法本曰：「空門何計此利。寮舍稍多但隨堂一齋一粥，欲
得三箇月道話，何必留房緡。俗之甚也。」

---

102 Bubbles and small bits of tea leaves were described as floating flowers or as ants the
color of yellow goose-down. In the poem "On Tea" 茶詞, Huang Tingjian 黃庭堅
(1045–1105) writes: "Valley waterfalls, the first spring is fragrant; / It has already
brewed until floating ants are a soft goose-down yellow." 谷簾第一泉香，已醮浮
蟻嫩鵝黃. See Huang Tingjian 2001, 343.

i.17 Banshe Diao Mode

Roaming at Night in the Palace
Junrui told him everything from the beginning,
"I am a poor scholar from Western Luo,
Roaming through every prefecture within the four seas to study.
I arrived in Puzhou, and
    so arrived at this monastery.

Since coming to this place, I've cut off any desire for the world of
    dust—
I want to rent a room here in which to read.
I'll pay the full monthly rent.
I inquire of you, Master,
    Will you grant this or not?"

"At the end of each month," said the student, "I will provide two strings
of a thousand cash to offset the rent. But I'm not sure if you will agree,
master."

i.18 Dashi Diao Mode

Sounds of Wu
Seeing the monk was inclined to respond favorably,
    the student spoke again with more persuasion:
He said, "Before I must go back,
    I'd like to stay here for a few months.
I want to review all the classics I have read."
If the abbot had not granted permission,
    there would be no tale to tell you now!

Cleverly inserted and effortlessly stitched together.

Dharma Source said, "We of the gates of emptiness make no such cal-
culation of profit. We have many monk's rooms. Simply join the host
for morning gruel and the noontime vegetarian meal. Since I want
three months of good conversation,[104] what is the need of rent? That
would just be vulgar."

103 In the poem "Dipping from the River to Brew Tea" 汲江煎茶, Su Shi writes: "Tea rain
is already turning—bubble feet where it is heated, / Pine winds suddenly begin—sound
when it is poured" 茶雨已翻煎處脚，松風忽作瀉時聲. See Su Shi 2010, 5116.
104 This line can also be read, "I desire that you hear my discourses about [perfecting]
the way [of the Buddha] for three months." See DJY08, 81.

（吳音子）

　　大師[10]曰：「先生錯，
　　　咱儒釋何分別。
　　若言着錢物，
　　　自家齋捨卻難借。
　　況敝寺其間多有寮捨，
　　　容一儒雅生韻又何礙也。」

生曰：「和尚雖然有此心，奈容朝夕則可矣；歲寒過有搔擾，愚意不留房緡，更不敢議。有白金五十星，聊充講下一茶之費。」

本不受。生堅納而起。本邀之，竟去。由是僧徒知生疏於財而重於義，過善之。

乃呼知事僧引於塔位一捨後，有一軒，清肅可愛，生令僕取行裝而至。

i.19 中呂調（碧牡丹）

　　小齋閑閉戶。
　　沒一個外人知處。
　　一間兒半，
　　　摒掠得幾般來清楚。
　　一到其間，
　　　絕去塵俗慮。
　　紙窗兒明，
　　　湘簟爾細
　　　　竹簾兒疏。

---

105 From *The Discourse on Salt and Iron* (鹽鐵論), "Wen Xue said, 'The ancients valued virtue and thought profit base; they esteemed righteousness and disesteemed material wealth.'" 文學曰：古者，貴德而賤利，重義而輕財. See Huan Kuan 1992, 56.

Sounds of Wu
The Grand Master replied, "You are wrong, sir
      what difference is there between a Confucian and a Buddhist?
If money were a real consideration,
      I'd find even my own room hard to rent.
And furthermore, so many monk-cells
      in our poor monastery are empty.
There's nothing to prevent ELEGANT!
      us from accepting a single Confucian student."

"Although you're so inclined, dear monk," the student replied, "that would only be suitable for a night or two. But when the weather turns colder, I will certainly be a bother. I must humbly profess that if I don't pay cash for the room, there is nothing else to discuss. I have fifty ounces of fine silver with me, which can be used to pay for a round of tea at one of your public sutra lectures."

Dharma Source would not accept it at first, but the student forced him to take it and stood up. Dharma Source tried to stop him, but the student left. From then on, all the monks and lay Buddhists knew that the student disregarded wealth and esteemed righteousness[105] and they praised him excessively.

And so, the Monastery Administrator was summoned to lead him to an apartment near the pagoda. It was a delightful place, both isolated and quiet. The student sent his servant to fetch the luggage.

i.19 Zhonglü Diao Mode

Blue-Green Peony
He casually closed the door to his little studio.
No outsider knew where he was.
A room and a half in size,
      he straightened it up until all was in order.
As soon as he entered that space,
      he abandoned any thought of the dusty world.
The paper-pasted window was bright,
      the mat woven from speckled bamboos was fine,[106]
            and slats of the bamboo shades were widely spaced.

106 Bamboo from the Xiang River. When the Sage King Shun died, his two consorts Ehuang 娥皇 and Nüying 女英 shed so many tears that they left indelible spots on the bamboo.

晚來初過雨。
有多少燕喧鶯語。
太湖石畔，
　有兩三竿兒修竹。
好寄閑身，
　眼底無俗物。
有幾扇兒紙屏風，
　有幾軸兒水墨畫，
　　有一枚兒瓦香爐。

（尾）
其餘有與誰為伴侶。
有吟硯紫毫箋數幅。
壁上瑤琴几上書。

閑尋丈室高僧語，
悶對西廂皓月吟。
是夜月色如畫，
生至鶯庭側近，

口佔二十字小詩一絕。其詩曰：

月色溶溶夜，
花陰寂寂春，
如何臨皓魄，
不見月中人。

詩罷，繞庭徐步。

i.20 中呂調（鵲打兔）
對碧天晴。
清夜月，
　如懸鏡。
張生徐步，
　漸至鶯庭。

瀟～散～是
鋪敘本色卻
便是淒涼況
味。

As a first rain passed at eventide,
Flocks of swallows twittered away amidst the chatter of orioles.
Beside the Lake Tai rockery
    were two or three stalks of tall bamboo.
It was the perfect place to rest his body,
    with nothing vulgar in sight.

There was a folding wind screen of several paper panels,
    a few scrolls of ink-wash paintings,
        and a single clay incense burner.

Freely and easily, this lays out the real flavor, but it also has the taste of a chillingly cold situation.

Coda
Of the rest, what would accompany him now?
An inkstone to use upon inspiration, a purple down-tipped
    brush, several sheets of paper,
A zither on the wall inlaid with precious gems, and books on his table.

In leisure he could seek out the abbot's chamber to chat with the
    exalted Buddhist,
And he could face the western chamber to intone poems on the white
    moon when melancholy.
This night the moonlit scene was bright as day,
And the student drew near the side of Oriole's courtyard.

There he extemporaneously chanted a little poem of twenty words:

A night flooded with the color of the moon,
A spring made silent and lonely by the shade of flowers,
Why, when approaching that white essence,
Do I not also see the woman of the moon?[107]

When the poem was done, he circled the courtyard with slow steps.

i.20 Zhonglü Diao Mode

The Hawk Takes the Hare
Facing the clarity of blue heaven,
The moon in the tranquil night
    like a mirror suspended,
Student Zhang walked slowly and
    gradually reached Oriole's courtyard.

---

107 Refers to the moon immortal Chang'e, who, in one tradition, is thought to be the
    wife of the archer Hou Yi. She stole from him an elixir of immortality, a gift from the
    Queen Mother of the West, and fled to the moon.

僧院悄，[11]
　迴廊靜。
花陰亂，
　東風冷。

颯～清風宛
身在此際。

對景傷懷，
　微吟步月，
　　淘寫深情。

詩罷躊躇，
　不勝情。
添悲哽。
一天月色，
　　滿身花影。
心緒惡，
　說不盡。
疑惑際 妙
　俄然聽。
聽得啞地門開，
　襲襲香至，
　　瞥見鶯鶯。

（尾）

臉兒稔色百媚生。
出得門兒來慢慢地行。
便是月殿里嫦娥也沒恁地撑。撑，方言謂美也。
　　　青天瑩潔，
　　　瑞雲都向鬢邊來；
　　　碧落澄暉，
　　　秀色並蠻眉上長。
　　　料想春嬌厭拘束，
　　　等閑飛出廣寒宮。
　　　容分一捻，
　　　體露半襟。
　　　軃羅袖以無言，
　　　垂湘裙而不語。

The monastery was quiet, and
     the winding corridor was still.
The flowers' shadows were chaotic,
     and the eastern wind was chill.
His heart was broken by the scene he faced
     and he softly chanted as he paced in the moonlight,
          giving vent to his deep emotions.

A rustling fresh breeze as if she were right there, right then.

Poem finished, he hesitated,
     unable to overcome his feelings,
Even more choked with grief.
A whole sky of moon-color
     covered his body with flowered shadows.
His mood darkened—
     too much for words.
And just on the edge of doubt and delusion EXCELLENT!
Suddenly he listened. . . .
He heard a door creak open—
     an unbroken drift of perfume reached him,
          and right before his eyes Oriole appeared.

Coda

With a tender face of a hundred kinds of charm,
She came out of the door and walked slowly along—
Not even Chang'e in her moon palace could be this hot. "HOT" IS DIALECT FOR "BEAUTIFUL."

     A clear sky of sparkling purity:
     auspicious clouds come to cluster at her temples.
     A blue void of clear radiance:
     the finest scenery spreads along her wrinkled brow.
     It seems this spring beauty is weary of being controlled,
     and has freely flown out of the Palace of Spreading Cold.[108]
     Her face just barely shows,
     Her body only reveals half of its form.
     She lets her silken sleeves droop and is silent,
     lets her silky woven skirt fall and says not a word.

[108] A legendary palace in the moon where beauties dwelt; it is also associated with Chang'e.

似湘陵妃子，

斜偎舜殿朱扉；

如月殿姮娥，

微現蟾宮玉戶。

i.21 仙呂調 （整花冠）

整整齊齊忒稔色。

姿姿媚媚紅白。

小顆顆的朱唇，

翠彎彎的眉黛。

疏～漸～，位
置迢遞。

滴滴春嬌可人意，

慢騰騰地行出門來。

舒玉纖纖的春筍，

把顫巍巍的花摘。

低矮矮的冠兒偏宜戴。

笑吟吟地喜滿香腮。

解舞的腰肢，

瘦岩岩的一搦，

簌簌的裙兒前刀兒短，

被你風韻韵煞人也猜。

穿對兒曲彎彎的

半折來大弓鞋。

（尾）

遮遮掩掩衫兒窄。

那些裊裊婷婷體態。

含情無限。

覷着剔團團的明月伽伽地拜。

不知心事在誰邊，

整頓衣裳拜明月。

佳人對月，依君瑞韻。

亦口佔一絕。其詩曰：

She is just like one of the consorts at the Xiang tumulus,[109]
clutching the red door-leaf of Shun's temple, half ajar,
or like Chang'e in the Hall of the Moon,
faintly appearing at the jade gate of the Toad Palace.[110]

i.21 Xianlü Diao Mode

Arranging the Flowered Hat
Prim and proper, just too lovely,
A beauty suffused with color.
A little round circle of vermilion lips,
    a green curve of eyebrows' kohl.
Brimming full, this spring beauty is so adorable,
    as she slowly walks out from the gate.
She extends her slender springtime shoots of jade,
    to pluck a quivering flower.

Imperceptibly her position moves further away.

The squat cap is perfectly worn,
With a slight smile, happiness suffuses her perfumed cheeks.
A waist made to dance,
    lithe and thin, barely a circle of the hands—
        swishing and rustling, the front panel of her skirt is
        short—
            her elegance is overwhelming!
And she wears a pair of curved
    arching shoes, a purlicue long![111]

Coda
The tunic hiding her body is tight,
She moves that lithe and limber little form
To make reverent obeisance while gazing at the perfectly round moon.

Unlimited passion on the verge of expression!

There was no way to know who occupied her mind
as she adjusted her clothing and prayed to the bright moon.
As the beauty faced the moon,
she also composed an answering poem on the spot,
to match Junrui's rhymes. The poem was:

---

109 The two consorts of Shun, Nüying 女英 and Ehuang 娥皇, wept for him at his tomb.
110 That is, the moon. Legend has it that a toad that lives in the moon swallows it during
    eclipses.
111 A purlicue is defined as the space between the thumb and the forefinger.

蘭閨久寂寞，
無事度芳春。
料得行吟者，
應憐長嘆人。

生聞之驚喜。

i.22 仙呂調（繡帶兒）

映花陰，
　　靠小欄。
照人無奈，
　　月色十分滿。
眼睛兒不轉。
仔細把鶯鶯偷看。
早教措大心撩亂。
怎禁那百媚的冤家，
　　多時也長嘆。

點染入神。

把張生新詩答和，
語若流鶯囀。
櫻桃小口嬌聲顫。
不防花下，
　　有人腸斷。

張生聞語意如狂。
相拋着大地苦不遠。
沒些兒忌憚。
便發狂言。
手撩着衣袂，
　　大踏步走至根前。
早見女孩兒家心腸軟。
唬得顫着一團。
幾般兒害羞赧。

每讀其轉換
處，如水窮山
盡，別出一段
煙波。

思量那清河君瑞，
　　也是個風魔漢。

My orchid chamber has long been lonely,
I have nothing to do to pass this fragrant spring.
I guess that the one who chanted as he walked
Will surely take pity on one who sighs so deeply.

When he heard this, Student Zhang was overjoyed!

i.22 Xianlü Diao Mode

The Embroidered Belt
Hidden in flowers' shadows,
    he leaned on the small balustrade.
Shining relentlessly,
    the moon was completely full.
His eyes never moved
As he stole a closer look at Oriole.
It drove this vinegar sack into turmoil.
How could he resist that predestined enemy, so graceful and
    charming?
    He sighed for a long while.
Perfectly matching Student Zhang's new poem,
    her spoken words flowed like the trill of an oriole.
Her beautiful voice trembled in her little cherry mouth—
And there was never a thought, there by the flowers,
    that someone's heart would break.

> *The finishing touches, applied to the point of spiritual resonance.*

When Student Zhang heard the intent of her words, he was like a
    madman.
Now there was hardly any distance between them
And without the slightest fear
He uttered wild words,
Gathered up the sleeves of his gown,
    and with steady steps strode right over.
We have already seen that this girl's feelings are tender—
He frightened her so much that she trembled all over,
With many embarrassed blushes!
Now, consider that Junrui from Qinghe
    was also a lunatic,

> *Every time I read places where he changes subjects, it's like rivers coming finally out of mountains to create distant misty waves.*

不防更被別人見。
　高聲喝道：「怎敢戲弄人家宅眷。」

（尾）

氣撲撲走得掇肩的喘。
勝到鶯鶯前面。
把一天來好事都驚散。

真所謂佳期難得，好事多磨。來的是誰。來的是誰。
張生覷，乃鶯之婢紅娘也。

鶯鶯問所以。

i.23 仙呂調（賞花時）

百媚鶯鶯正驚訝，
　道：「這妮子慌忙則甚那。
管是媽媽使來吵。」
紅娘低報：「教姐姐睡來呵。」

鶯忙紅淡張悶，
一～如畫。

（促鶯同歸。）

引調得張生沒亂煞。
「把似當初休見他。
越添我悶愁加。
非關今世，
管宿世冤家。」

（尾）

東風驚落滿庭花。
玉人不見朱扉亞。
「孩兒，莫不是俺無分共伊嘛。」

And didn't care if he was seen—
Suddenly a loud voice yelled out, "How dare you be so mischievous
*   with someone's daughter?"*

Coda
Gasping for air, running so fast that her breath shook her shoulders,
Suddenly she was there in front of Oriole,
Putting to flight this momentous and joyous occasion.

Truly, this is what is meant by the phrase, "A fine rendezvous is hard
to get, a happy event is often squashed." And who was it who came?
Who?[112] Student Zhang looked, and it was none other than Oriole's
maid, Crimson.

Oriole asked what she was doing.

i.23 Xianlü Diao Mode

Time to Enjoy the Flowers
Charming Oriole was truly startled,
And said, "Why is this little maid making such a fuss?
It must be that my mama has sent her here!"
Crimson reported in a low voice, "She's calling you in for bed."

Oriole fusses, Crimson is indifferent, the student is depressed: each of them is perfectly painted.

(She makes Oriole leave with her.)[113]

It all made Zhang crazed and befuddled,
"This makes me even more depressed
Than if I had never seen her.
And it's naught to do with this world,
      for she's a karmic enemy from my former lives."

Coda
The eastern wind shook down flowers to fill the courtyard,
The jade one disappeared as the vermilion leaf of the door
**   creaked shut.**
"Oh, child, could it be that I have no karmic lot to bring us
**   together?"**

112 Suspense point 4.
113 This phrase is set in smaller characters between stanzas of the song. It is written as an
     imperative and suggests that it indicates some form of directed physical movement.

生快快歸於寢,通宵無寐。

i.24 大石調 (梅梢¹²月)

劃地相逢,
　引調得,
　　人來眼狂心熱。
見了又休,
　把似當初,
　　不見是他時節。
惱人的一對多情眼,
　強睡些何曾交睫。
更堪聽
　　窗兒外面,
　　　子規啼月。

寫得平寂有韻。

此恨教人怎說。
　待拚了,
　　依前又難割捨。
一片狂心,
　九曲柔腸,
　　劃地悶如昨夜。
此愁今後知滋味,
　是一段風流冤業。
下梢管
　折倒了性命去也。

　自茲厥後,
　不以進取為榮,
　不以乾祿為用,
　不以廉恥為心,
　不以是非為戒。
　夜則廢寢,
　晝則忘餐。
　顛倒衣裳,
　不知所措。
　蓋慕鶯鶯如此。

Sullen and disgruntled, the student went back to his room. He did
   not sleep all that night.

i.24 Dashi Diao Mode

The Moon on Branch Tips of a Plum Tree
Suddenly they met,
     and it so stirred him up that
         his eyes went wild, and his heart grew hot.
He was finished as soon as he saw her—
     better, back in the beginning,
         had he never seen her at all.
Her passionate eyes brought only consternation—
     he tried to sleep but his eyelids never closed.
How could he bear listening to the cuckoo
     outside the window,
         chattering at the moon?

Written in a quiet ordinary way, but full of overtones.

How can one express such vexation?
     He wanted to be done with it,
         but as before, it was hard to give up.
A heart in turmoil,
     insides torn apart,
         he was as depressed as he'd been the night before.
"This taste of sadness will last forever,
     a karmic debt still owed to that enemy of a lover.
And the outcome of it all
     will surely ruin my life."

From then on, for him
there was no glory in the examinations
no use for a salary or wage,
no keeping a sense of honor or shame in his heart
no acting with respect to right and wrong.
At night he gave up sleep,
during the day he forgot to eat;
he put his clothes on backwards,
and never knew what he was doing.
This is how he yearned for Oriole.

i.25 大石調 （玉翼蟬）

前時聽
　和尚說，
　　空把愁眉斂。
道:「相國夫人
　從來性氣剛，
　　深有治家風範。」
怎敢犯。
尋思了
　空悶亂。
難睹鶯鶯面。
更有甚身心，
　書幃里做功課。
百般肖如風漢。

水乾了吟硯。
積漸里塵蒙了書卷。
千方百計，
　無由得見。
小庭那畔。
不見佳人門晝掩。
列翅着腳兒，
　走到千遍。
數幅花箋。
相思字寫滿。
無人敢暫傳。
正是：咫尺是冤家，
　渾如天樣遠。

　　　　客窗錯種疏疏竹，
　　　　細雨斜風故惱人。

i.26 雙調 （豆葉黃）

薄薄春陰，
　釀花天氣。

i.25 Dashi Diao Mode

A Jade-Winged Cicada
Back then he had listened
    as to the monk's explanation,
        and vainly wrinkled his sad brows.
The monk had said, "The wife of the Chancellor of State
    has always been unbending by nature and temperament
        and has strict protocols for running her house."
How dare he violate them?
After thinking it over,
    he felt empty, depressed, and confused.
It was so hard to get to see Oriole's face,
And now he had no mind
    to prepare lessons within his curtained study,
        for in every way he was an unhinged man.

The water dried up in his ink-stone,
Dust gradually settled over his books and scrolls.
He hatched thousands of plots, hundreds of plans,
    but could find no reason to see her.   '
Over in her little courtyard
He never saw the beauty, for her door was daytime shut.
With wavering steps
    he stumbled there a thousand times,
And filled reams of flower-patterned paper
With words of longing—
But there was no one to carry them to her.
True it is: "Your lover's house, a few feet away,
    is still as distant as the heavens."

        Outside of his window were randomly scattered
            bamboo,
        And a light rain and whipping wind seemed to vex him
            on purpose.

i.26 Shuang Diao Mode :

Bean Leaves Yellow
A light overcast spring,
    the season for brewing flowers.[114]

He begins once more from the monk's actual words. In anyone else's hand, this would be redundant. But here the more repetitive it is, the more it accords with one's sentiment, and the more ripples it creates.

---

114 That is, the flowers "brew" in their buds until ready to split open.

空齋無奈，只
合平～敘述纔
肖冷寂本色。

雨兒霏霺，
　風兒淅瀝。
藥欄兒邊鈎窗兒外。
妝點新晴，
　花染深紅，
　　柳拖輕翠。

採蕊的游蜂，
　兩兩相攜。
弄巧的黃鸝。
雙雙作對。
對景傷懷恨自己。
「病里逢春，
　四海無家，
　　一身客寄。」

（攬箏琶）
　窮愁淚。
　窮愁淚。
　掩[13]了又還滴。
　多病的情懷，
　　孤眠況味。
　說不得苦厭厭，
　　一個少年身己。
　都因為那薄幸種，
　　折倒得不戲。

　千般風韻，
　　一捻兒年紀。
　多宜。
　多宜。

At a dead end in the empty room. It is only appropriate to narrate this in an unremarkable manner before you can have the true color of cold

Rain, a cloud of drizzle,
    wind, blustery and blowing—
Beside the peony balustrade and
    outside the shutters,[115]
Dressing up the newly clearing day,
    flowers were dyed a deep red,
        and willows trailed their light green.

Plucking at pistils, roaming bees
    buzzed around in matching sets,
And clever little yellow orioles
Paired up two by two.
Struck sad by the scene he faced, he was vexed:
"Encountering spring sick
    and homeless within the four seas,
        a traveler lodges, a single soul."

Tuning the Strings
Tears of desolate sorrow.
Tears of desolate sorrow.
Wiped away, they fell again.
Feelings of such love-longing,
    the taste of sleeping alone.
An unspeakably painful depression
    in the body of this young man—
All because that capricious seed[116]
    had broken him down to this haggard state.

Her beautiful charm,
    her tender age—
Just perfect!
So perfect!

---

115 The shutters are for the balustrade, not the windows for their room. These are shutters hung on the outside of walkways or porticos that have a lattice railing. The shutters are suspended by "gooseneck" hooks from a horizontal axle at the top of each bay, between supporting posts and under an eave; they can be propped open by a pole set against the rail of the lattice work. Each bay has three shutters, and each shutter is divided horizontally into three sections with a square header of the same size (four sections total). Guo Zhongshu's 郭中恕 (d. 977) *Traveling on the River in Clearing After Snow* 雪霽江行圖 has clear pictures of a boat with such windows; see Ebrey 1999, 143.

116 The "seed" of his karma.

不惟道生得個龐兒美。
那堪更小字兒得愜人意。
蟲蟻兒里。
多情的鶯兒第一。
偏稱縷金衣。
你試尋思。
自家又沒天來大福，
　如何消得。

（慶宣和）
有甚心情取富貴。
一日瘦如一日。
悶答答孩地倚着個枕頭兒。
肖一似。
害的。

寫個帖兒倩人寄。
寫得不成個倫理。
欲待飛去欠雙翼。
甚時。
見你。

（尾）
心頭懷着待不思憶。
口中強道不憔悴。
怎瞞得青銅鏡兒裏。

千方百計，
無由得見意中人；
喪盡身心，
終是難逢忔戲種。

董詞之妙都於
無描畫中做出
幾尖新語。

Not only was she graced with a beautiful face,
But even more, her baby-name soothes one to hear, for
Among all small creatures
      the passionate oriole is the best and
So perfect for those golden-threaded clothes.[117]
Just think:
"I don't enjoy Heaven's great fortune—
      how can I ever be with her?"

Celebrating the Xuanhe Reign
What heart had he now to seize fame and glory?
Growing thinner every day and
Silently depressed, leaning on the pillow.
Just as if he had been
Injured.

He wrote letters, wanted to find someone to send them,
But his letters lacked all reason.
He wanted to fly away, but had not the wings—
"When?
Will I see you?"[118]

Coda
He longed for her in his heart until he couldn't recall her,
Made himself say, "I'm not all that haggard,"
But could he deceive that mirror of brass?

          Thousands of plans and plots—
          but still no way to see the one on his mind.
          Body and soul completely worn down—
          but impossible to see that delightful little karmic seed.

The marvel of Dong's writing is always to tease a few extremely novel phrases out of lackluster passages.

117 The yellow plumage of the oriole.
118 This entire last suite could also be read in the first-person voice as DJY08, 29–32 has translated it.
119 The strings slackened.
120 As he grew thinner.
121 In his lyric poem "Oriole" 鶯鶯, Qin Guan writes, "In the depths of night Crimson sends the clouds on their way" 紅娘深夜行雲送. Qin Guan 1985, 124.
122 From a poem by Li Bai 李白 (701–762), "Resentful Sentiments" 怨情: "The beauty furls the beaded curtain, / Sitting in the dark furrowing her moth-brows" 美人卷珠簾，深坐顰蛾眉. See Peng Dingqiu 1960, Vol. 6, 1882.

i.27 正宮 （虞美人纏）

> 霎時雨過琴絲潤。
> 銀葉龍香爇。
> 此時風物正愁人。
> 怕到黃昏。
> 忽地又黃昏。
>
> 花憔月悴羅衣褪。
> 生怕旁人問。
> 寂寥書舍掩重門。
> 手卷珠簾。
> 雙目送行雲。

（應天長）

> 兩眉無計解愁颦。
> 舊愁新恨。
> 這一番愁又新。
> 淹不斷眼中淚，
> 　搵不退臉上啼痕。
> 處置不下閑煩惱，
> 　磨滅了舊精神。

此段滋味少減，
然自去不得。

> 幾番修簡問寒溫。
> 又無人傳信。
> 想着後先斷魂。
> 書寫了數幅紙，
> 　更不算織錦回文。
> 我幾曾夢見人傳示，
> 　我虧你你虧人。

（萬金台）

> 比及相逢奈何時下窨。

123 From a poem by Xu Xuan 徐鉉 (916–991), "Sent as Matching Rhymes to Fang, Magistrate of Taizhou" 和方泰州寄: "The expelled traveler, anxious and lonely, again enters the capital, / Old sorrow and new vexations are equally hard to quell." See Fu Xuancong 1991, 101–102.

i.27 Zheng Gong Mode

The Beauty Yu: A Bound Suite
In a flash the rain had passed, the zither strings grew moist,[119]
Silver leaves: dragon-spittle incense turned to ash.
Scenes of this season truly made him sad—
Fear the approach of dusk and
Suddenly it is dusk once more.

Flowers were haggard, the moon was wan, silk clothes
    drooped.[120]
Worried someone would ask about him,
He closed the double door in his desolate study.
His hands rolled up the beaded curtain,
His eyes sent traveling clouds far away.[121]

Responding to Lengthening Days
He had no plan to relieve the sorrow, his brow furrowed,[122]
"New vexation on top of old sorrow—
But this time the sorrow is new.[123]
I cannot stop the tears in my eyes,
    or wipe away their streaks on my face.
I cannot quell this idle vexation,
    that has ground away my old spirit.

So many times, I've written notes to ask after her,
But there is no one to send my letters.
I think of her until my soul seems lost,
And I've written countless pages,
    but none count as a palindrome woven into brocade.[124]
I have often told her in my dreams:
    'I may treat you unfairly, but you have wronged me, too.'

The taste of this passage is a bit diminished but cannot be done away with.

A Platform of Gold
"The disappointment of our first encounter has now turned to
    despair.

---

124 Madam Su Hui 蘇蕙, the talented wife of Dou Tao 竇滔 (4th c.), wove a brocade
that included a palindromic poem (*Xuanji tu* 璇璣圖) expressing her love to send to
him after he was banished to the deserts of modern Xinjiang province. As DJY, 99
points out, this suite uses terms and allusions that are more normally associated with
women pining in their boudoir over distant lovers.

你尋思悶那不悶。
這些病何時可，
　待醫來卻又無個方本。
飲食每日餐三頓。
不曾飽吃了一頓。
一日十二個時辰。
沒一刻暫離方寸。

（尾）

　待登臨又不快閑行又悶。
　坐地又昏沈睡不穩。
　子倚着個鮫綃枕頭兒盹。

　　生從見了如花，
　　煩惱處治不下。
　　本待欲睡，
　　忽聽得櫳門兒低啞。
　　見個行者道：
　　「俺師父請吃碗淡茶。」
　　生攝衣而起，
　　勉就方丈，
　　與法本閑話。

i.28 正宮調（應天長）

前數幅寫盡
愁煩光景，至
此無可下手。
便捏出法本
閑話一段，轉
到紅娘大是作
家。

僧齋摒掠得好清虛。
有蒲團禪几、
　經案瓦香爐。
窗間修竹影扶疏。
圍屏低矮，
　都畫山水圖。
銀瓶點嫩茶，
　啜罷煩渴滌除。
有行者法師張君瑞，
、、、、、、、、
　、、、、、、、

Think about it! There's no way I could not be depressed.
When will this illness be cured?
If you bring in a physician, he'll have no prescription.
Three meals a day,
Yet I've never eaten my fill at one.
Twenty-four hours in a day,
But not a moment goes by that you don't appear in this square
    inch of my heart."

Coda
Desire he might to climb high and look down[125]**—no fun, and
    meandering was depressing.**
Sitting, he sank into a funk, and slept fitfully.
**He could only lie against his fine gauze pillow and occasionally
    nod off.**

        After the student saw the one like a flower,
        He couldn't control his agitation.
        He was trying to sleep
        When suddenly he heard the gentle creak of the door
        And saw an acolyte who said,
        "My master asks you to come have a cup of weak tea."
        The student gathered his clothes and rose,
        Forcing himself to go to the abbot's room
        And make idle conversation with Dharma Source.

i.28 Zheng Gong Mode

Responding to Lengthening Days
The monk's study had been tidied and was clean and uncluttered:
There were prayer mats and meditation armrests,
        sutra tables and tile incense burners.
Shadows of tall bamboo were thick and well-spaced in the
    window.
The surrounding screen was short and squat,
        and painted everywhere with patterns of mountains and
            waters.
A silver pitcher was brewing tender leaves of tea,
        and with a sip, both his troubles and thirst were gone.
**The acolyte, the Dharma Master, and Zhang Junrui were there
    by themselves, without any others.**

The several earlier passages have spelled out a scene of anxious worry that cannot be carried on at this point. So, he fabricates this section of desultory conversation with Dharma Source, and then moves on to Crimson. The mark of a great writer!

125 Also to compose poetry from that vantage point.

。。一個外人也無。。

許了林^雅下^閒做為侶。
說得言語：
真個不入俗。
高談闊論曉今古[14]。
一個是一方長老，
一個是一代名儒。
俗談沒半句。
那一和者也之乎、、
信道：「若說一夕話，
　勝讀十年書。」

（尾）。。。。。。。。

傾心地正說至投機處。
聽啞的門開瞬自覷。。。
見個女孩兒深深地道「萬福。」

　　　　桃源咫尺無緣到，
　　　、不意仙姬出洞來。

生再覷久之，乃向者促鶯之人也。

i.29 般涉調（牆頭花）
雖為箇侍婢，
、舉止皆奇妙。
那些兒鶻鴒、
　那^句些^俏兒掉。
曲彎彎的宮樣眉兒，
　慢鬆鬆地合歡髻小。

裙兒窄地，
　一搦腰肢裊。
百媚的龐兒，
　好那不好。

尾有煞尾有度
尾。煞尾如戰
馬收韁，度
尾如水窮雲
起。董西廂慣
露此手段～。

董詞此類甚夥，
然不厭目。

EXCELLENT! MEANINGFUL!
Each pledged to the other to become companions of the forest,[126]
To carry on conversations that truly eschewed the vulgar world.
Exalted conversation and wide-ranging discourse brought past and
    present to light.
One was an experienced abbot,
    the other would be the most famous scholar of his generation.
Not a half a sentence of vulgar chitchat,
And alike in their command of literate and literary conversation.
How true that "One evening's worth of conversation,
    is better than reading years of books."

Coda
Of like mind, they talked until they were on the same plane, and
They listened as the door creaked open and stared, blinking:
It was a young girl who said as she bowed deeply, "A myriad
    blessings, sires."

    The Peach Blossom Fount scarcely a foot away, yet no reason
        to go there,
    For unexpectedly a transcendent beauty emerged from that
        grotto.

The student took a second longer look, **and it was the girl who**
    had made Oriole leave.

i.29 Banshe Diao Mode

Flowers on the Wall
Just a maidservant,
    but her actions were still intriguing.
Those limpid orbs! Her beauty! *A NICE LINE!*
With curving brows done in palace style,
    her carelessly combed, loose lover's bun was small.

A skirt that swished along the ground,
    a hand-span waist slender and lithe.
A beautiful face
    finer than fine.
Tiny dots of vermillion lips,
    a pair of perceptive, darting eyes.

There are two kinds of codas: the abrupt and the transitional. The abrupt coda is like reining in a warhorse. The transitional coda is like clouds arising at the point where rivers end. Dong's Western Wing habitually reveals this method.

There are numerous phrases like this by Dong, yet they never tire the eye.

126 That is, those who met in the forest for deep discussions.

小顆顆的一點朱唇，
　溜沏沏一雙淥老。

不苦詐打扮，
　不甚艷梳掠。
衣服盡素縞，
　稔句色尖行為定有孝。
見張生欲語底頭，
　見和尚佯看又笑。

（尾）
道了個萬福傳示了。
姿媚地低聲道。
　「明日相國夫人待做清醮。」

法本令執事準備。紅娘辭去。

生止之曰：「敢問娘子：宅中未嘗見婢僕出入，何故。」

紅娘曰：「非先生所知也。」

生曰：「願聞所以。」

紅娘曰：「夫人治家嚴肅，朝野知名。夫人幼女鶯鶯，數日前，夜乘月色潛出，夫人竊知，令妾召歸。失子母之情，立鶯庭下，責曰：『爾為女子，容艷不常。更夜出庭，月色如晝，使小僧、遊客得見其面，豈不自恥。』鶯鶯泣謝曰：『今當改過自新，不必娘

She didn't trouble with makeup,
    she wasn't gorgeously turned out.
Her clothes were pure white silk
    and her careful actions clearly showed that she was in
        mourning. THIS LINE IS ACERBIC.
She saw Student Zhang and wanted to speak, but lowered her
    head,
    and seeing the monk, smiled and pretended to look at him
        instead.

Coda
After she said hello and relayed what business she had,
she spoke appealingly in a low voice,
"Tomorrow, Madam would like to do a Ritual of Deliverance."

Dharma Source ordered the Superintendent to prepare everything.
Crimson bid goodbye and left.

The student stopped her and said, "May I ask something? I've never
seen any servants, male or female, enter or exit your abode. Why is
that?"

Crimson replied, "That's not for you to know, sir."

"I would really like to know why," said the student.

Crimson said, "Madam Cui is very strict in her governance of the
household, and for that she's famous near and far. Her young daughter, Oriole, took advantage of the moonlight to slip out a few days ago,
and when she found out, she ordered me to fetch her back. Putting
aside all motherly affection, she made Oriole stand out in the courtyard and scolded her: 'You're just a girl, but you're unusually lovely.
Leaving our courtyard in the depths of the night, when the moonlight
is as bright as day, lets the younger monks and guests see your face.
Have you no sense of shame?' Oriole wept and begged pardon: 'I'll
correct my mistakes now and make a fresh start. There's no need
for you to worry yourself, Mother.' But her mother was so enraged
that Oriole dared not directly look at her. How much more trouble
would the uncontrolled comings and goings of a lesser woman be?"

自苦苦。』然夫人怒色，鶯不敢正視。況姨奶敢亂出
入耶。」

言訖而去。生謂法本曰：「小生備錢五千，為先父尚
書作分功德。」

師曰：「諾。」

中呂調（牧羊關）
適來因把紅娘問。
說夫人恁般情性。
「作事威嚴，
　治家廉謹。」
無處通佳耗，
　無計傳芳信。
欲要成秦晉。
天天除會聖。

悶答孩地倚着窗台兒盹[15]。
你尋思大小大鬱悶。
處治不下，
　擘劃[16]不定。
得後是自家採，
　不得後是自家命。
更打着黃昏也，
　兀的不愁殺人。

（尾）
黨或明日見他時分。、
把可憎的媚臉兒飽看了一頓。
便做受了這悽惶也正本。

She left once she had finished, and the student said to Dharma Source, "I have prepared five strings of cash to share the ritual on behalf of my late father, the Grand Secretary."

"Granted," said Dharma Source.

i.30 Zhonglü Diao Mode

Shepherd's Pass
He had just questioned Crimson
So she explained the temperament of Madam Cui:
"She is severe and strict
    and rules her household with integrity and caution."
No way now to communicate fine messages,
    no plan to send along fragrant letters.
Desire though he might to complete the alliance of Jin and Qin,[127]
Oh, Heaven, Heaven, if only he had some magic power!

He nodded off as he leaned despondently on the window ledge,
Just imagine how morose he was!
No way to deal with it and
    no certain way to end it.
"If I can do it, it's luck;
    if I can't, then it's life.
And now dusk is drawing near,
It makes me all too sad!

Coda
"If I can, when I see her tomorrow,
I'll sate my eyes with the beautiful face of that hateful one,
And that will compensate me for all this misery."[128]

The student said, "I'll see *you* tomorrow at the ceremony." But he was even more sleepless, thinking only of Oriole.

"Compensation" is "getting one's love requited," which is what Wang Jide means by his gloss of "being paid back."

127 These states made hereditary marriage alliances state policy. This later became a metaphor for arranging marriages between two different surnames.
128 Referring to Wang Jide's gloss of a line of the *Luo sining* aria in Book I, act 3 of the drama *Western Chamber*: "'Tonight in our poetic exchange, I saw her true feelings.' Comment: This means that he will surely gain her love, therefore he says, 'I will repay my capital expenditure with true love.'" See Wang Jide 1614, play 1, act 3, 29b.

生曰：「來日向道場里須見得你。」越睡不着，只是
想着鶯鶯。

i.31 中呂調（碧牡丹）
　　小春寒尚淺。
　　前嶺早梅應綻。
　　玉壺一夜，
　　　積漸裏冰澌生滿。
　　業重身心，
　　　把往事思量遍。
　　悶如絲，
　　　愁似織，
　　　　夜如年。

少此一段不
得。

　　自從人個別，
　、何曾考五經三傳。
　　怎消遣。
　　除告得紙和筆硯。
　　待不尋思，
　　　怎奈心腸軟。
　　告天天，
　　　天不應，
　　　、奈何天。、、、、

（尾）、、、、、、、、、
　　沒一個日頭兒心放閑。
　　沒一個時辰兒不掛念。
　　沒一個夜兒不夢見。

張生捱得個天曉，來看做醮，已早安排了畢。

i.32 越調（上平西纏令）

i.31 Zhonglü Diao Mode

Blue-Green Peony
A little spring:[129] only a light coolness,
Early plums on peaks ahead responded by splitting open their
buds.
A full night of a jade-pot moon
    that gradually filled with ice.

Karmic debts as well as wrongs weighed heavily on his mind   *Cannot do without*
    as he reflected on the past.   *this passage.*
Depression like silk threads,
    sorrow the very cloth they wove—
        a night as long as a year.

From the time they each went their own way   *The term* daxiao
    he touched neither the classics nor their commentaries.   *is saying "how*
                                                                 greatly."
"How can I carry on?
All I can do is take up paper, brush, and inkstone.
I may not want to ponder it
    but my heart and mind are weak.
I cry up to Heaven, 'Oh, Heaven,'
    But Heaven does not respond.
        Heaven gives no recourse.

Coda
"Not a day can my heart rest at ease,
Not an hour do I not think of her,
Not a night does she not appear in my dreams."

Zhang made it through to dawn and came to look at the ceremony,
which had already been arranged.

i.32 Yue Diao Mode

The Emperor Quells the West: A Bound Suite
The moon sank,
    roosters crowed,
        the eastern rim began to appear.

129 The tenth lunar month, an Indian summer. The passage here is derived from the first
    stanza of a lyric poem by Ouyang Xiu. See Qiu Shaohua 2001, 157.

月兒沈，
　雞兒叫，
　　現東方。
日光漸擁出扶桑。
諸方檀[17]越，
　不論城郭與村方。
一齊齊隨喜道場來，
　罷鋪收行。

登經閣，
　游塔位，
　穿佛殿，
　　立迴廊。
繞着聖位隨喜十王。
供壇高壘，
　寶花香火間金幢。
救拔亡過相公靈，
　、滅罪消殃。

（鬥鵪鶉）
　法聰收拾，
　　鼓鳴鐘響。
　眾僧雲集，
　　盡臨壇上。
　有法悟法空，
　　慧明慧朗。
　甚嚴潔，
　　甚磊浪。
　法堂里擺列着
　　諸天聖像。

次眾僧錯綜。

　整整齊齊，
　　自然成行。
　只少個圓光，
　　便似聖僧模樣。

Rays of light formed an orb as a sun emerged from the Fusang
     Tree.[130]
Lay benefactors from every quarter—
     city, borough, village, and ward—
Flocked together to sightsee at the ceremonial space,
     closing their shops and shutting down the guilds.

They climbed the sutra gallery,
     rambled by the pagoda,
          crossed through the Buddha Hall,
               and lingered in the corridors.
Round they went about the sacred statues,
     amusing themselves with the Ten Kings of Hell.
The offering altar was piled high,
     and precious flowers and incense dispersed under the golden
          canopies—
Thus, would they rescue the soul of the old Minister,
     extinguish his sins and dissolve all his misfortunes.

Fighting Quail
**Dharma Wit brought the preparations to a close—
     drums sounded and gongs echoed.
The congregation of monks formed like clouds
     and drew as close as possible to the altar.
There were Dharma Enlightenment, Dharma Emptiness,
     Wisdom Bright, and Wisdom Light.**   *An intricate order-
So solemn and pure,   *ing of the monks.*
     **so majestic they were—
Living statues of the Kings of Heavens,
     they arrayed themselves in the Dharma Hall.**

**In perfect rank and perfect row
     they naturally formed their lines,
Lacking only coronas of light
     to make them resemble sagely monks.
Dharma Source approached the altar,
     and the crowd looked up in anticipation.**

130 Stories about where the sun comes from are found in various myths; in one, nine
    ravens roost there, and each day one brings the sun across the sky.

法本臨壇，
　眾人瞻仰。
盡稽首，
　都合掌。
至心先把，
　諸佛供養。

（青山口）
　眾髧鬏簇捧着個老婆娘。
　頭白渾一似霜。
　體穿一套孝衣裳。
　年紀到六旬以上。
　臨壇揖了眾僧，
　　叩頭禮下當陽。
　左壁頭個老青衣
　　拖着歡郎。
　右壁個佳人。
　　舉止輕盈，
　　　臉兒說不得的搶。
　把^真蓋^雅頭^淡兒^語揭起，
　　不甚梳粧。
　自然異常。
　鬆鬆雲鬏偏，
　　彎彎眉黛長。
　首飾又沒，
　　着一套兒白衣裳。
　直許多韻相。

（雪裏梅）
　諸僧與看^晃人^炫驚^燿晃。
　瞥見一齊都望。
　住了念經，
　　罷了隨喜，
　　　忘了上香。

老寡嫩拖兒孥女光景絕似。

文章之妙，全在借客形主。若只寫崔之奇豔，張風狂，人皆能之。此却把眾和尚閙～攘～處，極力指畫，正為張生張本。

They all bowed their heads
    and pressed their palms together in front.
With a sincere heart he first
    paid obeisance to the various Buddhas.

Green Mountain Pass
A group of maidservants clustered around to support an old lady,
Her hair the color of frost,
Her body draped in mourning clothes—
Her years clearly more than sixty.
After she had bowed to the monks at the altar,
    she kowtowed and paid reverence to the Buddha.
On her left was first an old grisette
    dragging along Happy, Madam Cui's son, and
On her right, a beauty with
    movement so light and dainty,
        and a face of inexpressible beauty.

A near mimetic scene of the old woman dragging along her child and bringing along her daughter.

She lifted her veil TRULY WORDS THAT ARE ELEGANT AND MILD.
    But was not made up at all—
She was naturally beyond compare.
Loose and free, her clouds of tresses hung askew
    and curving brows of kohl-black were long.
Nothing to adorn her hair,
    dressed only in a long white gown—
Truly the image of elegance.

A Plum in the Snow
Both monks and onlookers were stunned by her brilliance,   FLASHY: BRILLIANT
And at first glance, they all fixed their eyes on her.
They stopped chanting the sutras,
    left off their sightseeing,
        forgot their offerings of incense.

The beauty of this passage is that it utilizes peripheral characters to describe the main characters. Anyone would be capable of writing about the rare beauty of Oriole or the lunatic behavior of Zhang. But here it uses extraordinary effort to describe the clamor and hubbub of the monks precisely. A foreshadowing of Student Zhang's behavior later.

From gentry, farmer, craftsman to merchant—
Everyone fell into turmoil.
No matter old, young, good-looking, vulgar—
    the whole altar space turned hot and wild.

The older monks stared madly and their hearts itched with desire,
The young ones rubbed their pates and shriveled from fear.

選甚士農工商。
　　一地裏鬧鬧攘攘。
折莫老的小的
　俏的村的，
　　滿壇裏熱荒。

老和尚也眼狂心癢。
小和尚每搯頭束項。
立掙了法堂。
　九伯了法寶，
　　軟癱了智廣。

（尾）
　添香侍者似風狂。
　執磬的頭陀呆了半晌。
　作法的闍黎神魂蕩颺。
　不顧那本師和尚。
　聒起那法堂。
　怎遮當。
　貪看鶯鶯鬧了道場。

　禪僧既見，
　　十年苦行此時休；
　　行者先憂，
　　二月桃花今夜破。

i.33　　餘者尚然，
　　張生何似。

大石調（吳音子）
　張生心迷着色事，
　　破了八關戒。
　佛名也不執，
　　舊時敦厚性都改。
　抖搜風狂，

Dharma Hall shivered,
Dharma Treasure was driven insane,
    and Wisdom Wide went limp.

Coda
The incense tenders seemed crazed,
The ascetics holding the chimes went blank for a while,
The preceptor of students performing the rituals felt his soul float
    away—
They paid no attention to that Buddhist Master Dharma Source,
But stirred up a ruckus in the ritual hall.
How could it be avoided?
Greedily eyeing Oriole, they created pandemonium in the whole
    sacred space!

Once the monks saw her:
ten years of arduous practice suddenly shuddered to a halt.
The acolytes were the first to worry:
tonight, a peach-blossom of the second month had burst open
    before their eyes.
With the rest like this, well then, what about Student
    Zhang?

i.33 **Dashi Diao Mode**

Sounds of Wu
Zhang's heart was so lost in her beauty
    that he would gladly violate all eight precepts.[131]
Buddha's very name dropped from his mind
    and his old mild and sincere disposition disappeared.
Riled up and frenzied,
    he played the madman.
He stirred up trouble,
Stirred up trouble!

擺弄九伯。
作怪。
作怪。

騁無賴。
傍人勸他，
　又誰偢倸。
大師遙見，
ヽ坐地不定害澀奈。
覷着鶯鶯，
ヽ眼去眉來。
被那女孩兒
不偢。
不倸。

（尾）
短命冤家薄情煞。
兀的不枉教人害，
少負你前生眼兒債。

抵暮，暮食畢，大作佛事。

i.34 般涉調（哨遍纏令）
是夜道場，
　同業大眾，
ヽヽ眾僧都來到。
寶獸爐中瑞煙飄，　ヽヽヽ
ヽ璀璀地把金磬初敲。
眾僧早躬身合掌，
ヽ稽首皈依佛ヽ法、僧三寶。
相國夫人煞年老。
虔心豈避辭勞。
鶯鶯雖是個女孩兒，
　孝順別人卒難學。
禮拜無休，
ヽ追薦亡靈，

Entirely shameless.   *"BRILLIANCE" HERE MEANS DAZZLING*
Well-intentioned advice from those around him
    went completely unheeded.
The abbot saw him from a distance
    and squirmed in his seat, embarrassed for him.
Gazing at Oriole
    Zhang sent her hints with eyes and brows,
But he was ignored by the girl,
Utterly ignored.

Coda
"Damned-to-early-death little enemy, so devoid of any feeling!
You make me suffer love's sickness for nothing—
I must still owe a debt to your eyes from some former life!"[132]

It turned to dusk, and when the evening meal was finished, an
    elaborate service was held.

i.34 Banshe Diao Mode

Whistling Song: A Bound Suite
The altar ground this night
    was packed with lay believers,
        and all the monks as well.
Auspicious smoke drifted from precious beast censers,
    and clinking and ringing, the metal chimes were struck first.
Already, the assembled monks
Had bent forward to join their palms in front, and
    bowed their heads to embrace
        the Three Treasures: the Buddha, the Law, and the
            Sangha.
The Minister of State's wife was quite old,
But too pious to abjure these tiring tasks.
Oriole might be just a girl,
    but was filial in a way that others could not match—
She knelt in supplication without rest, and
    recited scriptures and penitences for her father
        to rescue and free his lost soul.

But that troublemaking student
    sat there like a mad mischief-maker.

救拔先考。

那作怪的書生，
　坐間肖一似風魔顛倒。
大來沒尋思，
　所為沒些兒斟酌。
到來一地的亂道。
　幾曾懼憚，
　　相國夫人，
　　　不怕旁人笑。
盛說法，
　打匹似鬧唵諢，
　　正念佛作偈，
　　　把美令兒胡嘌。
秀才家那個不風魔，
　大抵這個酸丁忒劣角。
風魔中占得個招討。

正當敘事忽插數語，嬉笑怒罵，種～逼真。

（急曲子）
　比及結絕了道場，
　　惱得諸人煩惱。
智深着言苦勸，
　「解元休心頭怒惡。
譬如^妙這^語裏鬧鑊鐸。
把似書房裏睡取一覺。」

鑊鐸，喧鬧之意。

（尾）
　道着睬也不睬，
　　焦也不焦。
眼眯眯地伴呆着。
一夜葫蘆提鬧到曉。

葫蘆提，方言糊塗也。

日欲出，道場罷，眾僧請夫人燒疏。

He wasn't thinking,
    took nothing into consideration.
He spewed nonsense,
Showed no fear or trepidation
    about the Minister's wife, and
        didn't care who laughed at him.
Right at the peak of the explanation of the Dharma Law,
    he broke out with seemingly random vulgar jokes,
        and when they prayed to the Buddha and sang hymns,
        he wildly sang out songs of love.
Now, which young student isn't crazed?
    But this vinegary pedant was just too perverse!
He had claim on a military rank: General of the Army of Lunatics!

Right in the middle of his narrative he inserts these words. Laughable and funny or angry and cursing—everything rings true.

An Accelerando Song
By the time the ceremony was over,
    he had annoyed everyone there.
Wisdom Deep, trying to get him to do the right thing, said,
    "My Laureate, stop all this anger and hate in your heart!
Instead of rattling your pots here, FANTASTIC LANGUAGE!
    Why don't you go back to your study and sleep!"

"Rattling your pots here" means to create a noisy disturbance.

Coda
He paid no attention to what was said,
    heeded nothing,
And feigned slow-wittedness with sleepy, half-closed eyes—
The whole night was a muddle, he carried the ruckus on right through
    'til dawn.

"A muddle" is dialect for "a mess."

The ceremony ended as the sun was about to rise. The host of monks asked the Lady to burn the writ of salvation.

Endnotes

1   Reading 桿 for 捍.
2   In some editions, this has been mistakenly written or copied as 槎.
3   Reading 霸 as 灞.
4   Replacing 覽 with 賢.
5   Reading 鐘 for 鍾 here and afterward.
6   Uniformly changing 俏 to 肖 when used in simile structures here and hereafter.
7   Reading 年 for 正.
8   Reading 廝 for 廁.
9   Reading 佰 for 百.
10 Reading 大師 for 太師.
11 Reading 消 for 俏 .
12 Reading 梢 for 稍.
13 Reading 掩 for 淹.
14 Reading 今古 for 古今.
15 Reading 盹 for 肫.
16 Reading 劃 for 畫.
17 Reading 檀 for 壇.

董解元西廂 卷二
明 臨川湯顯祖義仍甫評

i.35/ii.1 商調（定風波）
  燒罷功德疏。
  百媚地鶯鶯不勝悲哭。
  似梨花帶春雨。
  老夫人哀聲不住。
  那君瑞醮臺兒旁立地不定，
   瞑子里歸去。

瞑子,調侃暗
地也.

  法本眾僧徒。
  別了鶯鶯夫人子母。
  佛堂里自監覷。
  覷着收拾鋪陳來的什物。
  見個小僧入得角門來，
   大踏步走得來慌速。

（尾）
  口苆目瞠面如土。
  唬殺那諸僧和寺主。
  氣喘不迭叫苦。

  天曉眾僧恰齋罷，忽一小僧，荒急來稱「禍事。」

Book II

Laureate Dong's Story of the Western Wing

ii.1/i.35 Shang Diao Mode[1]

Settling Windblown Waves
With the burning of the writs of merit finished,
The beautiful Oriole could not stop her sad weeping,
Her face like a pear blossom laden with rain.
The old madam's lamentations went on and on.
Junrui, who had been standing uneasily beside the ceremonial dais,
    slipped back to his room, keeping out of sight.

"Out of sight" is a sarcastic way of saying "unnoticed."

Dharma Source and all the acolytes
Parted from
    both mother and child,
And kept a watchful eye in the Buddha Hall,
Overseeing the gathering up of the implements that had been
    brought out.
Suddenly, they spied a young monk entering through the side door,
    bounding toward them, terribly flustered.

Coda
His mouth agape and his eyes bulging, his face the color of dirt,[2]
He shouted to all the monks and the Supervisor of the
    Monastery—
All the while panting, out of breath, crying of the suffering to
    come.

At daybreak the monks had finished the morning meal, when suddenly
a younger monk showed up agitated and crying out, "Disaster!"

---

1   In other editions, this is the last song of the first book.
2   In this case, the ocher color of loess.

ii.2/ii.1 仙呂調（剔銀燈）

> 堦下小僧報覆。
> 「觀了三魂無主。
> 塵閉了青天，
> 　旗遮了紅日，
> 　　滿空紛紛土雨。
> 鳴金擊鼓。
> 　擺槊搶刀，
> 　　把寺圍住。
>
> 為首強人英武。
> 見了早森森地怯懼。
> 裹一頂紅巾，
> 　珍珠如糝飯，
> 　　甲掛唐夷兩副。
> 靴穿抹 綠。
> 　騎匹如龍，
> 　　卷毛赤兔。」

（尾）

> 「彎一枝䆒鐙黃華弩。
> 搶柄籤箕來大開山板斧。
> 是把橋將士孫飛虎。」

3　Literally, "brushed green," an iridescent black, like dark and shiny hair.

4　"Red Harrier," the name of the horse that the stalwart Three Kingdoms general Lü 呂布 (161–199, byname Fengxian 奉先) rode, later became a common term for a magnificent steed. He praised his steed in the following words:

> This horse is out of the ordinary. The spots of blood that appear all over it are bright red, and its mane and tail are like fire, so it is called Red Harrier. The prime minister said that it is not called a red harrier because it is bright red, but it is called a harrier horse because it is used for hunting hares with a bow: when you are riding on dry land and it sees a hare, it will not start, so there is no need to rein it in or to make it hold firm for the bowshot. That's why it is

ii.2/ii.1 Xianlü Diao Mode

Trimming the Silver Lamp
At the foot of the steps, the young monk reported,
"After I saw it, my three souls were lost to me.
Dust shut off the blue sky,
    banners blocked the red sun
        and the air was filled with a rain of dust.
Ringing gongs and pounding drums,
Shaking spears and brandishing swords,
    they have surrounded the monastery.

The strapping man at their head is a martial hero,
And as soon as I saw him, I shriveled in fear.
Wrapped in a kerchief of red
    peppered with jewels,
        he wears a doubled suit of armor of the finest iron plating
          from Tang
The boots he wears are shiny black,[3]
    the horse he rides is like a dragon—
        a Red Harrier[4] with a curling mane.

Coda
"He cocks a leap-into-the-stirrup crossbow of yellow birch,[5]
And wields an open-the-mountains broadaxe as big as a
    winnowing basket—
He is Flying Tiger Sun, who held fast the bridge!"

called Red Harrier. He also said that when this horse comes to a river, it fords the water just as if it were on level land. When it reaches the middle of the river, [because] it doesn't eat grass or straw, it swallows fish and turtles. This horse can go a thousand li in a single day and can carry over eight hundred pounds. This is no ordinary horse!
See Idema and West 2012, 30, n. 34; and 40–43.

5   Reading 樺 for 華. From the *General Principles of Military Classics* (*Wujing zongyao* 武經總要), "Crossbows cocked by one person are adorned with black lacquer, and they are yellow and white birch, or birch the color of arsenic trisulfide. Somewhat smaller are the 'leap-into-the-stirrup' crossbow and the simple wooden crossbows. The leap-into-the-stirrup crossbow is also called 'little yellow.'" See Zeng Gong et al., 2018, 13.9a.

唐蒲關乃屯軍之處。是歲渾太師薨，被丁文雅不善御軍。
其將孫飛虎半萬兵叛，劫掠蒲中。如何見得。《鶯鶯本傳歌》
為證。歌曰，

> 河橋上將亡官軍，
> 虎旗長戟交壘門，
> 鳳凰詔書猶未到，
> 滿城戈甲如雲屯。
> 家家玉帛棄泥土，
> 少女嬌妻愁被虜，
> 出門走馬皆健兒，
> 紅粉潛藏欲何處。
> 嗚嗚阿母啼向天，
> 窓中抱女投金鈿，
> 鉛華不顧欲藏艷，
> 玉顏轉瑩如神仙。

一歌風艷。

ii.3/ii.2 正宮 （文序子纏）

> 諸師長，
> 　權且住，
> 　　略聽開解。
> 不幸死了蒲州，
> 　渾瑊元師。
> 把河橋將文雅，
> 　荒淫素無良策。
> 亂軍失統，
> 　劫掠蒲州，
> 　　把城池損壞。

---

6   Hun Jian 渾瑊 (736–800, also known as Loyal and Martial Prince of Xianning 咸寧
忠武王) was a descendent of the Hun tribe of the Tiele peoples from what is now
modern Ningxia and was originally named Rijin 日進. His father was a Regional
Commander during the mid-Tang, and father and son both fought in the Tang army
during the An Lushan Rebellion and in later insurrections against Emperor Dezong
(r. 779–805).

The Pu Pass area in the Tang dynasty was the site of a long-term military base. General Hun[6] had died that year and because the army was woefully mishandled under Ding Wenya,[7] Flying Tiger Sun had rebelled with some five thousand troops and pillaged Puzhong. How do we know? There is the "Song of Oriole's Original Story" as proof. It goes:

The Superior General holding the Yellow River bridge viewed the
    government forces as nothing,
Tiger flags and long halberds crossed at his encampment's main gates.
Phoenix rescripts by imperial hand had yet to arrive,
And weapons and armor filled the city like gathering clouds.
Silk and jade were cast aside in the mud,
Charming young wives and beautiful girls feared capture.
Out the door and onto ready horses, all the young men fled,
But where to secretly hide those rouged in red?
Wailing, mothers wept to Heaven,
Holding daughters in the window, they threw out golden hair
    ornaments;[8]
With white lead powder, they tried to conceal those beauties,
But their jadelike faces only revealed the jadeite sparkle of divine
    immortals.[9]

The entire song is elegant and gorgeous.

ii.3/ii.2 Zheng Gong Mode

Master Wen Xu: A Bound Suite
Now, my various masters in the audience,
    let us stop for a moment
        and listen as I explain:
Marshal Hun Jian
    unfortunately died in Puzhou.
And the general holding the bridge over the Yellow River, Ding
    Wenya,
    was dissolute and lacked any suitable strategy.
He lost control, and his army, bent on rioting,
    plundered Puzhou,[10]
        destroying the city walls and moat.

---

7   The only information on this general lies in texts involving Oriole and Student Zhang.
8   Hoping people would take them as payment to hide their daughters away.
9   Adding to their attraction. See Li and Wang 1985, 130.
10 While Puzhou would have been a large district, this refers to the walled city where the provincial offices were headquartered.

劫財物，
　奪妻女，
　　不能掙揣。
豈辨個是和非，
　不分個皂白。
南鄰北里成灰，
　劫掠了民財。
蒲城裏豈辨個後巷前街。
變做屍山血海。

（甘草子）
　驀無賴。
　驀無賴。
　於中個首將罪過迷天大。
　是則是英雄，
　臨陣披重鎧。
　倚仗着他家有手策。
　欲反唐朝世界。
　不來後是咱家眾僧採。
　來後怎當待。

（脫布衫）
　來後怎生當待。
　思量恁怪那不怪。
　猶然甚矮也不矮。
　彷彿近此中境界。

（尾）
　那裏到一個時辰外。
　埲埲騰騰地塵頭蔽日色。
　半萬賊兵騰到來。

氣色亦佳。

接句跌宕。

They looted money and property
    and wrested away wives and daughters
        who could not save themselves.
How could those soldiers know right from wrong
    or even distinguish black from white?
The southern neighborhoods and northern alleyways were all
    turned to ash,
    and looters stripped the people of their wealth.
In the walled city of Pu none could distinguish back alleys from
    main streets,
For it was all a mountain of corpses and a sea of blood.

The color of this passage is also superb.

Dried Licorice Root
Treacherous good-for-nothings!
Out of control thieves!
And in their midst, at their head, is a general whose
    transgressions rise to Heaven!
Yes, a brave hero he might be,
    approaching battle dressed in his doubled armor.

But he merely relies on the skills of others.
His sole desire is to overturn the world of the Tang.
If he doesn't reach us here, then we monks are all in luck.
But what if he comes?

Doffing the Cotton Shirt
"How can we withstand them?
Whatever we might think, there is no time to debate it,
Why are we still dilly-dallying?[11]
Because it seems they will reach the borders of this distric*t!*"

Coda
And sure enough, in less than an hour,
Billowing and swirling, clouds of dust rose to shut out the color
    of the sun—
Five thousand strong, the rebel soldiers were suddenly at the
    gate.

Flowing freely from one sentence to the next.

---

11 Following the interpretation of the line as explained in DJY, 121.

寺僧不及措手，惟掩戶以拒軍。賊以劍扣門，飛鏃入寺，
大呼曰，「我無他取，惟望一飯。」

典寺者與僧眾議，「欲開門迎賊，法堂廊宇，足以屯眾，
悉與會食，聊贈財賄，以悅眾心，庶惡人不生兇意。若不然，
恐斬關而入，不問老幼善惡，皆被殘滅。大眾可否。」

執事僧智深啓大師曰，「開門迎賊，於我何害。今寺有崔
夫人幼女鶯鶯，年少貌麗，亂軍既入，若不準備[1]，必被
虜掠而去。崔相姻親交朋，蒙恩被德，職司權路，不利
後事。雖被賊掠，皆我開門迎賊所致。執作同情，何辭
以辯。」

ii.4/ii.3 大石調 （伊州衰）

　　　佛堂里，
　　　　諸僧盡商議。
　　　開門欲迎賊。
　　　於中監寺道不可
　　　　對眾說及仔細。
　　　「亂軍賊黨，
　　　　儻或摅了鶯鶯，
　　　　　怎的備。
　　　朝野所知。
　　　　滿寺里僧人
　　　　　索歸逝水。」

The monks in the monastery had no time to do anything but close the gates to repel the army. The rebels knocked on the main gate with their swords, and flying arrowheads fell into the grounds. The rebels bellowed, "We will take nothing else, all we want is a meal."

The Comptroller of the Monastery[12] discussed this with the assembly: "I want to open the gates and welcome the rebels. There is plenty of space in the corridors and courtyard of the Buddha Hall to station the lot. We should provide them meals and give them presents as bribes, to mollify the group's desires, then hope that the bad lot among them will not resort to violence. If we don't let them in, I fear they will break the gates open and come in anyway, slaughtering everyone—young, old, good, or bad. What do all of you think?"

The Steward of the Monks, Wisdom Deep, petitioned the Grand Master, saying, "There's no harm to us, should we open the gates and let the bandits in. But now we have the young daughter of Lady Cui in residence, and she is young and beautiful. Once this uncontrollable army enters, if we are not prepared in advance[ii] she will be abducted and taken away. Minister Cui's relatives by marriage, friends, and those who have benefitted from his grace and virtue all occupy important offices and powerful positions—so this would do us no benefit later. Although it would be the bandits who abducted her, our opening the gates would have led to it. How would we explain away a charge that we conspired with them?"

ii.4/ii.3 Dashi Diao Mode

Yizhou Tremolo
In the Buddha Hall,
    the monks finished their deliberations.
And decided to open the doors and let the rebels in.
In their midst the Second Abbot said, "Impossible"
        and proceeded to explain in detail,
"Should this fractious army and band of rebels
        abduct Oriole
            how would we prepare?
Should everyone at court and abroad find out, then
        every monk and every person in this monastery would be
            nothing but water lost under a bridge."

---

12 The monk in charge of finances. See DDB entry for 監寺 in Muller 2012.

大師言道「如何是。

　　諸亂軍屯門首，

　　　　不能戰敵。」

眾中個和尚，

　　歷聲高叫如雷。

道「大師休怕。

　　眾僧三百餘人，

　　　　只管絮聒聒地。

空有身材，

　　枉吃了饅頭沒見識。」

（尾）

英氣英語。

　　把破設設地偏衫揭將起。

　　手提着戒刀三尺。

　　道「我待與群賊做頭抵。」

這和尚是誰，乃是法聰也。聰本陝右蕃部之後。少好弓劍喜遊獵。常潛入
蕃國，盜掠為事，武而有勇。一旦父母淪亡，悟世路浮薄，出家于此寺。

「大丈夫之志決矣。既遇今之亂，安忍坐視，非仁者之用心也。願得寺僧
有勇敢，共力破賊，易如振槁自斷。衆止一二作乱，餘必脅從。見目前之利，
忘返掌之災。我若敷陳利害，必使逆徒不能奮武作威，自令奔潰。」

ii.5/ii.4 仙呂調（繡帶兒）

　　不會看經，

　　　　不會禮懺。

The Grand Master said, "What's the right thing to do?
The fractious armies
    are camped at our gates
        and we can't battle such an enemy."
Then, from out of the crowd a single monk
    shouted with a voice like thunder and
Said, "Have no fear Grand Master!
    You and your three hundred monks
        just yammer on.
How useless that you've been given a body
    only to equivocate in indecision
        so you can mooch steamed buns off of us!"

Coda
He lifted the hem of his ragged monk's robe,
Raised his three-foot ordination knife,
And said, "I want to do battle with these rebels!"

Heroic senti-
ments and heroic
language.

Who was this monk?[13] It turned out to be Dharma Wit. He was originally descended from a foreign tribe in the western part of Shaanxi. When he was young, he loved archery, swordsmanship, and being out on the hunt. He often stole into foreign lands to rob and plunder. He was martial and he was brave. But one day his parents died, and the shallow triviality of the secular life became clear to him. So, he became a monk in this monastery.

"A real man, my mind is made up. Now that we've encountered this insurrection, to simply sit by while merciless cruelty goes on is just not how a humane person would act. I want to find some monks among us brave enough to fight fiercely and smash these rebels. It will be as easy as breaking a brittle branch! If only one or two of that mob wreak havoc, others will be compelled to follow. Seeing only the benefit before their eyes, they forget the disaster that will soon ensue. If I explain the risks carefully, those lackeys won't have the courage to fight, and they'll flee on their own."

ii.5/ii.4   Xianlü Diao Mode

The Embroidered Belt
He didn't know how to read the sutras,
    how to pray to the Buddha, or even be penitent for his sins.

13 Suspense point 5.

不清不淨，
　只有天來大膽。
一雙乖眼，
　果是釘人不斬。
自受了佛家戒，
　手中鐵棒，
經年不磨被塵，
　被塵暗。
凜凜有生氣。
腰間戒刀，
　是舊時斬虎誅龍劍。
一從殺割的眾生厭。
卦壁上，
　久不曾拈。

頑羊角靶盡塵緘。
生澀了雪刃霜尖。
高呼「僧行，
　有誰隨俺。
但請無慮，
　管不有分毫失賺。」
心口自思念。
「戒刀擧今日開齋，
　鐵棒有打鑿。」
立於廊下，
　其時遂把諸僧點。
「搊搜好漢每兀誰敢。
待要斬賊降眾，
　大喊故是不險。」

（尾）
「開門^肖但助我一聲喊。
戒刀擧把群賊來斬。
送齋時做一頓饅頭餡。」

He was unclean and impure—
    all he had was a boldness as big as the heavens,
And a pair of piercing eyes
    that never blinked when nailing a foe.
Since he had taken vows,
    the iron club he now held
        had lain untouched for years, covered in dust.
But the ordination blade at his waist
    was once a sword that beheaded dragons and tigers.
Having his fill of the slaughter of living beings
He had hung it up on a wall,
    and there it had remained long untouched.

Vivid and strong, possessing a life force.

Its sturdy ram's horn handle was completely sealed in dust.
The snow-keen blade and its frosty point were covered in rust.
He shouted out, "Monks!
    Who among you will follow me?
I'm asking you to think no more about it
    and can assure you that we have nothing to lose."
And he muttered his own heart's thoughts:
"*Today my ordination knife will begin again to feast on meat,
    and my iron club will be worn down to a tapered point.*"
In the portico of the hall he stood
    and began to count the monks one by one.
"Fine lads fierce and brave, who among you has the daring?
I have but to behead a rebel or two to make the lot surrender—
    a great battle cry will dispel all danger."

Coda   Just right!
"*When I open the gates, simply aid me with hearty battle yells,
And I have but to raise my ordination knife to behead a group of
    rebels.
When mealtime rolls around, I'll use their flesh as filling for steamed
    buns!*"

殺人肝膽，
翻為濟眾之心。
落草英雄，
翻作破賊之勇。
聰大呼曰
「上為教門。
下為僧眾。
當此之時，
各當勉力。
有敢助我退賊者，
出於堂右。」

須臾堂下近三百人。各持鐵棒戒刀。相應曰「願從和尚決死。」

ii.6/ii.5 雙調（文如錦）
細端詳。
見法聰生得搊搜相。
刁厥精神，
　蹺蹊模樣。
牛膀闊，
　虎腰長。
帶三尺戒刀，
　提一條鐵棒。
一疋戰馬，
　似敲了牙的活象。
偏能軟纏，
　只不披着介冑，
　　八尺堂堂。
好雄強。
似出家的子路，
　削了髮的金剛。

---

14 This section should be read against the last line of suite II.17, which describes the bloodied Dharma Wit after his battle as a penis emerging from a sexual encounter with a virgin.

His courage to kill, his liver and gall,
were turned into heart and a desire to save the masses.
A hero who had disappeared from the world
emerged again to be a champion who could smash the rebels.
Dharma Wit called out,
    "Above, for our religion,
    and below, for our sangha!
    Right now,
    each must exert himself.
    Those who dare to help me force the rebels withdraw,
    come out to the right of the hall."

In no time at all, close to two hundred men filled the courtyard, each carrying a bare wooden club and an ordination knife. They echoed in response, "We want to follow you, monk, to battle to the death."

ii.6/ii.5 Shuang Diao Mode

Patterned Like Embroidery
Look closely
And we will see Dharma Wit produce a menacing mien.
Brave and fierce of spirit
    and strange in appearance—
Thick as an ox's shank
    but elongated like a tiger's waist.[14]
He carried his three-foot-long ordination knife
    and lifted a single iron club in his hand.
His one warhorse
    was like a live elephant with tusks knocked out.
He bound himself pliantly[15] *as best he could—*
    all he was lacking was a helmet—
        and stood eight-foot tall and formidable.
How manly and strong—
Like a Zilu[16] who had become a monk instead,
    or a Vajra[17] shorn of hair!

---

15   According to DJY06, 54, n. 35, this was a protective wrapping for men without armor.
16   Zilu 子路 is known as the bravest, most martial, and most impetuous disciple of Confucius.
17   This seems to refer to the adamantine warrior (*jingang lishi* 金剛力士), the fierce warrior who battles ignorance and whose statue is found in most Buddhist temples. He bears the vajra pestle, an ancient club made of diamond-like material.

從者諸人二百餘，
　一個個器械不類尋常。
生得眼腦甌摳，
　人材猛浪。
或拿着切菜刀，
　幹麵杖。
把法鼓攂得鳴，
　打得齋鐘響。
着綾幡做甲，
　把鉢盂做頭盔戴着頂上。
幾個鬅頭的行者，
　着鐵褐直裰，
　　走離僧房。
騁無量。
道「俺咱情願，
　苦戰沙場。」

是闍黎慌忙赴闘模樣.

（尾）
這每取經後不肯隨三藏。
肩擔着掃帚藤杖。
簇捧着個殺人和尚。

執事者不及囑諭小心。聰已

率眾至門，
見賊勢大，
不可立退，
下馬登樓，
敷陳厲害，
以駭眾心。

Some two hundred followed him,
    each with a weapon that was not a normal kind.
Their eyes were deeply set and
    their bodies impressively huge.
Some carried cleavers,
    others rolling pins.
They beat the dharma drum resoundingly
    and rang the dinner gong.[18]
They used silken ceremonial streamers[19] *as armor*
    and wore their begging bowls for helmets on their heads.
Several members in the ranks,[20]
    wearing iron-colored straight cassocks of coarse fabric,
        ran out of the monks' cells
To show off their acts of merit,
Shouting, "We desire with all our heart
    to fight to the death on the sandy fields."[21]

This is the way monks get all riled up to go into battle.

Coda
These men, who would not have followed even Tripitaka[22] *after he*
    fetched the sutras,
Now shouldered brooms and waste-pans on rattan carrying poles,
And surrounded that homicidal monk.

    The Steward of the Monks didn't even have time to counsel them to
be careful. Dharma Wit had already

    led the crowd to the gate and
    seeing the force of the enemy was so great that
    they could not immediately be routed,
    he got off his horse and climbed a tower
    to lay out all the risks in detail
    and put fear in the rebellious soldiers' hearts.

18 Drums sounded the advance, gongs sounded retreat in battle.
19 With phrases from the sutras written on them.
20 Literally "acolytes with disheveled hair," postulants and acolytes waiting to enter the
    order, living on the grounds.
21 This is a fine example of the irony that often occurs in the text. Normally, monks
    would perform acts of merit to save souls from the world of red dust. Here, such acts
    are inversely applied to the battleground, or "sandy field," a term also applied to a
    deserted battlefield littered with the bones of the dead. This may also be a comment
    on the nature of the men who would seek sanctuary in a monastery.
22 A famous Tang dynasty monk who traveled to India.

ii.7/ii.6 般涉調（沁園春）

鐵戟侵空，
　繡旗映日，
　　遍滿四郊。
捧一員驍將，
　陣前立馬，
　　披烏油鎧甲，
　　　紅錦徵袍。
鼻偃唇軒，
　眉龐眼大，
　　擔一柄截頭古定刀。
如神道。
更胸高膀闊，
　胯大臀腰。

雄豪舉止輕驍。
馬上斜刀把寶鐙挑。
覰來手下諸軍校。
英雄怎畫，
　倜儻難描。
或短或長，
　或肥或瘦，
　　一個個精神沒彈包。
掂詳了。
縱六千來不到。
半萬來其高。

（牆頭花）

寺方五里，
眾軍都圍繞。
整整齊齊盡擺撥。
三停來系青布行纏，
折半着黃紬絮襖。

ii.7/ii.6 **Banshe Diao Mode**

Spring in the Princess's Garden
Iron halberds raised in the sky and
    embroidered flags aglow with sunrays
        filled the land outside the four main gates.[23]
They all crowded around a brave general
    who halted his horse in front of the formation.
He wore plate armor of oiled ebony
    and a battle robe of red brocade.
His nose was flat, his lips were raised and cleft,[24]
    brows bushy, eyes enormous—
        on his shoulder, level with his head, rested a sword from
           Guding.[25]
Like a god![26]

His chest rose high, and his thighs were wide,
    his hips wider than his rear or waist.
A powerful figure on horseback with nimble motions,
His sword picked at his jeweled stirrup.
He inspected the soldiers under his aegis—
With a heroic bravery hard to paint,
    and a calm ease hard to sketch.
Some short, some tall,
    some fat, some thin,
        but all of faultless mettle.
He finished counting them:
All together not quite six thousand,
But more than five.

Flowers on the Wall
The monastery was a square a mile and some around,
    and surrounded by a mass of soldiers
With lances arranged in perfect formation.
A third of them wore leggings of black cotton,
    and more than half wore ocher silk padded jackets.

---

23 Here begins a description of Flying Tiger Sun and his band.
24 He suffered from a harelip.
25 A town in Hebei known for its sword craftsmanship. Reading 古錠 for 古定.
26 Meaning the larger-than-life images of apotheosized generals, like the famous Guan
    Yu, whose statues were a regular feature of shrines.

鼕鼕的鼓響，
畫角聲繚繞。
獵獵徵旗似火飄。
催軍的聒地轟聲，
　納喊的揭天唱叫。

一時間怎堵當，
　從來固濟得牢。
牆壁若石壘，
　鐵裹山門破後砍。
待蹉踏怎地蹉踏，
　待奔吊如何奔吊。

（柘枝令）
板鋼斧劈群刀砍，
　一地裏熱鬧和鐸。
那法聰和尚，
　對將軍下情陪告，
「念本寺裏別無寶貝，
　敝院又沒糧草。
將軍手下有許多兵，
　怎地停泊。」

退陣時甘言。
勸誘.

（長壽仙衮）
「朝廷咫尺，
　不曉定知道。
多應遣軍，
　定把賢每征討。
不當穩便，
　恁時悔也應遲，
　　賢家試自心量度。」

那賊將聞斯語，
　心生怒惡。
「打脊的髡囚，

The echoing of the drums bellowed and boomed,
    the sound of their painted horns was sonorous and vibrant.
Flapping and snapping, battle flags were like flames afloat.
From being urged forward, the roar from the chariots rumbled
    across the ground,
    from those calling out battle cries, the chants lifted to the
        heavens.

How could the monastery stand against them now,
    even though it had always been secure!
The walls were like stone ramparts,
    the iron-clad gates were like smashed stone.[27]
If you wanted to trample it, how would you manage?
    If you wanted to scale it, how could you do it?

Chinese-Mulberry Branch Song
Steel broadaxes cleaved, a host of blades hacked—
    The whole place was alive with the din
As monk Dharma Wit carefully
    laid it out for the general:
"Our monastery has nothing of value,
    and our temple has no provisions for men nor for horses.
You have so many soldiers under your command, General,
    Why would you stop here?"

Getting their forces to withdraw, sweet words coax them into it.

Long-Life Immortals Tremolo
"The court is nearby
    and will know about this in no time.[28]
They will likely dispatch an army,
    a campaign that must punish your worthy men.
And when that causes you problems
    it'll be too late for regret—
        you, my worthy friend, need to think carefully about
            what will happen."

As soon as that rebel heard this pronouncement,
    his heart grew vile and angry,
"You bald, fit-for-beating shave-pated jailbird,

27 That is, difficult to break further.
28 Here, following the interpretation of DJY, 131, 133. But the passage may also be understood as "The court, so close, wouldn't know? They'd know it for sure."

怎敢把爺違拗。
俺又本無心，
　把你僧家混耗。
　甚花唇兒故來相惱。」

（急曲子）
「又不待奪賢寺宇，
　又不待要賢金寶。
眾軍飢困權停待，
　甚堅把山門閉着。
眾僧其間只有你做虎豹。
叨叨地把爺凌虐。」

顰眉宛肖。

（尾）
「你要截了手，
　打破腦。
雙割了耳朵牢縛了腳。
倒吊着山門上曬到老。」

聰曰，「公等息怒，願一一從命。且公等幾千人，與將軍
安　置飲食，敢告公等少退百步，使眾徐行，不至喧爭，
甚幸。」

將軍曰，「爾既許我，若不從命，非也。」於是軍退百步。
聰已下樓上馬。

ii.8/ii.7 黃鐘調（喜遷鶯纏令）
賊軍聞語。
約退三二百步。

why don't you follow your daddy's[29] orders?
I never had any intention
    to stir up you monks.
So why annoy me with this sweet talk?

An Accelerando Song
"I never wanted to snatch away your fine monastery,
    never desired your fine gold and jewels.
Our troops were tired and hungry, and we were just going to stop
    awhile,[30]
    so, what are you doing with the main gate closed?
You're the only violent one among all the monks,
Going on and on, savaging me, your father!

*Beard and eye-
brows to a tee!*

Coda
"You're going to have your hands cut off
    your skull smashed,
Your ears sliced off and your feet bound.
Then you'll be hung upside down from the main gate until you
    turn to jerky in the sun."

"Sire, you and the others please still your anger, we will abide by every order.[31] Since your troops number several thousand, please allow us to arrange food and drink for you, General, could you please withdraw two hundred paces? It would be best if we could have the multitude slowly pass by to be served without any squabbling."

"Since you have given in to me," said the general, "it would be wrong for me not to follow your directions." At this point the army withdrew two hundred paces, by which time Dharma Wit had already descended the tower and mounted up.

ii.8/ii.7 Huangzhong Diao Mode

Delighting in Orioles Aflight: A Bound Suite
The rebel army heard his speech
And withdrew several hundred paces.

---

29 A curse implying that the speaker has slept with the listener's mother.
30 A sarcastic rebuke, as travelers could always count on a meal and lodging at a monastery.
31 Here Dharma Wit speaks in a more formal mode of address.

下了長關，
　徹了大鎖，
　　兩扇門開處。
那法聰呼從者，
　「你但隨吾。」
喊得一聲，
　撲碌碌地離了寺門，
　　不曾見恁地蹺蹊隊伍。

盡是沒意頭，
　鄒搜男女。
覷賊軍，
　約半萬，
　　如無物。
那法聰橫着鐵棒，
　厲聲高呼。
「叛國賊，
　請個出馬決勝負。
不消得埋桿豎柱。」

（四門子）
「國家又不曾把賢每虧負。
試自心審腹。
衣糧俸祿是吾皇物。
恁咱有福。
好乾、好羞[2]。
方今太平徵戰又無。
好乾、好羞。
你做得無功受祿。

不幸蒲州太守渾瑊卒。
你便欺民叛國，
　劫人財產行氣魯。
更蹉踏人寺宇。
好乾、好羞。

The long bar on the gates was taken down and
    the great lock removed, then
        where the leaves of the two wing gates opened,
Dharma Wit rallied his followers,
    "Just follow me!"
It took only a single battle cry
    before they tumbled out of the monastery gates,
        a rag-tag troop like no one's seen before!

All a feckless and reckless
    band of men and women,
Who scorned those five thousand
    rebel troops
        as though they were nothing.
Dharma Wit laid his iron club across his saddle
    and shouted in harshest voice:
"Traitorous bandits,
    please send out a single mounted man to decide who wins and
        who loses!
It's useless to bury your spear handles or set up posts![32]

The Four Disciples
"The state never stinted on you worthy men—
Search your own hearts and consider:
Clothing, grain allotment, and salary, all from the emperor, and
Which all of you have had the great fortune to use.
So false! So shameful!
And now we are at peace with no campaigns in the offing.
So false! So shameful!
And you've done nothing of worth to merit that salary.

Unfortunately, Hun Jian, the Grand Protector of Puzhou, is dead,
And now you take advantage to bully the people and rebel against the
    state,
    stealing everything from everyone, running rampant.
On top of that, you stride into the precincts of monasteries!
So false! So shameful!

When cursing the force, vicious words to give them a verbal hiding.

32 That is, to set up a bivouac.

饅頭待要俺不與。
好乾、好羞。
待留着餵驢。」

（柳葉兒）

「譬如蹉踏俺寺家門戶。
不如守着你娘墳墓。
俺也不是廝唬。
孩兒每早早地伏輸。」

（尾）

「好也好教你回去。
弱也弱教你回去。
待不回去。
只消我這六十斤鐵棒苦。」

聰躍馬大呼「軍中掌領相見。」

一將出謂聰曰，「汝為佛弟子，當念經持戒，如何出粗惡。」

聰曰，「公等
　身充卒伍，
　忝預軍官。
且
　國家養爾，
　本欲安邊，
是以
　月終給粟，
　歲季支衣，
　四時無凍餒之憂，
　數口享福安之慶。
豈以
　一時失統，
　忘國重恩，
　大掠良民，
　敢殘上郡。

Want a steamed bun? You can't have one.
So false! So shameful!
  I'll keep them to feed our asses.

Willow Leaves
"Instead of striding into our monastery grounds
You should be standing by your own damn graves!
I'm not just making noise!
Boys, you'd better give it up and surrender!

Coda
"For better, I'll send you on your way,
For worse, I'll send you on your way.
And if you don't go on your way,
You'll enjoy the pain of my sixty-pound iron cudgel!"

Dharma Wit spurred on his horse and shouted, "Let me find the
leader of this troop."

A single general came out to cajole Dharma Wit, "You are a disciple
of the Buddha and should be reciting your sutras and minding your
vows. Why do you speak in such a vulgar way?"

Dharma Wit replied, "Well, sire, you and others
    fill out the ranks with your bodies,
    and, so unworthily, form part of the officer corps.
Moreover,
    the state takes care of you,
    desiring to secure its borders.
And for this
    they give you grain at the end of the month
    and clothing at the turn of the year.
    In the four seasons you have no worry about cold or hunger,
    Every one of you enjoys the blessings of fortune and safety.
How can you
    forget the deep grace the state has shown
    just because of a momentary loss of command
    and plunder the good people,
    daring to lay waste to our fine commandery?

　　　　朝廷咫尺，
　　　　旦夕必知。
　　　　命將統兵，
　　　　片時可至。
　　　　汝等作沙場之血，
　　　　汝族為叛國之囚。
　　　　族滅身亡，
　　　　有財何益。
　　　公等
　　　　宜熟計之。」

　　　賊將突馬出曰，「爾不為我備食，何說我眾。」

ii.9/ii.8 大石調（玉翼蟬）
　　　　賊頭領，
　　　　　聞此語，
　　　　　　佛也應煩惱。
　　　　嚼碎狼牙，
　　　　　睜察大小。
　　　「眾孩兒曹。
　　　　聽我教着。
　　　　只助我，
　　　　　一聲喊，
　　　　　　只一合，活把髡徒捉。」
　　　　眾軍聞言，
　　　　　鼕鼕擂戰鼓，
　　　　　　滴溜溜地雜彩旗搖。

　　　　連天地叫「殺」不住，
　　　　　齊吹畫角。
　　　　愁雲蔽日，
　　　　　殺氣連霄。
　　　　遂呼「和尚，
　　　　　休要狂獐等待着。
　　　　緊揞着鐵棒，
　　　　　牢坐着鞍轎。

The court is but a foot away and
sooner or later will hear the news.
They will commission a general to lead an army
And he will be here with due haste.
Your lot will offer up your blood to spill on the battlefield,
your band will become prisoners who rebelled against the state.
And, when your clans are exterminated, and your own bodies are gone,
what use will there be for all this wealth?
Sire, you and the others
should carefully think about what comes next."

The rebel general spurred his mount out and said, "You didn't prepare any food! How dare you harangue us?"

ii.9/ii.8 Dashi Diao Mode

A Jade-Winged Cicada
The leader of the bandits,
hearing these words—
why, even the Buddha himself would be annoyed—
Gnashed his wolf's teeth until they nearly fractured
and his eyes grew round and large.
"You, children,
listen to my orders*!*
Just spur me on
with a battle cry in unison, and
I'll capture this tonsured criminal alive."
Upon hearing him,
they beat the battle drums, they banged and boomed,[33]
they swished and swirled flags of many colors.

Shouts of "kill" and "death" filled heaven and earth,
and in unison, they blew their painted battle horns.
Clouds of sorrow blocked out the sun,
ethers of killing rose into the empyrean.
And he shouted, "Monk*!*
Stop being so arrogant and wait for me.
Hold tight to your iron club,
sit firmly in your saddle.

33 Drums were used to signal attack.

想着西方極樂。
見得十分是命夭。
略等我仁事與賢家，
　一萬刀。」

（尾）

掩耳不及如飛到。
馬蹄踐碎霞一道。
見和尚鼻凹上大刀落。

只聽得咶叮地一聲，和尚性命如何。

ii.10/ii.9 大石調（伊州衮纏令）

陰風惡。
戈甲遍荒郊。
殺氣黯青霄。
六軍發喊，
　旗前二馬相交。
法聰和尚，
　手中鐵棒眉齊，
　　快睹當[3]，
　咶叮地一聲，
　　架過截頭古定刀。

馬如龍，
　人如虎，
　　鐵棒輪，
　　　鋼刀舉，
　　　　各按六韜。
這一回，
　須定個誰強誰弱。
三合以上，
　賊徒氣力難迭，

Think about the ultimate joy of the Western Paradise,[34]
Because it seems your days here are numbered.
Let me just present to you, my worthy sir,
　　ten thousand blades!'"

Coda
In less time than it takes to cover your ears, he had flown to the
　　spot,
His horse's hooves trampled the road into a sunset of rainbow
　　dust,
And he let fall a great swipe, dead on the dip in the bridge of the
　　monk's nose.

All you could hear was the clang of the blade! And the monk's life?[35]

ii.10/ii.9 Dashi Diao Mode

Yizhou Tremolo: *A Bound Suite*
The dark wind was menacing.
Spears and armor filled the wild outskirts.
Ethers of killing blackened the blue empyrean.
Imperial troops let out their battle cries,
　　as the two mounts joined in front of the flags.
Monk Dharma Wit—
　　iron club in hand, held level with his brows—
　　　　was keen in his defensive moves.
Then with a great clang
　　he blocked the blow to the head by the Guding blade.

Horses like dragons
　　and men like tigers—
　　　　the iron cudgel whirled,
　　　　　　the steel blade rose—
　　　　　　　　each fought as taught by the manuals of war.
This was the moment
　　that would surely settle who was strong and who was not.
Thrice they joined,
　　until that bandit lackey could summon no more energy—

---

34 The Buddhist Heaven of the Pure Land Sect where those who have reached the end
　　of the wheel of rebirth will reside.
35 Suspense point 6.

怎賭當 [4]，
　辦得個架格遮截，
　　欲勝那僧人砑上砑。

（紅羅襖）
　苦苦的與他當，
　　強強地與他熬。
　似狡兔逢鷹鼠見貓。
　待伊揣幾合，
　　贏些方便，
　　　便宜廝鬧。
　欲待望本陣裏逃生，
　　見一騎馬肖如飛到。
　撚一柄丈二長槍，
　　騁麄豪，
　　　妝就十分惡。

　和尚果雄驍，
　　兵法暸曾學。
　搧過鋼槍，
　　刀又早落。
　不緊不慌，
　　不驚不怕，
　　　不忙不暴。
　不惟眼辨 與身輕，
　　那更馬疾手妙。
　盤得兩個氣一似擔椽，
　　欲遁逃，
　　　又恐怕諸軍笑。

（尾）
　把不定心中拘拘地跳，
　眼睜得七角八角，
　兩個將軍近不得腳。

　　　　六條臂膊，於中使鐵棒的偏強，

          how could he hold out?
               He managed a way to block the blows
                   but to best that monk now was doubly difficult.

Red Silk Padded Jacket
Tenaciously he faced him,
    and held him off with all his strength.
Like a crafty hare encountering an eagle, or a mouse seeing a cat,
He wanted to struggle long enough
    and gain enough advantage
        to find a proper moment to give a shout.
He wanted to run for his life to his own ranks,
    when there appeared a rider who came as though in flight—
Twirling a twelve-foot spear,
    giving rein to a rough heroism,
        he appeared as menacing as hell.

Now, our monk was indeed brave and fierce   *Stalwart indeed,*
    and had well mastered the arts of war.   *this Dharma Wit,*
He shunted the first's iron spear to the side,   *with no proclivity*
    and the other's sword already lay upon the ground.   *at all for rashness.*
Unworried, unhurried,
    not frightened or scared,
        neither rushed nor impetuous.
His eye was quick to advantage and his body light of movement,
    and his horse was nimble too, led by the deft handling of its
        reins.
He circled about with the two until, as one, their flagging
    breaths failed—
        and they both wanted to flee, yet
           feared their army's scornful laughter.

Coda
Unable to still the pounding palpitations of their hearts,
Eyes gaping so wide that crows' feet turned those round orbs to
    polygons—
Those two generals could not even draw near his feet.

Six arms, yet the one who wielded the iron cudgel was slightly stronger.

三個英雄，鬧裏戴頭盔的先歇。
使刀的對壘，使槍的好鬥。

ii.11/ii.10 正宮（文序子）

纔歇罷。
重披掛。
何曾打話。
不問個是和非，
　覷僧人便扎。
輕閃過捽住獅鬱，
　狠心不捨。
用平生勇力，
　抱入懷來，
　　鞍韉上一納。

聽得叫一聲「苦，」
　連衣甲。
頭攧得掉下。
奈何使刀的
　人困馬乏。
欲待掙揣些英雄
　不如赸撒。
何曾敢與他。
和尚爭鋒，
　望着直南下便迸。

（甘草子）

怎拿挈。
怎拿挈。
法聰覷了，
　勃騰騰地無明發。
彷彿趕相遮，
　叫聲如雷炸。
和尚何曾動着，
　子喝一聲

Three heroes, yet the one wearing a helmet to battle[36] was first to rest.
That sword fighter still squared off, the spearman was still aggressive.

ii.11/ii.10 Zheng Gong Mode

Master Wen Xu
Just a little rest,
And then armor was donned again.
Never a word exchanged,
Never questioning right or wrong, he
    glared at the monk, made a savage thrust.
Dharma Wit, deftly dodging,
Grabbed tight the other's Lion King buckle,
Then, using the whole of his hard heart
And all the strength he could muster,
    pulled the bandit into his embrace
        and held him tightly across the pommel.

The monk heard him shout, "Damn,"
Then, with clothes and armor both,
The bandit was thrown down head-first.
And what of the sword fighter—
    his body wearied and his horse tired?
As much as he wanted to eke out a bit more heroism
    he thought it wiser to go into full retreat.
He no longer dared cross swords with the monk—
But turned straight to the south and fled.

Dried Licorice Root
How to take him?
How could he be captured?
As Dharma Wit looked,
    his unseen fire[37] let loose, welling up in the skies.
He seemed to be right at his back
    as a shout rippled like a peal of thunder.
But the monk, never moving,
    simply gave a yell,

36 The one using the spear.
37 A Buddhist term for rage.

那時諕煞。

賊陣裏兒郎懣眼不扎。

道「這禿廝好交加。」

（尾）

怎禁那和尚高聲罵。

「打脊賊徒每怎敢反國家。

怕更有當風的快出馬。」

綉旗開隊，

臨風散幾百里朝霞，

戰鼓助威，

從地湧一千個霹靂。

直惱得這個將軍出馬。是誰。是誰。

ii.12/ii.11 仙呂調（點絳唇）

這個將軍，

英雄名姓非此此。

嫌小官不做，

欲把山河取。

狀貌雄雄，

人見森森地懼。

法聰覷。

「恐這人臉上，

常帶着十分怒。」

（台台令）

生得鄧虜淪敦着大肚。

眼三角鼻大唇龕。

額闊頦寬眉卓竪。

一部赤髭鬚。

也麼台台。

　　　one that instantly frightened
Those boys in the formation, squeezed their eyes shut and
Said, "That bald bastard can really fight!"

Coda
How could they endure that monk's loud cursing?
"Bandits who should be thrashed on the back! How dare you
　　　revolt against the state?
Should anyone else in there want to test the wind, come out
　　　now on your horse!"

　　　Embroidered flags unfurling, their ranks seemed
　　　a hundred miles of sunrise aura scattered before the wind,
　　　War drums egged on martial vigor—
　　　a thousand peals of thunder welled out of the ground.

　　　This only riled up another general to come forth on his horse. And
　　　who was it? Who?[38]

ii.12/ii.11 Xianlü Diao Mode

Dotting Crimson Lips
Now, this general's
　　　heroic name was not insignificant.
Despising minor posts, he did not hold them,
　　　but rather sought to seize the very mountains and rivers.[39]
His form and appearance were virile and vigorous,
　　　and as soon as anyone caught a glimpse, they shrank away in
　　　　fear.
Dharma Wit examined him closely,
"I fear the face of this fellow
　　　always betrays a fulsome rage."

Happy As Can Be
His big round belly jiggled when he walked,
His eyes were tri-cornered; his nose, huge; lips thick,
Forehead broad; chin, wide; eyebrows standing straight up;
And a full red beard. He was something to see.

38　Suspense point 7.
39　Meaning the empire.

（風吹荷葉）

　　雲雁徵袍金縷。

　　狼皮戰靴抹綠。

　　磊落身材宜結束。

　　紅彪彪地戴一頂紗巾，

　　　密砌着珍珠。

（醉奚婆）

　　甲掛兩副。

　　雄烈超今古。

　　力敵萬夫。

　　綽名喚孫飛虎。

（尾）

　　帶一枝鐵胎弩。

　　弧內插着百雙鋼箭，

　　　擔一柄簸箕來大開山斧。

　　　　　　適來壓路贏人，

　　　　　　不意棋逢對手。

ii.13/ii.12 般涉調（麻婆子）

　　飛虎是真英烈，

　　　法聰是大丈夫。

　　飛虎又能征戰，

　　　法聰甚是英武。

　　飛虎專心取寺宇。

　　法聰本意破賊徒。

本是對着意形　　　法聰有降賊策，

容。　　　　　　飛虎有叛國圖。

　　法聰使一條鑌鐵棒，

　　　飛虎使一柄板鋼斧。

　　恨不得一斧砍了和尚，

　　　恨不得一棒待搠殺飛虎。

Wind Blows the Lotus Leaves
A battle robe of clouds and geese threaded in gold,
And shiny black battle boots of wolf's hide,
An imposing physique, perfect for such decking out.
A rich red silk kerchief on his head,
    set with rows of tightly strung precious gems.

Drunken Mama Xi
Armor-dressed in doubled layers,
Brave and tough beyond all others,
Strength enough to battle ten-thousand ordinary men—
He was nicknamed "Flying Tiger Sun."

Coda
He carried a single crossbow with a stock of steel,
In his quiver were a hundred steel bolts, and
Slung over his shoulder was an open-the-mountain axe as big as
    a winnowing basket.

    Just as you block a chess run and think you've won,
    Before you know it, you run into a real match.[40]

ii.13/ii.12 Banshe Diao Mode

Pockmarked Crone
Flying Tiger was a true man of heroic deeds,
    but Dharma Wit was quite a man too.
Flying Tiger was capable of battle campaigns,
    and Dharma Wit, a brave soldier.
Flying Tiger had his mind set on taking the monastery,
    and Dharma Wit just wanted to smash the bandit lackeys.
Dharma Wit had a plan to make the bandits surrender,
    and Flying Tiger had a plot to rebel against the state.

They are matched opponents, hence the elaborate portrayals.

Dharma Wit used a club of the finest iron,
    while Flying Tiger used an axe with a head of flattened steel.
One itched to slice up a monk,
    the other itched to beat Flying Tiger to death.

40 Referring to *weiqi* 圍棋 (Japanese *go*) chess, in which you surround the opposition
    by blocking lines of movement to capture their territory.

不道飛虎慣相持，
　思量法聰怎當賭。
法聰尋贏便，
　飛虎覓走路。

（尾）
法聰贏，
　飛虎輸。
法聰不合趕將去。
飛虎攀番蹺蹬弩。

把夾鋼斧摠在戰鞍，
中靴入鐙，
扳番龍筋弩，
安上一點油，
搖番銅牙利，
會百步風裏穿楊，
教七尺來僧入怎。

那法聰喚做真實取勝，怎知是飛虎佯敗。

ii.14/ii.13 正宮（文序子）
將軍敗，
　有機變。
不合追趕。
趕上落便宜，
　輸他方便。
斜挑金鐙那身，
　十分陡健。
一聲霹靂，
　弩箭離弦。
渾如飛電。

法聰早，
　當此際，

Don't wonder if Flying Tiger could face him in battle,
    just wonder if Dharma Wit could hold him off.
Dharma Wit sought out an advantage,
    and Flying Tiger looked for way to flee.

Coda
Dharma Wit won,
    Flying Tiger lost—
But Dharma Wit should never have chased him for
Flying Tiger flipped around his foot-cocked crossbow.

    He took his steel-clad axe and stuck it against his saddle,
    centered his boots in their stirrups,
    flipped around the writhing-dragon crossbow
    put on a drop of oil,
    and wiggled the brass trigger cam.
    At a hundred paces he could pierce a willow branch in the wind,
    so how could he miss a seven-foot-tall monk?[viii]

    Dharma Wit was certain that he had truly won the battle. How could
he know that Flying Tiger had simply feigned defeat?

ii.14/ii.13 Zheng Gong Mode

Master Wen Xu
The general's defeat,
    was only a slick trick.
Dharma Wit should never have given chase, for
When he caught up, all advantage was quickly gone
    and he lost the upper hand.
Flying Tiger quickly twisted in his golden stirrups,
    deftly shifting his body.
There was the sound of a thunderclap
    as a crossbow bolt left the string
Exactly like a running flash of lightning.

But early on Dharma Wit—
    right at the critical juncture—

遙遙地望見。
果是會相持，
　能征慣戰。
不慌不緊不忙，
果手疾眼辨。
捽着寶勒，
　側坐着鞍轎，
　　吃地勒住戰驪。

（尾）

　剔團團的睜察殺人眼。
　嗔忿忿地斜橫着打將鞭。
　咭叮地拈折點鋼箭。

鐵鞭舉大蟒騰空，鋼箭折流星落地。賊眾大駭。

飛虎謂眾曰，「僧無甲，不可以短兵接戰，可以長兵敵。
如僧再追，汝必齊發弓弩，僧必潰矣。」

聰自度「賊有變，及馬困，不可久敵。」因謂眾曰，「汝等
退而保寺，我當衝陣而出，自有長策。」

ii.15/ii.14 中呂調（喬捉蛇）

　和尚定睛睃。
　見賊軍兵眾多。
　郊外列干戈。
　威風大。
　垓前馬上一個將軍坐。
　肩擔著鐵斧來也麼。

saw it all from a distance.
Now he was a true fighter,
    capable of long campaigns and accustomed to battle.
Unflustered, neither rash nor hurried—
    indeed, his hands were fast and his eyes quick to make sense of
        all they saw.
He drew rein using his decorated bridle,
    sat aslant on his cantle,
        and suddenly brought his white-bellied battle roan to a
            halt.
Coda
Round and wide he opened eyes ready to kill,
Full of rage he threw his general-killing whip straight out to the
    side, and
With a ringing sound snapped that tempered iron bolt in half.

A great python of an iron whip rose in the void and snapped the steel bolt into a thousand spark-stars that fell to the earth. The rebels were awestruck.

Flying Tiger told his multitude, "That monk has no armor,[41] so I can't get close and take him on hand to hand, but he can be bested by long-distance weapons. If he chases me again, you just fire your arrows and crossbow bolts as one, and he'll be done for."

Dharma Wit figured it out, "The rebels have something else planned and my horse is tiring. I cannot battle them much longer." And so, he spoke to his group, "You lot withdraw to protect the monastery. I will burst out of our formation through their lines. I have my own excellent plan!"

ii.15/ii.14 Zhonglü Diao Mode

Comically Catching a Snake
The monk fixed his glare
And saw that the traitorous troops were too numerous.
Shields and spears arrayed outside the walls were
Imposing and awesome.
At the front of the field on his horse sat a general,
Shouldering an iron axe, yes,

---

41 So is too nimble to defeat.

一個越添忿怒精神惡。

征戰瞇僂儸。
把法聰來⁵來便砍斫。
又砍不着。
法聰出地過。
誰人比得他驍果。
禁持得飛虎心膽破。
手親眼便難擒捉。

（尾）
　　賊軍覷了頻相度。
　　打脊的髡徒怎恁麼。
　　措手不及早攛過我。

龐豪和尚，
單身鏖戰，
勇如九里山混垓西楚霸，
獨自征敵，
猛似毛駝岡刺良美髯公。
全然不顧殘生，
走在飛虎軍內。

ii.16/ii.15 仙呂調（一斛叉）
　　亂軍雖然眾，
　　　望見僧人忽地開。
　　有若山中羊逢虎，
　　　却似獸逢豺。
　　弓弩如何近傍，
　　　鐵棒渾如遮箭牌。

And as his anger grew, he turned uglier in mettle.

The whole group of traitors rose to battle,
Rushed to chop up Dharma Wit
But never even came close.
Dharma Wit rushed past them—
None could match his bravery or stamina.
In frustration, Flying Tiger's heart and courage quailed, for
Dharma Wit's moves were so natural and his vision so clear that
    he was impossible to capture.

Coda
The rebel army looked and began to assess,
"How could that fit-for-a-beating shave-pated convict do all
    this?
How could he catch us so off guard that he slipped right by?"

    Rough champion of a monk!
    All by himself he went into battle
    As courageously as the King of Western Chu at the battle of Nine
        Mile Mountain.[42]
    He chose to go alone to challenge the enemy
    as fiercely as Beautiful Beard stabbed Yan Liang at Shaggy Camel
        Ridge.[43]
    He cared nothing for his own life,
    as he raced amidst
    Flying Tiger's army.

ii.16/ii.15 Xianlü Diao Mode

A Big Forkload
The rebellious army may have had the numbers
    but they parted the instant they spied the monk—
They were like goats on a mountain meeting a tiger
    or an animal encountering a wild dog.
How could they raise bows or crossbows up to their sides?
    Iron clubs now were simply no more than arrow-shields.

---

42 The king, the legendary Xiang Yu 項羽 (232–202 BCE), was defeated at Nine Mile
   Mountain, which led immediately to his downfall at the battle of Gaixia. See Sima
   Qian 1971, 37–74.
43 Yan Liang 顏良 (d. 200) was taken in battle by Lord Guan Yu (see n. 258), who was
   noted for his red beard. See Idema and West, 2016, 62–63.

馬過處連天叫苦，
　血污濺塵埃。

半個時辰突圍透，
　和尚英雄果壯哉。
上至頂門紅颭颭，
　事急怎生捱。
粗就箇曜州和尚，
　撞著搠搜孟秀才。
不合道渾如那話，
　初出產門來。

曜州和尚等
語是彼道中
一種故事。

末句太譃可
笑。
縱聰獨力不加，走出陣去。

賊兵把寺圍了，孫飛虎隔門大叫，「我第一待教兵卒吃頓
飯食。第二知崔相夫人家眷在此，來取鶯鶯。與我，大兵
便退，不與我，目下有災。」

人報崔氏子母，唬殺鶯鶯。

ii.17/ii.16 大石調（玉翼蟬）
　衝軍陣，
　　鞭駿馬。
　一徑地西南上迓。
　更不尋思，
　　手下眾僧行，
　　　身邊又無衣甲。
　怎禁他。
　諸賊黨，
　　著弓箭射，
　　　爭敢停時霎。
　眾僧三百餘人，
　　比及扣寺門，
　　　十停兒死了七八。

Where his horse passed cries of suffering rose to the heavens,
  and blotches of blood spattered the dust.

In no time at all he broke out of the encirclement—
  the bravery of this monk was stalwart indeed.
All the way to the tip of his head he was a vivid red,
  and he could never last another pitched battle.
He played the Monk of Yaozhou
  bumping into the fierce Scholar Meng—
I shouldn't say this, but he was just like that thing
  when it first comes out of a twat.

The Monk of Yaozhou and such is a story of their guild.

The last line is just over the top funny and laughable!

Though Dharma Wit's strength couldn't best them alone, he managed
to get out of their formation and escape.

After the rebels had surrounded the monastery, Flying Tiger Sun yelled
just outside the gate, "First, I want you to feed my soldiers a meal. Second, I know that Minister Cui's wife is here with her family, and I've
come to fetch Oriole. Give her to me and the soldiers will withdraw.
Don't, and there will be immediate disaster."

Someone reported this to Madam Cui and her children, and Oriole
was scared to death.

ii.17/ii.16 Dashi Diao Mode

A Jade-Winged Cicada
Headlong through their ranks
    he whipped his magnificent steed,
Fleeing in a beeline to the southwest.
Not a moment's thought did he give to
    those monks under his guidance
        who had no armor at all.
How could he be stopped?
That rebel horde
    loosed a rain of arrows from their bows
        in constant and uninterrupted flight.
And when those monks—three hundred or more—
    finally came to pound on the gates,
        only one was left from every four.

幾個參頭行者，
　著箭後即時坐化。
頭陀中劍，
　血污了袈裟。

幾個誦經五戒，
　是佛力扶持後馬踐殺。
一個走不迭和尚，
　被小校活拿。
唬得臉兒來
　渾如淬蠟[6]。
幾般來害怕。
　繡旗底飛虎道
　「驅來詢問咱。」

（尾）

欲待揪捽沒頭髮。
扯住那半扇雲衲。
屹搭搭地直驅來馬直下。

飛虎問曰，「我求一飯，汝輩拒我。」

入譚自住

僧曰，「大師欲邀將軍會食，執事者論及前相國崔公靈柩在寺。公有女鶯鶯，艷絕一時，恐公等虜去。崔公之親舊，權重朝野，致患在他時。」

寫寺僧被害
之狀淋漓盡
興。

飛虎笑曰，「適來法聰所言，真有鶯鶯。我想，河橋將丁文雅，好色嗜酒之外，百事不能動其情。我若使鶯鶯靚妝艷服獻之，文雅必大悅，可連師據蒲，雖朝廷興兵，莫我御矣。」

44 Older monks who oversaw ceremonials and the instruction of novices and wandering monks.

Several of the novice masters[44]
    struck by arrows, serenely passed away in seated pose,
The dhūta[45] *were put to the sword,*
    their cassocks smeared with blood.

Several practitioners of the five precepts[46] *chanted scriptures,*
    and, thus sustained by the power of the Buddha, were trampled
        by horses.
One monk, unable to flee and
    taken alive by a junior officer,
Was so frightened that his face
    turned the color of wax lees,
Utterly terrorized.
Underneath his embroidered banner, Flying Tiger barked,
    "Bring him over here for interrogation!"

Coda

The soldier tried to grab him by the hair, but there was none to be
    had,
So he grabbed one side of his ragged cassock
Twirled him tight and shoved him over to the general's horse.

> *Naturally perfect to devolve into humor.*

Flying Tiger interrogated him, "I sought a single meal, yet you denied even that."

The monk said, "The Grand Master[47] wanted to invite you to share a meal, General, but the Steward pointed out the fact that the coffin of the late Prime Minister Cui was in the monastery. Minister Cui had a daughter, Oriole, who is now the great beauty of the age, and he feared that you, sire, would capture her and take her away. The family and friends of Minister Cui wield power in court and in the provinces, and such an act would cause trouble for us later on."

> *The tracing of the condition of the monks who were harmed is done with a verve that completely satisfies.*

---

45 Literally, those who "have shaken the dust from their minds," who have no attachment to food, clothing, or shelter. See Muller 2012.

46 While this term can apply to monks and nuns, it also often applied to members of Buddhist households. The precepts are: no killing, no stealing, no debauchery, no lies, and no alcohol.

ii.18/ii.17 正宮 （甘草子纏令）

> 聽說破。
> 聽說破。
> 把黃髯撚定，
> 　徹放眉間鎖。
> 遂喚幾個小僂儸，
> 　傳令教攛掇。
>
> 隔著山門厲聲叫，
> 　「滿寺里僧人聽呵。
> 隨俺後抽兵便回去，
> 　不隨後您須識我。」

（脫布衫）

> 「得鶯鶯後便退干戈，
> 　不得後目前生禍。
> 不共你搖嘴掉舌，
> 　不共你鬥爭鬥合。」

（尾）

> 「寺牆兒便是純鋼裹。
> 更一個時辰打不破。
> 屯著山門便點火。」

僧眾聞之大駭。法本領被傷者，來見夫人，說及賊事。

Flying Tiger laughed and spoke to himself, "So, Dharma Wit was right, Oriole really is here. Let me think; the general guarding the Yellow River Bridge, Ding Wenya, can only be moved by his lust for sex and his desire for drink. If I make Oriole get all dolled up and then present her to him as a gift, Wenya will be overjoyed and we can merge our forces to occupy Puzhou. Even if the court launched a campaign, they wouldn't be able to fend us off."

ii.18/ii.17 Zheng Gong Mode

Dried Licorice Root: A Bound Suite
Done listening,
And having heard,
He fingered his yellow beard[48]
    and loosened the lock of anger on his brows.
He summoned several lackeys
    to transmit orders to urge on his troops.

Outside the main gate he shouted in his harshest voice,
    "All you monks in this monastery, heed this:
If you do as I say, I'll withdraw my troops and go back.
    Don't, and you'll come to know who I really am.

Doffing the Cotton Shirt
"If I get Oriole, then my soldiers will withdraw;
If I don't, then disaster will swiftly befall you.
I'm not going to chitter-chatter palaver with you anymore;
I'm not going to argue with you either.

Coda
"The walls of your monastery might be wrapped in purest steel,
But if I can't break through in an hour or two,
I'll blockade the main gate and start a fire."

The throng of monks became fearful after hearing this. Dharma Source led the monks who had been injured to visit Madam Cui and explained what was happening with the rebels.

---

47 In earlier passages, it was not the "Grand Master" but the Comptroller who wanted to issue the invitation ; the array of titles is meant to enforce the authority of the storyteller, rather than to give an accurate picture.

48 Formerly red, now ocher-yellow, from the loess dust stirred up in the battle.

夫人聞語僕地，誂倒紅娘與鶯鶯，連救多時稍甦。

鶯泣曰，「且以相公靈柩為念，鶯鶯乞從亂軍。一身被辱，
上救夫人殘年，下解寺災，活眾僧之命。願不以女子一身
見辱而誤眾人。」

ii.19/ii.18 道宮 （解紅）

　　　鶖聞人道。
　　　森森地唬得魂離殼。
　　　「全家眷愛，
　　　　　多應是四分五落。
　　　先人化去，
　　　　　不幸斯間遭賊盜。
　　　思量了。
　　　兄弟歡郎忒年紀小。
　　　隔門又聽得賊徒叫。
　　　指呼着鶯鶯是他待要。
　　　心頭肖如千刀攪。
　　　孤孀子母，
　　　　　沒處投告。

　　　心下徘徊自籌度。
　　　「只除會聖一命難逃。
　　　尋思到底，
　　　　　多應被他誅剿。
　　　我隨強寇，
　　　　　年老婆婆有誰倚靠。
　　　添煩惱。
　　　地闊天高沒處着。
　　　到此怎惜我貞共孝。
　　　多被賊人控持了。
　　　有些兒事體夫人表，
　　　「若惜奴一個，

正在張皇躊躇
中，又聞入賊
徒呼叫，故作
恐嚇光景。

When Madam Cui heard the news, she fell flat on her face. This scared Crimson and Oriole, who brought her back to consciousness after several attempts.

Oriole wept and said, "Out of consideration for the Minister's coffin, I request to go with the rebellious army. If my body is besmirched, then first it will preserve my mother's remaining years, and second it will dispel any calamity for the monastery and give life to the congregation. I don't wish to wrong a multitude of people just over my body being defiled."

ii.19/ii.18 Dao Gong Mode

Untying the Red
Suddenly hearing the report—
Trembling and so scared that her soul had left its husk, she said,
"My whole beloved family
    will be scattered to the wind.
First, my father died,
    and now comes the misfortune of encountering these
        bandits."
She thought it over:
"Little brother Happy is just so young,
And on the other side of the gate I can hear the bandit horde calling,
Calling out that it is Oriole that they want.
My heart feels pricked by a thousand blades.
Orphaned children and a widowed mother
    have nowhere to flee for help."

She thought and thought, trying to find a way—
"Only a miracle can save me.
I've thought of every possible way,
    but everything leads to extermination.
If I go with the bandits
    who will help my aged mother?
It's all so upsetting.
Earth is broad, heaven is wide, but there is no place for me to set a
    single foot—
At this point, how can I begrudge my chastity and filial piety?
The bandits are in charge.
I have some thoughts about this business I'll reveal to you, Mother:
If you cherish only me,

Just when everyone is alarmed and indecisive, Dong sticks in the yells of the rebels, purposely creating a fine scene of intimidating pressure.

　　有大禍三條

（尾）

　「第一我母親難再保。

　第二諸僧都索命夭。

　第三把兜率般的伽藍枉火內燒。」

夫人泣曰，「母禮至愛，母情至親。汝若從賊，我生何益？
吾今六十，死不為夭。所痛鶯鶯幼年未得從夫，孤亡蕭
寺。」言訖，放聲大慟。

ii.20/ii.19 大石調 （還京樂）

　　是時鶯鶯孤孀母子，

　　　抱頭哭泣號咷。

　放聲不住，

　　哭得他眾僧心焦。

　思量這回，

　　子母不能保。

　待覓個身亡命夭。

　又恐賊軍，

　　不知縷細

　　葫蘆提把寺院焚燒。

　「我還取次隨賊寇，

　　怕後人知道。

　這一場污名不小。

　做下千年恥笑。

　辱累煞我相公先考。

　我尋思，

　　這事體，

　　　怎生是着。

there will be three disasters:

Coda
"First, there's no further protection for you.
Second, all the monks will die before their time.
Third, for no good reason, this Tushita[49] *of a monastery will be*
*   reduced to ash."*

Madam Cui wept and said, "The rituals of a mother are perfect love, and the affections of a mother are the most intimate. What good is it for me to live if you're taken by the bandits? I'm sixty now, and if I die, it would not be before my time. What hurts me is that you, Oriole, are so young and have no prospects of marriage. And that you will perish in this monastery as an orphan." Finished speaking, she began to cry her heart out.

ii.20/ii.19 Dashi Diao Mode

Happiness of Returning to the Capital
At this juncture mother and child—widow and orphan—
    Wailed with their heads in their hands.
On and on they went,
    crying until the whole congregation began to be anxious,
Reflecting on this matter
    in which neither mother nor child could be protected.
They feared that the rebel army,
    not knowing the real story,
        would still stupidly burn down the monastery.
"If I'm willing to go with the bandits,
    I'm afraid posterity will find out:
The stain of this event on my reputation would be great—
It will become a source of humiliation and ridicule for the next
    thousand years,
And disgrace my deceased father, the Prime Minister too.

"Let me consider
    how this affair
        might work out right.

49 Fourth of the six heavens of desire in Buddhism and the home of the Future Buddha Maitreya in Pure Land Buddhism; an allusive way to say that the monastery is full of future Buddhas who will go out and teach the world.

夫人與大師，
　議論評度煩惱。
階前僧行，
　一謎地向前哀告。
擎拳合掌，
　要奴獻與賊盜。
指約不住，
　一地裏鬧钁鐸。
除死後一場足了。
欲要亂軍
　不生怒惡。
恁獻與妾身屍殼。
儘教他陣前亂刀萬斫。
假如死也名全貞孝。

（尾）

純是暗渡法.

　覷着墻址却待褰衣跳。
　眾人都唬得呆了。
　見墻下一人拍手笑。

「法聰施武，
寺中難可退賊兵 ；
不肖用謀，
破盡許多強寇眾 。」

鶯鶯褰衣望階下欲跳，欲跳，被夫人與紅娘扯住。忽聽階
下一人大笑，眾人皆覷笑者是誰。

ii.21/ii.20 黃鐘宮（快活爾纏令）
　子母正是愁，
　　大眾情無那。
　忽聞得一人語言，
　　稱將賊盜捉。
　一齊觀瞻，
　　見個書生，

My mother and the abbot
    discuss and deliberate but fret all the while,
While ranks of monks in front of the steps
    pitifully plead with my mother,
Bowing with hands clasped together.
    They want to give me to the bandits.
It's all out of control,
    the entire place is in a clamor—
Only my death is enough to end it.
If you want to blunt the rebel army's
    furious anger,
Then offer up my corpse to them,
And let them hack it to pieces in front of their formations.
If I must die, at least my reputation will remain whole and my
    chastity stay filial."

Coda

Seeing that she was gathering up her skirts on the steps, about to
    jump,
The whole crowd was stunned into silence.
And then beneath the steps someone appeared, clapping his hands
    and laughing.

Truly the method of the transitional coda.

"Dharma Wit employed his martial skill,
    but what's left inside the monastery can't dispatch the rebel troops.
I, this unworthy one, have a plan
    that can destroy this band of powerful brigands."

Oriole had gathered up her skirt and wanted to throw herself off the high stairs—but just as she moved to leap, Madam Cui and Crimson pulled her back. Then suddenly they heard a hearty laugh at the bottom of the stairs that made everyone look at who was laughing.

ii.21/ii.20 Huangzhong Gong Mode

Jolly Child: A Bound Suite
Daughter and mother were truly sad,
    and the congregation was moved by their helplessness.
Suddenly they all heard someone speak,
    claiming he could capture the rebels.
Everyone turned to stare in unison
    as a student came into sight,

　　　　出離人叢，
　　　　　　生得面顏相貌有誰過。

　　　　年紀二十餘。
　　　　身品五尺大。
　　　　疏眉更目秀，
　　　　　　鼻直齒能粗。
　　　　唇若塗朱。
　　　　臉似銀盤，
　　　　　　清秀的容儀，
　　　　　　　　比得潘安宋玉醜惡。

（出隊子）
　　　　卻認得是張生，

才點破。

　　　　　　僧人把他衣扯着。
　　　　低言悄語喚「哥哥。
　　　　又不比書房裏閒吟課。
　　　　你須見賊軍排列着。

　　　　賢不是九伯與風魔。
　　　　世言了怎改抹。
　　　　見法聰臨陣恁比合。
　　　　與飛虎衝軍惡戰討，
　　　　　　也獨力難加也走卻。」

（柳葉兒）
　　　　「你肌骨似美人般軟弱。
　　　　與刀後怎生掄摩。

借問難張生，
暗描他身貌輕
俊。巧甚。

　　　　氣力又無些個。
　　　　與疋馬看怎乘坐。
　　　　春笋般指頭兒十個。
　　　　與張弓怎發金鑿。
　　　　覷你人品兒矬矮。
　　　　與副甲怎地披着。」

emerging from the crowd,
with a face and features none could match.[50]

Just over twenty,
Five feet at full height,
With widespread brows, lustrous eyes,
a straight nose, large teeth,
And lips as though daubed with vermillion.
A face like the silver salver of the moon, and
deportment pure and fine—
next to him, Pan An and Song Yu would be ugly![51]

Sending Out the Dance Troupe
When he recognized it was Student Zhang,
the monk[52] tugged at his clothes
And said in a low whisper, "Brother,
This isn't the same as leisurely reciting lessons in your study,
You must have seen the bandit army lined up in rows!

Just beginning to reveal all.

My worthy sir, you're not insane,
But what you just said to the world can never be changed.
You saw Dharma Wit go into battle where he held his own,
Fighting fiercely with Flying Tiger and his raiding troops—
his lone strength was not enough to win, and so he fled.

Willow Leaves
"*Your flesh and bones are as weak and frail as a beautiful maiden*:
If we gave you a knife, how could you wield it?
You haven't the slightest strength:
Give you a horse, we'll see if you can mount it!
Ten fingers as delicate as bamboo shoots:
Give you a bow, how could you even shoot a metal awl?[53]
And seeing how short you are:
How could you wear a suit of plate armor?

Uses the pretext of finding difficulty with Student Zhang's physique to limn his elegant grace and to hint at his profound ingenuity. Very clever!

---

50 Both in good looks and in promise as augured through physiognomy.
51 See fn. 133.
52 Probably the Abbot, Dharma Source.
53 DJYo6, 58, n. 135 remarks, "metal awl: refers to an arrow." But perhaps the point of using the word "awl" has to do with the size of a projectile even a weakling could launch from a crossbow someone else had cocked.

（尾）

「你把筆尚猶力弱。
伊言欲退干戈。
有的計對俺先道破。」

笑者是誰？是誰？眾再覷，乃張珙也。

生言曰，「婦人女子，別無遠見，臨危惟是非泣而已。寺僧遊客，何愚之甚也。不能止此亂軍，坐定滅亡。倘用吾言，滅賊必矣。」

法本大師仰知生間世之才，必有奇划，可遏亂眾。

法本就見生而囑曰，「僧眾無脫禍之計，先生既有奇策，願除眾難。」

生笑曰，「師等佛家弟子，豈不悟此，生者死之原，死者生之路，生死乃人之常理。向者佛祖亦須入滅，況佛書分明自說因果。如師等前生行惡於賊，今生固當冤報，何能苟免耶？若前生與賊無因，今世不為冤對，又何懼也？」

故作不對科語單埋自己腳根。

師曰，「誠如是。但可惜寺門、佛殿、廊廡、鐘鼓、經閣，

Coda
"You can barely lift a writing brush on your own,
But you say you want to make spear and buckler retreat.
That plan you have—spill it to me first."

Who was it who laughed? Who?[54] The assembly took a second look, and it turned out to be Zhang Gong.

The student explained, "All women just weep at approaching danger, instead of having a plan. The monks and travelers in this monastery are idiots! You all are incapable of stopping this rebellious mob and just sit here, waiting to be exterminated. If you employ my plan, the destruction of the bandits is guaranteed."

Now Grand Master Dharma Source admired the student and knew that he was a talent of the age and surely would have a marvelous plan to halt the rebellious mob in their tracks.
Dharma Source went to see the student and urged him, "The assembly of monks has no plans to escape disaster, but since you already have a clever plan, Sir, I would like to eradicate the danger."

The student laughed, "**You, Master, and other disciples of the Buddha must be enlightened about this: 'Being born is the source of death, and death is the road to life.'[55] Life and death are constant principles of being human. In the past, even Buddha the progenitor also had to enter into extinction.[56] Moreover, the Buddhist books clearly speak about karmic cause and effect. You and the others must have done something bad to these rebels in an earlier life, and now in this life, you're being repaid for the injustices that you wrought. How could it be possible to avoid them? If you had no causal connection with the bandits in your earlier life, then you will face no unjust effects in this life, so what are you so afraid of?"**

He purposely has a scene of no direct responses. The language solely creates a foundation for his own point of view.

"It is truly so," said the Master. "But it is a pity that the Buddha halls, corridors and wings, bell tower and drum tower, as well as the sutra

54 Suspense point 8.
55 A paraphrase of lines found in several Buddhist sutras.
56 That is, nirvana.

計其營造，不啻百萬，一旦火舉，便為灰燼。願以功德為念。」

生愈笑曰，「師坐講《金剛經》，豈不知骨肉皮毛，亦非己有。性者，我也；身者，舍也。若當來限盡之後，一性既往，四大狼籍，妻子雖親，不能從其去；金珠雖寶，不可挈而行。是何佛殿鐘樓，欲為己有哉？」

師曰，「我等說道，不計生死，不恤寺宇。所悲者母子生離，故來上請。」

生曰，「夫人與我無恩，崔相與我無舊。素不往還，救之何益？」

僧曰，「子不救鶯鶯，即夫人必不使鶯鶯從賊。亂軍必怒，大舉兵來，先生奈何？」

生曰，「我自有脫身計，師當自畫。」

師又曰，「子為儒者，行仁義之教。仁者愛人，惡所以害之者，固當除害；義者循理，惡所以亂之者，固當除亂。幼闈孀母，皆欲就死，子坐而笑之，豈仁者愛人之意歟？

---

57 This is a truncated reference to the concept that "I am the Buddha-nature" (佛性我也), as discussed thoroughly in the *Compilation and Explanation of the* Mahāparin-inirvāṇa Sûtra. See CBETA T37n1763.18.

58 From the *Sutra of Perfect Enlightenment* (圓覺經), "My current body is a combination of the four great things. That which is called hair, skin, flesh, tendon, and bone, as well as the impure manifestations of marrow and brain, all return to earth; saliva, mucus,

galleries, cost millions of cash to construct. Should a fire touch off one day, they would all turn to ashes and cinders. I hope you will consider performing an act of merit."

The student laughed harder, saying, "You, Master, sit and lecture on the *Diamond Sutra*. How can you not know that your bones, flesh, skin, and hair do not belong to you? The nature is considered the 'I' and the body is discarded.[57] After one's time comes, and once the soul is gone too, then the four great things[58] all scatter. Although one's wife and children are dear, one cannot go with them; although gold and pearls are precious, one cannot take them with one. In this case, how can you consider the Buddha Hall or the bell tower to be your possession?"

"When we explain the Way," said the Master, "we calculate neither death nor life, nor do we feel sympathetic attachment to the physical monastery. What I was grieving about was the delivery of Madam Cui and her daughter. That's why I came to make my request."

The student replied, "Madam Cui has never shown any significant kindness toward me that would require a debt, and I am not a long-time acquaintance of Minister Cui. There have been no dealings between us, so what is the benefit of saving them?"

"If you do not save Oriole," said the monk, "then Madam Cui will certainly not allow Oriole to go off with the bandits. The rebellious troops will become enraged and turn against us en masse. Then what will you do?"

"I have a plan of escape for myself," said the student, "you should make your own."

Again, the Master spoke, "You are a Confucian scholar and carry out the way of benevolence and righteousness. To be benevolent is to love others and to hate anything that harms them. Therefore, you should root out the harm. Righteousness is to act in accord with principle and to despise all that disorders principle. Therefore, you should root out disorder. A young maiden and a widowed mother are both willing to go their deaths, yet you do nothing but laugh at them. How can this be

pus, and blood all return to water; the warm breath returns to fire; movement and action return to wind." See Zhou Qi 2023, *juan* 3, and see CBETA X0253.

且亂軍餘黨，恣為暴虐，子視而弗誅，豈義者循理之意
歟？古者叔段有不弟之惡，鄭伯可制而不制；黎侯有狄
人之患，衛侯可救而不救，《春秋》譏之。先生有安人退
軍之策，卷而懷之，責以《春秋》，未為得也。先生裁之。」

生又笑曰，「師知其一，不知其二。聞諸夫子曰，『君子有
勇而無義為亂，小人有勇而無義為盜』。故君子惡其勇而
無禮也。我雖負勇，他無所求，我何自舉也。又曰，『禮
聞來學，未聞往教』。是以君子不屑就也。」

ii.22/ii.21 般涉調（麻婆子）

大師頻頻勸，
　「先生好性撇。
眾人都煩惱，
　偏你恁歡悅。」
君瑞聞言越越地笑，
　「吾師情性好佯呆。
又不是儒書載，
　分明是聖教說

　『有生必有死，
　　無生亦無滅。』」

the meaning of 'those who are benevolent love others'? Moreover, this rebellious army and its various hangers-on will cut loose with atrocious violence. If you see it and do not punish it, can that be what is meant by acting in accord with principle? Among the ancients, Duan the Younger is detested because he did not act the way a younger brother should toward the elder; the Marquis of Zheng could have controlled him, but he did not. The Earl of Li was beset with troubles by the Di tribes, and the Marquis of Wei could have helped, but did not.[ix] In each case the *Spring and Autumn Annals*[59] censured them. You, Sir, have a plan to calm people and make the army retreat; but you roll it up and tuck it away in your robe. To impugn you by the values of the *Spring and Autumn Annals* is not off point—you decide."

Again, the student laughed and said, "You know only part of it, not the whole. I have heard this from Confucius, who said, 'As for a gentleman, if he possesses courage but no sense of righteousness, he will upset the order of things. If a small man has courage but no sense of righteousness, he will become a thief.'[60] Therefore, a gentleman despises bravery without a sense of ritual propriety. Although I may be overconfident about my own courage, there's nothing else I seek. How can I simply offer up the plans of my own accord? It is said moreover, 'In terms of ritual propriety, I have heard of students coming to study, but never of going out to teach.' Therefore, the gentleman never deigns to make the first move."

ii.22/ii.21 Banshe Diao Mode

Pockmarked Crone
The abbot tried to persuade him time and again,
    "You, sir, truly are an odd one.
The assembly is all in tumult
    and only you seem happy."
Hearing these words, Junrui kept laughing louder and louder.
    "By his nature, my abbot loves to feign being dense:
It is not found in the Confucian texts,
    but clearly in the teachings of Buddhism:

'If there is life there must be death,
    without life there is also no extinction.'

59 One of the Confucian classics, known for its terse, concise comments on political process.
60 *Analects* 17.23.

生死人常理，
　何須恁怕怯。
亂軍都來半萬餘，
　便做天蓬黑煞般盡刁厥。
但存得自家在，
　怎到得被虜劫。」

（尾）
「不須騎戰馬，
　不須持寸鐵。
不須對陣爭優劣。
覷一覷教半萬賊兵化做膋血。」

大師以生言語及夫人。

夫人曰，「誠如是？」夫人以禮見生，泣而言曰，

ii.23/ii.22 小石調（花心動）
「亂軍門外，
　要幼女鶯鶯，
　　怎生結果。
可憐自家，
　母子孤孀，
　　投托解元子個。」
張生聞語先陪笑，
　道「相國夫人且坐。
但放心，
　何須怕怯子麼。

不是咱家口大，
　略使權術，
　　立退干戈。
除去亂軍，
　存得伽藍，
　　免那眾僧災禍。
恁一行家眷須到三五十口，

Life and death are constant principles for a human being,
    there is no reason to be afraid.
If the whole army comes as five thousand or more
    as noisy and fierce as Tianpeng or Heisha,
So long as I'm here,
    we'll never be captured or taken away.

Coda
"No need to mount a warhorse,
    no need to carry an inch of iron.
No need to prove who is better or worse in a battle—
Just wait and I'll turn those five thousand bandits into lard and
    blood."

The old Abbot reported the student's words to Madam Cui.

"Really?" she cried. She greeted the student with proper ritual and
wept as she said,

ii.23/ii.22 Xiaoshi Diao Mode
The Flower's Heart Trembles
"A rebellious army is outside the gates,
    clamoring for my young daughter, Oriole—
        how can we bring it to an end?
My poor family,
    a widowed mother and orphaned children,
        I now place in your care, Laureate."
When Student Zhang heard these words, he first smiled at her,
    and said, "Madam widow, please sit for a moment,
        just relax.
What need is there to fear anything?

I'm not trying to boast,
    but I have a contingency plan
        that will immediately turn back spear and buckler.
I'll remove the rebel army,
    save the monastery,
        and rescue the congregation of monks from disaster.
Though you have a large household of forty or fifty,

大小不教傷著一個。
恁時節，
　便休卻外人般待我。」

才說出本懷。　夫人曰，「是何言也。不以見薄為辭，禍滅身安，繼子為親。」

生謂僧曰，「先令人傳報亂軍，鶯非敵他，當慈母別靈，理妝治服，少頃即至。願不見逼。」

亂軍稍緩。生曰，「亂軍不可以言說，人眾不可以力爭，但可威服。」

師與夫人皆曰，「孰為有威者？」

生曰，
「吾一故人，
以儒業進身，
武勇治亂，
內懷信義之心，
外有威嚴之色。
初典郡城，
賊盜悉皆去境，
再擢邊任，
塞馬不敢嘶南。
故知武備德修，
人歸軍仰。

臨軍常跨雪白馬，人目之曰『白馬將軍』，姓杜，名確。今鎮守蒲關，素得軍心，人莫犯之。與僕為死生之交。我有書藥，上呈夫人。」其略曰：，

I'll make sure that not one of them, young or old, will be
  injured.
Then, at that moment,
  please no longer treat me as an outsider."

Finally says what
he wants!

Madam Cui said, "What do you mean? Please don't quit because you
feel slighted! When the calamity is gone and we are secure, from that
point on, I'll treat you as a son." *ad lib.* here

The student told the monks, "First send someone to carry a message
to the rebel army that Oriole holds no grudge against him. She must
formally bid her mother goodbye, take leave of the coffin, and arrange
her makeup and clothes.[61] She will arrive shortly. We ask that we not
be put under duress, and that the rebel army relax its siege." He then
said, "The rebel army cannot be persuaded by words, and their numbers make engagement with them impossible. But they can be made
to submit by power."

The Abbot and Madam Cui both said, "Who holds any power here?"

"I have an old friend," said the student, "who
  became an official through the Confucian arts
  and settled disorder through military bravery.
  On the inside, his heart is full of trustworthiness and righteousness,
  and on the outside, he has an appearance that inspires awe.
  When he assumed a position in a provincial capital,
  the bandits and thieves all left the area under his control.
  When he was appointed to a border post,
  horses south of the northern passes dared not whinny.
  Therefore, we know
  his martial knowledge is complete
  and his virtue is that of a worthy man,
  so people admire him and the army looks up to him.

Leading his army to battle, he always sits astride a white charger, and
people have given him the appellation the 'White Horse General.' He
is Du Que, and he now guards Pu Pass. He has long since won the
hearts of his troops, and no one dares oppose him. We are brothers
sworn in life or death. I have here a draft letter I would like to show
you, madam." The gist of it goes:

61 To change from the unadorned funeral garb and plain makeup.

「辱游張珙書上半軍帥府，

　倉惶之下，
不備文章，
慷慨之前，
直陳利害。
　不幸
渾太師薨於蒲郡，
丁文雅失制河橋。
兵亂軍叛，
悉殘郡邑。
蒲州兵火，
盈耳哀聲。
生靈有懼死之憂，
黎庶有倒懸之急。

伏啓將軍，
天資神策，
人仰洪威。
有愛民治亂之謀，
奮斬將破敵之勇。
忍居住守，
安振軍城。
坐看亂軍，
肆兇暴惡。
公如不起，
孰拯斯危．

稍緩師徒，
恐成大亂。
　公至則
斬賊降眾，
守郡安民。
百里無虞，
一方甦泰。

Zhang Gong, who is out roaming, writes this missive to the headquarters of the Superior General of the army.

> Being in a rush
> I have not prepared a properly refined document,
> and before your generosity,
> I will simply state how the situation stands.
> Unfortunately,
> Grand Minister Hun passed away in Puzhou,
> Ding Wenya lost control of the bridge at the Yellow River,
> the soldiers went wild, and the army rebelled,
> wreaking havoc in prefecture and county.
> Puzhou fell to the flames of war
> and sounds of lamentation filled the ears.
> Living souls bear the fear of death,
> black-haired commoners feel the press of dire emergency.

> I humbly beseech you, General—
> Heaven has bestowed upon you sagely foreknowledge,
> and all raise their eyes to your awesome martial power.
> You have plans to care for the people and bring order to chaos,
> and the bravery to seize and behead generals to smash the enemy.
> If you hold back in your defensive posture,
> how can you rouse a city occupied by soldiers?
> If you sit and look at a mutinous army,
> you will let the treacherous loose to do violence and evil.
> If you do not rise up
> who can rescue us from this danger?

> Should you pause in the least in moving your troops,
> I fear it will bring great chaos.
> When you arrive,
> behead the traitors to quell the multitudes,
> protect the commandery and make the people secure.
> Then, for a hundred miles there will be nothing untoward,
> and the whole area will awaken to peace.

詔書將下，
必推退亂之功。
旌旆不行，
自受怯敵之過。
　今
賊兵見圍普救，
陋儒何計逃生。
　但願
上扶郡國，
下救寒生。
垂死之餘，
鵠觀來耗。
再生之賜，
皆荷恩光。

辱游張珙再拜良契將軍帥府足下。」

ii.24/iii.1 中呂調（碧牡丹纏令）

「是須休怕怖。
請夫人放心無慮。
亂軍雖眾，
　張珙看來無物。
俺有個親知，
　只在蒲關住。
與俺好相看，
　好相識，
　　好相與。」

祖宗非此仳，
　也非是庶民白屋。
不襲門蔭，
　應中賢良科舉。
是杜如晦的重孫，
　英烈超宗祖。

62　A practice begun in the Han dynasty of selecting people of virtue that was also a
feature of the Jin examination system. See Tuotuo 1975, Vol. 4, 1150.

An imperial rescript will be sent down
that will surely reward your merit in forcing them to withdraw.
If your battle banners are not set into motion
you will have the dishonor of fearing the enemy.
    At this moment
Puzhou monastery is surrounded by rebels.
What plans does this lowly Confucian have to escape with his life?
    I only hope that,
first, you will support the commandery and the state,
and second, you will rescue this poor student
suspended here on the verge of dying.
A crane will bring my missive—
the granting of a second life
will make each of us recipients of the brilliance of your grace.

Zhang Gong, who is out roaming, makes a second obeisance to you,
sir, my good friend at the Headquarters of the Superior General.

ii.24/iii.1 Zhonglü Diao Mode

Blue-Green Peony: A Bound Suite
"We should cease our trepidation and fear.
Madam, please relax, give it no further thought.
That rebellious army, though large in number,
    to my eye are nothing.
I have a close friend,
    now stationed at Pu Pass,
Who regards me well,
    knows me well,
        and is the closest of friends.

His ancestors are not insignificant.
They do not come from commoners' white-thatched dwellings.
But he did not avail himself of his family status,
    wanting to pass the examinations for the virtuous and
        capable.[62]
He's a great-grandson of Du Ruhui[63]
    and his brave actions surpass his ancestors.

---

63 Du Ruhui 杜如晦 (585–630, byname Keming 克明) was one of two famous chief
    counselors of the Taizong Emperor of the Tang. He was held up as a model minister
    of state.

開六鈞弓，
　閱八陣法，
　　讀五車書。」

（木魚兒）
　「初間典郡城，
　　一方盜賊沒。
　後臨邊地職，
　　塞馬胡兒不敢正覷。
　方今出鎮蒲關，
　　掌着軍卒。
　普天下好漢果煞數着。
　有文有武有權術。
　熟閑槍搠 快弓弩。
　　遮莫賊軍三萬垓，
　　　便是天蓬黑煞，
　　　　見他應也伏輸。」

（鶻打兔）
　「愛騎一疋白戰馬，
　　如彪虎。
　使一柄大刀，
　　冠絕今古。
　扶社稷，
　　清寰宇。
　宰天下，
　　安邦國。
　為主存忠，
　　願削平禍亂，
　　　開疆展土。

　自古有的英雄，
　　這將軍，
　　　皆不許。

He draws an eighteen stone-weight bow,
    reviews the methods of the Eight Formations[64]
      and has read five cartloads of books.

A Wooden Fish Sounding Board
"At the beginning, when he took charge of a commandery city,
    all the bandits and thieves disappeared from the area.
Then, when ordered to look after the frontiers,
    barbarian lads on border horses dared not look him in the eye.
Recently sent out to occupy Pu Pass,
    he controls a legion of soldiers.
Counted as the best of all brave men in the world,
He is learned, martial, and has a plan for every eventuality.
Proficient with thrusts of a spear, brilliant with bow or crossbow.
Even a million rebellious troops—
    even the Celestial Beacon star and the Black Killer of the
      North[65]—
      would surely bow in submission upon first sight.

The Hawk Takes the Hare
"The white charger he loves to ride is
    as powerful as a fierce tiger.
He wields a single-hafted battle-axe
    better than anyone now or before.
He supports the altars of grain,[66]
    cleanses the known world,
And ministers to all under heaven
    to secure the domain of the state.
He holds absolute loyalty to his lord,
    and desires to suppress internal chaos and disaster
      and to expand the territory of the state.

Many are the heroes from ancient times,
    but this general
      yields place to none.

---

64 The Eight Formations (*Bazhen tu* 八陣圖) is a treatise supposedly by the great tactician Zhuge Liang 諸葛亮 (181–234, byname Kongming 孔明).

65 Both sinister figures. On the Celestial Beacon, see Strickmann 2002, 101. For the deity Black Killer, see Davis 2001, 67–85.

66 The state; the fundamental sacrificial altars of an agrarian society.

> 壓着一萬個孟賁，
> 五千個呂布。
> 楚項籍，
> 蜀關羽。
> 秦白起，
> 燕孫武。
> 若比這個將軍，
> 兵書戰策，
>   索拜做師父。」

（尾）

> 「文章賈馬豈是大儒。
> 智略孫龐是真下愚。
> 英武笑韓彭不丈夫。」

夫人曰：「杜將軍誠一時名將，威令人伏。與君有舊，書至則必起雄師，立殘諸惡。關城相去幾數十里，若候修書，師定見遲留。」

生曰：「適於法聰出戰之時，已持此書報杜將軍矣。請夫人、

---

67 Meng Ben 孟賁 (d. 307 BCE) was a legendary general who was famous for such a sharp glare that it once scared men into jumping from their boat into a river.

68 See n. 183.

69 Xiang Ji 項籍 (232–202 BCE, byname Yu 羽), also known as the Hegemon Lord, contested with Liu Bang for control of the Qin empire. See Sima Qian 1971, 37–73; Guan Yu 關羽 (d. 220, byname Yunchang 雲長) fought on the side of the Shu during the contestations between Shu, Wu, and Wei, and later became deified. See Idema and West 2012, xvi, n. 10; Bai Qi 白起 a Qin general, also known as Gongsun Qi (332–257 BCE), conquered two central China domains. Sun Su is better known as Master Sun or Sunzi (ca. 544–497 BCE), author of Sunzi's *Art of War* (Sunzi bingfa 孫子兵法).

70 Referencing lines from the "Preface" to the *Wenxuan*; see Xiao and Knechtges 1982, 73–74, lines 41–42 and notes. Jia Yi 賈誼 (200–169 BCE) and Sima Xiangru are two famous writers of the early Han.

71 Sun Bin 孫臏 (d. 316 BCE), supposed descendant of Sunzi 孫子, served both Wei and Qi. In Wei, he was accused of treason and had his kneecaps removed. He escaped to

Better than ten thousand Meng Bens,[67]
    five thousand Lü Bus,[68]
or Xiang Ji of Chu,
    Guan Yu of Shu,
Bai Qi of Qin,
    or Sun Wu of Yan[69]
If compared to General Du—
    for texts on war or tactics in battle —
        all these men would acknowledge him as their teacher.

Coda

Or in terms of writing? Beside him Jia Yi and Sima Xiangru
    would pale.[70]
For military wisdom and strategy? Sun and Pang would seem
    simple.[71]
For courage and bravery? We would scorn Han Xin[72] and Peng
    Yue[73] as less than real men."

Madam Cui said, "General Du is truly famous, and all submit to his commands with awe. As a longtime acquaintance of yours, he'll surely dispatch a powerful force when he receives your letter, and immediately lay waste to all this evil. The walled city at the pass is only several tens of miles away, but if you wait to draft your letter, the troops will be delayed."

"I took advantage of the time when Dharma Wit went out to battle," said the student, "and have already had the letter delivered to General

Qi and helped them defeat Wei. Pang Juan 龐涓 (d. 342 BCE), once a fellow student and friend of Sun Bin, developed a jealous rivalry with him.

72 Han Xin 韓信 (ob. 196 BCE) devised the famous "ten-sided attack" (shimian maifu 十面埋伏) that annihilated Xiang Yu's army and led to Xiang's defeat at Gaixia. "Ten sides" refers to octants—the cardinal directions, the directions in between them—as well as above and below. Han's biography is found in English in "The Biography of the Marquis of Huai-yin," in Sima Qian 1971, 208–231.

73 Peng Yue was enfeoffed as Prince of Liang. Along with Han Xin and Ying Bu, he is known as one of the Three Great Generals of the Early Han (Hanchu san daming jiang 漢初三大名將). He was originally a fisherman in the lakes and marshes of Juye who fell in with some bandits. After some urging, he became their leader and then rose to prominence in the wars with Chu. Following the establishment of the Han, Peng and his family were killed by the new emperor because one of his underlings had falsely reported that Peng was planning to rebel. Idema and West 2012, 252, n. 29. See also "Biographies of Wei Pao and P'eng Yüeh," in Sima Qian 1971, 189–195.

大師待望於鐘樓之上，兵必至矣。」

ii.25/iii.2 大石調 （吳音子）

「相國夫人，
　　怕伊不信自家說。
請寬尊抱，
　　是須休把兩眉結。」
倚着闌干，
　　凝望時節。
寺宇周廻，
　　賊軍間列稍寧貼。

堪傷處，
　　見殺氣迷荒野。
塵頭起處，
　　遠觀一道陣雲斜。
五百來兒郎，
　　一個個刁厥。
似初下雲端來的，
　　驅雷使者。

（尾）

甲溜晴郊似銀河瀉。
繡旗颭似彩霞招折。
管是白馬將軍到來也。

夫人從長歡容，
大眾便生喜色。

ii.26/iii.3 越調 （鬥鵪鶉纏令）

天昏昏兮，
　　陣雲四合。
埒騰騰地，

Du. Madam and Grand Master, please go up into the bell tower and
watch for his imminent arrival. His soldiers will surely come."

ii.25/iii.2 **Dashi Diao Mode**

Sounds of Wu
"Madam widow of the Minister,
    I fear you don't believe me.
Please stop worrying,
    and don't knit your brows in fear."
She leaned against the railing
    her eyes fixed in expectation.
All about the monastery
    the rebel army had settled in.

What grieved her
    were ethers of death that obscured fallows and wilds.
Then, a sudden swelling of dust,
    and far away a line of war clouds appeared slanting across the
        sky—
Five hundred or more fine young men,
    all as fierce as fierce can be—
Seeming at first to be riders of the Thunder God
    emerging below the clouds.

Coda
As if the Milky Way had breached, sparkling armor flooded over
    the bright fields,
And embroidered flags rippled like a brilliant sunset tearing
    apart—
The army of the White Horse General had come at last.

    A happy look grew upon Madam Cui's face,
    An air of joy spread over the congregation.

ii.26/iii.3 **Yue Diao Mode**

Fighting Quail: A Bound Suite
Dusky and dark
    war clouds joined on four sides round,
Swirling and swelling
    dust filled the air as though shoveled up then sifted.

塵頭肖如皺籤。
栲栳大隊精兵，
　轉過拽腳慢坡。
六百來少，
　半千來多。
一心待把，
　群賊立破。

一字陣分開，
　盡都擺挪。
一個個精神，
　肖沒彈剝。
三十的早年高，
　六尺的早最矬。
把業龍擒捉，
　盡猛虎倒拖。
亂軍雖眾，
　望他怕他。

（青山口）
嘶風的驕馬弄風珂。
雄雄軍勢惡。
步兵卒子小僂儸。
擂狼皮鼓。
籤動金鑼。
森森排劍戟，
　密密列干戈。
待破賊軍
　解君憂
　　與民除禍。

簇捧着個將軍，
　狀貌雄雄，
　　古今沒兩個。
把金鐙笑踏，
　寶鞍斜坐。
腕下鐵鞭是水磨。

A large contingent of crack troops encompassed the field,
    turning past the impediment of a gradual slope—
Fewer than six hundred,
    but more than half a thousand—
All intent on
    smashing the horde of rebels forthwith.

They broke into a single-line formation,
    and all brandished spears.
The spirit of each man was
    faultless and beyond reproach.
The oldest was less than thirty,
    the shortest six feet tall.
They could seize a surly dragon
    or drag a tiger from its den by the tail.
The disorderly bandits may have had the numbers,
    but at first sight they cowered in fear.

Green Mountain Pass
Neighing in the wind, the proud horses shook their bridle jades;
Strong and virile, the horsemen were ferocious.
Foot soldiers, officers, men, and runners
Beat on wolf-skin drums
And shook metal gongs.
Swords and halberds were thick as a forest
    and spears and bucklers were packed tightly in rows.
Their only desire was to smash the rebel army,
    to relieve the sovereign's worry,
        and root out disaster on behalf of the people.

They clustered tightly around their general
    whose manly and vigorous form
        was unmatched in times past or present.
Laughing, feet in golden stirrups,
    he sat aslant a jeweled saddle.
The iron whip that dangled from his wrist was polished by a water
    stone.

脿背到恁來闊。
身材恁來大。
挾矢負弧，
甲掛熟銅，
袍披茜羅。

（雪裏梅 [7]）
行軍計若通神，
揮劍血成河。
莫道是亂軍，
便是六丁黑煞，
待子甚麼。

馬上笑呵呵。
把賊眾欲平蹉。
亂軍覷了道，
「這爺爺來也，
咱怎生奈何。」

（尾）
馬頷系朱纓，
栲栳來大一團火。
肩上鋼刀門扇來闊。
人似金剛，
馬似駱駝。
孫飛虎唬得來肩磨。
魂魄離殼。
自摧挫。
「只管為這一頓饅頭送了我。」

賊眾沒精神，
飛虎挫銳氣。

ii.27/iii.4 般涉調（牆頭花）
白馬將軍手下，
五百來人衣鐵。

如此英雄作尾
又着謔狀甚有
冷趣。

His shoulders and back were wide,
    his body size enormous.
Arrows were slung under his arm, with a wooden bow on his back;
    he had tempered bronze for armor
        and a cloak of madder red casually thrown on.

A Plum in the Snow
He put his battle tactics into motion as if blessed by divinity—
    as they wielded swords, blood turned to rivers.
And don't say, "it was just a rebel army," for
    even the Six Heavenly Ding generals under the Black Killer
        would be powerless against it.

Upon his horse, he laughed heartily,
And prepared to trample the rebel force.
Once the chaos-causing army saw him, they said,
    "Now that this old daddy's here
        what should we do?"

Coda
His horse's reins were tied with vermillion cords,
    their loop was as big as a basket, like a circle of fire.
The steel blade on his shoulders was as wide as the leaf of a door.
He was like a Vajra
    and his horse was like a camel.
Flying Tiger Sun was so scared his shoulders started to tremble.
His souls flew from his husk,
And he reproached himself:
"I've traded my life for a single meal of buns!"

> *How heroic this coda is. It also ends on a sarcastic note, and really carries a dry wit.*

    That horde of rebels lost all vitality;
    Flying Tiger's mettle had been dampened.

ii.27/iii.4 Banshe Diao Mode

Flowers on the Wall
Under command of the White Horse General
    some five hundred or more soldiers, clothed in armor,

一布地平原盡擺列。
覷一覷飛虎魂消，
　喝一聲群賊腦裂。

賊軍廝見，
　道：「咱性命合休也。」
半萬餘人看怎者。
又不敢睹個輸贏，
　又不敢爭個優劣。

賊軍肖似兒，
　來兵肖似爺。
來兵勢若龍，
　害怕的賊軍肖似鼈。
來兵似五百個僧人，
　賊軍似六千個行者。

（尾）
　把那弓箭解，
　　刀斧撇。
　旌旗鞍馬都不藉。
　回頭來覷着白馬將軍，
　　喝一聲爆雷也似喏。

杜將軍曰：「爾等以渾太師薨後，無人統制，丁文雅恣其
酒色，稍失訓練，因為掠剽，想無叛心。汝等父母妻子，
皆處舊營，一忘國恩，悉皆誅戮。我今親擁貔貅，振英武，
殺爾無主亂軍，易如刈草。但恐其間有非叛者，吾實不忍。」

又曰：「軍中不叛者，東向棄仗坐甲；叛者西向作隊，以
備死戰。」言訖，軍中皆棄仗向東坐甲。杜取孫飛虎斬之，

Were put in formation on the level plain—
Flying Tiger's twin souls disappeared at the sight,
  and with a single shout the rebels' heads split open.

The rebel army looked
  and said, "We're done for now."
And how did those five thousand men see it?
They dared not wager on a win,
  nor to fight to see who's best.

The rebel soldiers were just like children,
  and the rescue force exactly like their fathers.
The rescue force had the might of a dragon,
  while the fearful rebel troops were more like a soft-shelled turtle.
The rescue troops were like five hundred monks,
  while the rebel force was akin to six thousand acolytes.

Coda
The rebels dropped their bows and arrows,
  cast aside their swords and axes.
Neither battle pennants nor saddle horses were put to use.
Turning their heads to look at the White Horse General,
  in a voice like a roll of thunder, they bowed and yelled in unison,
   "As you command."

General Du remarked, "After Grand Master Hun passed away, there was no one to bring order to you lot, and Ding Wenya lost himself to wine and womanizing; he was remiss in his discipline and, consequently, you went on to plunder and raise hell. But I believe you did not have rebellion on your mind, because once you'd forgotten the munificence of the state and revolted, your parents, wives, and children still living in your former camps would all be executed along with you. If I had set my fierce troops to the task, and if I had stirred up their superb martial courage, then slaying the lot of you leaderless rebels would have been as easy as cutting grass. But I fear there may be some among you who did not want to rebel, so I truly cannot bear to inflict such punishment."

He went on, "Those in this troop who did not rebel go east to cast down your weapons and sit on your armor. Those who did mutiny, line up in formation on the west and prepare for a battle to the death." At that, the whole army cast down their weapons, headed eastward, and sat on

餘眾悉免。

張生與大師出寺邀杜。杜與生兄弟禮畢，執手入寺，置酒
於廊下，以道契闊。

生曰：「君今有功於國，有義於朋友，有恩於蒲民：只在朝夕，
朝廷必當重有封拜，即容上賀。」

ii.28/iii.5 仙呂調（滿江紅）
　　相邀入寺，
　　　滿寺裏僧人盡歡悅。
　「有義於知交，
　　　有恩於寺舍。
　　即時呈表聞帝闕。
　　功業見得凌煙閣上寫。
　　賞延後世，
　　　名傳萬劫。
　　不是降了群賊後，
　　　蒲州百姓，
　　　　幾時寧貼。
　　弟兄休作外，
　　　幾盞兒淡酒，
　　　　聊復致謝。」

　　白馬將軍飲了一杯。
　　道：「君瑞何須恁般惆悵。」
　　約退雜人，
　　　把知心話說。
　　三巡酒外紅日斜。
　　白馬將軍離坐起。

不過是平鋪文
字然非老手不
能。

their armor. Du seized Flying Tiger Sun and beheaded him, pardoning the rest of the group.

Student Zhang and the abbot went out of the monastery to greet Du. After the exchange of brotherly rites between Du and the student, they grasped hands and went into the monastery, where wine was set out in a veranda to honor their tribulations.

The student said, "Sir, today you have shown merit towards the state, righteous loyalty to your friends, and grace and beneficence to the people of Pu. In short order the court will surely award you substantial titles and fiefs. I would like to congratulate you."

ii.28/iii.5 Xianlü Diao Mode

A River Running Red
They invited him into the monastery
    where all the monks were overjoyed.
"You showed righteous loyalty to your friends,
    and beneficence for the monastery.
A memorial should be dispatched forthwith to be heard by the
    emperor,
For your merit should be inscribed on the walls of the Gallery that
    Spans the Mist.[74]
Rewards will extend to your later generations,
    and your name passed down for time eternal.
Had you not brought that horde of rebels to their knees,
    would the common folk of Puzhou
        ever find peace?
Let us be true brothers,
    so that with a few cups of weak wine
        we can take this opportunity to thank you again."

The White Horse General finished a cup and said,
    "Junrui, don't be such a stickler about formality.
Let's send the others away
    so we can speak as good friends should."
After three rounds of wine, the red sun declined,
And the White Horse General rose to leave his seat.

Merely a text of straightforward words, but only a seasoned writer can accomplish this.

---

74 A gallery in which Li Shimin 李世民 (598–649), founding emperor of the Tang, had portraits painted of twenty-four meritorious officers and officials who helped him found the dynasty. See Burkus-Chasson 2010, 163–255.

道：「先生勿罪，
　小官索去也。」
相送到山門外，
　臨岐執手，
　　彼此難捨。
更了一杯酒，
　「比及再回，
　　哥哥且略別。」

　　　　馬離普救搖金勒，
　　　　人望蒲關和凱歌。

生次日見大師曰：「昨日亂軍至寺，夫人禱我退賊之策，
願我繼親。未審親事若何。」

ii.29/iii.6 高平調（于飛樂）
　「念自家，
　　雖是個
　　　淺陋書生。
　於夫人反有深恩。
　是他家
　　先許了，
　　　先許了免難後成親。
　十分裏九分。
　多應待聘與我鶯鶯。

　「細尋思，
　　此件 [8] 事
　　　對面難陳。
　師兄略暫聽聞。
　既為佛弟子，
　須『方便為門。』
　不合上煩，
　　托付你作個媒人。」

He said, "Forgive me,
　　but I must leave."
Zhang accompanied him out of the main gate
　　holding hands as his departure neared,
　　　　as it was hard for each of them to bid the other
　　　　　　goodbye.
They finished a last cup:
　　"Until we meet again.
　　　　I part with you, brother, but only for the while."

Departing Universal Salvation, his horse shook his golden harness,
Off to Pu Pass, the men harmonized their victory song.

The next day, the student visited the abbot, saying, "When those chaotic rebels reached the monastery yesterday, Madam Cui begged for my plan to make the bandits withdraw, and then promised me her daughter's hand in marriage. I'm not certain how the marriage plans are going."

ii.29/iii.6　Gaoping Diao Mode

A Perfect Marriage
"I know
　　that I am
　　　　just a shallow student,
But in fact, I have done a deep favor for Madam Cui.
She's the one
　　who first uttered the oath
　　　　and granted marriage after Oriole's rescue.
It's a chance of nine in ten
That she'll betroth Oriole to me.

Thinking about it carefully,
　　this business
　　　　would be hard to discuss face to face with her.
Please hear me out, master:
Since you're a disciple of the Buddha
　　you surely know that 'expediency is the doorway!'[75]
I shouldn't bother you with this,
　　but please act as my go-between."

75　An oft-repeated twist in colloquial texts on the common Buddhist saying, "Compassion is the basis, expediency is the doorway" 慈悲為本方便為門; that is, any expedient means, if applied with compassion, can be used to lead people to enlightenment.

師笑許之曰：「先生少待，小僧徑往。」師詣夫人院，令人
報夫人。出請師坐。師乃勞問安慰，夫人陳謝而已。

師徐曰：「張生，義人也。當時獻退賊之策，夫人面許繼親。
張生托貧僧敬問一耗，未審懿旨若何。」

夫人曰：「張生之恩，固不可忘。方備蔬食，當與生面議。」
師喜而退，以夫人語報生。

ii.30/iii.7 高平調（木蘭花）

　　　那法師，
　　　　忙賀喜。
　　　道：「那每殷勤的請你。
　　　待對面商議。」
　　　張生曰：「今朝正是個成婚日。
　　　那家多應管準備。
　　　那就親筵席。

　　　又問道：「吾師，
　　　　那家裏做甚底。
　　　買了幾十瓶法酒，
　　　　做了幾十分茶食。」
　　　法師笑道：「休打砌。
　　　我道春了幾升陳米。
　　　煮下半甕黃齏。」

陳米、黃齏出
自法師，調生
甚妙。王實甫
用其意為。紅
語，而曰淘下
陳倉米云云。
滋味減少。

　　　生喜不自勝，整衣而待。

The master consented with a laugh, saying, "Wait here a bit, and I'll go directly there." The master then paid a visit to Madam Cui's compound and had someone notify her. She came out and asked the abbot to sit. The master then asked a few solicitous questions to console her, and she simply expressed her gratitude.

Speaking in an unhurried manner, the master said, "Student Zhang is a good and righteous man. When he offered his plan to make the bandits retreat, you promised a marriage pact right then and there. He has sent this poor monk to ask if there is any information, since he has not probed what your Ladyship's intent is."

Madam Cui replied, "The significant favor that Student Zhang did for us, for which we owe gratitude, can surely never be forgotten. I have just had a meal prepared and should discuss this personally with him." The abbot withdrew, delighted, and reported her words to the student.

ii.30/iii.7 Gaoping Diao Mode

Magnolia Blossoms
The abbot
profusely congratulated him
And said, "To have so enthusiastically invited you
Means she wants to discuss it face to face."
Student Zhang spoke, "This truly is the day to conclude the
      betrothal.
They should be getting prepared
For a marriage banquet."

He went on to ask, "Master,
      what have they already done?
How many bottles of the finest wine did they purchase?
How many dozens of nibbles and snacks did they make?
The Dharma Master laughed, "Don't kid yourself,
I would say they're hulling stale rice
And boiling up a half a vat of yellowed pickles!" [76]

The student was overcome with joy. He neatened his clothes and waited.

"Stale rice" and "yellowed pickles" here comes out of the master's mouth and is a marvelously clever poke at the student. Wang Shifu uses the sense of this but has Crimson speak the following: "Rinse off some stale rice from the state granary." The flavor is somewhat diminished!

[76] The passage to which the marginal commentary refers is from Play II, act 4; see Wang Shifu 2006, 139; for a translation of the passage and for its context in the drama, see Wang 1995, 170.

ii.31/iii.8 仙呂調（戀香衾）

梳裏箱兒裏取明鏡。
把臉兒掙得光瑩。
拂拭了紗巾。
要添風韻。
窄地羅衫長打影。
偏宜二色羅領。
沈郎腰道，
　　與絳條兒廝稱。

鈐口鞋兒樣兒整。
僧勒襪兒活淨。
扮了書闈裏
　　坐地不穩。
鏡兒裏拈相了內心騁。
窗兒外弄影兒行。
恨日頭兒不到
　　正南時分。

風魔景色。

（尾）

癢如如把心不定。
肚皮兒裏骨轆轆地雷鳴。
眼懸懸地專盼着人來請。

生更衣不作飯，專待來請。自早至晚，不蒙人至。生曰：
「法本和尚何相戲我至此。夫人亦待我薄矣。」

ii.32/iii.9 高平調（木蘭花）

從自齋時，
　　等到日轉過。
沒個人偢問，
　　酪子裏忍餓。
侵晨等到合昏個。
不曾湯個水米，

着此一誤殊
波瀾。

ii.31/iii.8 **Xianlü Diao Mode**

Quilt with the Fragrance of Love
He took out a bright mirror from his grooming box,
And prettied up his face until it glistened.
He brushed his gauze cap
To make himself appear more elegant.
His straight pongee tunic fit just right,
Perfect for silken over-lapels of two different colors.
His waist, thin as that of a young Shen Yue,[77]
      precisely fit a crimson sash.

His monk's shoes were perfect,
His Buddhist leggings pale and clean.
But there in the study after he dressed up
    he couldn't sit still.
After he looked in the mirror, his mind raced;
Outside the window, he strolled to make a show
And grumbled that the sun
    had yet to mark noontime.

All riled up in a frenzy.

Coda
He could not settle his itching heart,
And inside, his belly grumbled and growled like rumbling thunder,
He stared unblinking, waiting for someone to come and invite him.

The student changed clothes, and just waited for the invitation without making anything to eat. No one came all day. He said, "So Dharma Wit would go this far to make fun of me! And Madam Cui is treating me coldly."

ii.32/iii.9 GAOPING DIAO MODE

Magnolia Blossoms
From the time of the morning meal
    he waited straight until sunset,
But no one ever came, even to inquire about him,
    and he had to endure his hunger in private.
He had waited from the crack of dawn until the fall of dusk
And touched neither water nor rice—

A mistake like this adds to the suspense.

---

77 Shen Yue 沈約 (441–513, byname Xiuwen 休文) was a noted poet, statesman, and music theorist. He was also noted for being exceptionally thin. See Mather 1988.

便不餓損卑末。

「果是咱飢變做渴。
　咽喉乾燥，
　　肚兒裏如火。」
　開門見法本來參賀。
「您那門親事論議的如何。」

生作色曰 ：「我平日待師不薄，師何薄我如此。」

師曰 ：「不知我所以薄公者。」

生曰 ：「適來囑師問親，師報我以今日見請。

自朝抵暮，殊不蒙召。非師薄我何。」

師曰 ：「山僧過矣。夫人言明日作排，非今日矣。」

生笑曰 ：「兩句傳示，尚自疏脫，怎背誦《華嚴經》呵。禿屌。」

師笑而去。

生通宵不寐。須臾，日色清晨，果見紅娘斂衽道 ：「夫人
有請。」

ii.33/iii.10 仙呂調 （賞花時）
　　恰正張生悶轉加。
　　驀見紅娘歡喜煞。
　　叉手奉迎他。
　　連忙陪笑，
　　　道 ：「姐坐來麼。」　紅娘曰 ：「夫人使來，怎敢。」

wasn't poor old Zhang just destroyed by this hunger?

"And now my hunger has turned to thirst—
Throat parched and dry
    my stomach seems to be on fire."
Opening the door, Dharma Source appeared once more to
    congratulate him,
      "So, how did the conversation go about your wedding
        plans?"

The student flushed with anger, "I've always treated you well, Master. Why are you demeaning me like this?"

"I don't know how I've demeaned you," replied the master.

"Just a while ago," said the student, "I asked you to go and inquire about the marriage match, and you said I would be getting an invitation today. I waited from dawn to dusk but was never summoned. What is this, then, if not a humiliation?"

"It's my mistake," said the abbot. "**Madam Cui said tomorrow, not today!**"

Laughing, the student said, "Only two lines to transmit, and still you made a mistake—**how are you able to memorize and recite the Garland Sutra, you bald prick?**"

The master laughed and left.

Zhang didn't sleep all night long. Gradually, sunlight peeked into the new morning, and it turned out he did see Crimson, who straightened her lapels as a gesture of formality then said, "Madam Cui has an invitation for you."

ii.33/iii.10 Xianlü Diao Mode

Time to Enjoy the Flowers
Just as Student Zhang's depression was getting worse,
He was suddenly delighted by the sight of Crimson.
He bowed and welcomed her in,
Quickly smiled
    and said, "Big sister, will you sit?" Crimson said, "I've been sent by
        Madam Cui! no way!

「相國夫人教邀足下。
是必休教推避咱。
多謝解元呵。」
張生道 ：「依命，
　我有分見那冤家。」

（尾）
「不圖酒食不圖茶。
夫人請我別無話。
孩兒，管教俺兩口兒就親咲。」

紅娘笑而去。

ii.34/iii.11 雙調（惜奴嬌）
　絕早侵晨，
　　早與他忙梳裹。
備寫眼懸懸　不尋思虛脾真個。
處。　　你試尋思，
　　秀才家，
　　　平生餓。
　無那。
　空倚着門兒咽唾。

　去了紅娘，
　　會聖肯書幃裏坐不定一地裏篤麼。
　覷着日頭兒，
　　暫時間齋時過。
　「殺剁。
　又不成紅娘鄧我。」

生正疑惑間，紅娘再至，生與俱往見夫人。

ii.35/iii.12 雙調（惜奴嬌）
　再見紅娘，

The Wife of the Minister of State sent me to invite you, sir,
And to make sure that you come.
She has much to thank you for, Laureate."
Student Zhang replied, "I will comply with her request.
        At last, my chance to see my little karmic foe.

Coda
"I'm not thinking of wine and food, not thinking of tea,
For Madam Cui has asked me and will have nothing else to say
    but. . . .
Child! She's going to have the two of us seal the marriage pact."

    Crimson laughed and left.

ii.34/iii.11 Shuang Diao Mode

Cherishing My Love's Beauty
At the break of day, early morn,
        he was already getting himself all done up.
He never thought to question whether the invitation was genuine.   *Perfectly describes*
You, my audience, try and ponder this: *urgent, hopeful*
                                                                           gazing.
        young scholars on the rise
                spcnd thcir livcs hungry.
And, alas, nothing he could do—
But vainly lean against the door, with only saliva to fill his mouth.

Once Crimson left,
        only some miracle could keep him sitting there in his study.
Unable to keep still, he paced nervously about.
He looked where the sun might be,
        and already the time
                for the morning meal had passed.
"Damn it!
Has Crimson been taunting me too?"

    And, just as the student was totally perplexed, Crimson came again,
    and off he went with her to see Madam Cui.

ii.35/iii.12 **Shuang Diao Mode**
Cherishing My Love's Beauty
Seeing Crimson once more,

五臟神兒都歡喜。
請來後何曾推避。
逐定紅娘，
　見夫人，
　　忙施禮。
道「前日，想娘娘可來驚悸。」

相國夫人，
　謹陪奉張君瑞。
道 ：「輒敢便屈邀先輩。
子母孤孀，
　又無個，
　　別準備。
可憐客寄。
願先生高情勿罪。」

命生坐。茶訖，生起致辭曰 ：「前者兗人掩至，驚擾尊懷，
且喜雅候無恙。」

夫人稱謝，邀生坐，命進酒來。

ii.36/iii.13 仙呂調（賞花時）

體面都輸富貴家。
客館先來摒掠得雅。

好起句。

鋪設得更奢華。
簾垂繡額，
　芸閣小窗紗。

尺半來厚花茵鋪矮榻。
百和奇香添寶鴨。
飲膳味偏佳。
一托頭的侍婢，

the Deities of his Five Organs all rejoiced.[78]
When invited, he certainly wasn't going to demur
But followed closely behind Crimson, and
    seeing Madam Cui,
        he hurriedly greeted her formally,
Saying, "You must have been terrified the day before yesterday!"

Madam Cui, Wife of the Minister of State,
    attentively waited upon Zhang Junrui,
Saying, "I have asked you here rather rashly, sir,
But, as a mother with children, a widow with orphans
    we have nothing of note
        that we can prepare.
Please forgive us, since we are also travelers—
I pray, sir, that you will not find fault with what we offer."

She told the student to sit. When the tea was finished, the student rose
and made his speech, "The other day, when those fierce men suddenly
appeared, I know that you were startled and upset. I'm delighted that
you've suffered no lasting harm, madam."

Madam Cui thanked him, and then she welcomed him to sit and ordered
the wine brought in.

ii.36/iii.13 Xianlü Diao Mode

Time to Enjoy the Flowers
The elegance of the place surpassed the houses of the rich and noble.
The guest house was the first to be put in **elegant order,**
And was outfitted so it was even more opulent,
With hanging curtains and embroidered valences,
    rue-scented shelving, closed by doors of silken screens.[79]

Patterned, half-foot-thick cushions were spread on short
    couches, and
Precious incense filled a beautiful duck-shaped censer.
The taste of the refreshments was particularly fine,
And every single serving maid

What a great opening line.

---

78 His rumbling stomach. The abdominal cavity was thought to be inhabited by five
    spirits, each one assigned an organ.
79 A library, where rue discouraged insects and gauze windows barred dust.

盡是十五六女孩兒家。

（尾）

輕敲檀板送流霞。
壁間簇吊兒是名人畫。
如法；
膽瓶兒裏惟浸幾枝花。

生自思之 ：「鶯鶯必為我有。」

ii.37/iii.14 黃鐘調（侍香金童）
「不須把定，
不在通媒媾。
百媚鶯鶯應入手。」
鄭氏起來方勸酒。
張生急起，
避席只候。

一門親事，
十分指望着九。
不堤防夫人情性惱。
將下臉兒來不害羞。
欺心叢裏，
做得個魁首。

（尾）

把山海似深恩掉在腦後。
轉關兒便是舌頭。
許了的話兒都不應口。

道甚的來。夫人謂生曰 ：「妾之孤嫠，夫亡提攜幼稚。不幸屬
師徒大潰，實不保其身。弱子幼女，猶君之生也，豈可忘其恩
哉。」乃命弱子歡郎出拜。

was a girl of only fifteen or sixteen.

Coda
Lightly struck, aloeswood clappers accompanied "sunset-flow"
    wine,[80]
On the walls, hung in groups, were paintings by famous men.
Just as it should be:
    A few sprigs of flowers sat in long-necked vases.

Zhang thought to himself, "For sure, Oriole will be mine."

ii.37/iii.14 Huangzhong Diao Mode

Golden Lad Minding Incense
"No need for wedding gifts to the in-laws,
    no more sending of go-betweens, for
Adorable Oriole shall fall straight into my hands."
Madam Cui arose and just as she was about to make a toast.
Student Zhang forthwith arose
    and leaving his seat, respectfully waited.

Of the measure of his marriage plans
    he hoped nine of ten parts were done.
He was unprepared for the crafty nature of Madam Cui,
Who had the coldest of feelings and lacked all shame.
She was the queen
    of the deceitful and faithless.

Coda
Her debt of grace, deep as the ocean, she cast to the back of her mind.
She changed her plans, and with a tongue as her weapon,
She refused to acknowledge what she had promised before!

And what did she say? She told the student, "I am a lonely widow, my
husband died and left me to take care of young children. Unfortunately,
when the soldiers rose up in rebellion, I was most assuredly unable to
vouchsafe their lives. My young son and daughter owe their lives to
you. How could I forget your act of grace?"[81] She then ordered her son
Happy to come out and pay his respects.

---

80 The finest wine, supposedly drunk by immortals in Heaven.
81 Here the lines repeat those found in the original Tang short story nearly verbatim.

ii.38/iii.15 大石調（紅羅襖）

酒行到數巡外。
君瑞恩情試想，
　「自家倒大采。
百媚的冤家，
　風流的姐姐，
　　有分同諧。」
紅娘滿捧金卮，
　夫人道個「無休外。
想當日厚義深恩
　若山海。
怎敢是常人般待。」

如先描歡正為
鶯鶯張本。

低語使紅娘，
　叫「取我兒來」。
須臾至，
　鬒角兒如鴉頭緒兒白。
穿一領細衫，
　不長不短，
　　不寬不窄。

如此點綴真是
神手。

系一條水運條兒，
　穿一對兒淺面鈐口僧鞋。
都不到怎大小身材。
暢好台孩。
舉止沒俗態。

（尾）
怎不教夫人珍珠兒般愛。
居中中地行近前來。
依次第覷着張生大人般拜。

夫人指生曰 :「當以仁兄禮奉。」歡郎拜，生不受。

夫人令婢邀坐受拜。

ii.38/iii.15 DASHI DIAO MODE

Red Silk Padded Jacket
More than a few cups of wine were shared,
And Junrui examined his feelings:
 "Well, I've drawn the lucky card!
That adorable little karmic foe of mine,
  that romantic sister,
   is fated to find harmony with me."
Crimson filled the golden beaker
  and Madam Cui told him, "Don't be polite!
Considering that your gift of grace on that day
  was higher than the mountains and deeper than the sea
How could I even dare to treat you as an ordinary person?"

Then in a low voice she dispatched Crimson,
  telling her, "Go get my son."
He came in a bit,
  his double tufts of hair—a pair of ravens' heads—were
   wound with white ribbons,
Dressed in a fine gown
  just the right length
   and the perfect fit—
He had tied on a single shimmering sash
  and stepped into a shallow pair of monks' slip-on button-
   up shoes.
He was a slight lad
But truly carried himself well—
There was nothing of the common in his actions.

First describing Happy, but truly a foreshadowing of Oriole.

Only a divine hand can flesh it out like this.

Coda
How could Madam Cui help but love that little jewel?
With perfect decorum he walked forward
And flawless in form, made obeisances to Student Zhang just like an
  adult.

Madam Cui pointed to the student and told Happy, "You should treat
him with reverence as your honorable elder brother." Happy performed
his obeisances, but the student rose and refused to accept the bow.

Madam Cui then ordered a maidservant to invite Zhang to sit and receive the courtesies.

生自念之,「歡郎,鶯之弟也。我不與鶯繼親禮,而得
兄事,何濟。」似有慍色。

ii.39/iii.16 仙呂調 (樂神令)

君瑞心頭怒發,
忿得來七上八下。
煩惱身心怎按納,
誦薦薦地酪子裏罵。

夫人可來夾衩,
剛強與張生說話,
道 :「禮數不周休怪呵。
教我女兒見哥哥咱。」

夫人令紅娘命鶯鶯「出拜爾兄。」

久之,鶯辭以疾。

夫人怒曰:「張生保爾之命,不然,爾虜矣。不能報恩以禮,
能復嫌疑乎。」

又久之,方至。常服悴容,不加新飾,然而顏色動人。

ii.40/iii.17 黃鐘宮 (出隊子)

滴滴風流,
做為嬌更柔。
見人無語但回眸。
料得娘行不自由,
眉上新愁壓舊愁。

天、天悶得人來毂。

He thought to himself, "**Happy is Oriole's younger brother. If I'm not going to marry Oriole, what's the point of becoming his elder brother?**" He looked displeased.

ii.39/iii.16 Xianlü Diao Mode

Pleasing the Spirits
Anger burst from Junrui's heart,
So furious his whole body shook.
How could he suppress such frustration?
Silently grumbling and muttering, he cursed her.

But Madam Cui had moved on to another topic,
And kept on blathering to Student Zhang,
"Don't be upset that our courtesies are not satisfactory. . . .
"Tell my daughter to come out to greet her elder brother!"

Madam Cui ordered Crimson to summon Oriole: "Come out and make obeisance to your elder brother."

After a long time, Oriole declined, citing illness.

Madam Cui said angrily, "Student Zhang protected your life; if he hadn't, you would have been taken captive. Even unable to repay a debt of gratitude with the proper etiquette, can you still have such reservations?"

She finally came after a long while. Dressed in everyday clothes and looking tired, she had done nothing to adorn herself—yet her appearance could more than move a person.[82]

ii.40/iii.17 Huangzhong Gong Mode

Sending Out the Dance Troupe
"Every iota is refined and elegant,
Her actions now even more supple and charming.
Seeing me she is silent, with only the briefest glance.
I think she must have been pressured by her mother,
For on her brow, new sorrows crush the old.

Heaven, oh, Heaven, you have made us melancholy enough

---

82 The text here closely follows the original tale, with but a few changes.

把深恩都變做仇。
比及相面待追依，
　見了依前還又休，
　　是背面相思對面羞。

（尾）
　怪得新來可唧嘈。
　折倒得個臉兒清瘦。
　瘦即瘦。
　比舊時越模樣兒好否。

當初救難報恩，望佳麗結絲蘿 ；及至免危答賀，教玉容為
姊妹。此時張生筵上無語，情懷以醉。偷目覷鶯，妍態迥別。

ii.41/iii.18 南呂宮（瑤台月）
　「冤家為何。
　近日精神，
　　直恁的消磨。
　渾如睡起，
　　尚古子不曾梳裹。
　杏腮淺澹羞勻，
　　綠鬢瓏璁斜軃。
　眉兒細，
　　凝翠娥。
　眼兒媚，
　　剪秋波。
　　　嬌多。
　想天真不許
　　胭脂點污。

　謾言天上有姮娥，
　算人間應沒兩個。

---

83 Drawn-on, fan-shaped brows rising at a forty-five-degree angle.
84 Common hyperbole for a beautiful woman.

By turning deep grace to animosity.
I wanted to pursue the question of betrayal,
But having seen her now, I'll stop.
Truly, in absence there is longing, and in presence there is
    bashfulness.

Coda
"Amazing that she's even more beautiful now,
Worn down so much her face is drawn—
Well, thinner she may be
But her looks are even finer than before.

"At the beginning, my grace saved them from disaster, and I hoped this stunning beauty would tie the knot with me. But with the danger gone, the only dowry is to have this jade beauty as my sister." Student Zhang was silent at the feast mat, getting drunk on his longing. With stolen glances he looked at Oriole, whose beauty was truly extraordinary.

ii.41/iii.18 Nanlügong Mode

Moon on a Jade Terrace
"Why is my little karmic foe's
Spirit so listless
        these days?
It's like she just woke up
        and has yet to make herself up.
Her pale apricot cheeks are colored only by an even blush of
        embarrassment,
        her pinned-up black hair tangled and tousled.
Her brows are fine,
        little moth antennae of kingfisher green;[83]
Her eyes are enchanting,
        sending out autumn waves.
So much beauty—
No rouge should be allowed
        to pollute such naturalness.

She makes a lie of Chang'e in Heaven,[84]
And it is certain she has no peer in the human world.[85]

---

85 A cliché phrase for anything that is remarkable or fine, yet the citational context here revitalizes the phrase.

朱唇一點，
　小顆顆似櫻桃初破。
龐兒宜笑宜嗔[9]，
　身分兒宜行宜坐。
腰兒細，
　偏嫋娜。
弓腳小，
　繡鞋兒是紅羅。
輕挪。
伽伽地拜，
　百般的軟和。」

（三煞）
等得夫人眼兒落。
斜着淥老兒不住睃。
是他家伴不偢人，
　「都只被你個。
可憎姐姐，
　引得眼花心亂，
　　肖似風魔。

酒入愁腸醉顏酡[10]。
料自家沒分消他。
想昨來枉了身心，
　初間喚做。
得為夫婦；
　誰知今日，
　　卻喚俺做哥哥。

是俺失所算，
　謾摧挫。
被這個積世的老虔婆瞞過我。」

如何見得。有《鶯鶯本傳歌》為證。歌曰：
　此時潘郎未相識，
　　偶住蓮館對南北，

A little dot of vermillion lips,
    as tiny as newly split cherry blossoms, and
A face perfect for laughing or for anger,
    the perfect form whether afoot or at rest.
A waist as thin
    as a supple willow,
On arched feet so small and
    in embroidered slippers of the reddest silk gauze,
She moves lightly, then
Bows deeply,
    gentle as gentle can be.

The language about her spring-like face being suitable for anger or happiness is full of flavor.

Trebled Coda
He waited until Madam Cui looked away
Then shifted his gaze to stare at Oriole,
She's the one who feigned not noticing him!
    "All because of you,
My hateful little thing,
    luring me in until my eyes blur and my heart's in chaos—
        it's as though I've gone crazy.

Wine enters my grieving gut and my drunken face turns red.
I guess I'm not fated to enjoy her.
When I think of how thwarted my desire is,
    how, back then, we might be addressed as
Husband and wife—
    how could I foresee that now
        I'm to be called 'elder brother' instead!

I was wrong in my calculations,
    to suffer this setback in vain—
Deceived by this old virago who's wise to the ways of the world."

How do we know this? "Song of the Story of Oriole," is our proof. It says:

At that time young Master Pan[86] was still unknown,
Living alone in in his lotus rooms, separated by a distance.

---

86 Pan Yue, here of course referring to Student Zhang

潛嘆恓惶阿母心，
為求白馬將軍力。
明明飛詔五雲下，
將選金門兵悉罷。
阿母深居雞犬安，
八珍玉食邀郎餐，
千言萬語對生意，
小女初笄為姊妹。

鶯拜畢，因坐於鄭旁，凝睇怨絕，若不勝情。生目之，不
知所措。

ii.42/iii.19 商調（玉抱肚）
沒留沒亂，
　不言不語。
儘夫人問當，
　夫人說話，
　　不應一句。
酒來後
　滿盞家沒命飲，
　　面磨羅地甚情緒。
吃着下酒，
　沒滋味，
　　似泥土。
自心窨腹。
　「鶯鶯指望同鴛侶，
誰知道
打脊老嫗許不與。

可憎的臉兒堪捻塑，
　梅妝淺淺宜澹注。

Secretly moved by a mother's distressed heart,
He summoned the force of the White Horse General.
Edicts went out, bright with wisdom, from the five clouds above—[87]
The general was to be appointed at court; the fighting was all over.
Deep in her residence the mother dwelt, the dogs and chickens were
    settled.[88]
Then with the finest of foods, she asked the student to a banquet,
And expressed to him a thousand times,
"She's only just put her hair up in pins; she shall be your younger
    sister."[89]

Oriole finished her greetings, and then sat by Madam Cui. She gazed
into space resentfully, as though overwhelmed by her emotions. The
student eyed her but didn't know what he should do.

ii.42/iii.19 Shangdiao Mode

Jade Enwraps the Stomach
He was bewildered,
    utterly speechless.
No matter how much Madam Cui asked,
    or kept on babbling,
        he responded to nothing.
And after the wine was served
    he drank full cup after full cup, reckless,
        crestfallen, listless—what a mood!
He kept eating the snacks
    but they were as tasteless
        as mud.
He turned it over in his mind—
"Oriole had counted on being his faithful companion,
    but who could have expected
        that back-beating old witch would never assent?

My love's face is worthy of sculpting,
    a blossom of plum-color applied so lightly, perfect pale
        adornment—

---

87 From the emperor
88 That is, a place so peaceful one can hear only one's own dogs and chickens.
89 At fourteen, girls first pin up their hair in a rite of passage into adulthood. Wang
   Xuanbo 1985, 131.

唱呵好。
　風風韻韻，
　　捻捻膩膩，
　　　濟濟楚楚。
鶻鴒的淥老兒
　說不盡的搶，
　　儘人勞攘把我不覷。
咫尺半，
　如天邊，
　　謾長吁。
奈何夫人間阻。
苦煞人也天不管，
　剛待棄了，
　　爭奈煞腸肚。

（尾）
　婆婆娘兒好心毒。
　把如休教請俺去。
　及至請我這裏來，
　　卻教我眼受苦。

生因問鶯齒。

夫人曰 ：「十七歲矣。」

生徐以辭道鶯，宛不蒙對。生徬徨愛慕而已。欲結良姻，
未獲其 便，因乘酒自媒云，

「小生雖處窮途，
祖父皆登仕版，
兩典大郡，
再掌絲綸。
某弟某兄，
各司要職。

Oh, so fine!
With graceful bearing and refined movement,
    a sculpted body, delicately beautiful,
        dressed so exquisitely, she's comely and fair.
Intelligent sparkling eyes—
    an inexpressible rush of beauty that,
        despite all my attempts, refuses to look at me.
Half a foot away
    is as far as the rim of the sky—
        I heave my sighs in vain.
That old woman intercedes, obstructs.
She makes me suffer so, but Heaven doesn't care.
    Even should I want to cast her away,
        what then, of what now lies in my heart?

Coda
"That old woman's heart is pure poison.
Better that she had never invited me.
Because when she asked me to come here
    it was so I would suffer the pain with my own eyes!"

The student asked Oriole's age.

Madam Cui replied, "She is now sixteen."

The student slowly began to say a few words to Oriole, but she never felt obliged to answer. He could only uneasily admire her. Desiring to conclude a fine marriage, and finding no opportunity to do so, *he drunkenly acted as his own go-between*, saying,

"I may be in very difficult straits now,
but both my grandfather and father were officials,
both first in charge of their own district,
and then promoted to the Hanlin Academy.[90]
My cousins, older and younger,

---

90 An academic hall of higher learning.

惟珙
未伸表薦，
流落四方。

自七歲從學，於今十七年矣。十三學《禮》，十五學《春秋》，
十六學《詩》、《書》：前後五十餘萬言，置於胸中。

二九涉獵諸子。
至於禪律之說，
無不着於心矣。

後擬古而作相材時務內策，仗此決巍科，取青紫，亦不後
於人矣。不幸尚書捐館，數年置功名於度外，乃躬祭祀於
墓側。生事死葬之禮，於今畢矣。

今日
蒙聖天子下詔，

乃
丈夫寶貴之秋，
姑待來年，
必期中鵠。
願
不以自陳見責者，
東方朔求見武帝，
尚自媒書，
時異事同，
吾不讓矣。
今日
旅食蕭寺，
邂逅相遇，

each control an important office.
 It is only I
who has yet to be recommended,
and who drifts around the world.

I began studying at six, some seventeen years ago. At twelve, I studied the *Rites*, at fourteen, I studied the *Spring and Autumn Annals*, at fifteen I studied the *Book of Odes* and *Book of Documents*. Now I hold more than half a million words in my head.

At eighteen I made a foray into the Hundred Schools of Philosophy, and as for the theories of Chan and the Vinaya sects,[91] they are all firmly fixed in my mind.

Later, I imitated the ancient styles, hoping to become an official of ministerial talent to manage great affairs. With this, I'll be in the first class of graduates, seizing the blue and purple cords of a government seal and taking my place at the front. Unfortunately, my father passed away in office, and for several years[92] I put my hopes for a meritorious name aside for the annual mourning rituals, personally making sacrifices beside his grave. And now the rites of sacrifices are completed.

Now,
I have received the rescript sent down by the sagely Son of Heaven,[93]

 For it is
The autumn so treasured by a real man—
For now, I'm waiting for the coming year,
when I will certainly hit my target.
 I hope
you will not fault me for explaining all of this:
Dongfang Shuo sought audience with Emperor Wu of the Han,
to deliver his own letter of introduction.
The eras are different, but my actions are the same
And I will not yield.
 For the time being,
we are residing in this monastery,
where we have met by chance

91 Something like the School of Meditation and the School of Discipline.
92 The stipulated twenty-seven months of mourning for a deceased parent.
93 To hold the triennial examinations for Advanced Scholar.

特敘親禮者，
不自序行藏，
夫人焉知終始。
今因酒便，
浪發狂詞，
無罪。無罪。」

夫人曰：「先生之言，信不誣矣。然尚困布衣，必關諸命。」

生曰：「若承家蔭，踐仕途久矣。奈非本心。丈夫隱則傲世，起則沖天，況遇明時簡閱。然鶯鶯方年十七，未結良姻，敢問夫人，願聞所以。」

ii.43/iii.20 仙呂調（樂神令）

張生因而下淚以跪。
說道：「不合問個小娘子年紀。」
相國夫人道：「十七歲。」
張生道：「因甚沒佳配。」

夫人可來積世。
瞧破張生深意。
使些兒譬似閑腌見識。
着衫子袖兒掩淚。

夫人泣下，徐而言曰：「先生之言，深會雅意。鶯鶯女子，容質粗陋，如若委身足下，其幸有三：一則謾塞重恩，二則身有所托，三則佳人得配才子。妾甚願也。」

and have greeted each other with familiar courtesy.
If I had not narrated the facts of my life, madam,
how would you have known the fullness of them?
Today, with the aid of drink,
I have burst out with these wild words.
Please forgive me."

Madam Cui replied, "I believe what you've told me. But, you're still wearing the clothes of a student, and it is fate alone that will decide the outcome."

"If I had taken advantage of the privileges of my family,"[94] said the student, "I would have been on the official path long ago. But that is not my true will. When a real man is in seclusion, he has disdain for the world; when he arises, his fame soars to the heavens. How much greater to be selected through the examinations in such an enlightened age? Oriole is just sixteen, and has yet to make a fine wedding match. Dare I ask why?"

ii.43/iii.20 Xianlü Diao Mode

Pleasing the Spirits
In tears, Student Zhang knelt
And said, "I shouldn't ask, but how old is this young girl?"
The Wife of the Minister said, "Sixteen."
The student said, "Why does she not have a fine match made?"

Now Madam Cui had ample experience and was crafty—
She saw right through Student Zhang's real intentions.
And employed what could be called her seasoned expertise
As she concealed fake tears with the sleeves of her robe.

Madam Cui wept, and then slowly said, "Sir, your words are truly well meant. My daughter, Oriole, is crude and ugly, and should I promise her to you, sir, there would be three benefits. One is that it would help fulfill this deep debt of gratitude. Two is that she would have someone on whom to rely. And third, a beauty would get to be paired to a talented man. This is what I strongly desire."

---

94 That is, sought direct appointment to an office based on his father's rank and success.

言未已，生起謝曰：「無狀豎子，敢繼良姻。」

夫人急起謂生曰：「先相公秉政朝省，妾兄鄭相幼子恆，年今二十，鄭相以親見屬，故相不獲已，以鶯許之恆。鶯方及嫁，相公逝去，故未得成親。若非故相先許鄭相，必以鶯妻君，以應平生之舉。」

ii.44/iii.21 仙呂調（醍醐香山會）
　　　那張生聞說罷，
　　　　　喏喏地告退。
　　　夫人請「是必終席。」
　　　張生不免放身坐地。
　　　便是醍醐甘露酒怎再吃。

　　　不語不言，
　　　　　聞着酒只推磕睡。
　　　枉了降賊見識。
　　　歪着頭避着，
　　　　　通紅了面皮。
　　　筵席上軟攤了半壁。

鶯鶯見生敷揚己志，竊慕於己，「心雖匪石」，不無一動。

ii.45/iii.22 雙調（月上海棠）
　　　張生果有孤高節。

Before she finished speaking, the student rose and said, "This unworthy lad dares hope I might become a good match for her in marriage."

Madam Cui rose quickly and told the student, "When the former Minister held office at court, Heng, the son of my elder brother, Minister Zheng, was just twenty. Minister Zheng asked for a match and being a relative, the former Minister could not refuse, so he assented to the match of Oriole to Heng. Just as Oriole was about to get married, the Minister passed away, so it was never carried through. If the former Minister had not pledged the match to Minister Zheng, I would certainly have Oriole be your wife, to thank you for saving our lives."

ii.44/iii.21 Xianlü Diao Mode

Enlightened at the Meeting on Incense Peak
After Student Zhang heard this
    he stammered and asked to take his leave.
But Madam Cui urged, "Surely we must finish the feast."
And he had no choice but to surrender himself and sit.
Even if it was the finest brew of the sweetest dew, could he
    drink any more?

Speaking not a word,
    and sniffing the wine, he pushed it away and pretended to
        doze.
It was all for nothing now, his scheme to quash the rebels.
He turned his head to avoid her,
    his whole face suffused with red.
Half his body seemed paralyzed at the banquet.

When Oriole saw how the student expressed his own intention and determination, and how he had secretly admired her, "her heart was no stone,"[95] and she was undeniably moved.

ii.45/iii.22 Shuang Diao Mode

Moonlight Climbs up the Crabapple
Student Zhang held himself aloof from the others,

---

95 From the *Classic of Poetry* 詩經, "Cypress Boat" 柏舟: "My heart is not a stone, / It cannot be spun; My heart is not a mat, / It cannot be rolled up." 我心匪石，不可轉也。我心匪席，不可卷也.

許多心事向誰說。
　眼底送情來，
　　爭奪母親嚴切。
空沒亂，
　　愁把眉峰暗結。

「多情彼此難割捨。
　　都緣只是自家孽。」
席上正喧嘩，
　　不覺玉人低趄。
　鶯道：「休勸酒，
　　我張生哥哥醉也。」

鶯謂夫人曰：「兄似不任酒力。」

生開目視鶯微笑。

夫人曰：「本欲終席，先生似倦於酒。」令紅娘扶生歸館，生亦不答而去。

至舍，生取金釵一隻，以饋紅娘。

紅娘驚謂生曰：「妾奉夫人懿旨，送先生歸館，是何以物見賜。窺先生有意於鶯，不能通殷懃，欲因妾以敍意。不然，何賜之厚。」

生曰：「慧哉，紅娘之問。吾實有是心。娘子侍鶯左右，但欲假你一言，申予肺腑。如萬一有成，不忘厚德。」

So he had no one to whom to express all that was in his heart.
With lowered eyes he signaled his passions to Oriole
 but was no match for her mother's strict monitoring.
Bewildered for nothing,
 he sorrowfully knit his brow but kept it out of sight.

"With so much passion on either side, it's hard for us to part.
My karma alone accounts for this disaster."
The feast was at the height of boisterousness
When suddenly the jade one began to crumble.[96]
Oriole said, "Don't make him drink anymore,
 my brother Zhang is drunk."

Oriole said to Madam Cui, "It seems my brother cannot handle the wine."

The student opened his eyes and looked at Oriole with a faint smile.

Madam Cui said, "I wanted to finish up the banquet, but it seems you're worn out from drinking, sir." She ordered Crimson to escort the student back to his lodgings, and the student left without responding.

When they got there, the student took out a golden hairpin to present to Crimson.

Taken aback, Crimson said, "I simply carried out Madam Cui's decree to bring you back to your lodgings. Why would you give me anything? I can see that you have your mind set on Oriole. But, unable to communicate your true feelings, you want me to relay them. Otherwise, why would you be giving me such a lavish gift?"

The student replied, "**That's a brilliant question, Crimson. I do have that in mind.** You're always in service to Oriole; I just want to avail myself of a single phrase from you to tell her everything I'm feeling. If, by a one in a million chance, it's successful, I would never forget your profound virtue."

96 That is, passed out. From *New Account of Tales of the World*: "Ji Kang, as a person, towers majestically like a solitary pine; when he is drunk, he leans like a jade mountain about to collapse." Translation adapted from Liu and Mather 2002, 331. Ji Kang 嵇康 (223–262, byname Shuye 叔夜) was a talented poet and one of the "Seven Worthies of the Bamboo Grove" (竹林七賢), seven major poets of the third century.

紅娘笑曰 ：「鶯鶯幼從慈母之教，貞順自保，雖尊親不可
以非語犯，下人之謀，固難入矣。」

ii.46/iii.23 仙呂調 （賞花時）
　　　　「酒入愁腸悶轉多。
　　　　百計千方沒奈何。
　　　　都為那人呵。
　　　　知他你姐姐，
　　　　　　知我此情麼。
　　　　眼底閑愁沒處着。
　　　　多謝紅娘見察我。
　　　　與你試評度。
　　　　這一門親事，
　　　　　　全在你成合。

　　（尾）
　　　　「些兒禮物莫嫌薄。
　　　　待成親後再有別酬賀。
　　　　奴哥。
　　　　託付你方便之個。」

紅娘曰 ：「先生醉矣。」竟不受金，忿然奔去。生不勝怏怏。
況是無聊，又聞夜雨。

ii.47/iii.24 中呂調 （棹孤舟纏令）
　　　　不以功名為念，
　　　　　　五經三史何曾想。
　　　　為鶯娘。
　　　　近來粧就個躭浮浪。
趣甚。　　也囉。
　　　　老夫人
　　　　　　做事搊搜相。

Crimson laughed, "Oriole has followed her compassionate mother's instructions from youth. And, virtuous and compliant, she keeps careful watch over her own actions. Even those elders to whom she shows respect and love dare not offend her with inappropriate words. It would be hard indeed for a small person like me to broach my own thoughts."

ii.46/iii.23 Xianlü Diao Mode

Time to Enjoy the Flowers
"When wine enters a grieving gut, depression churns.
No matter how I've thought it out, no matter what I've tried, it
    all comes up blank.
And it's all because of her.
You know her: does your young mistress
    know my feelings?
All this pointless sorrow and nowhere to anchor it.
Thank you, Crimson, for your consideration,
But let me lay it out for you.
This whole marriage
    will come down to you.

Coda
"Don't resent the trifling nature of this small gift.
Wait until the marriage has happened and there will be other
    presents.
Sister,
I'm relying completely on you to find a way to make it happen!"

"You're drunk," said Crimson. Refusing to accept the gold, she hurried off in a huff. The student was dispirited, **made all the worse by ennui, and by hearing the nighttime rain.**

ii.47/iii.24 Zhonglü Diao Mode

Sculling a Solitary Boat: A Bound Suite
"No thought now about establishing a name,
    the Five Classics and Three Histories never come to mind.
All because of Oriole,
I've become flighty and neglectful of my duties.
Horrible!
The image of that pig-headed
    evil old woman—

Profoundly interesting.

做個老人家說謊。
白甚鋪謀退群賊，
　到今日方知是枉。
也囉。
一陌兒來，
　直恁地難偎傍。
死冤家無分同羅幌。
也囉。
　待不思量。
又早隔着窗兒望。
贏得眼狂心癢癢。
百千般悶和愁，
　盡總撮在眉尖上。
也囉。

（雙聲疊韻）
燭熒煌。
　夜未央。
轉轉添惆悵。
枕又閑，
　衾又涼。
睡不着，
　如翻掌。
謾嘆息，
　謾悒怏。
謾道不想。
怎不想。
空贏得肚皮兒裏勞攘。

淚汪汪。
昨夜甚短，
　今夜甚長。
捱幾時東方亮。
情似癡，
　心似狂。

A venerable person who still tells lies.
Why did I lay out the plan to make the bandits withdraw?
    Just to find today that it was all in vain?
Horrible!
Up to this point
    it's been hard to be by her side,
But my little karmic foe, are we not fated to share a bedchamber?
Horrible,
I don't even want to think about her,
Yet instantly find myself keeping watch from my window.
But that brings only wild eyes and a heart that itches and
    itches.
A thousand kinds of depression and sorrow
    are pinched together on the peak of my brows!
Horrible!

Alliteration and Rhyming
"The lamp flickers.
Midnight.
Little by little my despondency increases.
My pillow lies empty,
    my quilt is cold.
I can't sleep,
    but turn and toss and turn again.
My sighs are useless,
    and useless my emotional pain.
Useless to pledge that I won't think of her.
How can I not?
All I've won is a belly full of worry.

My teardrops keep flowing.
Last night was too short,
    and tonight is too long.
How much longer, now, before the east turns light?
I have the passion of the infatuated,
    and a heart that seems crazed.

這煩惱如何向。
待漾下，
　又瞻仰。
道忘了，
　是口強。
難割捨我兒模樣。

（迎仙客）
宜澹玉，
稱梅妝。
一個臉兒堪供養。
做為掙，
　百事搶。
只少天衣，
　便是捻塑來的觀音像。

除夢裏，
　曾到他行。
燒盡獸爐百和香。
鼠窺燈，
　偎着矮床。
一個孽相的蛾兒
　繞定那燈兒來往。

（尾）
淅零零的夜雨兒擊破窗。
窗兒破處風吹着忒飄飄的響。
不許愁人不斷腸。

　　早是夢魂成不得，
　　濕風吹雨入疏櫺。

異日，紅娘復至，曰：「夫人致意先生，今夜又候清勝。昨日
酒不終席，先生不罪，多幸。」

How can I stand such frustration?
I want to cast her out of my mind,
    but go on worshipping her.
I could say I've forgotten her,
    but that would be a lie.
I can never rid myself of the image of my love.

Welcoming the Immortal One
"Flawless, the palest adornment
    setting off her plum beauty spot.
A face to be worshipped like a bodhisattva—
Perfect in every action,
    beautiful in all things.
All she lacks are heavenly robes
    to be a newly sculpted image of Guanyin herself.

It was only in dreams
    that I could be with her.
Now the censer has burnt away all the fine incense and,
Cuddling up under a low couch,
    a mouse peeks at the lamp.
One miserable moth
    circles tight around and around the lamp.

Coda
"*Splattering, night rains strike the ripped paper window,*
And through those rips the wind sings, and paper flaps and snaps.
Unrelenting, it makes the sorrowful only more brokenhearted."

    First, the dream soul is unable to form,[97]
    Then the wet wind blows rain through the wide-spaced stiles.

The next day Crimson returned, and said, "Madam Cui extends her
best to you, sir. She hopes that you passed a pleasant night and hopes
you will forgive her for failing to bring the banquet to a proper close."

97 It is impossible to sleep.

生謝曰：「不才小子，過蒙腆餉。然昨者兇賊叩門，夫人以親
見許。以酒食饋我，令鶯娘以兄禮待，薄我何多。今當西歸
長安，與夫人絕矣。」

ii.48/iii.25 大石調（洞仙歌）
「當初遭難，
　與俺成親事。
及至如今放二四。
把如合下，
　休許咱家
　　你恁地，
　　　我離了他家門便是。

不如歸去，
　卻往京師。
見你姐姐夫人俱傳示。
『你咱說謊，
　我着甚痴心
　　沒去就，
　　　白甚只管久淹蕭寺。』
道得一聲『好將息』，

憤恨之狀。

　早收拾琴囊，
　　打疊文字。」

ii.49/iii.26 雙調（御街行）
張生欲去心將碎。
卻往京師裏。
收拾琴劍背書囊，
　道：「保重，紅娘將息。」
紅娘覷了高聲道：
　「君瑞先生喜。

思量此事非人力。

He thanked her and said, "For such an undeserving person as me, I was treated too well. But, when those violent rebels were knocking on the door, Madam Cui promised me a marriage; yet, when she served me wine, she had Oriole treat me as an elder brother. It was really demeaning. I should return to Chang'an now and break off any dealings with her."

ii.48/iii.25 Dashi Diao Mode

Song of Immortals in a Cavern
"Back then in the middle of a crisis,
    she promised a marriage to me.
But now she plays her dirty tricks.
It would have been better
    never to have promised—
        if she's going to act like this
            I'll just have nothing to do with her family.

Better to leave
    and go on to the capital.
When you see your sister and madam, tell them this:
'You've lied to me,
    but am I so infatuatcd
        that I won't leave?
            What's the point of hanging around this temple
                forever?'
Before they can say, 'Take care on the road,'
    I'll have already put my zither in its bag
        and gotten my books ready for the trip."

A description of deep rancor.

ii.49/iii.26 Shuang Diao Mode

Treading the Imperial Path
Heart about to shatter, Student Zhang wanted to leave
And go off to the capital.
He gathered his zither and sword, put his bookbag on his back,
    and said, "Take care of yourself, Crimson."
Crimson looked, then shouted,
"Master Junrui, congratulations!

I don't think this could come from human effort,

也是關天地。
這書房裏往日曒曾來，
不曾見這般物事。
只因此物，
不須歸去你有分學連理。」

逗出琴來絕奇。

紅娘曰：「妾不忍先生悽愴，謾為言之：世之好惡，乃知人之本情，順之則合，逆之則離。將有所謀，必有所好。今有一策，可使鶯啟門就此。願不以愚賤之言見棄。」

生曰：「我思面鶯之計，智竭思窮，尚不可得。今娘子有屈鶯就見之策，敢不聽命。雖赴湯火，亦願為之。乞賜一言，以慰愁苦。」

紅娘曰：「鶯鶯稍習音律，酷好琴阮。今見先生囊琴一張，想留心積有日矣。如果能之，鶯鶯就見之策，盡在此矣。」

生聞之，捧腹而笑。

ii.50/iii.27 仙呂調（戀香衾）

是日張生正鬱悶。
聞言點頭微哂。
道：「九百孩兒，
休把人廝哢。
你甚胡來我怎信。」
紅娘道：「先輩停頭，
只因此物，
有分成親。

婦女知音的從古少，
知音的止有個文君。
着一萬個文君，

but is a matter that must involve Heaven and earth!
How many times have I visited your study
    yet never remarked on this thing?
And because of it,
    you need not go back
        for you are destined to be like intertwining branches!"

*A marvelous novel-
ty to bring out the
zither in this way.*

Crimson said, "I can't bear to see you suffering, sir, so may I presume to speak? In the likes and dislikes of the world, one can know the basic emotions of any person. If one goes along with them, there is union; if one goes against them, there is separation. For a scheme to be good, there must be some enticement. Now I have an idea that will make Oriole open her door and realize this. I hope you won't disregard my humble plan."

"I've tried to think of a plan to meet Oriole and have exhausted every way I could think of, but nothing came to me," said the student, "If you have an idea that will tempt Oriole to come meet me, I will surely heed it. If I had to walk though boiling water or fire, I would do it. Please tell me something to soothe this bitter sorrow."

Crimson said, "Oriole knows something about music, and really loves the zither and the lute. Now that I've seen your covered zither, I presume that you have practiced it for a long time. If you can really play it, then the plan to get Oriole to come see you will be accomplished." When the student heard this, he held his belly and laughed.

ii.50/iii.27 Xianlü Diao Mode

Quilt with the Fragrance of Love
Student Zhang was miserably depressed that day,
And when he heard her words, he nodded and gave a little smile
As he said, "You crazy girl,
    don't try to put one over on me!
How can I believe such nonsense?"
Crimson said, "Just wait a second.
    It's precisely because of this one thing
        that you are predestined to marry."

Indeed, few women but one have understood music
    and that one was Zhuo Wenjun.
But could even ten thousand Wenjuns

怎比鶯鶯。
多慧多嬌性靈變，
平生可喜秦箏。
　若論彈 琴擘阮，
　　前後絕倫。」

（尾）
「等閑要相見、見無門。
着何意思，得成秦晉。
不須把定。
這七弦琴便是大媒人。」

紅娘曰：「如先生深夜作兩三弄，鶯聞必至，妾當從行。
如聞聲欵，乃鶯至矣。願先生變雅操為和聲，以詞挑之，
事必諧矣。鶯亦善賦者，恐因此而得成。先生裁之。但恐
先生不能耳。」

生曰：「吾雖不才，深善於此。」

Even come close to Oriole?
So clever, so charming, so changeable in mood,
    she found her greatest joy in stringed instruments—
In playing the zither or plucking the four-stringed guitar,
    she was without peer.

Coda
"In vain you wanted to see her, but there was no way.
How were you ever going to arrange a solid marriage pact?
No need now for betrothal presents
Because this seven-stringed zither will be your grand go-between."

Crimson spoke again, "If you can play two or three songs late at night, and Oriole hears them, she will certainly come. I'll be in attendance, and if you hear a cough, that means she's arrived. Then you should switch to an elegant tune to make lovely sounds and stir her with the lyrics, and you will surely succeed. Oriole is also skilled at composition. This will all lead to the fulfillment of this affair. Make your mind up, sir. I only fear that you won't be able to do it."

"I may not be talented," said the student, "but I'm really good at playing the zither."

Endnotes

1   Following DJY, 121 in understanding 不彷彿 as an error (or unknown usage) for the more common 不隄備.

2   *Ganxiu* 乾羞 can mean both "to be embarrassed for no reason," but also "to have not lived up to responsibilities and therefore to be ashamed." DJY07, 86 understands these lines as "excellent rice and excellent delicacies": "'*gan*' means dried grain and rice; '*xiu*' means fine delicacies." 「乾」，干粮飯食 ；「羞」，珍饈美味. This last phrase is also written as 珍羞美味. Thus, he produces a fine double entendre.

3   This line calls for a rhyme in the category of *xiaohao* 蕭豪 (*-au*) which does not occur here. I am, however, counting it as the end of a rhymed line.

4   This line also calls for a rhyme of *-au*; in both cases the phrase 睹當, to "withstand" or "defend" takes the place of an expected rhyme.

5   According to the pattern of this *qupai*, these should be two five-character lines, which were probably written as 把法聰來便斫，斫 又砍不着. The second 來 in the first line appears to be an accretion, perhaps due to an error introduced in transcription or printing.

6   In the text this is written as 蠟淬, which breaks rhyme here. DJY suggests it perhaps should be changed to 淬蠟, since *la* would be in the rhyme category. It is just as likely, however, that *zi* is an unintentional mis-transcription for the much more common *lazha* 蠟渣/蠟查 or *lacha* 蠟查/揸, all of which would also rhyme.

7   Reading 雪裏梅 for 雪兒梅.

8   Reading 仵 for 作.

9   DJY 04, 56b gives a longer version of this marginal note. It is unclear if it copied a different edition of the Tang Xianzu text, or if it was added to clarify the meaning of the circle-marked (italicized) text to which it referred: "This has a far deeper flavor than the passages like, "spring-like face" and "being suitable for anger or joy" 較宜嗔 宜喜春風面等語味深多矣."

10 The literate reader would recognize this as a line cobbled together from two lyric poems, one by Fan Zhongyan 范仲淹 (989–1015), and the other by Ouyang Xiu 歐陽修 (1007–1072): Fan, to the lyric pattern *Samaja* 蘇幕遮, titled "Embosoming the Past" 懷舊:

酒入愁腸，   Wine enters my grieving bowels,
化作相思淚   transforming into tears of love's longing.

Ouyang, to the lyric pattern *Ding fengbo* 定風波:

把酒花前欲問他， Holding wine before the flowers, I want
                  to ask him,

對花何吝醉顏酡。 Facing these flowers why begrudge your
                  drunken face turning red?

This is a superb example of how "catchy" phrases in the literary canon were appropriated into the world of colloquial literature.

11   Replacing 談 with 彈.

董解元西廂 卷三
明 臨川湯顯祖義仍甫評

iii.1/iv.1 雙調（文如錦）

「說恁心聰。
算來有分自家共。
若論着這彈琴，
　不是小兒得寵。
從幼小，
　撫絲桐。
啼烏怨鶴，
　離鸞別鳳。
使了千百貫現錢，
　下了五七年埃功。
曾師高士，
　向焚香窗下，
　　煮茗軒中。
對青松。
彈得高山流水，
　積雪堆風。

三百篇新聲詩意盡通。
一篇篇彈得，
　風賦雅頌。
古操新聲，
　循環無始終。
述壯節，
　寫幽悰。
閑愁萬斛，

看他自敘手段便
有指下風生之致

Book III
Laureate Dong's Story of the Western Wing

iii.1/iv.1 Zhonglü Diao Mode

Patterned Like Embroidery
"When you explain it like that, my heart brightens,
For perhaps we do have a destiny to be together.
And as for playing the zither—
    I'm not a child looking to curry favor, but
From the time I was little,
    on the stringed paulownia[1] I played
"Cawing Ravens," "Mournful Cranes,"
    "Simurghs Departing," and "Phoenix Leaving."[2]
I spent many thousands
    to put in five or six years of hard labor,
And studied with a fine master, until
    by a window where incense smoldered,
        or on a veranda where tea was brewed,
Or facing a verdant pine,
I could evoke high mountains and flowing waters,
    accumulating snow and massing winds.[3]

Looking at how Zhang describes his own skill, he possesses a perfect capability to "stir up the wind" with his fingers!

I fully understand all the tunes from the *Three Hundred Odes* to
    new sounds and poetic meanings,
Chapter by chapter I can play
    the Airs' expository style, the Elegantia, and the Hymns.[4]
Traditional zither tunes and new sounds
    I play round and round without end.
I can portray heroic resolve,
    describe deeply hidden feelings and

---

1   Paulownia wood was favored for making zithers.
2   All famous zither songs.
3   The finest music could evoke the power of landscape and forces of nature. The first phrase of this line refers the story of Bo Ya (伯牙) and Zhong Ziqi (鐘子期), the first a gifted zither player, the second his perfect audience. Whenever Bo Ya started to play his zither, Zhong would know precisely what Bo Ya's mental impulse for the song was; when Zhong Ziqi died, Bo Ya broke the strings on his zither, having lost his only audience. For a more detailed account, See Goh 2009, 45–69, and Berthel 2016, 259–70.

離情千種。
教知音的暗許，
　感懷者自痛。
今夜裏彈他幾操，
　博個相逢。
若見花容　　　　。
平生學識，
　今夜個中用。」

（尾）
「紅娘，我對你不是打閧。
你且試聽一弄。
休道你姐姐遮莫是石頭人也心動。」

紅娘歸。

iii.2/iv.2 仙呂調（賞花時）
去了紅娘悶轉加。

入情。

比及到黃昏沒亂煞。
花影透窗紗。
「幾時是黑，
　得見那死冤家。」

好綴。

先拂拭瑤琴寶鴨。
「只怕我今宵磕睡呵。」
先點建溪茶。
猛吃了幾碗，
　慚愧啞僧院已聞鴉。

（尾）

點景絕韻。

碧天涯幾縷兒殘霞。
漸聽得瑠瑠地昏鐘兒打。
鐘聲縈罷。
又成樓寒角奏《梅花》。

4　These are sections of the *Classic of Poetry*, informally known as the *Three Hundred Odes*.

5　A term also used to describe friends or lovers who are mutually attuned.

Idle sorrows in abundance,
    as well as a thousand kinds of emotions at parting.
Those who understand music[5] will be obliged to nod in silence,
    and those whom I move deeply will feel their own pain within.
Tonight, I will play several of those songs
    to win her over, the girl I met by chance.
And should I see that flowerlike visage, then
All that I have learned or known in my life
    will finally be put to its proper use on this night.

Coda
"Crimson, I'm not joking with you—
Just listen for a moment to a tune,
And even aside from your sister, a person of stone would be moved."

Crimson went back.

iii.2/iv.2 Xianlü Diao Mode

Time to Enjoy the Flowers
After Crimson left, his depression turned worse,
And when yellow dusk had settled, his heart was in turmoil   *Drawing us into*
As shadows of flowers penetrated the gauze of the window.   *the intricacies of*
"When will it get dark   *the scene.*
    and I can see that karmic foe of mine?"

First, he wiped off his treasured zither and the precious duck-   *Good*
    shaped censer,[6]   *embellishment.*
"I'm afraid I'll fall asleep this evening."
So, he brewed up some strong tea
And quickly downed several cups and then,
    oh joy! He heard ravens come to roost in the monastery.

Coda
A few threads of rosy hue on the blue sky's edge.
He gradually began to hear the striking of the evening bell.   *Elegantly enliven-*
And it had barely stopped   *ing the scene.*
When the cold horn on the watchtower played "Plum Blossoms."[7]

---

6 Incense was part of the ritual of playing music.
7 "Falling Plum Blossoms" 洛梅花 was played in military encampments as a signal to
   take rest.

是夜晴天澄徹，月色皓空，生橫琴於膝。

iii.3/iv.3 中呂調（滿庭霜）
　　　幽室燈清，
　　　　疏簾風細，
　　　　　獸爐香爇龍涎。
　　　抱琴拂拭，
　　　　清興已飄然。
　　　此個閣兒雖小，
　　　　其間趣不讓林泉。
句儁永。　初移軫，
　　　　啼烏怨鶴，
　　　　　飛上七條弦。

　　　循環。
　　　成雅弄，
　　　　純音合正，
　　　　　古操通玄。
　　　漸移入新聲，
　　　　心事都傳。
　　　一鼓松風瑟瑟，
　　　　再彈崑溜涓涓。
淡味。　空庭靜，
　　　　鶯鶯未寐寢，
　　　　　須到小窗前。

　　其琴操曰：
　　琴琴，軫玉，徽金。
　　其操雅，其趣深。
　　玄鶴集洞，啼烏繞林。
　　洗滌是非耳，調和道德心。

That night the sky was clear and deep, and moonlight was a transparent white. The student laid the zither across his knees as he sat cross-legged.

iii.3/iv.3 Zhonglü Diao Mode

Frost That Fills the Courtyard
In his dark and secluded room, the lamp burned bright,
through the bamboo weave of the curtains, the wind
was slight,
and in the censer, ambergris incense burned alight.
He embraced the zither and wiped it off,
an elegant mood already wafting up.
This little cell might be small,
but the delight it held was no less than a forest or a fount.
Then he first moved the bridges,[8]   *The flavor of these*
and "Cawing Ravens" and "Mournful Cranes"   *lines lasts forever.*
flew onto the seven strings.

Around and around,
Turning it into elegant tunes—
pure tones were perfectly matched
as older zither songs penetrated mysterious wonder.
Gradually he moved on to new sounds
to convey all that lay within his heart.
First, he thrummed, "Winds in the pines sough and sigh,"[9]
and second, plucked, "Spills from the cliffs drip and drop."[i]
The empty courtyard was quiet—   *A bland taste.*
if Oriole had yet to retire
she would surely come to listen by the little window.

His zither song went:

Zither, zither; bridges of jade; golden strings—
Its tune is elegant, its mood deep.
Black cranes gather in the grottoes, cawing crows circle the trees.
It cleans out ears used to judge rights or wrongs, harmonizes the mind
with the Way and its Power.

---

8   To tighten the strings.
9   A reference to an old Tang zither tune to the formal pattern "Wind Enters the Pines."

漱松風於石壁，迸遠水於孤岑。
不是秦箏合眾聽，高山流水少知音。
琅琅雅韻，寬遊子之愁懷，落落正聲，醒飲人之醉吟。

紅娘報鶯曰：「張兄鼓琴，其韻清雅，可聽否。」

鶯曰：「夫人寢未。」

紅娘曰：「夫人已熟寢矣。」

鶯潛出戶，與紅俱行。

iii.4/iv.4 中呂調（粉蝶兒）
iii.3/iv.3

何處調琴，
　惺惺地把醉魂呼醒。
正僧庭夜涼人靜。
羽衣輕。
羅襪薄，
　輕 ᵐⁱᵃᵒ 寒 ᵍᵘ 猶嫩。
夜闌時，
　徘徊月移花影。

尋聲審聽。
冷然出塵幽韵。
過空庭漸穿花徑。
躡金蓮，
　即漸到中庭。
待側近
　轉躊躇，
　　嚭嚭地把心不定。

Pine winds rinsing out stone cliffs, distant waters bursting out from
   isolated peaks.
This is not the famous twenty-five-string zither to which anyone can
   listen;
These high mountains and flowing waters are for the few who know.
Loud and clear the elegant tone that frees the wanderer's sorrowful
   heart;
Clear and pellucid the upright sound that wakes the drinker from a
   drunken dream.

Crimson reported to Oriole, "Brother Zhang is playing the zither, and
its tone is pure and elegant. Can we listen?"

"Is Mother asleep yet?" asked Oriole.

"Madam Cui is sound asleep already," said Crimson.

Oriole crept out the doorway, together with Crimson.

iii.4/iv.4 Zhonglü Diao Mode

Powdery Butterfly
Somewhere a zither played
   a pleasant melody that sobered her besotted soul.
A feathery light chemise,
Silken stockings, slight
   against the faint spring coolness.^{A fine line!}
 Midnight came and she
   hesitated as the moon shifted the flowers' shadows.

Seeking the sound, she listened carefully
   to its deep and serene tone rising loftily above the
      dusty world.
Crossing the courtyard, she moved gradually along a
   flowered path,
Walking on her little golden lotuses
   until she finally reached the courtyard's center.
She wanted to draw nearer
   but turned hesitantly,
      unable to quell her pounding heart.

（尾）

下語每出人意
表。

　　牙兒抵着不敢子聲。
　　側着耳朵兒窗外聽。
　　千古清風指下生。

　　紅娘聲欬於窗側。生聞之，驚喜交集，曰：「鶯即至矣。
看手段何似。」

iii.5/iv.5 仙呂調（惜黃花）
　　清河君瑞。
　　不勝其喜。
　　寶獸添香，
　　稽首頂禮。
　　「十個指頭兒。

嚀咐指頭顛狂
萬狀。

　　自來不孤你。
　　這一回看你把戲。

　　孤眠了一世。
　　不閑了一日。
　　今夜裏彈琴，
　　不同恁地。
　　還彈到斷腸聲，
　　得姐姐學連理。
　　指頭兒。
　　我也有福囉，
　　你也須得替。

iii.6/iv.6 仙呂調（賞花時）
　　寶獸沈煙裊碧絲。
　　半折兒梨花繁杏枝。
　　粧一膽瓶兒。

Coda

Cupping her cheek in her hand, she dared not make a sound
As she cocked an ear outside the window to listen.
From beneath his fingers arose airs from days long past.[10]

His use of language
always goes
beyond a person's
expectation.

Crimson coughed by the window and the student heard it. Surprised
and delighted, he said, "Oriole is here. Let's see what my skill is like."

iii.5/iv.5 Xianlü Diao Mode

Cherishing the Chrysanthemum
Junrui of Qinghe
Could not control his joy.
He added incense to his animal censer,
     kowtowed in utmost sincerity and said,
"Ah, my ten fingers,
I have never let you down,
So now let's watch your magic.

His lunacy in ex-
horting his fingers
is over the top.

I've slept alone my whole life
And never left you idle for a day.[11]
This night, though, you will play the zither,
     and not like all those other nights.
And if you can play a heart-rending sound
     you'll get your sister Oriole to long for intertwining branches.
Ah, fingers
I'll have all the luck
     and you will get a new assignment!"[12]

iii.6/iv.6 Xianlü Diao Mode

Time to Enjoy the Flowers
The incense in the precious censer spiraled up in blue threads.
Half-open pear blossoms, intricately intermixed with branches of
     plum,
Decorated a spherical, narrow-necked vase.

10 That is, his music holds the power that ancient music did to move the listener in a
    variety of ways, including romantically. "Fingers on the zither strings" is also a term
    for foreplay.
11 These lines have been omitted in the translation in DJY08, 105. DJY08, 162 also bowd-
    lerizes this passage, translating as, "I've slept alone my whole life, and played the
    zither every night." The lines clearly have a second-level reference to masturbation.
    Cf. DJY, 222.

冰弦重理。
聲漸辯雄雌。
說盡心間無限事。

聲欵微聞鶯已至。
窗下立了多時。
聽沈了一餉，
　流淚濕却燕脂。
（尾）
　也不彈雅調與新聲，
　　流水高山多不是。
　何似。
　　一聲聲盡說相思。

張生操琴歌曰：

　　　　　有美人兮　見之不忘，
　　　　　一日不見兮　思之如狂。
　　　　　鳳飛翺翺兮　四海求凰，
　　　　　無奈佳人兮　不在東牆。
　　　　　張琴代語兮　聊寫微茫，
　　　　　何時見許兮　慰我傍徨。
　　　　　願言配德兮　攜手相將，
　　　　　不得于飛兮　使我淪亡。

其辭哀，其意切，悽悽然如別鶴唳天。鶯聞之，不覺淚
下。但聞香隨氣散，情逐聲來。生知琴感其心，推琴而
起。

Those strings of ice were tuned again,[13]
Until it gradually defined male and female.[14]
To explain all the limitless matters of the heart,[15]

The sound of a cough barely heard; Oriole had arrived already.
She stood beneath the window for a long time
Listening quietly, intently,
        until flowing tears smeared the rouge on her cheeks.

Coda
He played no ancient tune or new songs,
        nor did he opt for flowing waters and high mountains,
What then?
Every single sound confessed love's longing.

Zhang's zither song said:

There is a beautiful woman, after one glimpse I cannot forget her;

A single day without seeing her, and I long for her as if mad.
Soaring high the phoenix flies, searching the four seas for its mate,
But alas that beauty is not on the eastern wall.[16]
I will string my zither in place of words, reveal my hidden thoughts.
When will you assent, and soothe these agitated longings?
I wish to speak of marriage, and to go hand in hand forever,
Should you be unwilling to fly away together, I will be destroyed.

The words were mournful and the intent sharp, as chilling as a departing crane calling in the heavens. Upon hearing it, Oriole wept involuntarily. All that could be perceived was perfume dispersing with her breath and passion pushing her with each sob. Knowing that the zither had moved her heart, Student Zhang pushed the zither aside and arose.

12 Literally "to get a substitute." See DJY, 223. See also Hong Jinfu 2016, 458.
13 A metaphor for fine zither strings. In legend there was an ice silkworm that, if covered with frost and ice, would produce wonderfully colored silk.
14 This refers to the zither song, "Parting Cranes" about the forced separation of a wife from her husband because she was unable to bear children.
15 A near verbatim use of the famous line in Bai Juyi's "Song of the Pipa" 琵琶行 about the power of the instrument: "It completely explains the limitless affairs in the heart" 說盡心中無限事.
16 See Book I, n. 107.

iii.7/iv.7 雙調（茭荷香）

夜涼天。

泠泠[1]十指，
　心事都傳。

短歌才罷，
　滿庭春恨寥然。

一个魆魆幽
恨，一个騰騰
熱腸。

鶯鶯感此，
　閣不定粉淚漣漣。

吞聲窨[2]氣埋冤。

張生聽此，
　不托冰弦。

火急開門月下覷，
　見鶯鶯獨自，
　　明月窗前。

走來根底，
　抱定款惜輕憐。

「薄情業種，
　咱兩個彼各當年。

休休，定是前緣。

今宵免得，
　兩下里孤眠。」

（尾）

女孩兒唬得來一團兒顫。

低聲道：「解元聽分辯。

你更做撏荒，敢不開眼。」

抱住的是誰。是誰。張生拜覷。

iii.8/iv.8 中呂調（鶻打兔）

暢忒昏沈，
　忒慕古，
　　忒猖狂。

iii.7/iv.7 Shuang Diao Mode

Ji he xiang
A cool night.
Chilled,[17] his ten fingers
    had relayed all that lay in his heart.
His short song just finished
    the courtyard was filled with the silence of springtime
      discontent.
Oriole was moved by the song
    and could not stop her powdered tears from overflowing.
She swallowed her sobs, drew in her breath, and buried her injustice.
Hearing her, Student Zhang
    no longer availed himself of the zither's strings.

One is silent and quiet with smoldering resentment; one is full of vigor with a burning heart.

As quick as fire he opened the door and looked in the moonlight,
    spying Oriole all alone
      beside the moonlit window.
He raced to her
    and embraced her with passion and tenderness,
"My heartless karmic seed,
    we are each at the appropriate age. . . .
Enough, enough; it is certainly foreordained
That tonight neither of us needs
    to sleep alone."

Coda
The girl suddenly shivered all over,
And said in a low voice, "Laureate, listen to me!
If you're going to embrace with such abandon,
Shouldn't you open your eyes first?"

Who was it he embraced? Who?[18] Student Zhang bowed and
    carefully looked.

iii.8/iv.8 Zhonglü Diao Mode

The Hawk Takes the Hare
Really—too dazed,
    too blundering,
      too out of control.

---

17 This expression (*lengleng* 泠泠) can also refer to the sound of an instrument that decays slowly.
18 Suspense point 9.

不問是誰，
　　便待³窩穰。
說志誠，
　　說衷腸，
騁奸俏，
　　騁浮浪。
初喚做鶯鶯，
　　孜孜地覷來，
　　　　却是紅娘。

有此一錯，倍
添悽惻。

打慘了多時，
　　痴呆了半晌。
惟聞月下，
　　環佩玎璫。
蓮步小，
　　脚兒忙，
柳腰細，
　　裙兒蕩。
齰齰的地心驚，
　　微微地氣喘，
　　　　方過迴廊。

（尾）
　　朱扉半開啞地響。
　　風過處惟聞蘭麝香。
　　雲雨無緣空斷腸。

生問紅娘曰：「鶯適有何言。」紅娘曰：「無他言，惟悽
怨泣涕而已。妾逆度之，似有所動。今夕察之，拂旦報
公。」紅娘別生歸寢，鶯已臥矣。

　　　　燭光照夜，
　　　　愁思攪眠。

iii.9/iv.9中呂調（碧牡丹）
　　夜深更漏悄。

Never asking, "Who?"
   he tries to get her in the sack,
Saying how sincere he is,
      laying all his heart on the line,
            giving free rein to his crafty schemes
                  and his frivolous flightiness.
He had first called her, "Oriole,"
   but on closer examination
      it turned out to be Crimson!

*This one mistake
doubles the grief he
will suffer.*

He froze in panic,
   dumbfounded for the longest time.
In the moonlight all he could hear
      was the tinkling of belt pendants.
Her lotus steps were tiny as
      her feet hurried away,
Her willowy waist fine as
      her skirt fluttered.
Her heart thumped with fright,
      her breath was lightly panting,
            as she finally passed through the winding corridor.

Coda
The vermillion gates half opened with a creak
And when the wind blew he could only smell her orchid musk.
The clouds and rain were never meant to be; he was
   brokenhearted for naught.

The student asked Crimson, "What did Oriole have to say?"

Crimson replied, "She said nothing. She was simply sad and wept. If I
were to surmise, it seemed something really moved her. I will investi-
gate tonight and report to you in the morning." Crimson bid the student
goodnight and went back to her bedchamber. Oriole had already gone
to bed.

   Candlelight glimmered in the night,
   Sad thoughts disturbed their sleep.

iii.9/iv.9 Zhonglü Diao Mode

Blue-Green Peony
Deep in the night the water clock was quiet,

鶯鶯更悶愁不小。
擁衾無寢，
心下徘徊籌度。
「君瑞哥哥，
　為我吃擔閣。
你莫不枉相思，
　枉受苦，
　　枉煩惱。

適來琴內排喚着。
即自家大段不曉。
自心思忖，
　怕咱做夫妻後不好。
奴正青春，
　你又方年少。
怕你不聰明，
　怕你不稔色，
　　怕你沒才調。

（鶻打兔）
　奈老夫人，
　　情性懆，
　　　非草草。
　雖為個婦女，
　　有丈夫節操。
　俺父親，
　　居廊廟。
　宰天下，
　　存忠孝。
　妾守閨門，
　　些兒恁地，
　　　便不辱累先考。

所重者，
　奈俺哥哥，

And Oriole even more depressed and sad.
Clasping the quilt in her arms, she was sleepless,
      her heart restless as she calculated:
"Brother Junrui
      you were wronged because of me.
Don't you long for me for nothing?
            Suffer for me?
                  Feel frustrated by me?

Of the call to temptation in your zither just now
I failed to understand the greater part.
But thinking about it,
      do you worry our marriage might go wrong?
I am in my youth
      and you are in your prime—
Do I worry you're not intelligent?
      Not striking?
            Not brilliant?

The Hawk Takes the Hare
"Alas, *old Madam Cui's*
      nature is too obstinate,
            but not rash.
She might be a woman
      but she has the principles and integrity of a strong man.
My father
      was a member of the court,
A minister of the realm,
      who put his loyalty and filial piety into action.
I keep to my boudoir
      but with what I've just been doing,
            would I not shame my father?

What is important here
      is that my brother

由未表。
適來恁地，
　把人奚落。
司馬才，
　潘郎貌。
不由我，
　難偕老。
怎得個人來，
　一星星說與，
　　教他知道

（雙聲疊韻）
　夜迢迢。
睡不⁴着。
寶獸沈煙裊。
枕又寒，
　衾又冷，
　　畫燭愁相照。
「甚日休，
　幾時了。
強合眼，
　睡一覺。
怎禁夢魂顛倒夜難熬。」

背畫燭，
　魆魆地哭，
　　淚滴了知多少。
哭得燭又滅，
　香又消。
轉轉心情惡。
自埋怨，
　自失笑。
自解嘆，
　自敦搦。
眼縣縣地，

全是沒頭沒緒
光景。

has yet to bring things to the surface.[ii]
And so, he just
    makes fun of me.
He has the talent of a Sima Xiangru
    and the looks of Master Pan Yue, yes,
But since it's not up to me,
    it'll be hard for us to grow old together.
How can I find someone
    to explain everything in detail
        to make him understand?"

Alliteration and Rhyming
The night dragged on and
She could not sleep.
Smoke from the precious incense censer wafted up.
The pillow was cool
    and the quilt was cold—
        in all, a dismal scene lit by a decorated candle.
"What day will it end,
    what time?
I force my eyes to close
    to sleep a bit.
How to keep my dreaming soul's infatuation from making this
    night unbearable?"

She turned her back on the decorated candle
    and softly cried
        endless tears.
She wept until the candle died out
    and the incense disappeared.
As her feelings gradually grew gloomier,
    She became resentful,
    she laughed at herself,
She grumbled about being alone,
    then she tossed and turned in bed.
Her eyes hungrily

A scene of utter confusion.

盼明不到。

（尾）

不撞曉鐘，故
言及行者貪
睡。

昏沈的侍者管貪睡着。
業相的明月兒不疾落。
慵懶的雞兒甚不唱叫。

鶯

通宵無寐，
抵曉方眠。
紅娘目之，
不勝悲感。
侵曉而起，
以情告生。

iii.10/iv.10 黃鐘宮（侍香金童纏令）
iii.9/iv.9

紅娘急起，
心緒愁無那。
忙穿了衣裳離繡閣。
如與解元相見呵。
一星星都待說與子個。

急離門首，
連忙開放鎖，
直奔書幃里來見他。
天色兒又待明也，
不知做什麼。
書幃里兀自點着燈火。

鶯之悶愁從自
己口中道出。
張之悶愁從紅
娘眼中看出。

（雙聲疊韻）

把窗兒紙，
微潤破。
見君瑞披衣坐。
管是⁵文字忙，
詩賦多。

looked for a dawn light that did not come.

Coda
"Acolytes sunk in their slumber care only for more sleep.
That damned moon won't set quick enough.
Why hasn't the lazy rooster made its raucous crow?"

The morning bell has yet to be rung, so it speaks about acolytes desiring to sleep.

    Oriole
        did not sleep the entire night,
        falling asleep only as morning came.
        Crimson eyed her and
        was grieved.
        She arose early and
        reported the situation to the student.

iii.10/iv.10 Huangzhong Gong Mode

Golden Lad Minding Incense: A Bound Suite
Crimson got up quickly,
    in an anxious state of mind.
She hurriedly threw on her clothes and left the embroidered
    gallery.
"If I see Master Zhang
    I'll tell him every little thing."

She quickly left the doorway,
    opened the lock on the courtyard gate,
        and raced straight to the study to see him.
The sky was about to turn light,
    and she didn't know what he was doing in there,
  Or why he had to light his lamp himself.

Oriole's depression was related by her own mouth; Zhang's depression is seen through the eyes of Crimson.

Alliteration and Rhyming
Moistening her finger, she
    poked a hole through the paper window
        and spied Junrui sitting there, draped in his clothes.
He wasn't busy composing
    or writing lots of poems or rhapsodies,

做甚閒功課。
見氣出不迭，
　口不暫合。
自埋怨，
　自摧挫。
一會家自哭自歌。

（出隊子）
　悄一似風魔。
　眉頭兒廝緊着。
　紅娘不覺淚偷落。
　相國夫人端的左。
　酷毒害的心腸忒煞過。

（尾）
　做個夫人做不過。
　做得個積世虔婆。
　教兩下里受這般不快活。

　　紅娘推開書齋，張生見了，且喜且驚。

iii.11/iv.11 仙呂調（勝葫蘆）
　手取金釵把門打。
　君瑞問「是誰家。」
　「是紅娘囉待與先生相見咱。」
　張生聞語，
　　速開門連問
　　　「管是您姐姐使來吵。
　昨日因循誤見他。
　咫尺抵天涯。

　一夜教人沒亂煞。」
一味真。　紅娘道「且住，
　　把鶯鶯心事，
　　　說與解元嗄。」

and he certainly wasn't studying for the examinations.
She saw him mutter on and on,
   his mouth never shutting for a second.
He was resentful
   and torturing himself—
      now weeping, now singing.

Sending Out the Dance Troupe
Just like a lunatic,
Eyebrows pinched tight,
Crimson couldn't help but let a teardrop fall.
"Madam Cui, the wife of a Minister of State, is truly off the mark,
For his heart has suffered too much of her tortuous poison.

Coda
"She can't just be a wife of status,
But is instead a conniving, experienced old witch,
Who's made the two of them really unhappy!"

   Crimson threw open the study door, and when Student Zhang saw her,
   he was surprised and delighted.

iii.11/iv.11 Xianlü Diao Mode

The Winning Gourd
She took the hairpin in hand and knocked on the door.
Junrui asked, "Who is it?"
   "It's Crimson and I want to see you!"
On hearing these words, Student Zhang swiftly opened up
   and followed with a quick remark,
      "You must have been sent by your sister!

Yesterday I hesitated too long and missed seeing her.
A single foot away might as well be as far as Heaven's edge—
And it drove me crazy all night."
   Crimson spoke, "Stop. . . .   *Pure sincerity.*
     I will tell you all there is to know
        about what lies in Oriole's heart."

紅謂生曰:「公勿憂。況姐姐之情,於公深矣,聽妾訴衷
腸。」

iii.12/iv.12 中呂調（古輪台）
    「莫心憂。
    解元聽妾話蹤由。
    俺姐姐夜來箇
      聞得琴中挑鬥。
    審聽了多時,
      獨語獨言搔首。
    手抵牙兒,
      喟然長嘆:
        『奈何茲母性惱搜。
    應難歡偶。』
    料來他一種芳心,
      盡知琴意,
        非不多情,
          自僝自僽。
    爭奈他家不自由。
    我團着,
      情取個從今後為伊瘦。」

    張生聞語,
      撲撒了滿懷裏愁。
    「想料死冤家
      心中先有。
    琴感其心,
      見得十分能勾。
    教俺得來,
      痛惜輕憐,
        繡幃深處效綢繆。
    盡百年相守。
    據自家冠世文章,
      謫仙才調,
        胸卷江淮,

Crimson told the student, "Don't fret, sir. Sister has deep feelings for you. Let me tell you right from the bottom of my heart."

iii.12/iv.12 Zhonglü Diao Mode

Old Bögör
"Do not fret,
Laureate, and listen as I trace it all out:
Last night my sister
    listened to the flirtations stirring from the zither
And, after listening carefully for a long time,
    started muttering to herself and scratching her head.
Cheek resting in her hand,
    she sighed,
        'Alas, my compassionate mother has such a stubborn
           nature,
She makes it impossible to become a loving couple.'
I think that fragrant heart of hers
    completely understood the meaning of your tune.
        She is full of feeling
           and was frustrated and resentful about it all.
But she doesn't have the freedom to act
And I surmise
    her emotions will mean she'll grow thinner every day because of you."

When Student Zhang heard her words,
    he completely shed the sorrow that filled his breast.
"I had imagined that my sworn enemy
    already held me in her heart,
So, when the zither stirred
    my success was certain!
Let me get her
    and I'll cherish her and treat her tenderly
        as we share our congress deep within the embroidered
           curtains.
We'll be together for a hundred years.
We'll rely on my unsurpassed literary skill,
    my talent and tenor like the banished immortal,[19]
        my breast as capacious as mighty rivers,

---

19 A reference to the famous Tang poet, Li Bai 李白 (702–761), whose unrestrained behavior earned him the nickname of "Banished Immortal."

　　　　腸撐星斗。
　　臉兒又清秀。
　　怎不教
　　　那稔色的人人掛心頭。

（尾）
　　他家肯方便覷個緣由。
　　知咱家果有。
　　相如才調，
　　　肯學文君隨我走。」

　生曰：「情已動矣，易為政耳。」因筆硯作詩一首。

iii.13/iv.13 雙調（御街行）
　　文房四寶都拈至。
　　先把松煙試。
　　墨池點得兔毫濃，
　　　拂拭錦箋一紙。
　　筆頭灑落相思淚，
　　　盡寫心間事。

　　也不打草不勾思。
　　先序幾句俺傳示。
　　一揮揮就一篇詩，
　　　筆翰與羲之無二。
　　須臾和淚一齊封了，
　　　上面顛倒寫一對鴛鴦字。

　張生謂紅娘曰：「敢煩持此達鶯左右。

　紅娘曰：「鶯素端雅，焉敢以淫詞致於前。然恃先生脫禍之恩，因鶯鶯慕郎之意，試為呈之。」

　持箋歸，置於妝台一邊。

20 Inkstone, ink, a brush of rabbit hair, and fine paper.
21 The ink, made from the smoke of burning pine resin.

my mind as brilliant as the constellations.
And since I'm also very good looking,
How could I not make that
    ripe beauty keep me ever present in her heart?

Coda
"I hope she's willing to find a reason—
Now that she knows I truly possess
The talent and tenor of Sima Xiangru—
    to emulate Wenjun and flee with me."

"Her emotions are already astir," said the student, "and now it will be easy to carry off." He took up a brush and inkstone to write a single poem.

iii.13/iv.13 Shuang Diao Mode

Treading the Imperial Path
The four treasures of the literati's study were brought forth.[20]
First, he tested the pine soot,[21]
And when the puddle of ink held thick to his rabbit-down brush,
    he spread out the brocade calligraphy paper.
The tip of the pen sprinkled tears of love
    as he wrote out the fullness of his heart.

He wrote no rough draft, never hesitated,
But first put down several lines to express his feelings,
Then brandishing stroke after stroke he finished the poem,
    with calligraphy to match that of Wang Xizhi.[22]
After sealing it with his tears,
    he wrote two words upside-down on the folded missive—
        "Mandarin Ducks."[23]

He told Crimson, "May I ask you to take this to Oriole?"

Crimson replied, "Oriole has always been extremely proper, how dare I present these lascivious words to her? But, given that you helped us escape disaster, as well as Oriole's admiration for you, I'll try and present it."

She took the letter back and placed it next to Oriole's makeup mirror.

22 Wang Xizhi 王羲之 (303–361, byname Yishao 逸少).
23 Symbols of true love, indicating this is a love letter.

鶯起理妝，見其簡而視之。

iii.14/iv.14 仙呂調（賞花時）

　　過雨櫻桃血滿枝。
　　弄色奇花紅間紫。
　　清曉雨晴時。
　　起來梳裹，
　　　脂粉未曾施。

　　把簡兒拈來抬目視。
　　是一幅花箋寫着三五行兒字。
　　是一首斷腸詩。
　　低頭一晌，
　　　讀了又尋思。

（尾）

　　覷着紅娘道：「怎敢如此。
　　打脊風魔虔妮子，
　　這妮子合死。」
　　臉兒上與一照台兒。
　　　照台一舉綬帶飛空，

照臺舉綬帶飛空，寶鑒響花磚粉碎。

紅娘急躲過曰：「死罪。死罪。」詩云：

　　　　相思恨轉深，
　　　　謾托鳴琴弄。
　　　　樂事又逢春，
　　　　花心應已動。
　　　　幽情不可違，
　　　　虛譽何須奉。
　　　　莫惡月華明，
　　　　且憐花影重。

When Oriole arose and put on her makeup, she saw the letter and read it.

iii.14/iv.14 Xianlü Diao Mode

Time to Enjoy the Flowers
Cherry trees after the rain: blood fills the branches,
Rare flowers that sport their colors: red mixed with purple—
A clear morning after the rain has gone.
Arising, she brushes her hair and puts on her robe,
**   with nary a bit of rouge or powder applied.**

She picks up the note and raises her eyes to look:
It is a piece of flowered paper with a few lines of writing.
A poem of a broken heart.
Lowering her head for a bit,
*   she ponders after reading. . . .*

Coda
She glares at Crimson, says, "How dare you!
Crazy little hussy, you're asking for a beating!
You little tramp, you deserve to die!"
She picked up the mirror stand and threw it at Crimson's face.

The stand and all its tassels and ribbons flew into the air,
The precious mirror itself rang out as it smashed the patterned pavers
    to pieces.[24]

Crimson quickly dodged and said, "Forgive me, I've done a terrible thing!" The poem itself read:

This lovesick anger grows ever deeper,
For naught I sounded it all out in a zither tune.
Pleasure is here as spring is too,
And the heart of the flower has already trembled in response.
Hidden feelings cannot be denied,
Why cling to a reputation that will mean nothing in the end?
Don't hate the luster of the moonlight,
But take pity on the weight of the flowers' shadows.

---

24 Chinese mirrors were made of polished bronze.

iii.15/iv.15 仙呂調〔繡帶兒〕

紙窗兒前，
　照台兒後。
一對兒小簡，
　掉在纖纖手。

又帶旁蓁。 拆開讀罷，
　寫着淫詩一首。
自來心腸懊。
更讀着恁般言語，
　你尋思怎禁受。
低頭了一晌，
　把龐兒變了眉兒皺。
道：「張兒淫濫如豬狗。
若夫人知道，
　多大小出醜。

不良的賤婢好難容，
　要砍了項上顱頭。
多應是你，
　廝迤廝逗。
兀的般言語，
　怎敢着我咱左右。
這回且擔免，
　若還再犯後。
孩兒多應沒訴休。
如今俺肯
　推窮到底胡追究。
思量定不必鬧合口。
且看當日
　把子母每曾救。」

　　（尾）
　「如還沒事書房裏走。
　更着閒言把我挑鬥。
　我打折你大腿縫合你口。」

iii.15/iv.15 Xianlü Diao Mode:

The Embroidered Belt
In front of the papered window,
    behind the mirror,
A little letter
    had fallen into tiny, delicate hands—
After opening it and reading
    she saw it contained a salacious poem.
Always a bit obstinate and contrary,
And now reading such language—
    Just imagine! How could she endure it?
She lowers her head for an instant,
    her expression changes and her brows knit,
And she says, "Brother Zhang is as randy as a pig or a dog!
It would be a fine spectacle
    If my mother found out.

Again, he brings in a peripheral description.

I can't stand such a worthless servant—
    I'd like to cut that ass's head off your neck.
It was you, more than likely,
    who enticed him to write it.
How dare you leave such a thing
    lying around in my presence?
I'll let it go this time,
    but if you ever commit such an error again,
Child, you'll have no place to complain.
That I'm willing now
    to let go of pursuing this to the end
And have decided not to add my voice to the fray—
Is only because I've considered that day
    when he saved us both, mother and child.

Coda
"If you go to his study again without good reason,
And stir up any more idle words to provoke me,
I'll break your legs and stitch up your mouth."

鶯曰：「非汝孰能持詩至此。我以兄有活命之恩，不欲明
言。今後勿得。」

紅娘謝罪。

鶯曰：「我不欲面折。」因筆左側，書於箋尾，令紅娘：
「持此報兄，庶知我意。」

紅娘精神失措，手足戰慄，趨至生前。生驚問之。

iii.16/iv.16 仙呂調（點絳唇）
　　　鶯見紅娘，
　　　　涙汪汪地眉兒皺。
　　　生曰：「可憎姐姐，
　　　　休把人傛僽。

驚恐倉皇。　　百媚鶯鶯，
　　　　管許我同歡偶。
　　　更深後與俺相約，
　　　　欲學文君走。」

　　　（尾）
　　　紅娘聞語道「休針喇，
　　　　放二四不識娘羞。
　　　待要打折我大腿、縫合我口。」

紅娘曰：「幾乎累我。」

生曰：「何故。」

紅娘盡訴鶯鶯意。

生驚曰：「奈何。」紅娘示箋。

生視之，微笑曰：「好事成矣。」

Oriole spoke, "No one else but you could have brought this poem here. Because of my brother's grace in saving us, I do not want to speak about this openly. Don't ever do it again!"

Crimson apologized for her offense.

Oriole said, "I don't want to settle this in person." She picked up the brush at her left and added a note to the bottom of his letter, and ordered Crimson, "Take this back as a reply to my brother. Hopefully he will understand what I mean."

Crimson was scared out of her wits, and she trembled as she hurried to face the student. Alarmed, the student questioned her.

iii.16/iv.16 Xianlü Diao Mode

Dotting Crimson Lips
Startled by the sight of Crimson,
*   her tears welling up and eyebrows furrowed,*
The student said, "Lovable sister,
*   stop torturing me.*

Beguiling Oriole,
*   certain to be my partner in love,*
Will make a pact with me tonight
*   to elope with me like Wenjun would."*

Frightened and
panic-stricken.

Coda
When Crimson heard this, she said, "Fool,
Don't be so damn ludicrous and shameless—
She wants to break my legs and stitch up my mouth."

Crimson spoke, "You nearly implicated me!"

"Why do you say that?" said the student.

Crimson told him everything Oriole was thinking.

"What shall we do?" cried the student in alarm. Crimson showed him the letter.

The student looked at it and said with a slight smile, "This fine affair is carried off!"

紅娘曰：「鶯適甚怒，卻有何言。」

生指詩悉解其意：「題其篇曰：《明月三五夜》。其詩曰：

待月西廂下，
迎風戶半開，
拂牆花影動，
疑是玉人來。

今十五日，鶯詩篇曰：《明月三五夜》，則十五夜也，故有『待月西廂』之句。『迎風戶半開，』私啓而候我也。『拂牆花影動』者，令我因花而逾垣也。『疑是玉人來』者，謂我至矣。」

紅娘笑曰：「此先生思慕之深，妄生穿鑿，實無是也。」言訖而去。生專俟天晚。

iii.17/iv.17 黃鐘宮（出隊子）

愁則怨月之不落，喜則怨日之不轉。

咫尺抵天涯。
病成也都為他。
幾時到今晚見伊呵。
業相的日頭兒不轉角。
敢把愁人刁虐殺。

鄧將軍謂日也。

假熱臉兒常欽定，
把人心不鑒察。
鄧將軍你敢早行麼。
咱供養不曾虧了半恰。
枉可惜了俺從前香共花。

25 This appellation must stem from the myth of Kuafu 夸父. From the *Classic of Mountains and Seas* (*Shanhai jing* 山海經): "Kuafu. . .chased after the sun and ran to where it sets. He became thirsty and wanted to drink, so he drank from the Yellow River and the Wei River. The water from the Yellow River and the Wei River was not sufficient for him so he went north to drink from the Grand Lake. But before he reached it, he died of thirst on the road. He threw down his staff, which became transformed

Crimson said, "Oriole was as mad as she could be, what could she have possibly said?"

The student pointed to the poem and gave a thorough explanation of its meaning, "She's titled the poem 'In the Bright Moonlight of the Night of the Third Five.' And the poem reads:

> Waiting for the moon by the western wing,
> Greeting the breeze, the gate half opened.
> Brushing the wall, flowers' shadows move,
> Could it be the Jade One coming?

Now, today is the fifteenth of the month. Oriole's title reads 'In the Bright Moonlight of the Night of the Third Five,' which is the night of the fifteenth. So she has the line, 'Wait for the moon by the western wing.' 'Greeting the breeze, the gate half opened,' means she will secretly open it and wait for me. 'Brushing the wall, flowers' shadows move,' tells me to jump over the wall beneath the flowers; 'Could it be the Jade One coming' means that I will get there."

Crimson laughed and said, "Your yearning is so deep that you've willfully distorted the reading. This isn't what it means." Finished speaking, she left. The student could do nothing but wait for the night to lengthen.

iii.17/iv.17 Huangzhong Gong Mode

Sending Out the Dance Troupe
"A single foot away might as well be as far as Heaven's edge:
All this lovesickness is because of her.
When will this night be dark enough to go to her?
This damned sun just won't turn the corner,
And instead tortures this grieving one.

Sad, he resents that the moon won't set; happy, he resents that the sun won't move.

That false warmth of its face refuses to move,
** unable to mirror the human heart.**
Oh, General Deng, can you move no faster?[25]
I've never stinted in my sacrifice to you,
But all the incense and flowers I lavished were worth nothing.

General Deng refers to the sun.

into the Deng Forest." See Yuan Ke 1983, 238 and Strassberg 2002, 178. There is no "general Deng" mentioned anywhere, but in one of the Daoist pantheons there is a Grand Marshal Deng, who was a thunder god.

（尾）

一刻兒沒巴避抵一夏。
不當道你個日光菩薩。
沒轉移好教賢聖打。

是夕一鼓才過，月華初上，生潛至東垣，悄無人跡。

iii.18/iv.18 中呂調（碧牡丹）

夜深更漏悄。
張生赴鶯期約。
落花薰砌，
　香滿東風簾幕。
手約青衫，
　轉過欄乾角。
見粉牆高。
「怎過去，」
　自量度。
又愁人撞着。

又愁怕有人知道。
見杏梢斜墮褭。
手觸香殘紅驚落。
欲待逾牆，
　把不定心兒跳。
怕的是月兒明，
　夫人劣，
　　狗兒惡。

就疊上三結句，
大有折趣。

（尾）

照人的月兒怎得雲蔽却。
看院的狗兒休唱叫。
願劣相夫人先睡着。

Coda
"A notch on the gnomon[26] equals a summer,
You may be called the 'Sunlight Bodhisattva,'
But if you refuse to move, the Buddha himself will beat you!"

That night the moon rose just after the first drum.[27] The student secretly went to the eastern wall, where it was quiet without a soul around.

iii.18/iv.18 Zhonglü Diao Mode

Blue-Green Peony
Night deepened and the water clock was the only sound
As Student Zhang went to his tryst with Oriole.
Flowers had fallen to scent the steps,
    their fragrance filled curtains brushed by the easterly wind.
His hand gathered up his blue robe and,
    as he turned the corner of the balustrade,
He saw the whitewashed height of the wall—
"How can I ever get over that?"
    he thought to himself.

He worried that he would run into somebody,
Worried someone would find out.
Then he saw a tip of apricot branch hanging over
    and as his hands touched its fragrance, its tattered red fell,
      startled.
He wanted to climb the wall,
    but he could not quell his leaping heart.
What he feared were: the brightness of the moon,
    the fierceness of Madam Cui,
      and the viciousness of the dog.

Piling on three concluding sentences—brightness of the moon, fierceness of Madam Cui and viciousness of the dogs—adds much fun to the twists and turns.

Coda
"Why did the clouds covering the shining moon withdraw so
    suddenly?
Let the watchdog in the compound not bark.
I just hope fierce Madam Cui went to sleep first!"

26 Roughly fifteen minutes.
27 Around 9 pm.

iii.19/iv.19 黃鐘宮（黃鶯兒）

君瑞。
君瑞。
牆東里一跳，
　在牆西里撲地。
聽一人高叫道「兀誰。」
生曰：「天生會在這裏。」

聞語紅娘道「踏實了地。
兼能把戲。
你還待要跳龍門，
　不到得恁的。」

見其人，乃紅娘也。紅娘曰：「更夜至此，得無嫌疑乎。」

iii.20/iv.20 雙調（攬箏琶）

紅娘曰：「君瑞好乖劣。
半夜三更，
　來人家院舍。
明日告州衙，
　教賢分別。
官人每更做擔饒你，
　須監守得你幾夜。」

張生聞語，
　急忙應喏。
「聽說。
聽說。
不須姐姐高聲叫，
　懷兒里兀自有簡帖。
寫着『啓戶迎風，
　西廂待月。』

iii.19/iv.19 Huangzhong Gong Mode

Yellow Oriole
Ah, Junrui,
Junrui.
A leap from the eastern side
    and you plop flat on the ground to the west,
Only to hear someone yell, "Who is it?"
The student replied, "I was sent to this tryst by Heaven's will!"

Hearing this, Crimson spoke, "Well, get two feet on the ground,
And then you can put on your little show.
Here you want to go and jump the Dragon's Gate,[28]
    but you can't even manage this!"

He looked to see who it was, and it turned out to be Crimson. She said,
"Isn't it sort of suspicious that you would show up here at midnight?"

iii.20/iv.20 Shuang Diao Mode

Tuning the Strings
Crimson spoke, "You're disgusting, Junrui,
Coming around at midnight
    to sneak into someone else's compound!
We'll report you to the provincial yamen tomorrow
And make you, my worthy gentleman, explain it all there.
Even if the officials let you off,
    they'll keep you in jail a few nights."

When Student Zhang heard these words,
    he answered in response:
"Listen to me.
Listen please,
There's no need for you to shout so loud.
There's an invitation right here in my robe,
On which is written 'opening the gate to welcome the wind,'
    and 'wait for the moon by the western wing.'

28 That is, to pass the examinations. From the story of carp that swim up the Yellow
   River to attempt to leap over the "Dragon's Gate" at the top of a waterfall where the
   Yellow falls off the loess plain. The carp turn into dragons if they succeed.

明道暗包籠，
　　是您姐姐。
紅娘，你好不分曉，
　　甚把我攔截。」

（尾）

即用其語作
尾，味更悠
長。

「今宵待許我同歡悅。
快疾忙報與您姐姐。
道『門外玉人來也。』」

怎見得有簡帖期生來。有《本傳歌》為證。歌曰：

丹誠寸心難自比，
寫在紅箋方寸紙，
寄與春風伴落花，
彷彿隨風綠楊里。
窗中暗讀人不知，
剪破紅綃裁作詩，
還怕香風易飄蕩，
自令青鳥口銜之。
詩中報郎含隱語，
郎知暗到花深處，
三五月明當戶時，
與郎相見花間語。

生反復解詩中之意。紅娘曰：「先生少待，容妾報之，容妾報之。」

倏忽，紅娘奔至，連曰：「至矣。至矣。」張生但歡，心謂得矣。

及乎至，則端服嚴容，大怒生曰：「兄之恩，活我之家，厚矣。是以慈母以弱子幼女見托。奈何因不令之婢，致淫

It clearly states a hidden fact:
    it's from your big sister.
Crimson, you just don't get it—
    why are you standing in the way?

Coda

"Tonight, she has assented to share her joy with me,
So, as fast as you can, tell your sister,
'The Jade One is here outside the door!'"

> *To immediately use Oriole's own words in writing the Coda makes the flavor last on and on.*

How do we know that there was an invitation for the student? The "Ballad of Oriole" is evidence. It reads:

An inch of loyal vermillion heart is hard to match,
Written on crimson paper hatched in one-inch squares;
He cast his words on the spring breeze to fall with blossoms
That seemed to follow the wind, scattering among the green poplars.
She read it secretly within her windows, so no one knew,
And scissored the crimson silk into the shape of poetry.
Still afraid the fragrant breeze could easily send it awry,
She had her own little bluebird take it in her beak.
The poem requited the fine young man and harbored subtle allusion
That he understood, and he came secretly to where the flowers were thick.
On the third fifth of the month, when the moon is bright, there, before
    the door,
She would meet the fine young man and speak with him amidst the
    flowers.

The student repeatedly explained the poem, then Crimson said, "Just wait a moment and let me tell her, just wait for me to tell her."[iii]

In a flash Crimson raced to him to say over and over, "She's coming, she's here." Student Zhang was overjoyed, and his heart told him he had won.

Just before she reached him, she straightened her clothes and put on a stern face. Angrily she told the student, "Your kind act to save my family was great indeed, brother. Therefore, my compassionate mother entrusted her young son and daughter to you. But, alas, you relied on this unworthy maid to send me words that were lascivious and licen-

佚之詞。始以護人之亂為義，而終以誨淫之語為謀。以謀
易亂，奪彼取此，又何異矣。誠欲寢其詞，則保人之奸不
貞，明之於母，則背人之惠不祥，將寄詞婢僕，又懼不得
發其真誠：是用託諭短章，願自陳啓。猶懼兄之見難，因
鄙靡之詞，以求必至。非禮之動，能不愧乎。願兄懷廉恥
之心，無及於亂，使妾保護廉之節，不失於貞。」

iii.21/iv.21 般涉調 （哨遍纏令）
　　　是夜鶯鶯，
　　　　　從頭對着張生，
　　　　　　　一一都開解。
　　　「當日全家遇非災。
　　　夫人心下驚駭。
　　　與眷愛。
　　　家屬盡沒
　　　　逃生之計，
　　　　　　彷彿遭殘害。
　　　謝當日先生奇謀遠見，
　　　　坐施了決勝良策。
　　　極深恩重若山海。
　　　不似尋常庶人般待。
　　　認義做哥哥，
　　　　厚禮相欽，
　　　　　　未嘗懈怠。

　　　念兄以淫詞，

tious. So, your act of righteousness in the beginning that protected me from disorder[29] now ends with you plotting the same thing, using words that would inspire me to licentious behavior. To substitute your own plot for disorder is merely to replace one for the other—how is it any different? I really wanted to put those words to bed, but to protect another's perfidy wouldn't be proper. It would also be wrong to turn my back on your kindness and bring this to my mother's attention. I wanted to entrust a servant to deliver my words, but I feared I wouldn't be able to express my true feelings. That's why I relied on a short note full of metaphors—I wanted to explain it to you in detail. Afraid that you wouldn't be able to interpret it, however, I used my own base words to ensure you would come. How can one not be shamed by actions that violate ritual? Brother, I hope that you retain a heart of integrity and a sense of shame and not let in thoughts of corruption. Let me to retain a proper measure of honesty and not lose my chaste virtue."[30]

iii.21/iv.21 Banshe Diao Mode

Whistling Song: A Bound Suite
That night Oriole
    faced Student Zhang, and from the top,
        explained things clearly one by one:
"On that day, the whole family faced real disaster.
My mother was terrified that,
In addition to her family members,
Everyone in the household would be exterminated—
    and, with no plan to escape,
        it seemed we were doomed to suffer.
Thankfully, your extraordinary stratagem and foresight
    set in motion superb tactics to assure victory.
Such all-encompassing kindness is as great as the very mountains
    and seas,
And you shouldn't be treated as if you were a simple, ordinary
    person.
In acknowledgment of your righteous actions, you were
    designated 'elder brother,'
        and we treated you in proportion with profound respect—
            never less than diligent about it.

When I think, brother, of your salacious words

---

29 May also be read as "protecting me from rape."
30 This portion of text found nearly verbatim in "The Tale of Yingying." Cf. Hightower 1973.

適來侍婢遺奴側。
解開遂披讀，
　　兀然心下疑猜。
故恰才。
令人詐以
　　新詞相約，
果是先生屆。
　　料當日須曾讀
先聖典教，
　　五常中禮義偏大。
弟兄七歲不同席，
　　今日特然對兄白。
豈不以是非為戒。」

（急曲子）
　　「思量可煞作怪。
　　夜靜也私離了書齋。
　　走到寡婦人家裏，
　　　　是別人早做賊捉敗。
　　此言當記在心懷。
　　知過後自今須改。」

（尾）
　　「莫怪我搶，
　　　　休怪我責。
　　我為個妹妹你作此態。
　　便不枉了教人喚做秀才。」

張生去住無門，紅娘精神失色，精神失色。

iii.22/iv.22 般涉調（夜遊宮）
　　言罷鶯鶯便退。
　　兀的不羞殺人也天地。

and how you dispatched my maid to leave them by my side—
When I opened it to read those words—
        suspicion and doubt suddenly stirred in my heart.
And so,
I sent someone
To arrange this tryst with my own words,
        And, sure enough you have proved my point!
You must have read the canonical teachings of the Former Sage,[31]
        in which ritual and righteousness hold the primary place.
From the age of six a brother may not share the same mat with a
        sister.[32]
        I'm making a special effort to explain this to you today.
Why are you not constrained by right and wrong?

An Accelerando Song
"Reflect on the real mischief you have done,
Leaving your study illicitly in the middle of a quiet night,
Walking over to a widow's home—
        anyone else would have been nabbed as a thief.
You should mark my words
And acknowledge your faults.
You must change your actions of your own accord.

Coda
"Forgive my intervention and
        don't blame me for scolding you—
I'm just a little sister, but if you act like this
Then won't identifying you as 'a scholar' be useless?"

    Student Zhang had no escape, and Crimson had lost all her color,
    lost it all.

iii.22/iv.22 Banshe Diao Mode

Roaming at Night in the Palace
Her words over, Oriole quickly withdrew.
Oh, Heaven, he was dying of embarrassment.

---

31 Confucius.
32 An approximation of the line from the "Family Rules" (Neize 內則) section of the
    Records of Rituals (禮記).

好插。

怎禁受紅娘廝調戲。
道「成親也，
　先生喜喜。

賤妾是凡事庸輩。
詩四句不知深意。
只喚做先生解經理。
解的文義，
　羞爭知快打詩謎。」

紅娘曰：「羞殺我也。羞殺我也。」

張生自笑，徐謂紅娘曰：

iii.23/iv.23 仙呂調（繡帶兒）
　「你尋思，
　甚做處。
　　不知就里，
　直恁衝衝怒。
　　把人請到，
　是他做死地相搶，
　　大小大沒禮度。
　　　俺也須是你個哥哥，
　看人似無物。
　　據恰才的做作，
　心腸料必如土木。
　　剛誇貞烈，
　　把人恥辱。
　這一場出醜，
　　向誰伸訴。

紅娘姐姐你便聰明，
　　當初曾救他子母。
誰知到今

How could he bear Crimson's satirical jab: *Marvelous*
She said, "You're going to get married—   *insertion.*
    Happiness, happiness to you, sir![33]

"I'm just a lowly servant of the most ordinary kind,
And simply didn't know the deeper meaning of the quatrain.
Only those called "Sir" know the principles of classical exegesis,
And can explain the correct meaning of the text!
Oh, the embarrassment! That you would struggle so to crack a
    poetic riddle!"

Crimson said, "So embarrassing, so embarrassing!"

Student Zhang laughed to himself, and slowly told Crimson,

iii.23/iv.23 Xianlü Diao Mode

The Embroidered Belt
"You need to consider
    what her actions were.
She didn't understand what I meant,
    and immediately flew into a rage.
She invited me here,
    and was hell-bent on explaining everything—
        but with a complete lack of propriety.
I am her older brother, after all,
    yet she regarded me as a nothing.
Based on her actions just now,
    her heart must be made of earth or wood.
To brag about her chaste virtue
    just to make me feel ashamed!
But there are none to whom
    I can complain about this unpleasant scene.

Now, sister Crimson, you are intelligent
    enough to see,
        in the beginning, I did save mother and children.
Who could have guessed that

---

33 A clever visual pun, creating in effect the word 囍 (*xi*), "doubled happiness," used
   for congratulations on a marriage.

把恩不顧。
恰才據俺
　對面不敢支吾。
白受恁閒驚怖。
細尋思吾也乾白，
　俺捹撥那孟姜女。
之乎者也，
　人前賣弄能言語。
俺錯口兒又不曾還一句。
　這些兒羞懶，
怎能擔負。」

（尾）
　「如今待欲去又關了門戶。
　不如咱兩個權做妻夫。」
　紅娘道「你莽時書房裏去。」

生帶慚色，久之方出。

iii.24/iv.24 般涉調（蘇幕遮）
　那張生，
　　心不悅。
　過得牆來，
　　悶悶歸書舍。
　壁上銀釭[6]半明滅。
　床上無眠，
　　愁對如年夜。

　寸心間，
　　愁萬疊。
　非是今生，
　　盡是前生業。

she would now disregard that kindness?
I just
    stood face to face with her without equivocation,
And impassively suffered such idle terrorizing—
Think about it carefully, I came off clean,
    but provoked Meng Jiangnü,[34]
Who, in the finest literary language,
    just flaunted how glib she is right in front of me.
Yet I never replied with a single phrase.
This kind of shame
    I cannot shoulder.

Coda
"I want to leave, but the gate is locked.
Wouldn't it be better if you and I hooked up for now as husband
    and wife?"
"It's time," said Crimson, "for you to go back to your study."

The student was abashed, and it was a while before he left the garden.

iii.24/iv.24 Banshediao Mode

Persian Sprinkling Dance
Now, Student Zhang
    was troubled.
After getting back over the wall
    he despondently returned to his study.
The silver lamp sconce on the wall flickered between bright
    and dark.
Sleepless on his bed
    he sadly faced a year-long night.

In that little inch of his heart
    sorrows piled up by the tens of thousands.
"It's not something from this life.
    It's all my karma from lives long past.

34 Fictional character Meng Jiangnü (孟姜女, literally the Eldest Daughter of the Jiang
family). Her new husband, Fan Xiliang 范喜良, was dispatched to help build the Great
Wall during the reign of the First Emperor of Qin. Meng traveled a great distance
to take him some winter clothes, but discovered he was already dead. Her powerful
weeping caused the wall to crumble and reveal her husband's body.

有眼何曾暫交睫。
　　淚點兒不乾，
哭向西窗月。

（柘枝令）
　　花唇兒恁地把人調揭。
　　怎對外人分說。
　　當初指望做夫妻，
　　　誰知變成吳越。
　　頓不開眉尖上的悶鎖，
　　解不開心頭愁結。
　　是前生宿世負償伊，
　　也須有還徹。

（牆頭花）
　　當初指望，
　　　風也不教洩。
　　事到而今已不藉。
　　莫不是張珙曾聲揚，
　　　莫不是別人曾間諜。

　　群賊作孽，
　　　早忘了當時節。
　　及至如今賣弄貞烈。
　　孤恩的毒害婆婆，
　　　負心的薄情姐姐。
　　親曾和俺詩韻，
　　　分明寄着簡帖。
　　誰知是咭咥，
　　　此恨教人怎割捨。
　　情詩兒自今休吟，
　　　簡帖兒從今莫寫。

（尾）
　　不走了，廝覷者。

I have eyes but have never closed them.
My tears undried,
I weep, facing the moon in the western window.

Chinese Mulberry Branch Song
Her clever mouth playfully reprimanded me.
How could I explain it to anyone not involved?
At first, I hoped we would be a couple,
     but who could know she would become a bitter enemy?[35]
I can't open the lock of depression on my brows,
     or untie the knot of sorrow in my heart.
If it is a debt from a former life or a previous incarnation that
    I owe you,
     it should be paid in full by now.

Flowers on the Wall
"What I hoped for in the beginning
     can never be revealed, even to the wind.
Now that it has happened, there can be no remorse.
Could it be that I made it too public?
     Or that someone else intervened?

A mass of rebels raised alarm—
     but she's already forgotten that,
And now she makes a parade of chaste resolve.
One is a cruel, poisonous old woman who turned her back on
    a favor
And the other a fickle little heartbreaker of a sister.
You matched the rhymes of my poem
     and plainly sent me a note—
Who knew it was all a trick?
     and how can this rancor ever be expelled?
I will never again chant a poem of love,
     and from this point on never write any other love notes.

Coda
"*I'm not going anywhere, so let's just see what happens.*

---

35 Or, "play the state of Yue to my state of Wu." These states were bitter enemies in a
    prolonged conflict in the early sixth century BCE. This is in distinction to his earlier
    use of Qin and Jin, which formed an alliance based on intermarriage.

神天報應無虛設。

休、休、休負德孤恩的見去也。

不禁憤毒。

張生勉強棄衣而臥。

iii.25/iv.25 黃鐘宮（出隊子）

他每孤恩。

適來到埋怨人。

見人扶弱騁精神。

幸自沒嗔剛做嗔。

渾不似那臨危忙許親。

花言巧語搶了俺一頓。

俺耳邊佯不聞。

歸來對這一盞惱人燈。

明又不明昏又不昏。

你道教人怎不斷魂。

（尾）

忽起波濤。

早是愁人睡不穩。

約來到二更將盡。

隔窗兒驀聽得人喚門。

生啟門觀，喜不自勝。是誰。是誰。

伴愁單枕，

翻成並枕之歡。

淹淚孤衾，

變作同衾之樂。

是誰。是誰。乃鶯鶯也。

生驚問「適何遽拒我。」

Divine Heaven's retribution wasn't readied for nothing.   *Irrepressible*
Enough. Enough! Let's see what rewards lie ahead for those who   *rancor.*
    forget favor and virtue!"

Student Zhang forced himself to disrobe and lie down.

iii.25/iv.25 Huangzhong Gong Mode

Sending Out the Dance Troupe
"They spurned a favor
And in the end played it as though *they* were the aggrieved.
My support for them in their weakness just allowed her free rein,
And turned what was a blameless act into angry condemnation.
How unlike making that hasty marriage pact when danger reared its
    head!

Her flowery words and sweet lies had me for a while,
But I pretended that my ears didn't take it in.
Back I come to face this annoying lamp,
Flickering between light and dark, dim and yet not dim.
Tell me, how could one not find it soul-crushing?

Coda   *Suddenly waves*
The sad one slept, but not soundly,   *begin to stir.*
And it was near the end of the second watch[36] when,
Outside the window, he suddenly heard someone call at the door.

The student opened the door to look, and was overjoyed. Who was
it? Who?[37]

    A single pillow shared only with sorrow
    Turned into a pillow shared in happiness.
    A lonely quilt soaked with tears
    Turned into a shared quilt of joy.

Who was it? Who was it? It turned out to be Oriole.

Shocked, the student asked her, "Why did you just reject me so ve-
hemently?"

36 9 p.m. until 11 p.m.
37 Suspense point 10.

鶯鶯答曰：「以杜謝侍婢之疑。」生擁鶯至寢。

iii.26/v.1 仙呂調（繡帶兒）

喜相逢。

笑相擁。

抱來懷裏，

　埋怨薄情種。

「適來相見，

　不得著言相諷。

今夜勞合重。

你也有投逹人時，

　姐姐煞起動。

傳言送簡，

　分明許我效鸞鳳。

誰知一句兒不中用。

甚廝迤廝逗，

　把人調弄。」

鶯鶯聞此，

　道謝相從。

著笑把郎供奉。

耳朵兒畔，

　盡訴苦悰。

臉兒粉膩，

　口邊朱麝香濃。

錦被翻紅浪，

　最美是玉臂相交，

　偎香恣憐寵。

鶯鶯何曾改，

　怪嬌痴似要人摣縱。

丁香笑吐舌尖兒送。

撒然驚覺，

　衾枕俱空。

一路說來，渾
如真境。到此
忽指破是夢。
令觀者心魂俱
眩。

"To prevent my maid from becoming suspicious." He steered her toward the sleeping space.

iii.26/v.1 Xianlü Gong Mode

The Embroidered Belt
Joyfully they met,
And he embraced her with a smile.
He gathered her in his arms,
    murmuring his dismay to that heartless little karmic seed:
"When we met just now
    you shouldn't have reproached me so.
But tonight, I'm especially thankful.
You need that moment, too, when you rush to another—
    and at no little effort.
The words you sent in your missive
    clearly meant for us to imitate the simurgh and the phoenix.[38]
Who could know that you didn't mean a single word?
Oh, such enticing language
    just to have fun at the expense of another!"

Hearing this, Oriole
    begged forgiveness and became compliant.
With a smile, she took his head in her hands
And next to his ear
    told him all that troubled her heart.
Her face was smooth and powdered,
    the rim of her mouth vermillion, her musky perfume thick.
The embroidered quilt rolled waves of red
    and sweetest to them both were their jade-white arms
        entwined,
            as nestling in her perfume, he let his tender passion free.
How Oriole had changed—
    so strangely charming and yearning for him to take her
        tenderly.
A little clove, with a smile she offered him the tip of her tongue. . . .
Suddenly he awoke with a start—
    quilt and pillow were both empty.

The entire aria has spoken of it as if it were a reality. Only at this point does he lay bare that it was a dream. This leaves the observer's heart and soul bewildered.

---

38 A euphemism for having sex.

（尾）

瑠瑠的聽一聲蕭寺擊疏鐘。
玉人又不見方知是夢。
愁濃。
楚臺雲雨去無蹤。

疏鐘敲破合歡夢，
曉角吹成無盡愁。

iii.27/v.2中呂調（踏莎行）

辣浪相如，
　薄情卓氏。
因循墮了題橋志。
錦箋本傳自吟詩。
張張寫遍鶯鶯字。

沈約一般，
　潘郎無二。
算來都為相思事。
「鶯鶯你還知道我相思。
甘心為你相思死。」

生自此行忘止，食忘飽，舉措顛倒，不知所以。久之成疾。

大師竊知，徑來問病，曰：「佳時難得，春光正妍。何事縈心，致損天和如此。」

生曰：「非師當問。」

Coda
Then, ringing, he heard the slow striking of the monastery bell,
And with the jade one disappearing, he knew it had been but a
*   dream.*
His sorrow was heavy.
From the terraces of Chu, rain and clouds had disappeared without
*   a trace.*

Sporadic ringing of the bell sundered a dream of shared pleasure;
Morning horns blew up into a sorrow without end.

iii.27/v.2 Zhonglü Gong Mode

Song of Treading the Sedge
An uninhibited and indulgent Sima Xiangru,
        and a fickle Zhuo Wenjun.
Writing his ambitions on the bridge[39] fell away,
And on embroidered paper he gave vent to poems he chanted only to
*   himself.*
Scribbling page after page with "Oriole, oriole, oriole."

He was just like Shen Yue,[40]
        and no different than Master Pan,[41]
All because of love's longing.
"Oriole, do you still know my love?
For you, I would happily die of love's longing."

After this he fell into a daze, barely eating, doing everything backwards, and appearing uncomprehending. After a while, this turned
into an illness.

When the Abbot heard about it, he went immediately to ask him about
his sickness. "Good seasons are hard to come by and spring's radiance
is at its peak. What has troubled your heart so much that your natural
temperament should decline like this?"

"Not something you should ask about," replied the student.

39 When he was summoned to the capital, Sima Xiangru inscribed a message on the
    gate of a bridge north of Chengdu saying that he would return only if successful.
40 See Ch.2, n. 77.
41 On Pan Yue's prematurely grey hair, see Ch. 1, n. 66.

iii.28/v.3 仙呂調（賞花時）

> 過雨櫻桃血滿枝。
> 弄色的奇花紅間紫。
> 垂柳已成絲。
> 對許多好景，
> 　觸目是斷腸詩。

> 稔色的龐兒憔悴死。
> 欲寫相思除非天樣紙。
> 寫不盡這相思。
> 怕[7]愁擔恨，
> 　孤負了賞花時。

（尾）

> 「不明白擔閣的如此。
> 欲問自家心頭事。
> 願聽我說似。
> 這心頭橫儻個海猴兒。」

即用賞花時三字入本曲。古人多用此法。

大師笑曰：「以一女子，棄其功名遠業乎。」

生曰：「僕非不達。潘郎多病，宋玉多愁，觸物感情，所不免矣。」

師知其不可勉，但曰：「子慎湯藥」而去。自是廢寢忘餐，氣微嗜臥。

夫人想生病，令紅娘問候。張生聲絲氣噎，

問紅娘曰：「鶯鶯知我病否。你來後，又甚詩詞簡帖。」

紅娘道「又來也那。你又來也。」

iii.28/v.3 Xianlü Diao Mode

Time to Enjoy the Flowers
Cherry trees after the rain: blood fills the branches,
Rare flowers that sport their colors: red mixed with purple—
Weeping willows had formed their withes.
Now he faced so much beautiful scenery that
     in his eyes could become verse of the brokenhearted.

His handsome face was now haggard.
To write down his love would take a piece of paper as big as Heaven,
For this love longing was a never-ending text.
Burdened by sorrow and rancor
     he spurned this season of appreciating flowers

He immediately takes the three words of the title Time to Enjoy the Flowers *and puts them into the song. This is a style used often by the ancients.*

Coda
"I don't understand how it reached this point.
You want to know what's troubling my heart?
You want to listen to my explanation?
There's a little sea monkey stretched out over my heart!"[42]

The Abbot laughed, "Are you really going to throw away your reputation and your long-term enterprise because of a single girl?"

"I'm not unaware," said the student. "But Master Pan was often ill, and Song Yu was often sad. You can't avoid being affected by things."

The Abbot knew he could not be pushed, so he simply said, "Be careful with the remedies you use." And then he left. From that point on, the student gave up sleeping and forgot to eat. His breathing became weak and all he wanted was to lie down.

Madam Cui took note of the student's illness and dispatched Crimson to check on him.

In a thready voice and with choked breath, he asked Crimson, "Does Oriole know I'm sick? But you're here—does that mean there will be poems or letters?"

Crimson spoke, "There you go again!"

---

42 "Sea monkey" (*haihou* 海猴) is an affectionate term, being a twist on the phrase "good child" (*haohai* 好孩).

iii.29/v.4 高平調 （糖多令）

「光景迅如梭，
　慊慊愁悶多，
　　思量都為奴哥。
不顧[8]深恩成間闊。
大抵是那少年女奴。
也囉。

舊恨怎消磨。
新愁沒奈何。
不防憂損天和。
怎吃受夫人看冷破。
雲雨怎成合。
也囉。」

iii.30/v.5 中呂調 （牧羊關）

「白日且猶自可，
　黃昏後是甚活。
對冷落書齋，
　青熒燈火。
一回家和衣睡，
　一回家披衣坐。
共誰閑相守。
與影兒廝伴著。

心頭病怎成恁麼。
幾日來氣微嗜臥。
舌縮唇乾，
　全無涕唾。
針灸沒靈驗，
　醫療難痊可。
見您姐姐與夫人後，
　一星星說與呵。」

iii.29/v.4 Gaoping Diao Mode

Tang duo ling
"Time passes by, fast as a shuttle thrown in a loom,
      and I am sick and tired of all this gloominess.
            I believe it's all down to your sister,
Letting a rift grow between us by not considering my deep
      kindness.
It's all that little lady's doing.
Oh, yes.

How can old rancor be wiped out?
And what about this new sorrow?
I never thought fretting would so ruin my nature.
How can I bear Madam Cui's chilly see-all vision?
Or bring the clouds and rain together?
Oh, how?

iii.30/v.5 Zhonglü Diao Mode20

Shepherd's Pass
"I can keep myself together in daylight,
      but how do I go on living after dusk?
Facing the desolate study
      and the blue flickering lamp,
I sleep in my clothes,
      sit with them draped over my shoulders.
Who will abide with me in these idle moments?
Only my shadow keeps me company.

How did my heart's illness turn ever worse?
For the last few days, sapped of energy, all I want is to lie down.
My tongue has contracted, my lips are parched,
      and I have no spittle at all.
Neither needle nor moxa work,
      and the physician's treatments bring no cure.
When you see your sister and Madam Cui
      tell them everything in excruciating detail!

說得酸鼻。　　　（尾）

「沒親熟病染沈痾。
可憐我四海無家獨自個，
怕得工夫肯略來看覷我麼。」

紅娘亦為之沾灑，曰：「妾必為郎伸意，但恐鶯鶯情分薄耳。」欲去，生止之。

iii.31/v.6 南呂（一枝花）

紅娘將出門。
喚住低聲問。
「孩兒，你到家道與鶯鶯。
都為他家害得人來病。
咱家乾志誠。
不望⁹他家，
　　怎地孤恩短命。

我見得十分。
難做人。
待死後通些靈聖。
閻王問『你甚死，』
　　我說實情。
從始末根由，
　　說得須教信。
少後三二日，
　　多不過十朝，
　　　須要您鶯鶯償命。

說得酸鼻。
到此不容不
出盡言。

（尾）

「待閻王道俺無憑准。
抵死護生斷不定。
也不共他爭。
我專指着伊家做照證。」

Coda
"*No family, no one close, as this illness spreads and worsens.*
Poor me, with no home in the wide world, utterly alone—
Perhaps with a little push from you, might they come look in on me?"

Said in a way that
makes one want
to cry.

Crimson, too, wept for him, saying, "I will certainly pass along
your wishes, but I worry that Oriole's affection for you is not deep
enough." She was about to leave when the student stopped her
and said. . . .

iii.31/v.6 Nanlü Diao Mode

A Sprig of Flowers
Crimson was about to leave his room,
When he called her to stop and asked her in a low voice,
"Child, when you get back, tell Oriole
That my illness is all her fault
And that I was sincere in intent, but it came to nothing.
I never expected that she
      would be such an ungrateful and miserable[43] person.

I see clearly now
That it will be hard to keep going.
Wait until I die and communicate with the spirits.
Yama[44] will ask me, 'How did you die?'
      and I will set the record straight.
I'll explain all the reasons
      from beginning to end, until he completely believes it.
Then in three or four days—
      certainly, no more than ten—
         he'll have your Oriole repay the debt with her life.

Coda
"*Wait until King Yama says I have no evidence,*
And that, for the life of him, he can't decide,
I won't argue with him—
I'll just point to you as witness to the truth."

Reaching this
point, he cannot
but express himself
fully.

43 Literally "short-lived," a curse against ungrateful lovers.
44 King of Hell.

紅娘曰:「休攀絆。」去無多時,紅娘曰:「夫人、姐姐
至矣。」生亦不顧,但張目而已矣。

iii.32/v.7 大石調 (感皇恩)
　　　　張君瑞病懨懨
　　　　　擔帶不去。
　　　　說不得淒涼,
　　　　　覰不得淒楚。
　　　　骨消肉盡,
　　　　　只有那筋皮膚。
　　　　又沒個
　　　　　親熟的
　　　　　　人抬舉。

　　　　有些兒閑氣,
　　　　　都做了短嘆長吁。
　　　　便吃了靈丹怎痊癒。
　　　　盡夫人存問,
　　　　　半晌不能言語。
　　　　目間淚汪汪,
　　　　　多情眼,
　　　　　　把鶯鶯覰。

鶯撫榻謂生曰:「兄之病危矣。不識病甚。願速言之。」

iii.33/v.8 黃鐘宮 (降黃龍袞纏令)
　　　　「自與兄別來,
　　　　　彷彿十餘日。
　　　　甚陡頓肌膚消瘦
　　　　　添憔悴。
　　　　儘教人問當,
　　　　　不能應對。
　　　　眼兒裏。
　　　　空恁淚汪汪地。

Crimson said, "Don't implicate me as an accomplice." Then after leaving briefly, Crimson returned and said, "Madam Cui and your sister are here."

The student paid them no heed, just glared with wide, angry eyes.

iii.32/v.7 Dashi Diao Mode

Moved by the Emperor's Grace
Zhang Junrui, weak and exhausted by his illness,
    couldn't bear the load anymore.
His unspeakable misery
    and grief were too unbearable to observe.
He had wasted away to nothing,
    nothing left but tendons and skin,
With not a single
    person close enough to care
        or look after him.

A bit of pointless anger
    had turned into sighs and groans.
Even that magic cinnabar elixir couldn't cure him.
After Madam Cui's questions
    he was speechless for a second,
His tears welled up,
    and with eyes full of passion
        he looked intently at Oriole.

Patting his bed, Oriole said to the student, "You seem terribly sick. Why you are ill? Quick, tell me what it is."

iii.33/v.8 Huangzhong Gong Mode

Descending Yellow Dragon, Tremolo: A Bound Suite
"Brother, I parted from you
    seemingly ten days or so ago.
Why this sudden thinning of skin and flesh,
    and such fullness of pallor?
I ask about it,
    but you seem incapable of a response.
Yet your eyes
Have vainly shed these copious tears.

尚未知傷着甚物，
　直恁不能起。
願對着夫人，
　一一說仔細」。
料來想必。
定是些兒閑氣。
　自瘦得個
清秀臉兒不戲。

（雙聲疊韻）
　有甚愁，
　消沈圍。
　潘鬢慵梳洗。
　眼又瞑，
　　頭又低。
　子管裏長出氣。
　細覷了，
　這病體。
　　好不忘，
　怎下得。
　　多應是為我後恁地細思憶。

　何處疼，
　那面痛，
　　教俺沒理會。
　管腹脹滿，
　　心閉塞，
　　　快請個人調理。
　便道破，
　　莫隱諱。
　到這裏。
　命將逝。
　鶯鶯有個藥兒善治。

I still don't know what has so harmed you
    that you can't rise from your bed.
I want you to explain to Madam Cui
    every little thing in detail.
I suspect
That it must be just pointless anger
That's caused you to starve yourself
    until your fresh and fine face became so haggard.

Alliteration and Rhyming
"What sorrow
    has thinned that span of Shen's waist?
Or made you too lazy to wash and comb those locks of Pan Yue?
Your eyes are dim
    your head is drooping,
And all you do is moan and groan.
After looking closely:
    this sickly body—
I can't put it out of my mind,
    how can it be borne?
It's likely because after we met you longed for me so.

Where does it ache,
    which side is in pain?
You make it hard for me to know.
Is it because your belly is swollen[45]
    or your heart is stopped up?
        Quick, call someone in to help you recuperate.
Then tell that person everything,
    and hide nothing.
You've come to the point
Where your life might pass away.
But I have the perfect cure."

45 With emotions.

（刮地風）

　　生曰：「多謝伊來問當俺，
　　　　縱來後何濟。
　　自家這一場腌臢病，
　　　　病得來蹺蹊。
　　難服湯藥，
　　　　不停水米。
　　不頭沉，
　　　　不腦熟，
　　　　　脈兒又沈細。
　　知他為個甚，
　　　　吃藥後難醫。

（尾）

　　「妹子夫人記相識。
　　多應管命歸泉世。
　　這病說不得悶懨懨一肚皮。」

　　鶯曰：「妾有小藥，能治兄心間鬱悶。少頃，令紅娘專獻
藥至。」

　　生勉勞謝。

　　夫人曰：「先生好服湯藥，我且去矣。」

　　生見夫人與鶯欲去，生勉強披衣而起。

iii.34/v.9 高平調（木蘭花）

　　那張生，
　　　聞得道。
　　把旋闌兒披定，
　　　起來陪告。
　　東傾西側的做些醃軀老。
　　聞生沒死
　　　的的陪笑。

A Ground-Scraping Wind
The student said, "Thanks for coming to see me,
    but what cure can your visit offer?
This foul illness of mine
    has had a strange effect on me.
I find it hard to subdue with decoctions,
    and I can't stomach food or drink.
My head isn't heavy
    and there's no fever,
        but my pulse is sunken and thready.[46]
Who knows why this illness
    is so hard to cure even after ingesting herbal remedies?

Coda
"Sister, Madam, please remark well—
This is probably because my life is destined to return to the world
    below.
This illness is a bellyful of inexplicable, moody unhappiness.

Oriole said, "I have a little herbal remedy that can cure all the gloom
in your heart. In a bit, I'll have Crimson bring it to you."

The student struggled to thank her.

Madam Cui said, "Be sure to take your medicine, sir. And now I should
leave."

Seeing that Oriole and Madam Cui were about leave, the student struggled to his feet, throwing on a robe.

iii.34/v.9 Gaoping Diao Mode

Magnolia Blossoms
When Student Zhang
    heard this
He threw his long robe on securely
    and rose to tell them something.
Wobbling side to side, his body a strange sight,
Barely half alive,
    he delivered an affable smile,

---

46 The classic signs of the depression stemming from longing.

「相國夫人您但去，
　把鶯鶯留下，
　　勝如湯藥。」
紅娘聞語把牙兒咬，
「怎得條白練，
我敢絞殺這神腳。」
　夫人與鶯俱去，生目送之。

iii.35/v.10 黃鐘宮（降黃龍袞）
iii.33/v.8

添得許多曲
折，覺覽之不
窮。

那相國夫人，
　探看了張君瑞。
便假若鐵石心腸
　應粉碎。
子母每行不到
　窗兒西壁。
只聽得書舍裏。
一聲僕地。

是時三口兒轉身，
　卻往書幃內。
驚見張生，
掉在床腳底。
赤條條地。
不能收拾身起。
口鼻內。
悄然沒氣。

（尾）
相國夫人道得「可惜。
早是孩兒一身離鄉客寄。
死作個不着墳墓鬼。」

令紅娘救，少頃稍蘇。令一僕馳入蒲，請醫人至，令看其
脈。

醫曰：「外貌枯槁，其實無病。」

"Madam of State, why not go alone
and leave Oriole here—
that would be better than any medicine."
Hearing these words, Crimson gnashed her teeth:
"Where can I find a strip of silk
to strangle this halfwit?"[iv]

The student's eyes followed Madam Cui and Oriole as they left.

iii.35/v.10 Huangzhong Gong Mode

Descending Yellow Dragon, Tremolo
After the Wife of the Minister of State
had paid a visit to Zhang Junrui—
Why, even a heart of iron or stone
would crumble to nothing.
Mother and child had yet to reach
the western side of the window
When from the study they heard
something drop to the floor.

The trio turned around
to go back into the study,
Where they were alarmed to see Student Zhang
slumped by the foot of the bed,
Stark naked.
They couldn't even straighten his body,
And both his mouth and nose
were silent, without a sign of breath.

He has added so many twists and turns that one has the feeling it can never be read in full.

Coda
The Wife of the Minister of State spoke, "How sad!
First, he left home as a solo traveler,
And after death he'll be a wandering ghost, unbound to his family's
graves."

She had Crimson try to save him and in a short while he revived a bit.
Then she sent a servant into Puzhou to summon a doctor, and when
he arrived she asked him to take Zhang's pulse.

The physician said, "Well, he looks withered and haggard, but in fact,
he's not sick at all."

iii.36/v.11
iii.33/v.8 黃鐘宮（黃鶯兒）

奇妙。

奇妙。

郎中診[10]罷，

嘻嘻的冷笑。

道「五臟六腑又調和，

不須醫療。」

又問生曰「先生無病，何瘦弱如此。

為個甚肌膚渾如削。」

張生低道「我心頭橫著這鶯鶯。」

醫人曰「我與服瀉藥。」

醫留湯一點，夫人賜錢二千。醫退。

夫人曰：「宜以湯藥治，不可自苦如此。」夫人與鶯既歸，無一人至。

生曰：「所望不成，雖生何益。」強整衣巾，以條懸棟。

iii.37/v.12
iii.33/v.8 仙呂調（六么實催）

情懷轉轉難存濟。

勞心如醉。

也不吟詩課賦，

只恁昏昏睡。

恰恁時才合眼，

忽聞人語，

啞地門開。

卻見薄情種

與夫人來這裏。

着他方言語，

把人調戲。

不道俺也識你，

恁般圈圓，

iii.36/v.11 Huangzhong Gong Mode

Yellow Oriole
Wonderful,
Wonderful!
After the physician took his pulse,
**   he chuckled sardonically,**
Saying, "His internal organs are in harmony
**   and he needs no treatment."**
He questioned the student again, "You aren't sick, so why are
**   you wasting away?"**
"Why does it seem that your very flesh is being pared away?"
Student Zhang replied in a low voice,
"My heart is clogged up by an Oriole."
"Well," said the physician, "I'll prescribe you a purgative!"

The physician left him a small infusion. Madam Cui paid him with two
strings of cash, and the physician withdrew.

Madam Cui said, "You should take this infusion to cure yourself. You
cannot punish yourself like this." Once she and Oriole had gone back,
no one else came.

The student said, "All that I desired did not come to pass. What's the
point of living?" He stirred himself to put his clothes and head scarf in
order, then hung a silk braid from the rafter.

iii.37/v.12 Xianlü Diao Mode

Minor Sixth Accelerando
His feelings were in such turmoil, it was hard to continue on,
Drunk as he was with anxiety.
Writing no poetry, penning no rhapsodies
**   all he could was sleep in a stupor.**
He was just about close his eyes when he heard someone
**   talking.**
The door creaked open
**   and he saw that heartless seed**
**   and Madam Cui arrive.**

"Let her use deceitful words
    to make fun of me,
You never thought I'd recognize
That snare of yours;

慢長吁氣空垂淚。
念向日春宵月夜，
　迴廊下，
　恁時初見你。

（六么遍）
　向花陰底潛身立。
　漸審聽多時，
　　方見伊端的。
　腰兒稔膩。
　裙衣翡翠。
　料來春困把湖山倚。

回首絮叨。
　偏疑。
　沈香亭北太真妃。

　好多嬌媚諸餘美。
　遂對月微吟，
　　各有相憐意。
　幽情未已。
　忽觀侍婢。
　請伊歸去朱門閉。
　堪悲。
　只怨阿母阻佳期。

（哈哈令）
　伊家只在香閨。
　小生獨守書幃。
　縱寫花箋無人寄。
　忍輕離也哈哈。
　斂愁眉也哈哈。

（瑞蓮兒）
　咫尺渾如千萬里。

47　That is, Precious Consort Yang, Emperor Xuanzong of the Tang's favorite consort. They once were viewing peonies outside the Aloeswood Pavilion. Li Bai wrote a series

now I uselessly sigh, shed tears in vain,
And think about that spring night when,
      in the winding corridor on a moonlit night,
         I first saw you.

One Minor Sixth Section of the Great Song
"You hid your body in the shadows of flowers.
I drew closer and listened carefully
      before you revealed yourself at last.
Your waist was voluptuously fine,
Skirt and chemise the color of kingfisher green.
I thought perhaps it was spring lassitude that made you lean
      against the rockery,
But even then I suspected
You might be the True Consort, north of the Aloeswood
      Pavilion.[47]

So many delicate charms and all else beauty.
Our faces both turned to the moon, we whispered our poems,
      each with a true affection
And deep feeling still unabated.
Suddenly I saw your maid
Urging you to go back, where the vermillion gates closed.
Ah, such unbearable sorrow!
How I resent your mother for preventing our fine tryst.

Guffawing Song
"You were in your fragrant boudoir,
And I kept within my study curtains, alone.
Scribble I might on flowered paper, but there was no one to deliver
      the poems.
No easy parting to bear—*alas, alas,*
My sad brows knit together—*alas, alas.*

Auspicious Lotus Song
"One foot away from you was like thousands of miles.

A long-winded recapitulation.

of three poems on the occasion, the last of which contained the lines "Releasing the infinite regret of the spring wind, / She leaned upon the balustrade north of Aloeswood Pavilion" 解釋春風無限恨，/ 沈香亭北倚闌干. In the context of the poem, the first line of the couplet would refer to Emperor Xuanzong, who was infatuated with her.

誰知後來遇群賊。
子母無計皆受死。
難閃避。
怎時節，
　是俺咱可憐見你那裏。

（哈哈令）
蒲關巡檢與我相知。
捉賊兵免了災危。
怎時許我為親戚。
不望把心欺也哈哈。
好昧神祇。
也哈哈。

（瑞蓮兒）
刁鐙得人來成病體。
爭如合下休相識。
三五日來不湯個水米。
教俺難戀世。
對照埋怨。　到此際。
兀誰可憐見我這裏。

（尾）
把一條皂條梁間系。
大丈夫死又何悲。
到黃泉做個風流鬼。

iii.38/v.13 雙調 （御街行）
iii.33/v.8
張生是日心將碎。
猛把殘生棄。
手中把定套頭兒。
滿滿地兩眼兒淚。
思量人命也非小可，
果是關天地。

夫人去後門兒閉。

Who would have thought we'd encounter that horde of rebels?
Children and mother without any plans, all ready to accept death.
Hard to escape, indeed!
But it was that moment
      when I felt sympathy for you.

Laughing Song
"The Military Commissioner of Pu Pass, a friend of mine,
Captured the rebels and saved you from disaster.
When will I be accepted as part of your family.
I never expected to be deceived like this—*alas*.
You even fooled the spirits—*alas*.

Auspicious Lotus Song
"You thwarted me at every turn until I grew sickly.
It'd be better had I never known you.
For days I've touched no water or food,
And I have no love left for the world of the living—
At this moment of crisis,
Who will feel sorry for me?

Bitter resentment over the stark contrast between the promise and reality.

Coda
"I'll tie a black silk braid between the rafters—
What real man grieves over his death?
I'll reach the Yellow Springs[48] and be a ghost of love."

iii.38/v.13 Shuang Diao Mode

Treading the Imperial Path
That day, Student Zhang's heart was about to shatter,
And suddenly he wanted to end his life.
He firmly grabbed the noose
As his eyes swelled with tears.
Consider for a moment—a human life is no small thing
Because it involves both Heaven and earth.

The door was closed after Madam Cui left,

---

48 Yellow Springs (黄泉): hell, the underworld.

又沒甚東西。
驀一人走至猛推開，
　不覺勝[11]來根底。
舒開刺繡彈箏手，
　扯住張君瑞。

雖云禍福無門，
大抵死生由命。
當日一場好事
，頃刻不成，
後來萬里前程，
逡巡有失。

拽住的是誰。是誰。紅娘也。

謂生曰：「先生惑之甚矣。妾若來遲，已成不救。」曰：
「鶯自視郎疾歸，泣謂妾曰：『鶯之罪也。因聊以詩戲
兄，不意至此。如顧小行、守小節，惧兄之命，未為德
也。』令妾持藥見兄。」

iii.39/v.19 中呂調（古輪台）
iii.33/v.8
　　那紅娘
　　對生一一說行藏。
　　「俺姐姐探君歸，
　　　愁入蘭房。
　　獨語獨言，
　　　眼中雨淚千行。
　　良久多時，
　　　唱然長嘆。
　　低聲切切喚紅娘。
　　都說衷腸。
　　道『張兄病體尫羸，
　　　已成消瘦，

Nothing and nobody were left to him now. . . .
Then suddenly someone arrived, threw open the door,
and before he knew it, was right in front of him.
Opening her hand adept at embroidery and the zither,
she stopped Zhang Junrui.

One might say,
Though fortune and disaster are not preordained.
Generally,
Death and life are determined by one's fate.
On that day this fine affair
was forestalled in an instant,
so that a future myriad miles away
was held back from certain loss.

And who was it who pulled him back? Who?[49] It was Crimson.

She told the student, "You've really lost it, sir. If I'd been a minute later, the deed would have been done." She went on, "When Oriole went back after seeing you so sick, she wept and told me, 'It's all my fault. It's because I thoughtlessly sent that poem to tease my brother; I never thought it would come to this. There's nothing virtuous about injuring him for such minor deeds and lesser principles.' And then she ordered me to bring some medicine to you."

iii.39/v.14 Zhonglü Diao Mode

Old Bögör
Crimson
Explained Oriole's conduct in detail.
"After your sister came back from visiting you,
        she went sorrowfully into her orchid chamber.
She mumbled, talking to herself
        as tears rained from her eyes in a thousand drops.
After a long, long time
        she uttered an extended sigh.
Then in a low voice she earnestly called me over
And explained everything she was holding inside.
She said, 'Student Zhang is growing weak and frail,
        gaunt and haggard,

49 Suspense point 11.

不久將亡。
都因我一個，
　而今也怎支當。
我尋思，
　顧甚清白救才郎。』

當時聞語，
和俺也恓惶。
　遣妾將湯藥
來到伊行。
　卻見先生，
　這裏恰待懸梁。
些兒來遲，
　已成不救，
　　定應一命見閻王。
人好不會思量。
試覷他此個帖兒，
　有些湯藥，
　　教與伊服，
　　　依方修合，
　　　　聞着噴鼻香。
久服後，
補益丹田助衰陽。」

（尾）
　一天來好事裏頭藏。
　其間也沒甚諸般丸散。
　寫着個專治相思的聖惠方。

乃一短簡，外封曰：「小詩奉呈才兄文几，鶯鶯謹封。」
生取古鼎，令添香，置諸筆几之上。

謂紅娘曰：「往者以褻慢而見責，今日敢無體乎。」遂拜之。

and will soon perish.
It's all because of me—
    how can he go on anymore?
I have thought it over and
    will sacrifice my purity to save him.'

Hearing these words,
    even I was alarmed.
She dispatched me to bring some medicine
    over to you.
But what did I see? You, sir,
    about to hang yourself from the rafters.
Had I been a minute later
    it would have been too late for rescue
        and you would have been sent off to see King Yama.
You can't think straight—
Now, look here at this little slip of paper,[50]
    there is some medicine there
        which I'm supposed to make you take.
            All prepared according to prescription,
                you can smell its perfume burst in your nose.
If you take this over time, then
    it will supplement your cinnabar field and aid your
        deteriorating yang."[51]

Coda

A Heaven-sent wonder was hidden inside.
There were no pills or powders,
But a miracle prescription written solely to cure love's longing.

It was just a short missive, sealed on the outside with, "A short poem sent specially to my talented brother's desk. Carefully sealed, Oriole." The student took an ancient bronze tripod, filled it with incense, and placed it on top of his writing desk.

He told Crimson, "Before, I was upbraided for being insincere. Dare I act without the correct ritual today?" He then bowed to the missive.

---

50 The same term is used for "missive," "letter," or "note" and for a "spill," a folded slip
     of paper that holds prescription powders.
51 That is, it will increase his vitality and virility.

iii.40/v.15 高平調（木蘭花）
iii.33/v.8

急添香，
　忙禮拜。
躬身合掌，
　以手加額。
香煙上度過把封皮兒拆。
　明窗底下，
　款地舒開。
不知寫着甚來?
讀罷稿
　幾回喝采。
十分來的鬼病，
　九分來痊瘥。
紅娘勸道「且寧耐。
　有何喜事
恁大驚小怪。」

張生遂展開，讀了鶯鶯詩，喜不自勝，其病頓愈。詩曰：

勿以閑思想，
摧殘天賦才。
豈防因妄幸，
卻變作君災。
報德難從禮，
裁詩可當媒。
高唐休詠賦，
今夜雨雲來。

都來四十字，治病賽盧醫。

iii.41/v.16 仙呂調（滿江紅）
iii.33/v.8

清河君瑞，
　讀了嘻嘻地笑不止。
也不是丸兒。
也不是散子。

iii.40/v.15 Gaoping Diao Mode[52]

Magnolia Blossoms
He quickly added incense
    and busily made reverential bows,
Bending his body forward, placing palm to palm
    and bringing both hands to his forehead.
Passing the paper through the incense smoke, he split the seal,
And beneath the bright window
    he carefully spread it out.

Don't you know what was written there?
After he read it,
    he gave a few appreciative shouts.
That ghostly illness
    seemed ninety percent cured.
Crimson counseled him, "Calm down!
What could be such good news
    to make you overreact like this?

He opened it fully and after reading Oriole's poem, he was happy beyond belief and his illness was suddenly cured. The poem read:

Do not destroy your Heaven-bestowed talent
Because of some vague apprehension,
How can I keep your kindness toward me
From turning into a disaster for you?
When repaying such deep virtue, it's hard to observe the rites.
So I crafted this poem to serve as our matchmaker.
On Gaotang intone no rhapsody,
For tonight, clouds and rain will call upon you.

Those few words[53] were a brilliant physician that could cure any illness.

iii.41/v.16 Xianlü Diao Mode

A River Running Red
Junrui from Qinghe
    laughed and laughed after he read it.
It wasn't pills,
And wasn't powders,

---

52 Restoring the mode name, which is missing in all early texts.
53 The original says, "Those forty characters. . . ."

寫遍幽期書體字。
疊了舒開千百次。
念得熟如本傳，
　弄得軟如故紙。
也不是閑言語，
　是五言四韻、
　　八句新詩。
若使顆硃砂印，
　便是偷情帖兒。
私期會子。

儘紅娘問而不答。
驀兒紅娘詢問着，
　道「若洩漏天機，
　　是那不是。」
情事如畫。
「是您姐姐，
　今宵與我偷期的意思。
說與你也不礙事。」
紅娘聞語吸地笑，
道「一言賴語，
都是二四。
沒性氣閑男女，
不道是啞你，
你喚做是實志。
你好不分曉，
　是前來科段，
　　今番又再使。」

生曰：「汝欲聞此妙語，吾能唱之，而無和者，奈何。」

紅娘曰：「妾和之，可乎。」

張生曰：「可。」

iii.42/v.17　仙呂調（河傳令纏）
iii.33/v.8
　「不須亂猜。

Only fine calligraphy describing a secret tryst.
He folded and unfolded it a thousand times,
Reciting it until he knew it by heart
     and fiddling with it until it was soft as old paper.
They weren't just idle words
     but eight five-character lines,
          a new poem in four rhymes.
And had it been stamped with a vermilion seal,
     it would clearly be a summons to a secret love affair,
An entry ticket to a private tryst.

No matter how often Crimson asked, he would't answer.
Suddenly Crimson began interrogating him:
     "It's revealed the secrets of Heaven,
          has it?"
"It's your sister's
     wish to have a secret rendezvous with me tonight.
I suppose it's not a problem if I tell you about it."
As soon as she heard this, Crimson snorted and laughed,
     "The whole of it is a lie,
          a falsehood, a fib.
A tepid and useless pair, you two—
     it's not just that she's deceiving you,
          but you mistake it as authentic desire!
You're clueless—
     the trick she played on you before
          is about to be employed again.

The truth of the matter is as clear as it could be.

     "If you want to hear these marvelous words," said the student, "I can sing them, but alas I have no one who can do the harmony."

     "I can," said Crimson. "How about that?"

     "Fine," said Student Zhang.

iii.42/v.17 Xianlü Diao Mode

Spread by the River Song: A Bound Suite
"No need to guess wildly.

這詩中意思，
略聽我款款地開解。
　誰指望是他
劣相的心腸先改。
想咱家
　不枉了
　　為他害。

紅娘姐姐且寧耐。
是俺當初堅意，
　這好事終在。
一句句唱了，
　須管教伊喝采。」
那紅娘道「張先生，
　快道來。」

（喬合笙）
休將閑事苦縈懷,和「哩哩囉。哩哩囉。哩哩來也。」
取次摧殘天賦才。和
不意當初完妾命，和
豈防今日作君災。和
仰酬厚德難從禮，和
謹奉新詩可當媒。和
寄語高唐休詠賦，和
今宵端的雨雲來。和
（尾）
那紅娘言「休怪。
我曾見風魔九伯、
不曾見這般個神狗乾郎在。」

生謂紅娘曰：「自向來飲食無味，今日稍飢。想夫人處必
有佳饌，煩汝敬謁，不拘多寡，以療宿飢，可乎。」

紅娘諾而往。頃而至，持美饌一盤。生舉箸而罄。

Just listen to the meaning of this poem
    as I slowly unpack it for you.
Who would have expected that her
    hard heart would be the first to change?
I suppose I
    have not been hurt by her
        in vain.

Bear with me, Sister Crimson,
It's because I was unyielding in the beginning
    that this fine event will now happen.
After each line that I sing
    I ask you to weigh in with your harmony."
Crimson said, "Mister Zhang,
    bring it on!"
Clever Harmonizing
"Don't let vague apprehensions turn your feelings bitter, (*lililuo*
    lililuo lililai ye)
Or destroy your Heaven-bestowed talent; (*lililuo lililuo lililai ye*)
You wanted to save my life to start with, (*lililuo lililuo lililai ye*)
How could I let it turn into disaster now? (*lililuo lililuo lililai ye*)
When repaying such deep virtue, it's hard to observe the rites,
    (*lililuo lililuo lililai ye*)
So I respectfully offer up this poem as our matchmaker. (*lililuo*
    lililuo lililai ye)
I have sent my words to Gaotang, don't make any rhapsodies,
    (*lililuo lililuo lililai ye*)
For tonight, truly, the clouds and rain will pay a visit. (*lililuo lililuo*
    lililai ye)"

Coda
Crimson said, "Don't blame me, but,
While I've seen some loonies in my time,
I've never seen a fool's fool like you before!"

The student told Crimson, "Food didn't sound tempting before, but
I'm a little hungry now. There must be some good food at Madam
Cui's place. Could I ask you to bring me a little to assuage my hunger?"

紅娘曰：「吃得作得，信不誣矣。」

^{iii.43/v.18}
^{iii.33/v.8}中呂調（碧牡丹）

> 小詩便是得效藥。
> 讀罷頓然痊較。
> 入時衣袂，
> 　脫體別穿一套。
> 煞懶懶做些蜷軀老。
> 問紅娘道。
> 「韻那不韻，
> 　俏那不俏。」
>
> 鏡兒裏不住照。
> 把鬢鬏掠了重掠。
> 口兒裏不住，
> 　只管吃地忽哨。
> 九伯了多時，
> 不覺的高聲道。
> 「呀囉曰齋時
> 　啞曰轉角。
> 啞曰西落。」

吳道子手段。

（尾）

> 紅娘覷了吃地笑。
> 俺骨子不曾移動腳。
> 這急性的郎君三休飯飽。

生贈金釵一隻而囑曰：「今夕不來，願相期於地下。」紅
娘謝生而歸。生送至階下，再三叮囑。

^{iii.44/v.19}
^{iii.33/v.8}仙呂調（勝葫蘆）

> 送下階來欲待別。

Crimson assented and went off. She was back shortly with a plate of fine food. The student raised his chopsticks and immediately finished it off.

Crimson remarked, "It's no lie—if you can eat, you can do anything."

iii.43/v.18 Zhonglü Diao Mode

Blue-Green Peony
That little poem was an efficacious medicine
And when he was done reading, he was suddenly cured.
He donned a fresh set
        of stylish clothes,
Then he twisted and turned, contorting his body,
And asked Crimson,
    "Is this elegant enough, do you think?
        Is it smart enough or not?"

He kept looking at himself in the mirror,
Smoothing his sideburns again and again.
And from his mouth
        came a persistent low whistle.
He had carried on crazily for a long time
        when he suddenly shouted,
"Oh, it's time for the daily meal!
        Ah, the sun has turned the corner of the building,
And oh, there's the sun setting in the west!" [54]

Coda
Crimson looked at him and sniggered,
"Before I have time to take a single step,
This impatient fellow has already downed three meals."

This is the way Wu Daozi dealt with things. [By getting rid of things he didn't like.]

He gave her a golden hairpin and warned her, "If she doesn't come tonight, we will have a date in the underworld."

Crimson thanked him and headed back. He went with her as far as the stairs and pleaded with her several more times.

iii.44/v.19 Xianlü Diao Mode

The Winning Gourd
He accompanied her down the steps and was about to part

---

54 Wu Daozi 吳道子, or Wu Daoxuan 吳道玄 (680–759), was a renowned painter.

又囑付兩三歇。

「待好事成合後別繳謝。

把目前已往，

　為他醃苦，

　　都對着那人說。

生死存亡在今夜。

不是我佯呆。

待有一句兒虛脾天地折。

是必你叮嚀囑付，

　你那可人的姐姐。

教今夜早來些。」

（尾）

　去了紅娘歸書捨。

　坐不定何曾寧貼。

　倚門專待西廂月。

是夜玉宇無塵，

銀河瀉露。

月華鋪地，

愈增詩客之吟，

花氣薰人，

欲破禪僧之定。

人間長夜靜復靜，

天上美人來不來。

生專待。

鼓已三交，

鶯無一耗。

iii.45/v.20 仙呂調（賞花時）
iii.33/v.8

　倚定門兒手托腮。

　悶答孩地愁滿懷。

　不免入書齋。

Then pleaded with her several times.
"When this wonderful affair succeeds, there will be other rewards.
Give her a full account
    of all my suffering and sorrows
        from the very beginning up to now.

Life and death, being and extinction, all hang in the balance tonight.
I'm not just pretending to be crazy,
And if one sentence be a lie, may heaven and earth be sundered.
You must entreat, implore, plead with
    that sweet little sister of yours
To get here as early as possible tonight!"

Coda
He went back to his study after Crimson left
But couldn't sit still, finding himself in constant motion.
Then, leaning against the door, he waited for the moon of the
    western wing.

    Not a speck of dust in the jade empyrean tonight:
    the Silver River[55] leaked drops of dew.
    Moon glow spread over the ground,
    providing fodder for the chants of poetic travelers.
    The fragrance of flowers saturated a person
    enough to break the concentration of a Chan monk.
    In the human world, the night was silent beyond silence,
    and in Heaven above, would such a beauty decide to come?
    The student concentrated on waiting.
    The drum sounded three times,
    but not a whisper of an oriole.

iii.45/v.20 Xianlü Diao Mode

Time to Enjoy the Flowers
He leaned firmly against the door, chin in hand,
As sorrow filled his bosom with gloom.
He had no choice but to go back into the study.

55 The Milky Way.

儻還負約，
　今夜好難捱。

此一番音耗
自是中間節
奏處。若鶯
立時便到則
太興盡矣。

悶損多情的張秀才。
忽聽得櫳門兒啞地開。
急把眼兒揩。
見紅娘斂袂，
　傳示解元咳。

（尾）
　「莫縈心且暫停寧耐。
　略時間且向書幃裏待。
　教先生休怪。
　等夫人燒罷夜香來。」

生隱幾小眠，有人覺之曰：「織女降矣，尚耽春睡。」生
驚視之，紅娘抱衾攜枕而至，謂生曰：「至矣。至矣。」
生出戶迎鶯，但見欲行欲止，半笑半嬌。生就而撫之，翻
然背面。

iii.46/v.21 大石調（玉翼蟬）
iii.33/v.8
　多嬌女，
　　映月來，
　　　結束得極如法。
　着一套衣服，
　　偏宜恁淡淨，
　　　烏雲軃玉簪斜插。
　好嬌姹。
　腳兒小，
　　羅襪薄，

"If she fails to keep this tryst,
      this will be a hard night to get through."

The depressed young Scholar Zhang, so full of passion,
Suddenly heard the door creak open
And quickly rubbed his eyes
And saw Crimson gathering her sleeves up to bow
      and signaling the scholar with a cough.

The news this time is delivered naturally at a medium tempo. If Oriole were suddenly to be there, then it would cause a loss of interest.

Coda
"Don't obsess. Just relax a bit for the time being.
Kill some time by waiting in your study.
She asks you not to take it amiss,
For she will come as soon as Madam Cui burns her incense
      tonight."[56]

The student was napping on his armrest when someone woke him up, crying, "The Weaving Girl has descended from the sky, and you're still stuck in your spring sleep!" Startled, the student looked, and saw it was Crimson bringing quilts and a pillow.

"She's coming, she's coming," she told the student.

He went out of the door to greet Oriole and saw that, while she wanted to walk toward him, she half-wanted to stop, smiling and bashful at the same time. He went to her and embraced her, as she turned her back to him.

iii.46/v.21 Dashi Diao Mode

A Jade-Winged Cicada
A beautiful girl
      reflected in the moonlight
            and dressed just right,
Wearing an ensemble
      perfect for such pale purity.
            Her loose cloud of raven hair was held at an angle by
                  jade pins.
How alluring!
Her feet were so small

56 She is praying to the full moon on the night of the fifteenth.

疑把金蓮撒。
更舉止輕盈，
　　諸餘裏又稔膩，
　　　　天生萬般溫雅。

甫能相見，
　　僻着個龐兒那下。
儘人問當，
　　佯羞不答。
萬般哀告，
　　手摸着裙腰兒做勢煞。
您不偢人，
　　俺怎敢嗔他。
自來不曾，
　　虧伊半恰。
薄情的媽媽，
　　被你刁鐙得人來，
實志地咱。

夜半紅娘擁抱來，脈脈驚魂若春夢。

_{iii.47/v.22} 大石調（洞仙歌[12]）
_{iii.33/v.8}
　　青春年少，
　　　　一對兒風流種。
　　恰似嬌鸞配雛鳳。
　　把腰兒抱定，
　　　　擁入書齋，
　　　　　道：「我女兒
　　　　　　休恁人前莊重。」

　　哄他半晌，
　　　　獨自疑春夢。
　　燈下偎香恣憐寵。
　　拍惜了一頓，
　　　　嗚咂了多時。

and her stockings so thin
        that one could think she was scattering golden lotuses.
Her movements were light and quick
    and all else was exquisite beauty,
        endless varieties of natural gentle grace.

She had barely seen him
    when she turned her face away.
No matter how much he asked her,
    she feigned embarrassment and would not respond.
He pleaded with her over and over,
    but she simply struck a pose with hands on hips.
"You ignore me,
    but how can I be angry?
I have never
    harmed you in the slightest.
You heartless mama!⁵⁷
    I've played the fool for you,
        sure and true."

Crimson delivered her at midnight.
Without a word, she startled his soul like a spring dream.

iii.47/v.22 Dashi Diao Mode

Song of Immortals in a Cavern
They were both young,
    a perfect pair of romantic karmic seeds—
It was as if a beautiful simurgh had mated with a fledgling phoenix.
He held her waist tight
    and guided her into his study,
        saying, "My girl
            don't put on such serious airs with me."

He tried to soothe her for a bit,
    but still felt it was all just a dream.
There, beneath the lamp, he gave himself free rein as he held
    onto her fragrance.
He caressed her with affection
    and kissed her for a long time.

---

57 A term of endearment for one's wife.
58 These lines are directly quoted from the original "Tale of Yingying."

緊抱着噇，
那孩兒不動。
更有甚功夫脫衣裳，
　便得個胸前，
　　把奶兒摩弄。

羞顏慵怯，力不能運肢體。曩時之端莊，不復同矣。張生
飄然，一旦疑神仙中人，不謂從人間至矣。

iii.48/v.23 中呂調（千秋節）
iii.33/v.8
　　良宵夜暖。
　　高把銀缸點。
　　雛鸞嬌鳳乍相見。
　　窄弓弓羅襪兒翻。
　　紅馥馥地花心，
　　　我可曾慣。
　　百般攔就十分閃。

　　忍痛處，
　　　修眉斂。
　　意就人，
　　　嬌聲戰。
　　浣[13]香汗。
　　流粉面。
　　　紅妝皺也嬌嬌羞，
　　　　腰肢困也微微喘。

月傳銀漏和更長，
郎抱鶯娘送舌香。

He held her tight and brushed her face with his lips.
Young Oriole didn't move a muscle.
There was no time to remove her clothes—
    he quickly found her breasts
        and began to stroke them.

> Embarrassed and timid, she could not move her limbs. The serious airs
> of former times would never be the same. Student Zhang was transport-
> ed, suspecting all morning that she was a divine being, not someone
> one would say was from the human world."[58]

iii.48/v.23 Zhonglü Diao Mode

Tang Xuanzong's Birthday Song
A fine night, one of warmth.
They lit the lamp high on its silver stand,
And the fledgling simurgh and charming phoenix were revealed to
    one another.
Over the raised arches of her bound feet, he unrolled her silk
    stockings
To uncover the trembling heart of her red and fragrant flower—
    "I've never done this."[59]
A hundred ways he tried to soothe her, and she dodged them all.

But, finally bearing the pain
    she drew her brows together.
And when she gave herself to him,
    she trembled as she moaned with pleasure.
She was bathed in a fragrant sweat
    that streamed over her powdered face,
Her red makeup now smeared; she was bashfully affectionate.
    Her body was tired, and she panted lightly.

> The moonlight carried the sound of a silver water clock, and the night
>   lengthened
> As the young man held Oriole and delivered a clove to her with his
>   tongue.

---

59 It is unclear here to whom the pronoun "I" refers to in this line. DJY06, 222 takes it
to refer to Oriole; DJY 07, 148, to Student Zhang; DJY, 293 and DJY08, 268 leave it
ambiguous.

一宵之事，張生如登霄漢，身赴蓬宮。

iii.49/v.24 仙呂調（臨江仙）
iii.33/v.8

　　　燕爾新婚方美滿，
　　　愁聞蕭寺疏鐘。
　　　紅娘催起笑芙蓉。
　　　巫姬雲雨散，
　　　宋玉枕衾空。

　　　執手欲言容易別，
　　　新愁舊恨無窮。
　　　素娥已返水晶宮。
　　　半窗千里月，
　　　　一枕五更風。

　　　怎見得有如此事來。有唐元微之《鶯鶯傳》為證：
　　　「紅娘捧鶯而去，終夕無一言。張生辨色而興，自疑於心曰：
　　　『豈其夢耶。豈其夢耶。』所可明者。妝在臂，香在衣，淚光
　　　熒熒然猶瑩於衽席布而已。」

iii.50/v.25 羽調（混江龍）
iii.33/v.8

　　　兩情方美，
　　　　斷腸無奈曉樓鐘。
　　　臨時去幽情脈脈，
　　　　別恨匆匆。
　　　洛浦人歸天漸曉，

For Student Zhang, the whole night had felt as if he had ascended to the Milky Way, and that his body had raced to the Palace of the Immortals.

iii.49/v.24 Xianlü Diao Mode

Approaching the River Sylph
The wedding night had just ended perfectly for the couple
    when, sadly, they heard the well-spaced knell of the
        monastery bell.
Crimson urged Oriole to rise, and she smiled like a hibiscus
    opening to the sun.
Then, gone were the clouds and rains of the goddess
    leaving Song Yu's pillow and quilt empty.

Holding hands, wanting to speak—this was no easy parting,
    and new sorrow, like old regrets, seemed unending.
Chang'e returned to her Crystal Palace—[60]
The distant moon halfway down the window,
    a single pillow, and the fifth watch breeze.[61]

And how do I know this happened? There is Yuan Zhen's "Tale of Oriole" as proof:

"Crimson took Oriole back, and she was silent that whole evening.

Student Zhang arose as soon as it was light enough to see. He was still half in doubt: 'Was it a dream? Just a dream?' But what clarified things were her makeup on his arm, her fragrance on his clothes, and the glistening radiance of tears lingering on his bed."

iii.50/v.25 Yu Diao Mode

Dragon that Muddies the River (Dredge)
Their passions had just reached a climax,
    when, alas, that heart-rending morning bell sounded.
Separation approached as their secret passions pulsed and
    throbbed,
        the vexation of parting harried them.
The Goddess of the Luo River went back, the sky gradually grew
    light,

60 Alluding to the fact Oriole is still dressed in white mourning garments.
61 The fifth watch ends at 5:00 a.m.

楚台雲斷夢無蹤。
空回首，
　閒愁與悶，
　　應滿東風。

起來搔首，
　數竿紅日上簾櫳。
猶疑慮。
實曾相見，
　是夢裏相逢。
卻有印臂的殘紅香馥馥，
　偎人的粉汗尚融融。
鴛衾底，
　尚有三點、
　　兩點兒紅。

生取紙筆，遂寫詞二首。詞畢，又賦《會真詩》三十韻。

iii.51/v.26 仙呂調（朝天急）
iii.33/v.8
錦箋和淚痕，
　一齊封了。
欲把鶯鶯今夜約。
殷勤把紅娘告。
「休推托
　專專付與多嬌。
姐姐便不
　可憐見不肖。
更做於人情分薄。
思量俺日前，

the clouds of Chu's Terrace disappeared, and the dream left
    no trace behind.[62]
He looked back to no avail,
    as pointless sorrow
        filled the eastern wind.

He rose and scratched his head,
    the red sun rising high in the curtained window.
He still doubts—
    had he really experienced it
        or had he met her in dream?
Still, a smudge of fragrant red was stamped on his arm, and
    the powdery sweat from their embrace was still warm,
And, beneath the mandarin duck quilt
    there remained
        two or three droplets of red.

Zhang took up paper and brush and wrote two lyric poems. Then he
composed "A Poem of Encountering the True One," in thirty rhymes.

iii.51/v.26 Xianlü Diao Mode

Worried About Seeing the Emperor
The patterned stationery and the streaks of his tears
    were sealed up together.
Wanting to meet Oriole that night,
He eagerly beseeched Crimson,
"Don't make excuses,
    just turn this over to my charming one.

Even if Sister Oriole
    merely looks upon this unworthy one with pity,
Even if she really has no feelings for me,
She should think of what I did before—

---

62 Fu Fei 宓妃, the daughter of the mythical Fu Xi 伏羲, drowned in the Luo River 洛
河, and became the "spirit of the Luo" (*Luoshen* 洛神). Chu Terrace refers to the
legend of the King of Chu, who roamed on Gaotang, and fell asleep there. While
asleep he was visited by a deity who proffered a mat, shared it with him, then said as
she left, "I reside on the sunny side of Shamanka Mountain, on the perilous peaks. At
the break of day I am the morning clouds and at the end of daylight I am the driving
rain. Morning after morning, evening after evening I am on Sun Terrace."

　　　恩非小。
　今夕是他不錯。

　　　道與冤家休負約。
　　　莫忘了。
　　　如把濃歡容易抛。
　　　是咱無分消。
　　　你莫辭勞。
　　　若見如花貌。
　　　一星星但言我道。」

（尾）
　　　「我眼巴巴的盼今宵。
　　　還二更左右不來到。
　　　您且聽着。
韻語。　隄防牆上杏花搖。」

　　紅娘歸，以詩詞授鶯。鶯看之，愈喜愈愛。詞曰：

　　　司馬傷春候，
　　　　文君多病時。
　　　殘紅簌簌褪胭脂，
　　　恰恰流鶯，
　　　　催日上花枝。

　　　釋悶琴三弄，
　　　　消愁酒一巵。
　　　此時無以說相思，
　　　　綵筆傳情，
　　　聊賦會真詩。

　　右調《南柯子》。又詞曰：

that was no little act of kindness.
Tonight, it is she who must make the right judgment.

Tell that little enemy of mine, 'Don't betray the tryst
    and don't forget.'
If she can so easily cast away this intense pleasure,
Then it is not my lot in life to enjoy it.
Don't say it's too much trouble.
And when you see that face like a flower,
    repeat to her every single word I have spoken.

Coda
"I will keep my eyes wide open for tonight.
And if she's not here sometime around the second watch,
   Then you start listening
   And prepare for the apricot branches beyond the wall to shake."

The last line of the coda is very refined.

Crimson went back and gave Oriole the poem and the lyrics. Oriole
read them, growing happier and more in love. The lyrics read:

The coming end of spring pained Sima Xiangru,
    and troubled Zhuo Wenjun as well.
Tattered red rustles, now the color of fading rouge,
While a warbling, flitting Oriole
    rose to a flowering branch to urge on the morning sun.

Three tunes on the zither to relieve my depression,
    and a flagon of wine to dissolve my sorrow.
Now with nothing else at hand to explain love's longing,
    and with my brush of many colors to speak for my passion,
I casually compose the poem "On Meeting a Transcendent Being."

That lyric above is to the pattern "Southern Branch." The second lyric
reads:

雲雨事，
　都向會真誇。
麝墨輕磨聲韻玉，
兔毫初點色翻鴉，
書破錦箋花。

詩句麗，
　造化窟中挐。
俊逸參軍非足羨，
清新開府未才華，
寄與謝娘家。
詩曰：

微月透簾櫳，
螢光度碧空。
遙天初縹緲，
低樹漸蔥蘢。
龍吹過庭竹，
鸞歌拂井桐。
羅綃垂薄霧，
環佩響輕風。
絳節隨金母，
雲心捧玉童。
更深人悄悄，
晨會雨濛濛。
珠耿光文履，
花明隱繡龍。
寶釵行彩鳳，
羅帳掩丹虹。
言自瑤華圃，
將朝碧玉宮。

Our congress of clouds and rain,
    shall be amplified in "On Meeting a Transcendent Being."
In ink of musk lightly ground are tones and rhymes of jade;
Where the rabbit down first touches, the color turns raven black,
And my calligraphy crushes paper's embossed flowers.

The poetic lines are beautiful,
    stolen from the cave of the Shaper of Things.
The handsome, poised Canjun[63] is unworthy of praise,
  The fresh Kaifu[64] falls short of his brilliant genius;
  I send this now to the house of Miss Xie.[65]

The poem read:

A faint moon filters through the doorway curtains,
Flickers of fireflies transit to the azure void;
The distant heavens are dimly seen at first;
Little by little, low trees gain lush definition.
Dragon puffs pass through courtyard bamboos,
Simurgh songs brush the paulownia trees by the well;[66]
Her fine silk suspends a thin mist,
And belt pendants tinkle in the light wind.
Crimson tallies follow the Golden Mother, and the cloud's heart sur-
    rounds the Jade Lad; [67]
As the watch deepens, people fall quiet, and at morning's return she
    meets the misty rain.
Bright gems shone on patterned shoes,
Vivid flowers obscured embroidered dragons,
A precious hairpin set a colored phoenix flying,
A silk curtain covered a vermillion rainbow;[68]
He says, "From the Arbor of Jade Flowers,
I was going to morning court at the Palace of Azure Jade,

---

63 A title of Bao Zhao 鮑照 (414–466, byname Mingyuan 明遠), a prolific writer of poetry and rhapsodies, best known for his "Rhapsody on the Ruined City" 蕪城賦.
64 A title held by Yu Xin 庾信 (513–581, byname Zishan 子山), also a master of the rhapsody form.
65 Xie Daoyun 謝道韞 (ca. 340–400, byname Lingjiang 令姜) was a talented poet and scholar; by analogy, a female literary genius.
66 Describing the sound of the wind in bamboo, and the rustling of leaves sounding like a song.
67 Oriole is trailed by Crimson and attended by her young brother.
68 A silken veil over her face.

因游洛城北，
偶向宋家東。
戲調初微拒，
柔情已暗通。
低鬢蟬影動，
回步玉塵蒙。
轉面流花雪，
登床抱綺叢。
鴛鴦交頸舞，
翡翠合歡籠。
眉黛羞偏聚，
唇朱暖更融。
氣清蘭芷馥，
膚潤玉肌豐。
無力慵移履，
多嬌愛斂躬。
汗光珠點點，
髮亂綠鬆鬆。
方喜千年會，
俄聞五夜窮。
留連時有限，
繾綣意難終。
慢臉含愁態，
芳詞誓素衷。
贈環明運合，
留結表心同。
啼粉流清鏡，
殘爐遶暗銅。
華光猶冉冉，
旭日漸曈曈。
乘鶩還歸洛，
吹簫亦上嵩。
衣香猶染麝，
粉膩尚殘紅。

Because I roamed north of Luo City,
By chance I went toward Song Yu's eastern neighbor."[69]
Though teasing flirtation was thwarted at first,
Her pliable passions were already silently conveyed.
Her loose chignon, the movement of a cicada's shadow,
Her returning steps imprinted in dust of jade;[70]
Turning her face, she let flow a flurry of flowers,
Mounting the bed she clutched folds of silk,
And we sported there as mandarin ducks,
Necks entwined, halcyon jade in a cage of our union's pleasure.
The kohl of her eyebrows knitted in embarrassment,
The vermeil of her lips warmed and melted,
And her breath was pure with the fragrance of orchid,
Her skin lustrous, her flesh firm as jade.
Exhausted, she lazily shifted her sandals.
So delicate, she loved to spoon,
Glistening sweat, gem drop by gem drop,
Her hair was mussed, a freely tangled black.
As we enjoyed this rare meeting to the fullest,
Suddenly we heard the fifth night watch run its course.
We dallied, though time was limited,
Entangled there by a passion hard to end.
A tinge of dolor on her languorous face,
With fragrant words she pledged unending love,
Bestowed a ring to promise reunions,
And left a corded knot to symbolize hearts entwined.
Powder from weeping flowed over the clear mirror,
The lamp's last light circled the dark bronze,
And as its brilliance was still fading away,
The rising sun gradually began to brighten.
Riding a wild duck, one returned to the Luo River;
Playing his pipes, the other ascended Mount Song.
His clothes were fragrant, still dyed by her musk,
Powdery rouge still stained red.

---

69 He was originally going to the Buddha Hall but stumbled into the western wing. The idiom comes originally from Song Yu's "Rhapsody on the Lecher Deng Tuzi," which relates how Song Yu showed no interest in a beautiful girl next door, even when she climbed on the wall separating their households to be admired. Song Yu paid no attention to her for three years. Junrui, of course, did precisely what Song Yu did not.

70 Signifying hesitation.

幕幕臨塘草，

飄飄思渚蓬。

素琴鳴怨鶴，

晴漢望驚鴻。

海闊誠難度，

天高不易衝。

行雲無處所，

蕭史在樓中。

鶯鶯異之。索箋擬和，佇思久之，閣筆不下，擲筆自笑

曰：「才不逮於郎矣。」

iii.52/v.27 大石調（吳音子）
iii.33/v.8

鶯鶯從頭讀罷，

縮首頓稱賞。

「此詩此韻，

若非神助便休想。

着甚才學，

和您文章。

休強。

休強。

果非常。

做得個詩陣令騷壇將。

收拾雲雨，

為郎今夜更相訪。

消得一人，

因君狂蕩。

不枉。

不枉。

（尾）

豈止風流好模樣。

The grass[71] teems thick at the pond's edge,
Rolling and turning, the tumbleweed[72] longs for a sandy spit.
A plain zither gives voice to a resentful crane,
Toward the clear Han[73] she gazes long, awaiting the startled swan.
The sea is wide and truly hard to transit,
The heavens are high and not easy to reach.
Traveling clouds[74] remain nowhere,
But Xiao Shi is in his loft.

Oriole marveled at the poem and took up a piece of stationery with
the intention of writing a response. She thought for a long time but
couldn't even start. She put her brush down and laughed, "I am just
not as talented as he is."

iii.52/v.27 Dashi Diao Mode

Sounds of Wu
After Oriole finished reading it from the top,
     she lowered her head and praised it over and over.
"This poem, these rhymes,
     would be impossible without divine help!
What talent would it take
     to respond to his verse?
I won't even try!
I won't even try!

Truly he is extraordinary,
**He's the commander of a poetic brigade, the leader of a circle
     of poets.**
Let me get the clouds and rain ready
     for I will visit this gentleman again tonight.
And I alone will enjoy
     my man's wild lack of restraint.
It's worth it!
Worth it!

Coda
He's not just romantic and handsome,

71 Her heartfelt thoughts.
72 The roaming man.
73 That is, the Milky Way
74 The goddess who moves in the clouds.

更一段兒怎錦繡心腸。

道個甚教人看不上。

次夜，張生啓門伺鶯，多時方至。

似姮娥離月殿，

如王母下瑤台。

iii.53/v.28 正宮（梁州纏令）
iii.33/v.8

玉漏迢迢二鼓過。

月上庭柯。

碧天空闊鏡銅磨。

啞地聽，

櫳門兒響，

見巫娥。

對郎羞懶無那。

靠人先要偎摩。

寶髻挽青螺。

臉蓮香傳，

說不得媚多。

（應天長）

欲言羞懶顫。

多時方語，

低謂「粉郎呵。

鶯鶯的祖宗你知麼。

家風清白，

全不類其他。

鶯鶯是閨內的女，

服母訓怎敢如何。

不意哥哥因妾病，

憫憫地染沈痾。

兩低語入
情。

But also blessed with a talented heart and mind—[75]
Is there anything not to admire?"

The next night Student Zhang opened the door to wait for Oriole. After a long time, she finally arrived.

She was like Chang'e leaving the moon palace,
Like the Queen Mother descending from her jasper terrace.

iii.53/v.28 Zheng Gong Mode

Liang Prefecture: A Bound Suite
The jade water clock dripped on and on until the second drum
    had passed
And the moon had climbed the branches of the courtyard trees.
The azure sky stretched empty and wide—the moon was a
    bright, clean mirror.
He heard a creak—
    the door made a sound
        and there appeared the goddess.

She was shy and languid in response to the student,
Leaning against him, first desiring to cuddle.
Her bun was coiled like a green sea-snail shell,
Her face gave off perfume of lotus—
    indescribable beauty and charm.

Responding to Lengthening Days
Wanting to talk, shy and trembling, her voice quaked,
But finally, she was able to speak,
    softly saying, "My beloved,
Do you know who my ancestors are?
The spotless purity of our family tradition
    is completely different from all others.
I was a virgin from the maiden's quarters,
    and never dared deviate from my mother's teachings.
I never expected you would fall ill because of me
    and be stricken with such a wasting affliction.

Entering into passion through two softly spoken sentences.

---

75 Literally, "a heart and mind of brocade and embroidery."

思量都為我咱呵。
肌膚消瘦，
　瘦得渾似削，
　　百般醫療終難可。
鶯鶯不忍，
　以此背婆婆。
婆婆知道除會聖，
　雲雨怎得成合。
異日休要逢別的，
　更不管負人呵。」

（甘草子）
　「聽說破。
聽說破。」
張生低告道
　「姐姐言語錯。
　休恁廝埋怨，
休恁廝奚落。
　張珙殊無潘沈才，
輒把梅犀玷污。
　負心的神天放不過，
休麼奴哥。」

（梁州三台）
　鶯鶯色事，
　　尚兀自不慣，
　　　羅衣向人羞脫。
抱來懷裏惜多時，
　貪歡處嗚損臉窩。
辦得個嗽着摸着。
偎着抱着。
輕憐痛惜一和。
恣恣地覷了可喜冤家，
　忍不得恣情嗚喊。

And when I consider that it was all because of me!
Your flesh and muscle grew thin,
  just as if pared away—
    and no treatment could cure it.
I could not bear it
  and so, I turned my back on mother.
Should she have known—unless there was some miracle—
  our union could never have come to pass.
In the days to come, don't find another,
  and what's more, don't be a fickle-hearted lover."

Dried Licorice Root
"Listen now,
Listen now,"
Student Zhang told her softly,
  "You are wrong to say all this.
Don't complain
  and accuse me like this.
I, Zhang Gong, don't have the talent of a Pan An or Shen Yue,
  who could freely sully the petals of any old plum blossom.[76]
Heaven never lets a fickle lover get off free—
  does that put an end to it, lover?"

Liang Prefecture: Three Terraces
Uninitiated in the ways of sex, Oriole
  was still unaccustomed
    and embarrassed to remove her silken clothes in front
      of him.
He embraced her and caressed her a long while,
  but as passion rose, he kissed her dimpled face.
They kissed, they fondled,
They embraced, they held each other in their arms.
With tender love and heartfelt affection, together as one—
After looking at his lovable enemy, without restraint
  he let his passion loose and kissed her with abandon.

This describes the emotional expressiveness of a girl on her first sexual encounter. But this is the second night. It would have been perfect if used on the first night.

76 To engage in casual sexual relations.

（尾）

鶯鶯色膽些來大。
不慣與張生做快活。
那孩兒怕子個怯子個閃子個。

iii.54/v.29
iii.33/v.8 仙呂調（點絳唇纏令）

殢雨尤雲，
　靠人緊把腰兒貼。
顫聲不徹。
肯放郎教歇。

檀口微微，
　笑吐丁香舌。
噴龍麝。
　被郎輕嚙。
卻更嗔人劣。

（風吹荷葉）

只被你個多情姐。
噉得人困也怕也。
痛憐嗚損胭脂頰。
香噴噴地，
軟柔柔地，
酥胸如雪。

（醉奚婆）

歡情未絕。
願永遠如今夜。
銀台畫燭，
笑遣郎吹滅。

（尾）

並頭兒眠，
　低聲兒說。
　夜靜也無人窺竊。
有幽窗花影西樓月。

Coda
Oriole became a little braver.
But, still not used to pleasure with the student,
The girl was still trepidatious and dodged his every move.

iii.54/v.29 Xianlü Diao Mode

Dotting Crimson Lips: A Bound Suite
Lost in heavy rain and dense clouds
    they leaned against each other, waist pressed to waist.
Her trembling voice murmuring on and on,
She willingly let him proceed without cease.

Her sandalwood-scented lips opened slightly
    and with a smile she stuck out her clove of a tongue
And exhaled the scent of musk.
He lightly nibbled at it
But was chided again for being mischievous.

Wind Blows the Lotus Leaves
She was so deeply passionate
That he kissed and kissed until, worn out, he was afraid to go on.
He lovingly nibbled at her rouged cheeks until her makeup was
    ruined.
Exuding a perfumed scent,
    soft and pliant,
        her creamy breasts were white as snow.

Drunken Mama Xi
Their loving passion yet unbroken,
They wanted eternity to be like this night.
With a smile she sent him to blow out
    the patterned candle on its silver stand.

Coda
They slept together with heads touching
    and spoke in soft voices.
The night was still, there was no one to spy on them—
A darkened window, shadows of flowers, and the moon in the
    western loft.

　　　　　紅娘至，促曰：「天色曙矣。」

iii.55/vi.1 仙呂調（戀香衾）
iii.33/v.8
　　　　　一夕幽歡信無價。
　　　　　紅娘萬驚千怕。
　　　　　且恐夫人
　　　　　　　暗中知察。
　　　　　暫不多時雲雨罷。
　　　　　紅娘催定如花。
　　　　　把天般恩愛，
　　　　　　　變成瀟灑。

　　　　　君瑞鶯鶯越偲的緊，
　　　　　紅娘道：「起來麼娘呵。」
　　　　　戴了冠兒把玉簪斜插。
　　　　　欲別張生臨去也，
　　　　　　　偲人懶兜羅襪。
　　　　　「我而今且去，
　　　　　　　明夜來呵。」

　　　　（尾）
留連往復。
　　　　　懶別設的把金蓮撒。
　　　　　行不到書窗真下。
　　　　　兜地回來又說些兒話。

　　　　　自是朝隱而出，暮隱而入，幾半年矣。夫人見鶯容麗倍
　　　　　常，精神增媚，甚起疑心。夫人自思，「必是張生私成暗
　　　　　約。」

iii.56/vi.2 雙調（倬倬戚）
iii.33/v.8
　　　　　相國夫人自竇約。
　　　　　「是則是這冤家沒彈抱[14]。

Crimson arrived to hurry them, "It's getting light outside."

iii.55/vi.1 Xianlü Diao Mode

Quilt with the Fragrance of Love
A night of secret love is surely priceless,
But Crimson was alarmed and apprehensive,
Fearful that Madam Cui would surreptitiously find out.
In no time at all, the storm of rain and clouds had passed
And Crimson urged the one like a flower to go back.
Their blissful love and affection
    turned to somber sadness.

Junrui and Oriole held each other tighter
As Crimson said, "Get up, girl!"
Crimson put on Oriole's cap and pushed the jade hairpin in.
About to leave the student, on the verge of going
Oriole held him close, **then half-heartedly pulled on her silk**
    stockings.
"I'm leaving now for a while,
    but I will come again tomorrow night."

Coda
Reluctantly she pushed her golden lotuses into her sandals,[77]
But had yet to reach the study window
When, suddenly, she returned to say something else to him.

Reluctant to part, she goes and then returns.

For nearly half a year she would leave him secretly every morning and return secretly every night. Seeing how Oriole's face seemed more beautiful, and she was growing even more spirited and charming, Madam Cui began to suspect something.

She thought to herself, "It must be that Student Zhang has secretly brought off a tryst."

iii.56/vi.2 Shuang Diao Mode

Boundless Sorrow
The Wife of the Minister of State figured it out on her own.
"It's a fact that this little lover has been faultless in the past,

---

77 An alternate understanding of this line would be, "Reluctantly she set her golden lotuses into motion."

陡恁地精神偏出跳。
轉添嬌。
渾不似，
　　舊時了。
舊日做下的衣服件件小。

眼慢眉低胸乳高。
管有兀誰廝搬着[15]。
我團着。
這妮子
　　做破大手腳。」

鶯以情繫心，戀戀不已。夫人察之，是夕私往。

iii.57/vi.3 大石調（紅羅襖）
iii.33/v.8
　　　君瑞與鶯鶯，
　　　　來往半年過。
　　夜夜偷期不相度。
　　沒些兒斟量，
　　　沒些兒懼憚，
　　　　做得過火。
　　鶯鶯色事迷心，
　　　　是夜又離香閣。
　　方信樂極悲來，
　　　　怎知覺，
　　　　　若場天來大禍。

　　那積世的老婆婆。
　　其時暗猜破。
　　高點着銀缸堂上坐。
　　問侍婢以來，
　　　兢兢戰戰，
　　　　一地裡篤麼。
　　問：「鶯鶯更夜如何背游，
　　　私地有誰存活。」
　　諸侍婢莫敢形言，

But why is her spirit so much more alive?
And why even more charming?
It's so unlike the way
    she acted in the past.
The clothes we made before are all too tight,

Her eyes are tired, her brows droop, and her breasts are fuller.
Who is it who seduced her?
I bet it's that little wench
    who has urged *that* cat out of the bag."

Oriole, smitten with passion, had only love on her mind. Madam Cui
had noticed this and stealthily went out one evening.

iii.57/vi.3 Dashi Diao Mode

Red Silk Padded Jacket
Junrui and Oriole
    had been carrying on for half a year or more,
Meeting night after night, oblivious to everything.
They gave it not the slightest thought,
    felt not the smallest bit of trepidation,
        and carried on far too long.
Oriole was blinded by desire
    as she left her perfumed chambers again that night—
True indeed, "Grief comes when joy reaches its zenith!"
    How could they be aware
        of the impending scene of great disaster?

The old woman with her world of experience,
Had secretly guessed the right time.
She sat in the main hall, with lamps lit on high
And questioned all the female servants,
    who trembled and shook in fright,
        nervously shifting about.
She asked, "Why does Oriole go out late at night against my orders?
    Who keeps her company in some private place?"
None of the maidservants dared give it form in words

約多時，
　　有口渾如鎖。

（尾）
　　相國夫人高聲喝。
　「賤人每怎敢瞞我。
　　喚取紅娘來問則個。」

一女奴奔告鶯，鶯急歸。見夫人坐堂上，鶯鶯戰慄。

夫人問紅娘曰：「汝與鶯更夜何適。」

紅娘拜曰：「不敢隱匿。張生卒病，與鶯往視疾。」

夫人曰：「何不告我。」

答曰：「夫人已睡，倉猝不敢覺夫人寢。」

夫人怒曰：「猶敢妄對，必不捨汝。」

iii.58/vi.4 中呂調（牧羊關）
iii.33/v.8
　　夫人堂上高聲問。
　「為何私啟閨門。
　　你試尋思，
　　　早晚時分。
　　迤逗得鶯鶯去，
　　　推探張生病。
　　恁般閒言語，
　　　教人怎地信。

　　思量也是天教敗，
　　　算來必有私情。
　　甚不肯承當，
　　　抵死諱定。
　　只管廝瞞昧，
　　　只管廝咭哮。

and time passed—
>they had mouths, but they were locked tight.

Coda
The Wife of the Minister of State yelled,
"Good for nothings! How dare you deceive me?
Call Crimson here so I can question her myself!"

A maidservant rushed to tell Oriole, and Oriole immediately returned. Seeing her mother sitting in the hall, she began to tremble.

Madam Cui questioned Crimson, "Where did you and Oriole go tonight?"

Crimson bowed and said, "I don't dare keep you in the dark. Student Zhang was very ill, and Oriole and I went to check on his symptoms."

Madam Cui asked, "Why didn't you tell me?"

"You were already asleep," answered Crimson, "and we were in such a hurry we didn't dare wake you in your bedchamber."

Angrily, Madam Cui said, "You dare lie to me again? I won't let you get away with it."

iii.58/vi.4 Zhonglü Diao Mode

Shepherd's Pass
In the hall the mother shouted her questions:
"Why did you decide to open the boudoir door?
Think carefully now
>about what time it was
When you lured Oriole away
>on the pretext that Student Zhang was ill.
How could anyone believe
>such a meaningless lie?

On second thought, since it is Heaven that brought this destruction,
>I surmise that romance must be involved.
Why don't you take responsibility
>instead of refusing to confess?
All you do is try to hide it
>by lying to me.

好教我禁不過，
　這不良的下賤人。」

（尾）

　「思量又不當口兒穩。
　如還抵死的着言支對，
　教你手托着東牆我直打到肯。」

　　　　紅娘徐而言曰：「夫人息怒，乞申一言。」

iii.59/vi.5
iii.33/v.8
仙呂調（六么令）

　「夫人息怒，
　　聽妾話蹤由。
　不須堂上，
　　高聲揮喝罵無休。
　君瑞又多才多藝，
　　咱姐姐又風流。
　彼此無夫無婦，
　　這時分相見，
　　　夫人何必苦追求。

　一對兒佳人才子，
　　年紀又敵頭。
　經今半載，
　　雙雙每夜書幃里宿。
　已恁地出乖弄醜，
　　潑水再難收。
　夫人休出口，
　　怕旁人知道，
　　　以頭贏得自家羞。」

　　（尾）

　　「一雙兒心意兩相投，
　　夫人白甚閒疙皺。
　　休疙皺。
　　常言道『女大不中留。』」

There is no way I'm letting you off,
    you good-for-nothing little tart.

Coda
"Think about it—shouldn't you keep your mouth shut?
Because if you keep on lying to me no matter what
You'll have your hands against the eastern wall, and I'll beat you
    until you're willing to give it up!"

    Crimson spoke slowly, "Cease your anger, madam, let me say a word
    in my defense."

iii.59/vi.5 Xianlü Diao Mode

Song of a Green Waist
"Stop your rage, madam,
    and let me explain what happened.
There's no need to sit here in the hall
    shouting and yelling and cursing me no end.
Junrui is talented and artistic,
    and our sister is elegant and dashing.
Neither is married or betrothed,
    so why must you ferret everything out
        about their encounters?

They are matched as a beauty and a talented scholar,
    and are just at the perfect age.
For half a year now within the curtains of his study
    they have slept together as a couple.
They've already done the deed—
    spilled water can never be gathered back up.
So, stop bruiting it about
    lest outsiders come to know
        and you become the first to own your shame.

Coda
"A perfect pair with hearts and mind in accord,
What good is your anger?
Let your anger go.
As the proverb says, 'A daughter who is grown is not worth keeping.'

「當日亂軍屯寺，夫人、小娘子皆欲就死。張生與先相無舊，非慕鶯之顏色，欲謀親禮，豈肯區區陳退軍之策，使夫人、小娘子得有今日。事定之後，夫人以兄妹繼之，非生本心，以此成疾，幾至不起。鶯不守義而忘恩，每侍湯藥，願兄安慰。夫人聰明者，更夜幼女潛見鰥男，何必研問，是非禮也。夫人罪妾，夫人安得無咎。失治家之道。外不能報生之恩，內不能蔽鶯之醜，取笑於親戚，取謗於他人。願夫人裁之。」

紅娘可與定
大事。

夫人曰：「奈何。」

紅娘曰：「生本名家，聲動天下。論才則屢被巍科，論策則立摧凶醜，論智則坐邀大將，論恩則活我全家。君子之道，盡於是矣。若因小過，俾結良姻，通男女之真情，蔽閨門之餘醜，治家報德，兩盡美矣。」

iii.60/vi.6 般涉調（麻婆子）
iii.33/v.8
　　「君瑞又好門地，
　　　姐姐又好宗祖。
　　君瑞是尚書的子，
　　　姐姐相國的女。

"When the rebel army camped around the monastery, you and your daughter were facing death. Student Zhang had no connections with your husband. If he had not been enthralled with Oriole's beauty and had not wanted a marriage with her, then how could he have so meticulously laid out a plan to have them withdraw and keep you and your daughter alive? After the revolt was quelled, you made him part of the family, but only as an elder brother to a younger sister, and that was never what was on his mind. He became ill over the slight, nearly to the point of being bedbound. Oriole couldn't forget such a kindness and still maintain her integrity, and she hoped to soothe him with each dose of medicine. Madam, with your intelligence, there's no need to pursue the question of what happens when a young girl slips off at midnight to visit an unmarried man. Indeed, it is not proper. You can blame me, but how could you be guiltless? You have lost the right way to run a household. Outside of the household, you couldn't repay the student's kindness, inside the household, you can't conceal Oriole's unsavory behavior. You will reap the scorn of your relatives and the slander of others. I would like you to consider all this, madam."

"What's to be done?" asked Madam Cui.

Crimson truly is someone with whom one can make big decisions.

Crimson said, "The student is from a noted family whose reputation is widely known. In terms of his talent, he has always placed highest in examinations; in terms of his strategy, he quickly did away with evil; in terms of his military knowledge, he sits and receives great generals; and in terms of his acts of grace, then he has given life to your whole family. He embodies the Way of the gentleman. Should you allow them to marry in spite of his minor trespass, then you will accommodate the true feelings between a man and a woman, and you will conceal the scandal of the boudoir. You will regain control of the family and repay virtue at the same time, a perfect ending for both."

iii.60/vi.6 Banshe Diao Mode

Pockmarked Crone
"Junrui is from a good family,
       and our sister has a good lineage;
Junrui is the son of the head of the Secretariat,
       and our sister is the daughter of a Minister of State.

姐姐為人是稔色，
　　張生做事忒通疏。
姐姐有三從德，
　　張生讀萬卷書。
姐姐稍親文墨，
　　張生博通今古。

姐姐不枉做媳婦，
　　張生不枉做丈夫。
姐姐溫柔勝文君，
　　張生才調過相如。
姐姐是傾城色，
　　張生是冠世儒。」

（尾）

「着君瑞的才
　　着姐姐的福。
咱姐姐消得個夫人做。
張君瑞異日須乘駟馬車。」

夫人曰：「賢哉，紅娘之論。雖然如此，未知鶯之心下何似。恐女子之性，因循失德，實無本心。」

令紅娘召之，「我欲親問所以。」

鶯鶯羞悌而出，不敢正立。

iii.61/vi.7
iii.33/v.8
般涉調　（沁園春）
　　是夜鶯鶯夫人[16]，
　　　半晌無言，
　　　　兩眉暗鎖。
　　　多時方喚得鶯鶯至，

Our sister is a woman of beauty,
and Student Zhang knows how to get things done.
Our sister has the virtue of the Three Abidings,[78]
and Student Zhang has read ten-thousand books.

Our sister has some familiarity with writing,
and Student Zhang is highly knowledgeable about the past
and the present.
Our sister will make the perfect wife,
and Student Zhang will make the perfect husband.
Our sister is milder and more considerate than Zhuo Wenjun,
and Student Zhang more talented a writer than Sima Xiangru.
Our sister has a beauty that can topple cities,
and Student Zhang is a scholar for the ages.

Coda
"There is Junrui's talent,
and our sister's good fortune,
Our sister will certainly become a matriarch herself,
And some day to come, Zhang Junrui will be riding in a four-horse
carriage!"

Madam Cui said, "That's a worthy speech, Crimson. That all may be so, but I still don't know Oriole's mind. I worry that a young girl will simply go along with losing her virtue, without it being her own will." She sent Crimson to summon her. "I want to personally ask her what her reasons were."

Oriole emerged, embarrassed and anxious, not daring to adopt a formal posture.[79]

iii.61/vi.7 Banshe Diao Mode

Spring in the Princess's Garden
That night Madam Cui
was speechless for a long time,
her brows locked in silence.
Time dragged on before she called Oriole to her—

78 Women were expected to obey their father when young, their husband when married, and their eldest son once widowed.
79 Lest she appear defiant. Cf. DJYo8, 163.

　　羞低着粉頸，
　　　愁斂着雙蛾。
桃臉兒通紅，
　　櫻唇兒青紫，
　　　玉筍纖纖不住搓。
不忍見，
　　盈盈地粉淚，
　　　淹損鈿窩。

六十餘歲的婆婆。
　　　道「千萬擔饒我女呵。
子母腸肚終須熱。
着言方便，
　　撫卹求和。
事到而今，
　　已裝不卸，
　　　潑水難收怎奈何。」
都閒事，
　　這一場出醜，
　　　着甚達摩。

（尾）
　　「便不辱你爺便不羞見我。
　　我還待送斷你子個。
　　卻又子母情腸意不過。」

夫人曰：「事已如此，未審汝本意何似。願則以汝妻生，
不願則從今斷絕。」

鶯鶯待道「不願」來，是言與心違。待道「願」來後，對
娘怎出口。卒無詞對。

夫人又問。

14

Oriole bowed her powdered neck with shame,
  sorrowfully knitting her twin moth brows.
Her peach-like face was flushed full red,
  her cherry lips were a dark purple,
    and the delicate jade shoots of her fingers never stopped
      fidgeting.
It was unbearable to witness,
  the overflowing, powdery tears
    smothering her dimpled appliqué.

The sixty-year-old woman
Said, "Of course, I will forgive you.
In the end, the bond between mother and child always remains
  warm.
Let's speak of an expedient way
  to calm ourselves and find harmony.
It's happened and now
  that cart's already been packed—[80]
    and spilled water cannot be gathered back up.
Of all the crazy things,
  this scene of you making a fool of yourself—
    how are we going to deal with it?[81]

Coda
"Better you had not shamed your father,
  better had you never been embarrassed to see me.
I'd still like to take your head off,
Yet I cannot overcome those feelings between mother and child."

Madam Cui said, "What's done is done, but I have yet to ask about your true desires. If you desire this, then I shall marry you to the student, but if you don't, then you must cut it off right now."

If Oriole were to say, "I don't want it," the words wouldn't be true to her heart. But how could she say, "I do want it," to her own mother? In the end, there was nothing she could say.

Her mother questioned her again.

80 Roughly equivalent to "shut the stable door after the horse has bolted."
81 Literally, "what Dharma can be used."

iii.62/vi.8 雙調 （豆葉黃）
iii.33/v.8

　　　　「我孩兒安心，
　　　　　省可煩惱。
　　　　這事體休聲揚，
　　　　　着人看不好。
　　　　怕你個室家是廝落。
　　　　你好好承當，
　　　　　咱好好的商量，
　　　　　　我管不錯。

　　　　有的言語，
　　　　　對面評度。
　　　　凡百如何，
　　　　　老婆斟酌。」
　　　　女孩兒家見問着。
　　　　半晌無言，
　　　　　欲語還羞，
　　　　　　把不定心跳。

　　　（尾）

宛然畫出。　　可憎的媚臉兒通紅了。
　　　　對夫人不敢分明道。
　　　　猛吐了舌尖兒背背地笑。

　　　　　　　願郎不欲分明道，
　　　　　　　盡在回頭一笑中。

　　　拂旦，令紅娘召生小飲。生懼昨夜之敗，辭之以疾。

iii.63/vi.9 仙呂調 （相思會）
iii.33/v.8

　　　　君瑞懷羞慘。
　　　　心只自思念。
　　　　「這些醜事，
　　　　　不道怎生遮掩。」
　　　　「紅娘莫恁把人乾廝咭。

iii.62/vi.8 Shuang Diao Mode

Bean Leaves Yellow
"Set your mind at rest, child,
    and don't fret.
Don't bruit this affair about
    and make us look bad to others—
I fear you'll be the object of ridicule.
Take responsibility for what you've done.
    We will find a solution,
        and I'll forgive it all.

If you have something to say to me,
    let's discuss it face to face,
No matter what it is,
    I'll take it into account."
When the girl heard this
She was silent for a long while,
    wanting to speak but too embarrassed,
        and unable to control her beating heart.

Coda
That little darling's face flushed full red,
She dared not explain it clearly to her mother.
Suddenly she stuck out her tongue and laughed with her back turned.

Portrayed as if it were right before your eyes.

She wanted the young man but did not want to say it clearly,
    Yet, it was all expressed in that momentary laugh when she turned
        her head.

When morning approached, Crimson was dispatched to invite the student to come have a drink. The student was terrified about the debacle of the night before, and he begged off, saying he was ill.

iii.63/vi.9 Xianlü Diao Mode

Love Rendezvous
Junrui was ashamed,
And he'd been mulling things over in his mind:
"I wonder if this whole mess
    can somehow be covered up?
Crimson, don't poke fun at my expense!

我到那裡
　　見夫人吵，
　　有甚臉。

尋思罪過
　　蓋為自家險[17]。
算來今日，
　　請我赴席後爭敢。」
紅娘見道，
　　道「君瑞真個欠。
我道你，
　　佯小心，
　　　妝大膽。」

真可與定大
事。

紅娘曰：「但可赴約，別有佳話。」

生驚曰：「如何。」

紅娘以實告生。生謝曰：「誠如是，何以報德。」

曰：「妾不敢望報。夫人與鄭恆親。雖然昨夜見許，未足
取信。先生赴約，可以獻物為定。比及鶯鶯終制以來，庶
無反覆，以斷前約。」

生曰：「善。然自春寓此，迄今囊橐已空矣，奈何。」

iii.64/vi.10 仙呂調（喜新春）
iii.33/v.8
　　　　「草索兒上，
　　　　　都無一二百盤纏。
極意形容酸子　　　一領白衫
逆旅之蕭然之　　　　又不中穿。
狀。　　　　夜擁孤衾三幅布，
　　　　　晝欹單枕是一枚甎。
　　　　只此是家緣。

How could I save face
    when I get there
        and see Madam Cui?

I know that this offense
    rightfully accrues to me.
So today I think
    I dare not accept the invitation."
Hearing this, Crimson replied,
    "Junrui, you truly are a fool!
I'd say you
    are feigning caution
        so that you can pretend to be brave."

She truly is one with whom to make big decisions

Crimson said, "Just go. There will be some good news."

Zhang perked up and said, "What is it?"

Crimson gave him a true account of what had happened. He thanked her, saying, "If that's all true, then I am in your debt."

She replied, "I dare not look forward to any repayment. Madam Cui, however, is kin with Zheng Heng. While she might have given permission last night, it's not yet to be trusted. **You should go to the meeting and present her something as an engagement gift.** She won't have any chance, then, to change her mind and break off the engagement before Oriole finishes the mourning period for her father."

"Wonderful," said the student. "But since I've stayed here since spring, my purse is now completely empty. What should I do?"

iii.64/vi.10 Xianlü Diao Mode

Delight in Springtime Anew
"On my grass-braid string
    are no more than a few hundred for travel expenses.
I have one plain robe
    not worth wearing.
By night I hug a quilt made for one, only three layers of cotton thick.
By day I lean on a single pillow, and it is a brick.
These are my only possessions.

A perfect imitation of the student's voice describing the miserable condition of a sourpuss scholar in an inn.

要酒後，
　廚前自汲新泉。
要樂當筵。
自理冰弦。
要絹有壁畫兩三幅，
　要詩後卻奉得百來篇。
只不得道着錢。」

紅娘曰：「先生平昔與法聰有舊，法聰新當庫司，先生歸而
貸之，何求不得。」

生聞言而頓省，遂往見聰。

iii.65/vi.11　大石調（驀山溪）
iii.33/v.8
　　　張生是日，
　　　　叉手前來告。
　　　「有事敢相煩，
　　　　問庫師兄不錯。
　　　相公的嬌女，
　　　　許我作新郎，
　　　　　這事體，
　　　　　　你尋思，
　　　　　　　定物終須要。

　　　小生客寄，
　　　　沒個人挨靠。
　　　剛準備些兒，
　　　　其外多也不少。
　　　不合借索。
　　　總賴弟兄情，
　　　　如借得，
　　　　　感深恩，
　　　　　　是必休推托。」
　（尾）
　　　法聰聞言先陪笑。
　　　道「咱弟兄面情非薄，

If I want some wine,
    I draw water from the spring in front of the kitchen.
If I want music on the mat,
    I play the cold strings myself.
If you want silk, I have only two or three hanging scrolls.
Should you want poetry, I can offer up hundreds of verses.
Just don't speak of money."

Crimson said, "You seem to have been friends with Dharma Wit for a while, and he is the new head of the pawnshop here. Go back and borrow it from him. He'll grant you anything."

Enlightened by her words, the student went off to see Dharma Wit.

iii.65/vi.11 Dashi Diao Mode

Jumping Across a Mountain Stream
That day Student Zhang
    came with folded hands to say,
"There is something I must trouble you with,
    and I hope you sir, as Master of the Pawnshop, will forgive me.
The minister's lovely daughter
    has accepted me as her spouse,
        and please consider that
            for this arrangement
                an engagement gift is a must.

I am just a traveler lodging here
    and have no one on whom to rely.
I've managed to put together a bit for everyday use,
    but beyond that I have nothing.
I shouldn't ask you, but. . . .
Given our brotherly affection,
    I feel I can borrow from you.
        I would be deeply appreciative of your considerable grace—
            please, you must not decline!"

Coda
Dharma Wit laughed pleasantly when he first heard these words,
And said, "We do share a strong bond as brothers,

子除了我耳朵兒愛的道。」

生曰:「如有餘資,煩貸幾索,甚幸。

聰曰:「常住錢不敢私貸。貧僧積下幾文起坐,盡數分付足下,勿以寡見阻。」取下五十索。聰曰:「幾日見還。」

生指期拜納。

iii.66/vi.12 **雙調**(荽荷香)
iii.33/v.8
　　　　忒孤窮。
　　　　要一文錢物,
　　　　　　也擘划不動。
　　　　法聰不忍,
　　　　　　借與五十貫青銅。
　　　　「幾文起坐,
　　　　　　被你個措大倒得囊空。
　　　　三十五十家攛來,
　　　　　　比及償到,
　　　　　　　　是幾個齋供。」

　　　　君瑞聞言道「多謝,」
　　　　　　起來叉手,
　　　　　　　　着言倍奉。
　　　　「若非足下,
　　　　　　定應難見花容。
　　　　咱家命里,
　　　　　　算來歲運亨通。
　　　　多應魚化為龍。
　　　　恁時節奉還,
　　　　　　一年請俸。」

摹口角直至是。

　　(尾)
　　　　法聰笑道:「休打閧。
　　　　不敢問利息輕重。

So, you say nothing my ears do not find pleasant."

The student said, "If you have the money, may I trouble you to borrow a few strings? That would be superb."

Dharma Wit said, "I dare not make the decision to loan out our communal money. But I have managed to scrape together a bit of cash of my own, and I'm happy to give that to you. Please don't be put off by the meagre amount." He took out a full fifty strings. Then he asked, "How long before you can return it?"

The student indicated a time and then thanked him.

iii.66/vi.12 Shuang Diao Mode

Leaves of Lotus and Water Caltrop are Fragrant
He was so alone and in dire straits,
And couldn't even muster
    a single coin.
Dharma Wit couldn't bear it
    and loaned him fifty strings of blue coppers:[82]
"Ah, my last bit personal cash,
    emptied out of my bag by a poor student, was
Scrounged up from thirty or so families,
    until it was enough—
        ah, so many services for the dead!"

Hearing this, Junrui said, "Many thanks,"
    and rose to salute his friend with a bow,
        speaking in an ingratiating way,
"If it weren't for you,
    it would have been impossible to see that face like a flower.
My fate
    has been cast to be favorable for the coming year,
And it is certain that this fish will transform into a dragon.
When that happens, I will repay you
    with a year's worth of my salary."

Coda
Dharma Wit laughed and said, "Don't be silly,
I don't care about interest at all,

He carries the bickering all the way to here.

82 Copper coins turned blue from oxidation.

這本錢苟年得用。」

生以錢易金，赴夫人約，坐不安席。

酒行，夫人起曰：「昨不幸相公歿，攜稚幼留寺，群賊方興，非先
生矜憫，母子幾為魚肉矣。無以報德。雖先相以鶯許鄭恆，而未受
定約。今欲以鶯妻君，聊以報，可乎。」

iii.67/vi.13 大石調（玉翼蟬）
iii.33/v.8
　　　　夫人道：
　　　　　「張解元」，
　　　　　　美酒斟來滿。
　　　　道：「不幸當時，
　　　　　群賊困普救，
　　　　　　全家莫能逃難。
　　　　賴先生，
　　　　　便畫妙策，
　　　　　　以此登時免。
　　　　今日以鶯鶯，
　　　　　酬賢救命恩，
　　　　　　問足下願那不願。」

　　　　夫人曰：「如先生許，則滿飲一盞。」

　　　張生聞語，
　　　　急把頭來暗點。
　　　「小生目下，
　　　　身居貧賤。
　　　粗無德行，
　　　　情性荒疏學藝淺。
　　　相公的嬌女，
　　　　有何不戀。
　　　何以夫人苦勸。」
　　　吃他一盞，

But I'll have to use the principal in a year or so."

The student changed the money for gold, and went to Madam Cui's; but he couldn't sit still.

As the wine was poured, Madam Cui rose and said, "The Minister of State has, unfortunately, recently passed away, and I have brought my children to reside here in the monastery. If it were not for your compassion, sir, I and my children would all have been victimized.[83] I have no way to repay your virtue. Although the former minister had promised Oriole to Zheng Heng, no firm commitment was made. Would it be all right with you if I marry Oriole to you, sir, in reciprocity?"

iii.67/vi.13 Dashi Diao Mode

A Jade-Winged Cicada
"Young Master Zhang,"
        pronounced Madam Cui
                as she filled his cup to the brim with fine wine.
"When we had the misfortune
        of a horde of bandits laying siege to Universal Salvation
                none of our family could escape.
We relied on you, sir,
        to sketch out a marvelous plan
                by which we were immediately saved.
Today, with Oriole
        I reciprocate your worthy grace in saving our lives
                and ask you, sir, 'Do you so desire?'"

She said, "**If you assent, sir, then please drink this cup of wine.**"

When he heard these words, Zhang
        quickly nodded agreement.
"Right now, this impoverished student
        is living in a poor and humble way.
I have no true virtuous conduct and,
        indolent by nature, have accrued little learning or art.
The comely daughter of a Minister—
        what's not to love?
There's no need to persuade me."
He drank the cup of wine

---

83 Literally, "turned into fish and meat."

忽地推了心頭一座山。

生取金以奉夫人曰：「貧生旅食，姑此為禮，無以微見
卻。」

夫人不受，曰：「何必乃爾。」

好幫襯。

紅娘曰：「物雖薄，禮不可廢也。」夫人受金。生拜堂
下。

夫人曰：「然鶯未服闋，未可成禮。」

生曰：「今蒙文調，將赴選闈，姑待來年，不為晚矣。」

夫人曰：「願郎遠業功名為念，此寺非可久留。」

生曰：「倒指試期，幾一月矣。三兩日定行。」夫人以巨
觥為壽。生飲訖。令紅娘送生歸。

生謂紅娘曰：「不意有今日。」

答曰：「適鶯聞夫人語親，忻喜之容見於面。聞郎赴文
調，愁怨之容動於色。」

生曰：「煩為我言之。功名世所甚重，背而棄之，賤丈夫
也。我當發策決科，策名仕版，謝原憲之圭竇，衣買臣之
錦衣，待此取鶯，愜子素願。無惜一時孤悶，有妨萬里前
程。」

紅娘以此報鶯，亦不見答。自是不復見矣。後數日，生

84　"Hovel" is literally a small triangular window dug through the walls of a packed-earth
dwelling. Yuan Xian 元憲 (ca. 520 BCE) was one of Confucius' seventy-two disciples
who lived happily in poverty. Zhu Maichen 朱買臣 (ob. 115 BCE) rose from rags to

and instantly a mountain of worry toppled from his heart.

The student gave the gold to Madam Cui, saying, "I'm just a poor student on the road, but I hope you can accept this as a betrothal gift. Please do not be put off by its meagerness."

She did not accept it, saying, "There's no need."

Crimson interrupted, "**It's only a slight offering, but the rites cannot be set aside**." Madam Cui accepted the gold, and the student paid his proper respects.

What great help she is.

Madam Cui said, "Since Oriole has yet to finish the mourning period, we cannot hold the wedding now."

"Since the examinations are only a month away," said the student, "I will need to leave in a few days." Madam Cui toasted him with a large flagon of wine and the student drank it all. Then she ordered Crimson to escort him back to his room.

"I never expected this day," the student told Crimson.

"When Oriole heard Madam Cui speak of the marriage," she replied, "a look of delight appeared on her face. But when she heard you would be going to take the capital examinations, she seemed sad and resentful."

"Please explain to her," said the student, "that a meritorious reputation is something that the world values. Only a sad excuse for a man would give up such a chance. I shall certainly do well in the examinations and my name will be listed on the rolls of official service. Then I can bid the hovel of Yuan Xian goodbye and don the brocade robes of Maichen.[84] I shall then marry Oriole and fulfill my long-held desire. We can't let a moment of loneliness stand in the way of a promising career."

Crimson relayed this to Oriole, but she offered no reply. They did not see each other after that. Several days later, as the student set off, and

---

riches when he attracted the attention of the Han Emperor Wu, who sent him back to become magistrate in his hometown, saying, "To not return to your hometown after becoming rich and noble is like walking around at night in brocade robes."

行，夫人暨鶯送於道，法聰與焉。經於蒲西十里小亭置
酒。

　　　　悲歡離合一樽酒，
　　　　南北東西十里程。

Madam Cui sent Oriole off to send him on his way. Dharma Wit was also there. They set out a parting feast at the ten mile pavilion west of Puzhou.

> The sorrow and happiness of separation and meetings: one pitcher of wine,
> North and south, east, and west: ten *li* of the first leg of the journey.

Endnotes

1   Reading 冷 for 泠

2   Here, reading 飲氣 for 窨氣. Cf. Kim et al., 226.

3   The original character, 眾 makes no sense here; replacing with 待.

4   Reading 睡不着 for 睡後着.

5   是 is often used for 甚.

6   Reading 釭 for 缸.

7   Reading 拍 in place 怕.

8   Reading 顧 in place of 願.

9   Replacing 不忘 with 不望. Cf. DJY, 265, Zhang Haimei, *Jindai zhu-gongdiao cihui*, 182.

10   Reading 診 for 疹.

11   Replacing 騰 with 勝.

12   Replacing 哥 with 歌.

13   Replacing 腕 with 涴.

14   Replacing 觱剝 with 彈抱.

15   Understanding 廝搬着 as 相伴着.

16   For some reason 鶯鶯 has been written in Tang's edition instead of 夫人, which is clearly demanded by the lines that follow, and which occurs in other editions.

17   The use of 險 here offers two possible interpretations: first, "I consider that the offense I have committed makes it dangerous for me now to go to have drinks," and secondly, "My own role in this offense is insidious, and not clearly out in the open, and is something I brought on myself." Cf. DJY, 223.

董解元西廂 卷四
明 臨川湯顯祖義仍評

iv.1/vi.14 大石調（玉翼蟬）

　　蟾宮客。

　　赴帝闕。

　　相送臨郊野。

　　恰俺與鶯鶯，

　　　鴛幃暫相守，

　　　　被功名使人離缺。

　　好緣業。

　　空悒怏，

　　　頻嗟嘆，

　　　　不忍輕離別。

　　早是怎，

　　　淒淒涼涼受煩惱，

　　　　那堪值暮秋時節。

　　雨兒乍歇。

　　向晚風如溧[1]冽。

　　那聞得衰柳蟬鳴淒切。

　　未知今日別後，

　　何時重見也。

　　衫袖上盈盈，

　　　搵淚不絕。

　　幽恨眉峰暗結。

　　好難割捨。

　　縱有千種風情，

　　　何處說。

點染處跌宕烟
波。

　　　（尾）

　　　莫道男兒心如鐵。

　　　君不見滿川紅葉。

　　　盡是離人眼中血。

Book IV

Laureate Dong's Story of the Western Wing

iv.1/vi.14 Dashi Diao Mode

A Jade-Winged Cicada
That traveler to the Toad Palace[8]
Went off to the imperial capital,
Accompanied by a send-off party on the verge of the fields.
"Oriole and I shared only
    a moment in our love nest
        when my need to make a name split us apart.
What fine karmic fate!
I am fruitlessly depressed,
    sighing over and over,
        not taking this parting so lightly.
I have already
    accepted this dismal bedevilment,
        but can I stand the season of late autumn, too?

The rains have stopped.
To face the evening wind is to feel chilled to the bone,
And there's the cold shrill of cicadas in the withering willows.
After today's parting no one knows
    when we will see each other again.
Sleeves of my robe are soaked
    by unstoppable tears that can never be wiped away.
A deep rancor secretly knots the peaks of my brows.
It's so hard to pull us apart.
Even if there were a thousand kinds of romantic feeling,
    whom could I tell?

Coda
"Don't say a man's heart is like iron,
Can't you see the red leaves filling the stream?
They're blood from the eyes of those who must part."

The places where he has embellished the text are full of twists and turns.

---

1   A palace in the moon.

iv.2/vi.15 越調（上平西纏令）

　　　　景蕭蕭，
　　　　　風淅淅。
　　　　雨霏霏，
　　　　　對此景怎忍分離。
　　　　僕人催促，
　　　　　雨停風息日平西。
　　　　斷腸何處唱《陽關》，
　　　　　執手臨岐。
　　　　　蟬聲切，

　　　　蟬聲細。
　　　　　角聲韻，
　　　　雁聲悲。
　　　　望去程依約天涯。
越令人斷腸。　且休上馬，
　　　　　苦[8]無多淚與君垂。
　　　　此際情緒你爭知，
　　　　　更說甚湘妃。

　　（鬥鵪鶉）
　　　　囑付情郎，
　　　　　「若到帝裏。
　　　　帝裏酒釅花穠，
　　　　　萬般景媚。
　　　　休取次共別人，
　　　　　便學連理。
　　　　少飲酒，
　　　　　省遊戲。
　　　　記取奴言語，
　　　　　必登高第。

　　　　專聽着伊家，
　　　　　好消好息。

iv.2/vi.15 Yue Diao Mode

The Emperor Quells the West: A Bound Suite
The scenery was cold and lonely,
    as the wind rustled and sighed.
Rain fell hard and fast—
    faced with such a scene, how could they bear to part?
Servants urged and pushed—
    the rains had stopped, the wind was calm, and the sun was
        level in the west.
Where do the heartbroken sing "Yang Pass?"[2]
    Where they approach a fork in the road, hand in hand.

Sounds of the cicada were shrill,
    and sounds of the cricket muted.
The sound of the evening horn decayed,
    and sounds of geese were full of grief.
Gazing at the road ahead, it seemed to run to heaven's edge.
"*Wait, don't mount your horse yet,*
    for I fear I will have no tears left to shed for you.
How can you understand my heartfelt thoughts now,
    much less those of the consorts of the Xiang."[3]

*Makes one
even more
brokenhearted.*

Fighting Quail
She counseled her sweetheart,
    "When you get to the capital
There will be strong wine and heady flowers,[4]
enchanting prospects of every kind.
Don't willfully join with another
    to imitate love's twining branches.
Don't drink too much,
    and cut back on your fun.
Remember my words
    and you will surely pass with high marks.
I will do nothing but wait
    for your wonderful news.

2   This poem by Wang Wei 王維 (d. 761), "Sent to Yuan the Second on his Commis-
    sion to Anxi" 送元二使安西, is perhaps the most famous parting song in the poetic
    repertoire: "Morning rain in Wei City moistens the light dust, / Green on green at
    the hostel, willow's color is new; / I urge you, sir, drain one more cup of wine, /
    Going west out of Yang Pass, there will be no old friends."
3   See Book I, n. 149
4   That is, good-looking women.

專等着伊家，
　寶冠霞帔。
妾守空閨，
　把門兒緊閉。
不拈絲管，
　罷了梳洗。
你咱是必。
把音書頻寄。」

（雪裏梅花）

囑咐罷却便慰
解。慰解罷却
又囑咐。悲戀
徘徊。

「莫煩惱莫煩惱，
　放心地放心地。
是必。
是必。
休怎，
　做病做氣。

俺也不似別的。
你情性俺都識。
　臨去也，
　　臨去也，
且休去，
　聽俺勸伊。」

（錯煞）

先囑咐飲酒閑
遊，後及早晚
茶飯。女心事
固有輕重。

「我郎休怪強牽衣。
問你西行幾日歸。
着路裏小心呵，
　且須在意。
省可裏晚眠早起。
冷茶飯莫吃。
好將息。
我倚着門兒專望你。」

Wait for that
    hat of jewels and auroral cape.[5]
I will abide in my empty boudoir
    and keep my door tightly closed.
I will play no stringed instruments
    and don no makeup.
And you must
Constantly send me letters.

Plum Blossoms in the Snow
"Don't fret, don't worry.
Rest easy, don't stress.
What must be
Must be.
And don't
    create problems or blow off steam.

*Finished coun-
seling him, she
then consoles him.
After consoling
him, she counsels
him again. She
oscillates between
compassion and
concern.*

I'm not like any other,
I know your disposition well.
You're about to leave
    about to leave. . . .
        Don't leave me yet
           But listen to my counsel!

Double Coda (Complex)
"Sweetheart, don't get upset because I tugged at your clothes—
I wanted to ask, 'When will you return from your journey to
    the west?'
Be careful on the road,
    be attentive to everything.
Don't sleep late or get up too early.
Don't eat or drink anything cold!
Take good care of yourself—
I'll do nothing but lean on the doorframe and look longingly for
    you!"

*She first counsels
him about drink-
ing and roaming
about; then she
counsels him about
time and food.
There are things
more or less impor-
tant in the mind of
females.*

5   Only a woman with an officially conferred title was allowed to wear clothing and
accessories that noted her status. Cf. Wang Yong 1981, 2.18.

生與鶯難別。夫人勸曰「送君千里，終有一別。」

iv.3/vi.16 仙呂調（戀香衾）

苒苒徵塵動行陌。

杯盤取次安排。

三口兒連法聰，

　外更無別客。

魚水似夫妻正美滿，

　被功名等閒離拆。

然終須相見，

　奈時下難捱。

君瑞啼痕污了衫袖，

　鶯鶯粉淚盈腮。

一個止不定長吁，

　一個頓不開眉黛。

君瑞道「閨房裏保重」，

　鶯鶯道「途路上寧耐」。

兩邊的心緒，

　一樣的愁懷。

張囑鶯，鶯囑
張。僕人促
張，夫人促
鶯。怎地匆
匆。

（尾）

僕人催促怕晚了天色。

柳堤兒上把瘦馬兒連忙解。

夫人好毒害。

道「孩兒每回取個坐車兒來。」

生辭夫人及聰。皆曰「好行。」夫人登車。生與鶯別。

iv.4/vi.17 大石調（驀山溪）

離筵已散，

It was hard for the student and Oriole to part. Madam Cui urged them,
"You could accompany him for a thousand miles, but you'd still have
to part."

iv.3/vi.16 Xianlü Diao Mode

Quilt with the Fragrance of Love
Fine, feathery dust stirred on the traveler's path
And cups and trays were scattered about.
There were the three of them, and Dharma Wit made four—
    no one else was there.
A new couple now, husband and wife, like fish in water, but
    pointlessly torn apart by his need to make a name.
Though they would certainly reunite in the end,
    it was still hard to bear the moment at hand.

The traces of Junrui's weeping had stained the sleeves of his
    gown,
        and powdery tears covered Oriole's cheeks.
One could not stop his long sighs,
        the other could not relax her brows of kohl.
Junrui said, "Take care of yourself, darling,"
        and Oriole replied, "Have patience on the long road."
Tangled thoughts filled separate hearts,
        equal in their misery.

Coda
The servants urged them to part, lest daylight be gone,
And they busily prepared his skinny nag there on the willowed
    bank.
Madam Cui, heartless as ever,
Said, "Child, pick a cart to ride back in."

The student bid goodbye to Madam Cui and Dharma Wit, and they
both replied, "Have a safe trip." The old woman got in the cart, and
the student parted from Oriole.

Zhang counsels Oriole, Oriole counsels Zhang. The servants pressure Zhang, Madam Cui pressures Oriole. Such a hurried rush!

iv.4/vi.17 Dashi Diao Mode

Jumping Across a Mountain Stream
With the parting banquet already dispersing,

再留戀應無計。
煩惱的是鶯鶯，
　受苦的是清河君瑞。
　頭西下控着馬，
車向馱坐車兒。
　辭了法聰，
別了夫人，
　把樽俎收拾起。

臨上馬，
　還把徵鞍倚。

依戀延捱。

低語使紅娘，
　「更告一盞以為別禮」。
鶯鶯君瑞。
彼此不勝愁，

恁地無言，只
堪哽咽。

　廝覷者，
　　總無言，
　　　未飲心先醉。

（尾）
滿斟離杯長出口兒氣。
比及道得個「我兒將息」。
一盞酒裏。
白冷冷的滴嗀半盞兒淚。

夫人道「教郎上路，日色晚矣。」鶯啼哭，又賦詩一首贈
郎。詩曰

　　　棄置今何道，
　　　當時且自親。
　　　還將舊來意，
　　　憐取眼前人。

iv.5/vi.18 黃鐘宮（出隊子）
最苦是離別。
彼此心頭難棄捨。
鶯鶯哭得似痴呆。

there was no reason for them to tarry there.
Oriole was upset,
    Junrui of Qinghe suffered.
He pointed his horse toward the west,
    and the wagon pointed east.
After he said his goodbyes to Dharma Wit
    and parted from Madam Cui,
        the plates and dishes were gathered up.

About to mount his horse,
    he still leaned against the saddle   *Stalling, reluctant*
And in a low voice dispatched Crimson,   *to leave.*
    "Announce one more stirrup cup for the parting rites."
Oriole and Junrui—
Equally victims of sorrow—
    looked at each other,
        speechless,
            hearts already drunk before they drank.

Coda
The stirrup cup poured full, the two sighed and sighed,
Before he was able to say, "Take care, my love,"
    Into their cups of wine
Fell useless, chilly tears, to half fill the cup.

Madam Cui said, "Let him get on the road, it's getting dark." Oriole wept
bitterly and composed another poem to give to the student. It read:

Cast aside now, what should I say?
I was the one who drew close back then.
Take up your old feelings once again
And treat with sympathy the one before your eyes.[6]

iv.5/vi.18 Huangzhong Gong Mode

Sending Out the Dance Troupe
The bitterest taste is that of separation,
And neither could find it in themselves to abandon the other.
Oriole cried herself crazy,
As tear tracks on her cheeks turned bloody.

6   "The one before your eyes" normally means a new lover. Cf. DJY, 334.

臉上啼痕都是血。
有千種恩情何處說。
夫人道「天晚教郎疾去。」

怎奈紅娘心似鐵。
把鶯鶯扶上七香車。
君瑞攀鞍空自攧。
道得個「冤家寧耐些」。

（尾）

讀者不容不目
斷矣。

馬兒登程坐車兒歸舍。
馬兒往西行坐車兒往東拽。
兩口兒一步兒離得遠如一步也。

iv.6/vi.19 仙呂調（點絳唇纏令）

美滿生離，
　據鞍冗冗離腸痛。
舊歡新寵。
變作高唐夢。
回首孤城，
　依約青山擁。

一味寂寞。

西風送。
戍樓寒重。
初品《梅花弄》。

（瑞蓮兒）

衰草萋萋一徑通。
丹楓索索滿林紅。
平生蹤跡無定着，
　如斷蓬。
聽塞鴻。
啞啞的飛過暮雲重。

（風吹荷葉）

憶得枕鴛衾鳳。

She had a thousand types of love and kindness, but where to
    express them now?

Madam Cui spoke, "It's getting late, tell him to get along."
With no choice left, Crimson's heart turned to iron
As she pushed Oriole onto the perfumed cart.
Clambering into the saddle, Junrui pretended to stumble,
Just long enough to be able to utter, "My precious, be patient."

Coda
The horse got on the road, the wagon returned to the monastery,
The horse headed west, those in wagon were pulled to the east;
Their steps took them further and further apart.

The reader cannot avoid watching them until they disappear.

iv.6/vi.19 Xianlü Diao Mode

Dotting Crimson Lips: A Bound Suite
**After such beautiful fullness now came a separation as long as a
    lifetime—**
      **clinging to the saddle, full of thoughts, his parting heart
        ached.**
Old pleasures and new favors
Now became only a dream of Gaotang.
He turned his head back to lonely Puzhou,
    seemingly embraced by the green mountains.
A western wind saw him on his way.
Cold doubled in the watch tower
As they began to play the "Plum Blossom Song."

All a taste of loneliness.

Auspicious Lotus Song
Withering grasses were still luxuriant, parted by a single path;
Vermillion maples rustled slightly, filling the forest with red.
His trek through this world never found a place to settle,
    and he was as rootless as a tumbleweed.
He listened to geese from northern passes
    honk and honk as they flew through layers of clouds.

Wind Blows the Lotus Leaves
He remembered the pillow and quilt of shared love—

今宵管半壁兒沒用。
觸目淒涼千萬種。
見滴流流的紅葉,
淅零零的微雨,
　率剌剌的西風。

（尾）

驢鞭半裊,
　吟肩雙聳。
休問離愁輕重。
向個馬兒上馱也馱不動。

離蒲西行三十里,日色晚矣,野景堪畫。

iv.7/vi.20 仙呂調（賞花時）

落日平林噪晚鴉。

單寫景孤冷荒
涼。

風袖翩翩吹瘦馬。
一徑入天涯。
荒涼古岸,
　衰草帶霜滑。

瞥見個孤林端入畫。
離落蕭疏帶淺沙。
一個老大伯捕魚蝦。
橫橋流水,
　茅舍映荻花。

（尾）

駝腰的柳樹上有漁槎。
一竿風斾茅檐上掛。
澹煙瀟灑,
橫鎖着兩三家。

生投宿於村店。

Tormented tonight by an unused half.
Ten thousand kinds of lonely desolation met his eye,
As he saw red leaves swirling and whirling,
    and felt light rain sprinkle and spatter
        as the western wind needled and stung.

Coda
His donkey whip held at half mast,
    his shoulders hunched[7] as he chanted.
Don't ask about the weight of separation's sorrow:
Put that bundle on a horse's back and it would be unable to move.

He had traveled west of Puzhou some thirty miles, and it was already getting late. The scenery of the wilds was worthy of painting.

iv.7/vi.20 Xianlü Diao Mode

Time to Enjoy the Flowers
A setting sun, level forest, cawing evening crows;
Setting his sleeves flapping, the wind blew on his skinny nag—
A path directly into Heaven's edge.
An aged riverbank was deserted and chilly,
    sere grass slippery with a covering of frost.

Simply describes the scene as forsaken loneliness, isolated and deserted.

A glimpse of a faraway forest fit for painting—
A plaited twig fence, sparse and empty, covered by shallow sand,
An old uncle catching fish and shrimp,
A bridge athwart running water,
    and a thatched hut set against silvergrass blooms.

Coda
On a crook-trunked willow a fishing raft was hung,
And a single wine flag dangled from a pole stuck in thatched eaves.
A thin, delicate mist
    locked itself across two or three homes.[8]

The student lodged in a village inn.

---

7 Known as "poet's shoulders," since poets often hunched as they recited their poems.
8 This song adapts and redistributes the metrical patterns of the song "Pure Clean Sand" 天淨沙 and makes repeated lexical and metrical gestures to the famous poem "Autumn Thoughts," an anonymous early song. See West 2021.

iv.8/vi.21 越調（廳前柳纏令）

蕭索江天暮，
　投宿在數間茅舍，
　　夜永愁無寐。
謾咨嗟，
　床頭上怎寧貼。
倚定個枕頭兒越越的哭，
　哭得悄似痴呆。

語語涼。

畫櫓聲搖拽，
　水聲嗚咽，
　　蟬聲助凄切。

（蠻牌兒）

「活得正美滿，
　被功名使人離缺。
知他是我命薄，
　你緣業。
比似[23]他時，
　再相逢也，
這的般愁，
　兀的般悶，
　　終做話兒說。

料得我兒今夜裏，
　那一和煩惱唓嗻。
不恨咱夫妻
　今日別。

向後愁預先准
備。

動是經年，
　少是半載，
　　恰第一夜。

（山麻皆）
「淅零零地雨打芭蕉葉。
急煎煎的促織兒聲相接。
做得個蟲蟻兒天生的劣。

iv.8/vi.21 Yue Diao Mode

Willow at the Front of the Courtyard: A Bound Suite
Deserted and quiet, as the sky darkened over the river
 he stopped to lodge among some thatched cottages but,
  as night dragged on, he could not sleep for sadness.
He heaved melancholy sighs—
 no way he could lie still on the bed.

He lay back against the pillow, weeping more and more,   *Every word is*
 crying himself crazy.   *forlorn.*
The sound of painted sculls turned and creaked,
 the sound of the river was muffled sobs,
  and the sound of the cicada bolstered the mournful cold.

Barbarian Shield
"I was living in a state of bliss,
 when the need for a reputation tore us apart.
Who knows, was it because of my meager fate?
 Or your karmic retribution?
Compared to our time back then,
 when we meet again,
This sorrow,
 this depression,   *Getting ready.*
  will be nothing more than a topic for conversation.

I imagine that on this night, my love,
 you're dealing with a bout of terrible vexation.
But feel no rancor for the parting
 of husband and wife today—   *Preparing ahead of*
A year or more for sure,   *time for the sorrow*
 at best six months,   *to come later.*
  and this is only the first night.

Mountain Hemp Stalks
"Spattering rain pounds the banana leaves,
Anxious sounds of the cricket[9] follow one after another.
Such a Heaven-sent vileness to be this insect,

---

9 Identified by its kenning here as "the urger of weaving," since its call resembles the
 sound of shuttle constantly thrown in a loom.

特故把愁人做脾瞥。
更深後越切。

恨我寸腸千結。
不埋怨除你心如鐵。
淚痕兒淹破人雙頰。
淚點兒怕搵不迭。
是相思血。

無端入夢。　　（尾）

「兀的不煩惱煞人也。
燈兒一點甫能吹滅。
雨兒歇。
閃出昏慘慘的半窗月。」

西風怯雨眠難熟，
殘月窺人酒半醒。

iv.9/vi.22 南呂宮（應天長）

無語悶答孩地，
　　慢兩淚盈腮。
清宵夜好難捱。
一天愁悶怎安排。
役損這情懷。
睡不着，
　　萬感勉強的把旅捨門開。
披衣獨步在月明中，
　　凝睛看天色。

澹雲遮籠素魄。
野水連天天竟白。
見衰楊折葦，
　　隱約映漁台。
新愁與舊恨，
　　睹此景，
　　　　分外增煞。

極曠極幽，似
真似幻。

Suffocating the sorrowful,
Ever more intense as the night wears on.

I hate that every inch of my gut has a thousand knots,
Only the iron-hearted could bear this without complaint.
Tear stains have flooded my cheeks,
Teardrops unlikely to ever be wiped away—
They are the blood of love's longing.

Coda
"It's driving me crazy,
Just enough of the lamp's flame left to blow out.
The rain stops
And suddenly a dim and dusky moon emerges halfway up the window."

Enters a dream state for no reason.

A west wind blows, he shrinks from the rain,[10] **sleep remains fitful.**
A crescent moon peeks, yet he is only half sobered from drinking.

iv.9/vi.22 Nanlü Gong Mode

Responding to Lengthening Days
Wordless, depressed,
      Tears covering his cheeks—
Such a quiet night was hard to endure.
How could he deal with a sorrow that could fill the heavens?
He was worn down by his feelings and
Unable to sleep.
      Thousands of emotions forced him to open the doors,
Throw on his clothes, and walk in the moonlight,
      staring up at the color of the sky.

Thin clouds enwrapped the pale moon in a diaphanous globe.
The river in the wilds linked to the sky, which was white as well.
He could see withered willows and broken reeds
      where appeared the faint reflection of a fishing jetty.
New sorrow joined to old vexations,
      and in watching this scene,
            both swelled beyond measure.

Exceptionally clear, exceptionally murky; it seems real and it seems illusory.

10 An adaptation of the cliché "to fear the wind and shrink from the rain," (怕風怯
雨) or to be extremely sensitive and delicate.
11 "White" also meaning "empty" or "blank," as in the empty illusions of a dream.

白柳陰裏忽聽得有人言，
　　低聲道「快行麼娘咳。」

（尾）
張生覷了失聲道「怪」。
見野水橋東岸南側
兩個畫不就的佳人映月來。

　　鞋弓襪窄，
　　行不動，
　　步難移。
　　語顫聲嬌，
　　喘不迭，
　　頻道「困。」
　　是人是鬼俱難辨，
　　為福為災兩不知。

生將取劍擊之，而已至矣。因叱之曰「爾乃誰人唬秀才。
」月影柳陰之下，定睛細認。^云_云。

iv.10/vi.23 雙調（慶宜和）
　iv.9/vi.22
　　　「是人後疾忙快分說，
　　　　是鬼後應速滅。」
　　　入門來取劍取不迭。
　　　兩個來的近也。
　　　近也。
　　　君瑞回頭再覷些。
　　　半晌痴呆。

　　　回嗔作喜唱一聲喏，
　　　　卻是姐姐。
　　　那姐姐。

熟視之，乃鶯、紅也。生驚問曰「爾何至些。」鶯曰「適
夫人酒多寐熟，妾與紅娘計之曰。『郎西行，何日再面。

In the umbra of the white[11] willows, he heard someone say
in a whisper, "Hurry up, my girl."

Coda
Student Zhang looked and without thinking, uttered, "Strange!"
For there by the bridge on the south side of the river's eastern bank,
Two unimaginably beautiful women were approaching in the light of
the moon.

> Shoes arched, socks tight,
> they could hardly walk
> or move their feet.
> Words quavering, voices charming,
> they panted and panted
> and kept saying, "So tiring!"
> It was hard to tell if they were person or ghost.
> Was it good luck or misfortune?

The student was about to get out his sword to strike them, but they had already reached him. He yelled, "Who's that scaring me?" In the shade of the willow under the waning moon, he scrutinized them.[ad lib]

iv.10/vi.23 Shuang Diao Mode

Celebrating the Xuanhe Reign
"If you're human, explain yourself at once,
    and if you're a ghost, begone!"
He went in the door to get his sword, but it was too late.
They were already too close,
Too close.

Junrui turned his head around for another look and
    in no time at all, he was dumbstruck.
Going quickly from anger to joy, he recognized them,
And cried, *"Aha! It's you, sister!*
Both sisters!"

> He looked closely, and it turned out to be Oriole and Crimson. Startled, he questioned them, "How did you get here?" Oriole said, "Mother had a bit too much to drink and is sleeping soundly. Crimson and I thought about it and said to each other, 'He's gone west; when will we see him

紅日。「郎行不遠，同往可乎。」』妾然其言，與紅私渡河而至此。」

生攜鶯手歸寢。未及解衣，聞群犬吠門。生破窗視之，但見火把照空，喊聲震地，聞一人大呼曰「渡河女子，必在是矣。」

iv.11/vi.24 商調（定風波）

好事多妨礙。
恰拈了冠兒，
　鬆開裙帶。
汪汪的狗兒吠，
　順風聽得喊聲一派。
不知為個甚，
　唬得張生變了面色。
真個大驚小怪。

火把臨窗外。
一片地叫「開門」，
　倒大驚駭。
張生隔窗覷，
　見五千餘人，
　　全副執戴。
一個最大漢，
　提着雁翎刀，
　　厲聲叫道
　　　「與我這裏搜猜。」

（尾）

柴門兒腳到處早蹉開。
這君瑞有心掙揣。
向臥榻上撒然覺來。

閃出一夢，略一點染便爾警覺。沒把鼻光景。

again?' Then Crimson said, 'He hasn't gone far, can we go on with him?' I seconded her proposal, so we secretly crossed the river to get here."

The student took her by the hand and returned to his sleeping chamber. He hadn't even had time to loosen her robe before he heard a pack of dogs yapping at the door. The student broke through the paper window to look. He saw torches lighting up the sky and heard shouting that shook the earth. Someone yelled, "Those girls who crossed the river must be here!"

iv.11/vi.24 Shang Diao Mode

Settling Windblown Waves
Good things are always frustrated—
He had just taken off her headdress,
      and loosened the belt of her robe,
When the dogs barked
      and he heard a string of shouts on the wind.
He didn't know what it was
      but it scared him pale.
It was such a fright!

Suddenly, out comes a dream. It begins to be embellished, but then the student wakes in a fright. It becomes a baseless scene.

Torches approached his window
And they yelled as one, "Open the door,"
      really scaring him.
He looked out the window
      and saw more than five thousand men
            in full armor, with weapons and helmets.
The largest among them
      lifted a goose-feather blade
            and shouted in an angry voice,
                  "Search this place for me."

Coda
The brushwood door split wherever they kicked.
Junrui had a mind to struggle against them. . . .
When he suddenly woke up in bed.

12 In legend, magpies fly up to Heaven and form a bridge across the Milky Way. From the story of lovers who inhabit the constellations Altair and Vega, and who are allowed to meet only once a year, on the seventh day of the seventh month, when magpies form a bridge for them to cross the Heavenly River (known in the West as the Milky Way) to meet.

無端怪鵲高枝噪，
一枕鴛鴦夢不成。

坐而待旦，僕已治裝。

iv.12/vi.25 仙呂調（醉落魄纏令）
酒醒夢覺。
君瑞悶愁不小。
隔窗野鵲兒喳喳地叫。
把夢驚覺人來，
　不當個嘴兒巧。

悶打孩似吃着沒心草。
越越的哭到月兒落。
被頭兒上淚點多少。
媚媚的不乾，
　揾也揾[4]得着。

（風吹荷葉）
枕畔僕人低低道。
「起來麼解元天曉。」
也把行李琴書收拾了。
聽得幽幽角奏，
　噹噹地鐘響，
　忔忔地雞叫。

只將山高水
杳，描畫一遍
無數惝惶。

（醉奚婆）
把馬兒控着。
不管人煩惱。
程程去也，
　相見何時却。

（尾）
華山又高。
秦川又杳。

For no reason the marvelous magpie[12] chattered on the high branches,
A single pillow of mandarin ducks: the dream was incomplete.

He sat and waited for dawn. His servant had already packed.

iv.12/vi.25 Xianlü Diao Mode

Drunk and Down on My Luck: A Bound Suite
Sobering up and coming out of his dream,
Junrui woke with melancholy.
Beyond his window, magpies chattered raucously in the wilds,
Startling him from his dream—
> **they shouldn't be such chatterboxes.**

He was as depressed as if he had eaten no-heart greens,
And wept until the moon set.
There were so many tears that the top of his quilt
Had gradually become so saturated
> **it had to be wrung dry.**

Wind Blows the Lotus Leaves
Beside his pillow, the servant said in a low voice,
"Get up, Laureate, the skies are growing bright."
He had already arranged the luggage, zither, and books.
Zhang could hear the muffled horn play,
> **the ringing echo of the bell,**
>> **and the raucous crowing of the rooster.**

Drunk and Down on My Luck
The servant had Zhang's mount ready,
Paying no attention to how troubled the student was.
Stretch by stretch, he went on his way—
When would he return and see her again?

Coda
Mount Hua was high,
And the streams of Qin distant and dim.

He adapts the height of the mountain and the far reach of rivers to describe the many trials and tribulations he faced on the way.

過了無限野水橫橋。
騎着瘦馬兒圪登登的又上長安道。

> 行色一鞭催瘦馬，
> 羈愁萬斛引新詩。
> 長安道上，
> 只知
> 君瑞艱難。
> 普救寺中，
> 誰念
> 鶯鶯煩惱。

鶯自郎西邁，憔悴不勝。乘間詣郎閱書之閣，開牗視之，非復曩日。鶯轉煩惱。

iv.13/vi.26 黃鐘宮（侍香金童纏令）

> 才郎自別，
> 劃地愁無那。
> 裊裊爐煙縈綠瑣。
> 濃睡覺來心緒惡。
> 衣裳羞整，
> 霧鬢斜軃。

> 香消玉瘦，
> 天天都為他。
> 「眼底閒愁沒處着。
> 是即是下梢相見咱。
> 大小身心，
> 時下打疊不過。」

（雙聲疊韻）

件件傷神。

> 「吟硯乾，
> 黃卷堆，
> 冷落了讀書閣。
> 金篆鼎寶獸爐，
> 誰爇龍涎火。

He passed over uncountable bridges across streams in the wild,
As riding his skinny nag, he clopped along the road to Chang'an.

Pressed for time, his single whip urged on his skinny nag.
Thousands of bushels of traveler's sorrow drew out new poems.
On the road to Chang'an,
We only know of the hardships of Junrui.
But in the Monastery of Universal Salvation,
Who thought about Oriole's sadness?

From the time her lover headed west, Oriole had become haggard and
drawn. She slipped away to the gallery where she had read, **opened
the door bolt to look, but it wasn't like before.** She became sadder
and more vexed.

iv.13/vi.26 Huangzhong Gong Mode

Golden Lad Minding Incense: A Bound Suite
From the moment she parted from her talented lover,
      sorrow became as insufferable as it was before.
Wafting up in a spiral, smoke from a censer laced through the
      window's green latticework,
And she slept soundly, but woke in a terrible state of mind,
      her clothes all askew
            and her misty coils of hair drooping to the side.

Her perfume vanished; her jade body daily grew thinner—
      all because of him.
She struggled with the pointless sorrow.
"**Although we are sure to see each other in the end,**
This heart of mine
      is ever unsettled now.

Alliteration and Rhyming
"**The inkstone dry,**   *Everything harms*
      yellow scrolls stacked up—   *her soul.*
            what a cold and lonely study.
The golden seal-script-inscribed tripod, the precious animal
      censer—

幾冊書，
　有誰垛。
粉箋暗，
　被塵污。
俏沒人照覷子個。」

（刮地風）
「薄幸的冤家好下得，
　甚把人拋躲。
眉兒澹了教誰畫，
　哭損秋波。
琵琶塵暗，
　懶拈金撥。
有新詩，
　有新詞，
　　共誰酬和。
那堪對暮秋，
　你道如何。」

（整金冠令）
「促織兒外面，
　鬥聲相聒。
小即小，
　天生的口不曾合。
是世間蟲蟻兒裏的活撮。
叨叨的
　絮得人怎過。」

以下亦能詞者
可辦。

（賽兒令）
「愁麼。
愁麼。
此愁着甚消磨。
把腳兒摀了耳朵兒搓。
沒亂煞，
　也自攛挫。

who is here to light the ambergris incense?
Several fascicles of books—
　　who shall stack them?
The pink bookmarks
　　are besmirched with dust.
Now there is no one to take care of it all.

A Ground-Scraping Wind
"That hard-hearted, insincere lover of mine,
　　how could he just cast me aside?
My eyebrows grow faint, who shall paint them?[13]
　　Weeping has injured my limpid eyes.[14]
The *pipa* grows dim with dust,
　　and I languidly hold the golden pick.
There are new poems,

Unbearable to recollect or to re- member.

　　new lyrics,
　　　　but no one here to share them.
How can I bear facing this late autumn?
　　Just tell me how.

Adjusting a Ritual Cap of Gold
"Outside, crickets
　　fight with grating sounds.
Small they might be

What follows is also something someone capable of writing lyrics can manage.

　　but their Heaven-bestowed mouths have never been closed.
They are the most hateful creatures of the insect world.
On and on,
　　they drone until it's unbearable.

Song of the Passes
"Sorrowful.
Miserable.
What can ever dispel this grief?
I stamp my feet, rub my ears—
No help at all,
　　I just wear myself down.

13　Zhang Chang's 張敞 (d. ca. 47 BCE) wife had suffered an injury in childhood that
　　left one of her eyebrows incomplete. Zhang lovingly drew on her eyebrows every
　　morning before going to court.
14　Literally, "my autumn ripples."

塞鴻來也那。
塞鴻來也那。」

（柳葉兒）

「淅冽冽的曉風簾幕。
滴流流的落葉辭柯。
年年的光景如梭。
急煎煎的心緒如火。」

（神仗兒）

「這對眼兒，
　這對眼兒，
　　淚珠兒滴了萬顆。
止約不定，
　恰才淹了，
　　撲簌簌的又還偷落。
勝秋雨點兒多。」

（四門子）

些兒鬼病天來大。
何時是可。
羅衣寬褪肌如削。
悶答孩地獨自個。
空恨他。
空怨他。
料他那裏與誰做活。
空恨他。
空怨他。
不道人圖個甚麼。

（尾）

把寶鑒兒拈來強梳裹。
腮兒被淚痕兒浥破。
甚全不似舊時節風韻我。

The border geese are already here.
The border geese have already come.

Willow Leaves
"Soughing and sighing, the morning wind penetrates the
   curtains,
Rustling and whispering, falling leaves drop from their
   branches.
The scenes of each year pass like a shuttle thrown,
The simmering, anxious threads of my heart seem to be on fire.

A Guard of Spirits
"These eyes,
      these eyes
            have shed countless tears.
Uncontrollable—
      just ceasing and then,
            pittering and pattering, they stealthily start again,
More numerous than the drops of autumn rain.

The Four Disciples
"When will this ghostly illness, greater than the heavens,
Ever be cured?
My clothes hang loose, my flesh seems pared away.
Listless and depressed and all alone,
I hate him pointlessly,
Resent him pointlessly.
I guess he is making his life with someone else now—
I hate him pointlessly,
Resent him pointlessly.
I don't understand what he's planning on, anyway.

Coda
"I'll take up my precious mirror and force myself to get ready for
   the day—
My cheeks are ruined by traces of tears—
Can I bear losing the graceful and charming person I used to be?

自季秋

　　與郎相別，杳無一信。

　　早是離恨，又值冬景。

　　白日猶聞，清宵更苦。

iv.14/vi.27 中呂調（香風合[5]纏令）

　　煩惱知何限。

　　悶答孩地，

　　　獨自淚漣漣。

　　身心俏似顛。

　　相思悶轉添。

　　守着燈兒坐[6]，

　　　待收拾做些兒閒針線。

　　奈身心不苦歡。

　　不苦歡。

　　一雙春筍玉纖纖。

　　貼兒裏拈線。

　　把繡針兒穿。

　　行待紝針關。

　　卻便紝針尖。

　　欲待裁領衫兒段。

　　把繫着的裙兒胡亂剪。

　　胡亂剪。

（石榴花）

　　覷着紅娘，

　　　認做張郎喚。

　　認了多時自失笑，

　　　「不惟道鬼病相持，

　　　　更有邪神繳纏。

　　苦苦天天。

　　此愁何時免。

　　鎮日思量敫萬千遍。

From late autumn
    when I parted from my lover,
    there have been no letters, just silence.
    Already beset by the rancor of parting
    I now face this world of winter.
    Daytime is all right,
    but the still nights are ever more bitter."

iv.14/vi.27 Zhonglü Diao Mode

Fragrant Winds Converge: A Bound Suite
Is there ever an end to this vexing sorrow?
Listless and depressed,
    her tears ceaselessly flowed when alone.
Body and mind as though crazy,
Love sickness layering depression upon depression,
She sat by the lamp
    wanting to while the time away with needle and thread,
But alas, her heart was not happy.
Not happy at all.

Her hand's ten bamboo shoots of spring, fine as delicate jade,
Plucked a thread from the sewing box
To thread the embroidery needle.
But, trying to thread it,
She mistook point for eye.
She wanted to cut out a section of collar for a robe,
But in a daze trimmed the skirt she was wearing.
Dazed, she trimmed it instead.

Pomegranate Flowers
Looking at Crimson
    she mistakenly called her, "Master Zhang,"
And, realizing her mistake, laughed at herself:
    "Not only is this ghostly illness a constant presence,
        but I seem beset by evil spirits too.

Suffering! Good heavens!
When will I escape this sorrow?
He's always on my mind, never leaves my thoughts.

算無緣得歡喜存活，
　　只有分與煩惱為冤。

到此夢亦
〔不〕成。

　　譬如對燈悶悶的坐，
　　　把似和衣強強的眠。
　　心頭暗發着願。
　　願薄幸的冤家夢中見。
　　爭奈按不下九曲回腸，
　　　合不定一雙業眼。

（尾）
　　是前世裏債、
　　　宿世的冤。
　　被你擔閣了人也張解元。

明年，張珙廷試，第三人及第。

iv.15/vii.1 正宮 （梁州令纏[7]）
　　步入蟾宮折桂花。
　　舉手平拏。
　　《長楊[8]》賦罷日西斜。
　　得意也。
　　掀髯笑、
　　　喜容加。

　　才優不讓賈馬。
　　金榜名標高甲。
　　蹤跡離塵沙。
　　青雲得路，
　　鳳沼步煙霞。

（甘草子）
　　最堪嘉。

15 Literally, "settle the nine bends of my intestines."
16 The third in rank of successful examination candidates was called "the flower-plucking gentleman." In the performance world, pursuit of a woman was often

I must lack the karma to abide in happiness,
    and am destined to merely complain about my fate.

It's like sitting and miserably facing a lamp
    or making yourself sleep with clothes on.
In my heart I secretly express my desire:
I want to see that heartless lover in my dreams.
But try as I might, I can't quell my sadness,[15]
    or close this damned pair of eyes.

At this point the dream also does not form.

Coda
"It's a debt from a former life,
    some injustice from lives long past.
I have been abandoned by you, Laureate Zhang."

The next year Zhang Gong took the examinations and passed as third from the top.[16]

iv.15/vii.1 Zheng Gong Mode

Liang Prefecture: A Bound Suite
He strode into the Toad Palace and snapped off a cassia blossom,
Easily picking it by simply raising his hand.
His examination rhapsodies[17] were finished, and sun was yet to set.
And he was pleased,
Laughing as he stroked his beard,
    his face full of happiness.

Superb talent the equal of Jia Yi or Sima Xiangru,
He was in the highest category of names on the Golden Plaque.[18]
Gone now from the world of dust and sand,
He had found the road to the clouds in the sky,
    and at the Phoenix Pond[19] would walk in a misty aurora.

Dried Licorice Root
A wonderful,

represented as a quest for success in the examinations, and of course the flower also signifies his lover.

17 Literally, the "Rhapsody on the Changyang Palace" 長楊宮賦, by the noted Han dynasty writer Yang Xiong 揚雄 (53–18 BCE); here a metonymy.
18 Register of successful candidates.
19 A metonymy for the Central Secretariat, one of the primary organs of the state bureaucracy.

最堪嘉。
一聲霹靂，
　果是魚龍化。
金殿拜皇恩，
　面對丹墀下。
正是男兒得志秋，
　向晚瓊林宴罷。
沈醉東風裏，
　控驕馬。
鞭裊蘆花。

蓦地打着

（脫布衫）
　追想那冤家。
　獨自在天涯。
　怎知此間及第，
　　修書索報與他。

　有多少女孩兒，
　　卷珠簾騁嬌奢。
　從頭着眼看來，
　　都盡總不如他。

　不敢住時霎。
　即便待離京華。
　官人如今是我，
　縣君兒索與他。

　偏帶兒是犀角。
　幞頭兒是烏紗。
　綠[9]袍兒當殿賜，
　待把白衫兒索脫與他。

（尾）
　得個除授先到家。

20 The site where Song emperors once fêted newly enfranchised candidates. Chalcedony refers to the bluish color of conifers covered in snow.

Admirable success.
A peal of thunder—
    truly a fish transforming into a dragon.
At the golden halls he paid his homage to imperial grace,
    standing face to face beneath the vermillion steps.
In this autumn when a man truly realizes his ambition,
    toward evening, he finished up the Feast in the Chalcedony
        Grove.[20]
Deeply inebriated by an eastern wind,[21]
    he took control of his proud mount
And let his whip trail through catkins of reeds.[22]

Doffing the Cotton Shirt   *He suddenly hits*
He recollected, then, his lover,   *on it.*
Alone out there at heaven's edge.
"She can't have learned my success.
    I should write a letter and report it to her.

There have been so many girls who,
    furling beaded curtains, have shown off their arrogant
        excesses.
I have looked them over from head to toe,
    yet none of them are her equal.

I cannot linger a second.
I must leave the capital with all due speed.
I am now an official
    and that will make her a Lady of the County.

My belt inlaid with rhinoceros horn,
My cross-tailed cap is raven-black silk.
A green robe[23] was bestowed on me at the imperial hall,
    so I'll take off this plain one to give to her.[24]

Coda
I'll go back home before I get an assignment,

---

21 Inappropriate to autumn, the eastern or spring breeze signifies a new life on the
    horizon.
22 Literally "reed flowers." As one of the top three candidates, he would have his
    choice of "the flowers of Chang'an," or the young daughters of high ministers.
23 Of officialdom.
24 A subtle gesture to the title of this song ("Doffing the Cotton Shirt").

引着幾對兒頭答。

見俺那鶯鶯大小大詐。

珙賦詩一絕，令僕人赴鶯鶯報喜。

iv.16/vii.2 雙調（御街行）

須臾喚得僕人至。

「囑付你些兒事。

指點如畫。

蒲州東畔十餘里。

有敕賜普救之寺。

法堂西壁。

行廊背後，

　　第三個門兒是。

見妻兒太君都傳示。

但道我擢高第。

教他休更許別人，

　　俺也則不曾聘妻。

相煩你。

且叮嚀寄語，

　　『專等風流婿』。」

生緘詩與僕，僕行。

鶯未知郎第，荏苒成疾。時季春十五夜。鶯思之，去年待月西廂之夜，感而泣下。

紅娘曰「姐姐今春多病，觸時有感，恐傷和氣。妾未知姐姐所染何患，當以藥理之，恐至不起。」

鶯鶯愈哭。

With my entourage two by two ahead,
Won't that be a wonderful way to greet my Oriole!"

The student composed a short four-line poem and sent the servant on
his way to report the good news to Oriole.

iv.16/vii.2 Shuang Diao Mode

Treading the Imperial Path
In no time at all he had summoned a servant boy,   *Directions as clear*
"I have an order for you: *as a drawing.*
Ten miles east of Puzhou
There is an imperially commissioned monastery, Universal
    Salvation—
West of the Dharma Hall,
Behind the corridor,
        the third door will be the place.

Relay this message to my wife's mother:
Just say I finished high up in the examinations,
And tell her not to betroth my wife to another
        because I have engaged myself to no other woman.
And I'll trouble you
To tell her these words:
        'Just wait on that elegant and handsome son-in-law.'"

He sealed up a poem, gave it to the servant, who set off.

Having no news yet of Zhang's success, Oriole took to her bed, sick.
That was the fifteenth night of the last month of spring.[25] Oriole thought
about this; it was this night last year that she had waited for the moon
in the western wing. She wept.

Crimson said, "You have been seriously ill this spring, and you've been
moved by the season's beauty. I fear it has upset the harmony of your
ethers. I don't know what anxiety has gotten hold of you, but it requires
medicine, lest you end up unable to rise again."

Oriole simply wept all the more.

---

25 When the moon is full.

iv.16/vii.2 道宮（憑欄人纏令）

憶多才。
自別來約過一載。
何日裏卻得同諧。
縈損愁懷。
怕黃昏愁倚朱欄，
　到良宵獨立空階。
趁落英遍蒼苔。
東風搖蕩，
　不簾飛絮，
　　滿地香埃。

欲問俺心頭悶答孩。
太平車兒難載。
都是俺今年浮災。
煩惱煞人也猜。
悶厭厭的心緒如麻，
　瘦嵒嵒的病體如柴。
鬢雲亂慵整瓊釵。
勞勞攘攘，
　身心一片，
　　沒處安排。

滋味大是尋
常。

（賺）

據俺當初，
把你個命般看待。
誰知道
到今贏得段相思債。
　相思債。

是前生負償他還着後噠。
你試尋思怪那不怪。
都是命乖。
爭奈心頭那和不快。
好難消解。

iv.17/vii.3 Dao Gong Mode

Someone Leaning on the Rail: A Bound Suite
"I recall that talented one.
It's been a year since we parted—
When will we get to share our harmony?
I'm wrapped in sad feelings, and I suffer.
Fearing the yellow dusk, I lean on the vermillion balustrade;
    in the long nights I stand alone on the empty steps.
I move toward falling blossoms spreading over the green moss.
The eastern wind stirs everything afloat,
    no screening out the flying floss
        that fills the earth with perfumed dust.

You want to ask about all this depression in my heart?
A freight wagon could not bear the load.[26]
And it all grew into a disaster that has plagued me this whole
    year—
It's driven me crazy.

A truly ordinary flavor.

Heavily depressed, my heart's thoughts are like tangled hemp;
    emaciated as a skeleton, this sick body is but firewood.
I'm too weary to stick a jeweled pin into the chaos of my clouds of
    locks.
Worn down and agitated,
    there's nothing I can do
        to settle this, the whole of body and heart.

Beguiling Song
"Once, back in the beginning,
I treasured you like my own life—
Who knew
    that that would win me only a debt of love's longing?
A debt of love's longing?

It's a debt incurred in a former life that I still need to pay.
Don't you think it's strange?
It's all just a miserable fate.
But alas, all that unhappiness in my heart
Is truly hard to purge.

---

26 This repeats the metaphorical use of sorrow as a heavy burden voiced by Student
    Zhang above, in suite IV.6/VI.19

近來這病的形骸。
鏡兒裏覷了後自澀耐。
傷心處，
故人與俺彼此天涯客，
天涯客。

我於伊志誠沒倦怠。
你於我堅心莫更改。
且與他捱。
下梢知他看怎奈。
悶愁越大。

（美中美）
　　困把欄桿倚，
　　羞折花枝戴。
　　這段閒煩惱，
　　　是自家買。
　　勞勞攘攘，
　　　不是自家心窄。
　　春色褪花梢[10]，
　　　春恨侵眉黛。
　　遙望着秦川道，
　　　雲山隔。

　　白日渾閒夜難熬，
　　　獨自兀誰採。
悶對西廂月，
　　　添香拜。
　　去年此夜，
　　　猶自月圓人在。
　　不似去年人，
　　　猛把欄桿拍。
　　有個長安信，
　　　教誰帶。

猛然提起。

My sick frame now
Makes me cringe when I look in the mirror.
And the most painful part is that
    that old acquaintance and I are both travelers at heaven's edge.
Travelers at heaven's edge.

My devotion to you has never faltered,
So don't you alter the loyalty you owe to me.
Together, we will bear it for the time being,
And see how it all turns out in the end.
This depressive sorrow is even greater now.

Beauty Within Beauty
"Tired, I lean on the railing
    and lazily snap off a flowering branch to wear in my hair.
I purchased this spell of pointless vexation
    all by myself.
My confusion and depression
    are not due to intolerance.
Spring colors fade on flowered branch tips
    and spring regrets infringe on the kohl of my brows.
I look far away at the road through Qin rivers,[27]
    separated by clouds and mountains.

Days are ordinary, nights hard to bear—
    all alone and companion to none,
I gloomily face the moon of the western wing
    and pray, adding ever more incense.
Last year on this night
    the moon was full, and you were here.
I am not the person I was that year. . . .
    Suddenly, I slap the railing—
I do have a letter to Chang'an
    but who will deliver it?

*She suddenly
begins to be stirred.*

27 That is, toward Chang'an.

（大聖樂）
花憔月悴，
　蘭消玉瘦，
　　不似舊時標格。
閒愁似海。
況是暮春天色。
落紅萬點，
　風兒細細，
　　雨兒微篩。
這些光景，
　與人妝點愁懷。

悶抵着牙兒，
空守定妝台。
眼也倦開。
淚漫漫地盈腮。
似恁淒涼，
　何時是了，
　　心頭暗暗疑猜。
縱芳年未老，
　應也頭白。

（尾）
紅娘怪我緣何害。
非關病酒
　不是傷春，
只為冤家不到來。

　　　　　　鶯對春時感舊恨，
　　　　　　為憶生漸成消瘦。

iv.18/vii.4 高平調（青玉案）
寂寞空閨裏。
能詞者易辦。苦苦天天甚滋味。
淅淅微微風兒細。

Music of the Great Sage
"Flowers shrivel, the moon grows pallid,
    orchids fade and jade grows thin[28]—
        all unlike the fullness of old times.
Pointless sorrow is like an ocean,
And even worse under skies of waning spring:
Myriad dots of fallen red—
    a fine, fine wind
        and the delicate winnowing of rain.
Scenes such as these
    fill a person with melancholy.

Downcast, head in hand,
    I look at my makeup stand in vain.
My eyes too tired to open,
    tears course down and flood my cheeks.
Will this dreary loneliness
    ever come to an end?
        My heart secretly harbors doubt.
Even though still young and in my prime
    my hair will have already turned white.

Coda
"Crimson wonders what it is that ails me.
It's not that I've had too much to drink,
It's not pain over spring's passing—
It's all because you haven't returned, my love."

    Oriole faced the spring season moved by old vexations,
    And grew ever thinner thinking of the student.

iv.18/vii.4 Gaoping Diao Mode

The Case of Unblemished Jade
Sad and lonely in her empty boudoir.
Bitter, bitter—O Heaven—what flavor is this?
Drizzling then whispering—the wind was a zephyr.

Easily accomplished by those who are capable poets.

---

28 While here a description of Oriole's perfume and body, this phrase can also mean
    "the integrity and chasteness of a woman."

薄薄怯怯，
　半張鴛被。
冷冷清清地睡。

憂憂戚戚添憔悴。
裊裊霏霏瑞煙碧。
　滅滅明明燈將煤。
哀哀怨怨不敢放聲哭，
　只管噆噆[11]嗳嗳地。

覆旦，靈鵲喜晴，鶯起。

iv.19/vii.5 仙呂調（滿江紅）
殘紅委地，
　靈鵲翻風喜新晴。
玉慘花愁，
　追思傳粉。
巾袖與枕頭兒都是淚痕。
一夜家無眠白日盹。
不存不濟，
　香肌瘦損。
「教俺縈方寸。
想他那裏
　也不安穩」。
「恰正心頭悶」。
見紅娘通報，
　「有人喚門」。[12]

門人報曰「張先生僕至。」夫人與鶯教召，須臾入。

Under a delicate, diaphanous gossamer of a thin
      sliver of a mandarin duck quilt.
Cold and chilly. Deserted and alone, she slept.

Disquieted and anxious, her looks grew haggard,
Coiling and thick, auspicious mists circled blue tiles.[29]
Now guttering, now glowing, the lamp was about to die out.
Lamenting, full of rancor and resentment, she dared not cry out,
      just sniffled and sighed.

The dark night over, it was dawn again. The prophesying magpies delighted in the clear sky.[30] Oriole arose.

iv.19/vii.5 Xianlü Diao Mode

A River Running Red
Tattered red shriveled on the ground
      as auguring magpies tumbled on the wind, delighting in the
         clear sky.
Her jadelike skin and flowered face were careworn and sad,
      her thoughts only about him, he of the whitest face.[31]
Headscarf, sleeves, and pillow all bore the stain of her tears.
Sleepless the whole night long, on and off the whole day, she
      dozed.
Life seemed pointless,
      as her perfumed body grew thin, then thinner.
"My mind is so troubled now
And I think that he
      must be uneasy there too."
She had just set aside the depression she felt
      when Crimson appeared to report,
         "Someone's calling at the gate."

The gate guard reported, "A servant of Student Zhang has arrived."
Madam Cui and Oriole had him summoned, and he immediately entered.

---

29 Likely the same tiles Zhang sang of in Book I, 1.5, and in 1.8.
30 The sporting and cawing of the magpie foretold good news.
31 From the story of He Yan 何晏, (ca.194–249, byname Pingshu 平叔), who wore
    white powder, though his face itself was even whiter than the powder. See Yiqing
    Liu 2002, 330.

僕使階前忙應諾，
　骨子氣喘不迭，
滿面征塵。
呼至簾前，
　夫人親問。
道「張郎在客可煞苦辛。
想見彼中把名姓等。
幾日試來，
　那幾日唱名。
得意那不得意，
　有何傳示、
　　有何書信。」
那廝也不多言語，
　覷着夫人賀喜，
　　喚鶯鶯做「縣君」。

一一描出。

僕以書呈夫人。紅娘取而奉鶯，鶯發書視之，止詩一絕。
詩曰

　　　玉京仙府探花郎，
　　　寄語[13]蒲東窈窕娘。
　　　指日拜恩衣晝錦，
　　　是須休作倚門妝。

鶯解詩旨曰「『探花郎』，第三也。『指日拜恩衣晝錦』
，待除授而歸也。」

夫人以下皆喜。自是至秋，杳無一耗。

He quickly paid his respects in front of the steps,
    still panting and out of breath,
        his face covered by the dust of travel.
He was called before the curtain,[32]
    where Madam Cui personally asked,
"This trip must be hard on Laureate Zhang.
I can imagine him there, waiting to see if he's on the list.
How long since he took the examinations?
    On what day was the pronouncement of names?
Was he pleased about how it turned out?
    What messages are there?
        Or what letters?"
That fellow didn't say much in reply—
    looking at Madam Cui, he offered congratulations,
        and called Oriole, "Lady of the County."

Highlighted one by one.

The servant presented a letter to Madam Cui, which Crimson took and handed to Oriole. Oriole opened the letter, but it was just one four-line poem:

    From the flower-plucking esquire in the precincts of the transcendent
        one[33] of the jade capital:
    I send these words to the modest sequestered woman in the East
        of Pu:
    "The day is at hand to thank the emperor for his grace, and to don
        daytime brocade,
    So stop now with the makeup of 'someone leaning on the door and
        waiting'."[34]

    Oriole understood that "plucking the flower" meant to come in third. And "The day is at hand to thank the emperor for his grace, and to don daytime brocade" meant that he was waiting for an appointment before returning.

---

32 As women, they could not meet a stranger face to face.
33 The emperor.
34 The early sense of "leaning on the door" referred to anxious parents awaiting a son's return, so the line means "don't wait for my return." To apply makeup also refers to making oneself up for the stage, hence to "play a role," which raises the possibility of reading this as "don't put on an act about waiting for me," poking fun at the poses adopted by separated lovers.

鶯修書密遣僕寄生，隨書贈衣一襲、瑤琴一張、玉簪一
枝、斑管[14]一枚。

iv.20/vii.6 越調（水龍吟）

露寒煙冷庭梧墜，
　又是深[15]秋時序。
空閨獨坐，
　無人存問，
　　愁腸萬縷。
怕到黃昏後，
　窗兒下甚般情緒。
映湖山側左，
　芭蕉幾葉，
　　空階靜散疏疏雨。

一自才郎別後，
　儘自家憑欄凝竚。
碧雲黯[16]澹，

楚天空闊，
　徵鴻南渡。
飛過蒹葭浦。
暮蟬噪煙迷古樹。
望野橋西畔，
　小旗沽酒，
　　是長安路。

（看花回）

想世上，
淒涼事，
　離情最苦。
　　恨不得，

插翅飛將往他行去。
地里又遠關山阻。

From Madam Cui on down, everyone was delighted. But from that time until the autumn, there was not even the simplest message.

Oriole crafted a letter and secretly sent a servant to deliver it to Zhang, accompanied by a set of clothes, a gem-set zither, a jade hairpin, and a writing brush of tear-stained bamboo.

iv.20/vii.6 Yue Diao Mode

Water Dragon Chant
The dew is chilly, the mist is cold, and the courtyard paulownia
    trees have shed their leaves—
        deep in autumn once more in the procession of the seasons.
Sitting alone in her empty room,
    with none to ask after her,
        her sad innards were myriad threads of thoughts.
She worried what the feelings in her heart would be like,
    there by the window when dusk fell.
Several leaves of the plantain were blown in and out of sight
    at the nearby pond and rockery
As a gentle rain fell sporadically
    on the silent and empty steps.

"Since my talented man left
    I have kept leaning on the balustrade to gaze out.
Glaucous clouds dim and dark—
    across the vast skies of Chu;
        migrating geese, crossing south,
Fly over reed-lined riverbanks.
Evening cicadas trill, mist obscures ancient trees.
Gazing west of a bridge in the fallows,
    I see the small flag of a wine-seller—
        that is the road to Chang'an.

Coming Back from Looking at Flowers
"To me, of all the dreary and lonesome
    moments of this world,
        feelings after separation are the most bitter.
How terrible that I cannot
    put on wings to fly to him.
The land between us is so distant
    and obstructed by many a mountain pass.

無計奈，
謾登樓空目斷，
故人何許。
密召得，
僕人至，
將傳肺腑。
連幾般
衣服。
——包將去。

是必小心，
休遲滯，
莫躭誤。
喚紅娘，
教拈與，
再三囑付。

（雪裏梅）

一路襯貼都有致。

「白羅素襜袴。
摺動的裰兒也無。
一領汗衫與裹肚。
非是取取。
是俺咱自做。

綿襪兒莫嫌薄。
燈下曾用工夫。
一針針刺了羨覷。
恐慮破後，
有誰重補。」

（揭鉢子）

「藍直系有工夫。
做得依規矩。
幽窗明淨處。
潛心下繡針，
着意分絲縷。

No plan is in the offing,
    I keep climbing up the tower to vainly gaze to heaven's edge.
        Where is my man?

Secretly I've summoned
    a servant here,
        to carry a heartfelt message,
Together with
    some clothing
Packed piece by piece for the trip.
'You must be careful,
    don't tarry
        and don't you dare delay.'"
She summoned Crimson
    to hand them to the servant,
        enjoining her several times:

A Plum in the Snow
"These plain trousers of white silk
Have not the slightest wrinkle from being folded.
This undershirt and sash for your robe
Are not just meaningless tokens,
But were made by me alone.

Don't find these silk stockings too thin,
As I spent endless effort under lamplight
And admired every stitch that I made.
I worry, if they got a hole
    who would be there to darn them?

Raising the Alms Bowl
"Laborious effort went into your blue robe,
Tailoring it to compass and rule.
In a clean bright spot by a sheltered window,
I plied the embroidery needle with devoted heart, and
    painstakingly separated every thread.

In this whole series, every moment of subtle comparison to her real feelings is precise and endlessly charming.

繡着合歡連理花，
雉[17]子兒交頸舞。

絨縧兒細絳州出，
宜把腰圍束。
青衫忒離俗。
裁得暢可體，
襖兒是吳綾，
　　件件都受取。
更與伊幾件物。」

（疊字三[18]台）
「簪雖小是美玉。
玉取其潔白純素。
微累纖瑕不能污。
渾如俺為你
　　俺為你心堅固。
你曾惜俺如珍。
　　今日看如糞土。

寫紫毫瑤琴，
更瀟灑多韻。

紫毫管未嘗有，
　　是九嶷山下蒼竹。
當日湘妃別姚虞。
眼兒裏淚珠。
淚珠如秋雨。
點點都畫成斑，
　　比我別離來苦。

瑤琴是你咱撫，
夜間曾挑鬥奴。
你悄似相如獻了上林賦，
成名也在上都。
在上都裏貪歡趣。
鎮日家耽酒迷花，
　　便把文君不顧。」

I embroidered flowers of shared joy with stems interlaced
And pheasants dancing with intertwined necks.

The soft-napped ribbon is fine, produced in Crimson Prefecture,
Perfect for cinching the span of your waist.
The black gown is beyond ordinary,
Tailored to fit your form.
Pendant cords are from the finest southern silk—
        please accept all these things,
For I have others to give you, too.

Three Terraces Reduplication
"Though small, the hairpin is of beautiful jade.
Jade for its unblemished white of purest clarity,
Unmarred by the slightest hint of a flaw—
Exactly how I
        made my heart firm and fast for you.
You once treasured me like the rarest jewel,
But today you just see me as a heap of dung.

Describing the purple down and gem-set zither is even more elegant and full of charm.

A brush of purple hare's down, matchless in the world,
        has a handle of mottled bamboo from Mount Jiuyi.
On that day when the consorts of the Xiang parted from King Shun
Their eyes were filled with pearls of tears,
Pearls of tears like an autumn rain that
Dyed these speckles drop by drop—
        their parting was even more bitter than mine.

This gem-set zither is the one you strummed
At night, the one that stirred me.
You are like a Sima Xiangru, after presenting his 'Rhapsody on
        Shanglin,'
Making your name in the capital.
In the capital you lust for amusing pleasures—
Drunk all day, bedazzled by the beautiful flowers,
        you pay your Wenjun no mind.

（緒煞）

「孩兒沿路裏耐辛苦。

若見薄情郎傳示與。

但道『自從別來，

官人萬福。』

一件件對他分付。

教他受取。

看是阻那不阻。

臨了教讀這一封兒墜淚書。」

那得不斷腸。

僕未至京。君瑞擢第後，以才授翰林學士。因病閑居，至秋未愈。

iv.21/vii.7 仙呂調（剔銀燈）

寂寞空齋清秋院宇。

瀟灑閑庭幽戶。

檻內芳菲，

黃花開遍，

將近登高時序。

無情緒。

憔悴得身軀。

有誰擡舉。

早是離情恁苦。

病體兒不能痊癒。

淚眼盈盈，

眉頭鎮蹙。

九曲回腸千縷。

「天遙地遠，

萬水千山，

故人何處。

（尾）

許多時節分鴛侶。

Double Coda (Continuing)
"Bear the trials of the road, my servant lad,
And if you see that heartless lover of mine, tell him,
'From the time we parted
you have enjoyed a thousand bounties.'
Repeat everything that I have said about each item
And make him take them all.
See if he refuses or not.[35]
And at the end, have him read this letter of fallen tears."

*How can one not
be broken-hearted
when reading this?*

The servant had yet to reach the capital when Junrui was appointed
an Academician in the Hanlin Academy because of his talent. Ill,
he lived quietly, but his illness lingered through autumn.

iv.21/vii.7 Xianlü Diao Mode

Trimming the Silver Lamp
A cold and lonely study sits empty,
A secluded room in a somber courtyard.
A wonderful fragrance within the gates
        of chrysanthemum in full bloom—
            it was near the time of climbing heights.[36]
But he was depressed and had no interest.
His body drawn and drained,
There was no one to care for him.

Already suffering so from the feelings of separation,
His body could find no cure.
Teary eyes filled to overflowing
        and the arch of his brows was permanently clenched.
In his very soul were a thousand tangled thoughts[37]—
"Heaven far and earth further,
        ten-thousand rivers and a thousand ranges away,
            where is my lover?

Coda
"Through many seasons, away from my faithful companion,

---

35 That is, whether he has rejected her.
36 The ninth of the ninth lunar month, called the Double Yang Festival, a time for
    gathering with friends and family to climb mountains and compose poetry.
37 Literally, "A thousand threads in the nine bends of his small intestine."

除夢裏有時曾去。
新來和夢也不曾做。」

IV.22/VII.8

生喜來擢第，
愁來病未愈。
那逢秋夜，
為憶鶯鶯，
杳然無一耗，
愁腸萬結矣。

正宮（梁州令斷送）
簾外蕭蕭下黃葉。
正愁人時節。
一聲羌管怨離別。
看時節。
窗兒外雨些些。

亦是詞詞人入
語。

晚風兒淅溜淅冽。
暮雲外徵鴻高貼。
風緊斷行斜。
衡陽迢遞。
千里去程賒。

（應天長）
經霜黃菊半開謝。
折花羞戴，
　寸腸千萬結。
捲簾凝淚眼，
　碧天外亂峰千疊。
望中不見蒲州道，
　空目斷暮雲遮。

38 This aria is a reworking of a rather famous lyric attributed to Zhao Ji 趙佶, the
Northern Song emperor Huizong 徽宗 (1082–1135, r. 1100–1126), supposedly written on his exile to the north after Jin conquered the Northern Song. For the original, see Zhu Decai 1997.

Only in dreams could I sometimes go to her,
But now I don't even dream."[38]

> The student was delighted he had passed the examinations
> but was sad that his illness had yet to be cured.
> Then he encountered autumn nights
> and, as he remembered Oriole,
> who was silent and sent no word,
> his sorrowful guts were tied into thousands of knots.

IV.22/VII.8 Zheng Gong MODE

Liang Prefecture Song: Final Suite
Pitter-pattering, yellow leaves fell outside the window—
Precisely the depressing season.
A single sound from a Tibetan flute brought the resentment of
    parting,
And just look at this moment:
Outside the window rain gently falls.

These are the insertions of a real writer of lyrics.

An evening wind whistles and sighs,
And beyond the moving clouds, migrating geese stay in close
    formation.
But when the wind kicks up, it breaks their serried ranks.
Hengyang is still far away,[39]
With a thousand miles left on their journey.

Responding to Lengthening Days
After the frost, half of the yellow chrysanthemums had withered,
He snapped off some flowers, but was ashamed to put them in his
    hair,
        every inch of his innards drawn tight in thousands of knots.
Furling the curtain, he set his teary eyes
        On a thousand layers of chaotic peaks at the edge of azure skies.
His field of vision revealed no road to Pu Prefecture,
        for his empty eyes were obstructed by the evening clouds.

---

39 From a poem by the Tang poet, Du Fu 杜甫 (712–770, byname Zimei 子美),
    "Hengyang geese from ten thousand miles away / Return north again this year" 萬
    里衡陽雁,今年又北歸. Hengyang is in Hubei Province, in the south of China. See
    Du Fu and Qiu Zhao'ao 1979, vol 4, 2059.

荒涼深院古台榭。

惱人窗外，
琅玕風欲折。
早是離人心緒惡，
閣不定淚啼清血。
　斷腸何處砧聲急
與愁人助淒切。

（賺）
點上燈兒，
　悶答孩地守書舍。
謾咨嗟。
鴛衾大半成虛設。
獨對如年夜。

守着窗悶悶地坐，
　把引睡的文書兒強披閱。
檢秦晉傳，
　檢不着翻尋着吳越。
把耳朵撦。

收拾起，
　待剛睡些。
爭奈這一雙眼兒劣。
好發業。
淚漫地會聖也難交睫。
空自擷。

似恁地淒涼
　恁地愁絕。
下場知他看怎者。
行志了，
　不覺聲絲氣噎。
幾時捱徹。

In this deserted and cloistered courtyard, amid old terraces and
    kiosks,

What annoyed him outside the window were
    green bamboos nearly snapping from the wind.
Already tormented by a heart of one separated,
    he had little control over his tears, all fresh blood.
Breaking his heart: from just where did the persistent sound of the
    fulling block[40] arise,
        abetting the misery and grief of the sorrowful?

Beguiling Song
He lit the lamp,
    and mindlessly attended to his study.
He sighed uselessly—
The larger half of a lover's quilt was rolled out for naught,
For he faced this year-long night alone.

Sitting by the window, gloomy and glum
    he made himself flip through books to bring him sleep.
He searched for a chapter on Qin and Jin,
    and not finding it, turned instead to one on Wu and Yue.[41]*He*
        pinched his ears in anxious confusion.

He began to put the books away
    wanting to sleep a little.
But, alas, his eyes were mischievous
And caused no end of trouble—
Tears so overflowed that even a saint couldn't keep his eyes shut.
He uselessly stamped his foot.

Such misery and
    such deep sadness—
Who knows how he'll wind up?
He did everything he could but
    ended up enervated and breathless.
When would it all end?

"He searched for a chapter on Qin and Jin, / not finding it, turned instead to one on Wu and Yue" reveals deep resentment.

40 Fulling blocks are used to beat clothes, here preparing them to be stored for
   winter.
41 Books on strife and warfare instead of amity and accord.

（甘草子）
　　我伴呆。
　　我伴呆。
　　一向志誠，
　　不道他心趄。
　　短命的死冤家，
　　甚不怕神天折。
　　一自別來整一年，
　　為個甚音書斷絕。
　　着意殷勤待撰個簡牒，
　　奈手顫難寫。

（脫布衫）
　　幾番待撇了不藉。
　　思量來當甚廝憋。
　　孩兒我須有見伊時，
　　咱對着惺惺人說。

（三台）
　　愁欹單枕，
　　夜深無寐，
　　襲襲靜聞沉屑。
　　隔窗促織兒泣新晴，
　　小即小，
　　叫得暢嗹嗻[19]。
　　向空階那畔，
　　叨叨地悄沒休歇。
　　做個蟲蟻兒，
　　沒些兒慈悲，
　　聒得人耳疼耳熱。

（尾）
　　越越的哭得燈兒滅。
　　慚愧啞秋天甫能明夜。
　　一枕清風半窗月。

Dried Licorice Root
"How stupid could I be?
How stupid could I be?
I've been sincere all along
  but it seems her heart has gone astray.
You due-for-a-short-life deadly enemy,
  why don't you fear the wrath of the spirits?
It's been a year since we parted
  so why are all letters cut off?
I want to write you a letter with all my heart,
  but alas my hand trembles so I cannot write.

Doffing the Cotton Shirt
"How many times I have wanted to discard you and couldn't.
But when I think of it, it's no more than a fit of pique.
Child, there is a time we will meet
  and I will explain it then, face to face."

Three Terraces
Sorrowful, he reclined on his single pillow,
  sleepless, deep in the night
    and in the silence, whiff by whiff, he could smell the ashes
      of aloeswood incense.
Outside the window, crickets sobbed at newly clearing skies,
  small they might be
    but called on and on.
Over by the empty steps
  they chirred as if they would never stop.
Just a little bug
  without the slightest sense of compassion,
    grating on peoples' ears until they hurt, until they
      burned.

He overuses these kinds of words.

Coda
More and more, he wept until the lamp gave out,
And, oh joy,[42] **autumn was starting to have clear nights—**
One pillow of freshening winds, half a window of moonlight.

42 Said in sarcasm.

生渴仰間，僕至，授衣發書。其大略曰

「薄命妾鶯鶯，致書於才郎文几。

柔婉悽惻。

去秋已來，
常忽忽如有所失。
於喧嘩之中，
或勉為笑語。
宵宵<?>自處，
無不淚零。
至於夢寐之間，
亦多敍感咽
離憂之思。
綢繆繾綣，
暫若尋常。
幽會未終，
驚魂已斷。
雖半枕如暖，
而思之甚遙。

一昨拜辭，
倏逾舊歲。
長安行樂之地，
觸緒牽情。
何幸不忘幽微，
眷念無斁。
鄙薄之志，
無以奉酬。
至於終始之盟，
則固不忒。

鄙昔中夕相因，
或同宴處。
婢僕見誘，
遂致私誠。
兒女之心，

Just as Student Zhang was hungrily longing, the servant arrived and gave him the clothes. Zhang opened the letter. The gist of it read:

Oriole, the ill-fated, sends this letter to the desk of the talented gentleman.

> From autumn of last year,
> I have been in a daze, as though I were lost.
> Amid the noise of daily life
> *I could perhaps banter with others,*
> *But night after night, when all alone,*   *Gentle and sweet;*
> *there was never a time I would not weep.*   *full of grief and*
> *And between dreams and sleep*   *pain.*
> *I also silently sobbed,*
> *rehearsing the anxieties of separation.*
> Our intimate lovemaking
> for that brief time[43] seemed normal.
> But our hidden tryst had yet to reach its conclusion
> when your soul[44] was sent flying, and the dreams ended.
> A half of the pillow might seem warm
> but I think of you as far away.
>
> One morning you bid me adieu
> and in a flash a year passed by.
> *In Chang'an, one can indulge in pleasures*
> *and chances for entangled relationships come easily.*
> *How fortunate I am that you remember me enough*
> *to still feel undying affection.*
> My petty ambitions can find
> no way of repaying you for that.
> As for our pact to share our lives together,
> it is firm and has not changed at all.
>
> Before, I met you late at night,
> or occasionally shared the same feast mat.
> My maidservant was enticed to send your messages,
> and in secret I committed myself to you.
> The hearts of young lovers

43 In the dream.
44 The *hun* or "light" soul could travel or be summoned free of the body.

不能自固。
兄有援琴之挑，
鄙人無投梭之拒。
及薦枕席，
義盛恩深，
愚幼之情，
永謂終托。

豈其既見君子，
而能以禮定情，
松柏留心，
致有自獻之羞，
不復明侍巾櫛，
歿身永恨，
含嘆何言。
倘若仁人用心，
俯遂幽劣，
雖死之日，
猶生之年。

如或達士略情，
捨小從大，
以先配為醜行，
謂要盟之可欺，
則當骨化形銷.
丹誠不泯，
因風委露，
猶託清塵。
存歿之誠，
言盡於此。

臨紙嗚咽，
情不能伸。
千萬千萬，
珍重珍重。

cannot be firm of their own volition,
how much more so when you seduced me with your zither,[45]
and I did not forestall you with a thrown shuttle![46]
Though, when I brought my pillow and mats to share,
your sense of obligation was strong, and your kind favor deep,
and in my naïve passion,
I thought I could rely on them to the very end.

"Having already met my love,"[47]
must a marriage match be made with ritual propriety?
My heart is as unchanging as pine or cypress,
to the point that I bore the shame of offering myself to you,
no longer to be a woman fit to marry.
I buried myself in eternal regret.
I can only sigh; what is there to say?
Should you, a humane person, give play to your heart
and consider acceding to the wishes of this low one,
then, were that also to be the day I die,
it would be worth a year of life.

Should a wise man such as yourself think lightly of this,
and discard my petty wishes to follow higher dictates,
considering grass weddings[48] to be vile,
saying that this compact, forced upon you, can be spurned,
then let my bones decay and my body disappear.
But the sincerity in my red heart shall never perish,
and instead, trailing the wind and tailing the dew,[49]
it shall be entrusted to the pure dust of your stride.
My perfect sincerity in life or death
is fully expressed in this.

I sob as I look at this letter-paper,
but my true feelings cannot be expressed.
Ten thousand times I say,
"Take care of yourself."

45 A comparison to Sima Xiangru and Zhuo Wenjun
46 From the story of a woman resisting the advances of a man by throwing her shuttle
    at him and breaking two of his teeth.
47 The first part of an ancient couplet, the second part being, "how should I not
    rejoice?"
48 Taking a wife informally, before the marriage is announced in the ancestral temple.
49 That is, like flowers and leaves being felled by spring winds and autumn's frost.

玉簪一枝，

斑管一枚，

瑤琴一張。

假此數物，

示妾真誠。

玉取其堅潤不渝，

淚痕在竹，

愁緒縈琴。

因物達誠，

永以為好。

心邇身遠，

拜會何時。

幽情所鍾，

千里神合。

秋氣方蕭，

強飯為佳，

慎自保持，

無以鄙為深念也。」

生發書，不勝悲慟。

iv.23/vii.9 大石調（玉翼蟬）

才讀罷，

　仰面哭。

淚把青衫污。

料那人爭知我，

　如今病未愈。

只道把他孤負。

好悽楚。

One jade hairpin,
one writing brush of tearstained bamboo,
one gem-set zither.
I avail myself of these few objects
to reveal my perfect sincerity.
Jade, because its hard luster never changes,[50]
The tear stains are on the bamboo,[51]
And threads of sorrow are strung on the zither—
these things express my sincerity to the fullest
and can forever be taken as symbols of what was good.
Our hearts are near,
our bodies distant,
and no time designated for us to meet again.
My secret passions desire
that our souls merge a thousand miles away.

Autumn has turned cold and severe,
and you should make sure to eat.
Take heedful care of yourself,
and don't think too deeply of me.[52]

Reading the letter, the student was overcome by grief.

iv.23/vii.9 Dashi Diao Mode

A Jade-Winged Cicada
Just finished reading,
          he raised his head to the heavens and cried,
Tears staining his black robe.
"I suspect she cannot know
          that I am still in the throes of illness, and
Can only say that I have turned my back on her.
So wretchedly sad!

50 Faithfulness.
51 She means "as mine are on this paper." Since she mentions "purple down" above, we
   know that, while "round bamboo" is sometimes used to describe a tea roller, here it is
   a brush.
52 Several places have been changed in this text from the original Tang short story
   to make it fit its performance context and the time: the season of the year, for instance, and small inflections that change this from a final parting letter to one only of
   separation.

空悶亂，
　　長嘆吁。
此恨憑誰訴。
似恁地埋怨，
　　教人怎下得，
　　索剛拖帶與他前去。

讀了又讀。
一個好聰明婦女。
其間言語。
都成章句。
寄來的物件，
　　斑管瑤琴簪是玉。
竅包兒裏，
　　一套衣服。
怎不教人痛苦。
眉癒眉攢，
　　斷腸腸斷，
　　　這鶯鶯一紙書。

生友人楊巨源聞之，作詩以贈之。其詩曰

　　　　　清潤潘郎玉不如，
　　　　　中庭霜冷葉飛初。
　　　　　風流才子多春思，
　　　　　腸斷蕭娘一紙書。

巨源勉君瑞娶鶯。君瑞治裝未及行，鄭相子恆至蒲州，詣
普救寺，往見夫人。

夫人問曰「子何務而至於此。」

恆曰「相公令恆，慶夫人終制，成故相所許親事矣。」

夫人曰「鶯已許張珙。」

恆曰「莫非新進張學士否。」

I worry and fret in vain,
    and all I can do is sigh.
Who is there to listen to my rancor?
Such resentment toward me—
      how can I bear it?
          Better I set out with my illness to return to her side.

Done reading, I read it again—
What an intelligent woman—
Her every word a paragraph.
The things she sent:
    a tear-stained brush, a gem-set zither, a comb of jade,
And peeking inside the bag,
    a complete set of clothes.
Doesn't it anguish me,
Make my eyebrows furrow?
    My heart breaks, sundered
        by this single letter from Oriole.

He cries as soon as he reads it, then reads it again and again; he cannot keep himself from reading it over and over.

Yang Juyuan, a friend of Zhang's, heard about this and wrote a poem to send to the student. The poem read:

Fresh and lustrous is Esquire Pan, even more than jade,
Frost chills the center of the courtyard: the start of the leaves' fall.
A romantic talented one, full of spring thoughts,
And a broken-hearted beauty, with a letter of a single page.

Juyuan urged Junrui to take Oriole as his wife.

Junrui got his things in order, but he had yet to leave when Minister Zheng's son, Heng, reached Puzhou and visited the monastery to pay a call on Madam Cui.

Madam Cui asked, "What business brings you here?"

"My father ordered me to celebrate the end of your mourning, madam," said Heng, "and to complete the marriage that Minister Cui had promised."

"But Oriole is already promised to Zhang Gong," replied Madam Cui.

Heng said, "Would that be the newly advanced Academician Zhang?"

夫人曰「珙新進，未知除授。」

恆曰「珙以才授翰林學士，衛吏部以女妻之。」

iv.24/vii.10南呂宮（一枝花纏）

這畜生腸肚惡，

全不合神道。
着言廝間諜，
　忒奸狡。
道「張珙新來，
　受了別人家捉。
本萌着一片心，
　待解破這同心，
　　子腳裏他家做俏。」

鄭氏聞言道。
「怎地着。」
攧損紅娘腳。
鶯鶯向窗那畔
　也知道。
九曲柔腸，
　似萬口尖刀攪。
那紅娘方便地勸道。
「遠道的消息，
　姐姐且休縈懷抱。」

（傀儡兒）
「妾想那張郎的做作，
　於姐姐的恩情不少。
當初不容易得來，
　便怎肯等閒撇掉。
鄭恆的言語無憑准，
　一向把夫人說調。

為姐姐受了張郎的定約
那畜生心頭熱燥。

於夫人着惱處
略，特詳鶯鶯
忙恨。紅娘閒
解方合本情。

"Gong is newly advanced through the examination system," said Madam Cui, "but I hadn't heard that he's been given a position in the bureaucracy."

"Gong was appointed Hanlin Academician," said Heng. "Minister of Personnel Wei has arranged a marriage for him and his daughter."

iv.24/vii.10 Nanlü Gong Mode

A Sprig of Flowers: A Bound Suite
This beast was bad through and through,
    lacking any morals at all.
He spoke only to sow discord,
    and he was just too crafty!
He said, "Just recently, Zhang Gong
    was betrothed to another family.
All along he nurtured the intention
    of untying this lover's knot
        to prance around in someone else's family."

Hearing this, Madam Cui cried,
    "How could he do this!"
Crimson stamped her foot so hard it hurt,
And by the window, Oriole
    also heard him,
And the nine loops of her tender gut
    seemed to be ripped by thousands of knives.
Seizing her opportunity, Crimson encouraged Oriole,
"Don't concern yourself over rumors
    from faraway places.

The part where Madam Cui is vexed is shortened; but it is particularly detailed where Oriole becomes preoccupied. It reverts to the facts of situation only when Crimson casually offers an explanation.

Puppets
"I think that everything Master Zhang has done
    shows his compassion and tenderness toward you.
You weren't easy to get in the beginning,
    so how could he just casually toss you aside?
There's no basis for Zheng Heng's words;
    they were just to provoke your mother.

That beast's heart is fuming
    because you accepted Master Zhang's proposal.

對甫成這一段虛脾，
望姐姐肯從前約。
等寄書的若迴路便知端的，
目下且休，
秋後便了。」

（轉青山）

鶯鶯儘勸，
全不領略，
迷留悶亂沒處着。
「上梢裏只喚做
百年偕老。
誰指望是他沒下梢。
負心的天地表。
天地表。

待道是實，
從前於俺無弱。
待道是虛甚音信杳，
為他受苦了。
多多少少。
爭知他恁地情薄。
只是自家錯了。
自家錯了。

且疑且悔，總
之是怨。

（尾）

孤寒時節教俺且充個「張嫂」。
甚富貴後教別人受郡號。
剛待不煩惱。
呵吁的一聲僕地氣運倒。

讒言可畏，
十分不信後須疑。
人氣好毒，
一息不來時便死。

He's created this fictional scenario
    in the hopes you'll be willing to accept the earlier compact.
Just wait until the answer to your letter arrives, and then you'll know
    for sure.
      So just stop right now,
          and things will become clear in the end."[53]

Return to the Green Mountains
Try as she might to counsel Oriole,
    she comprehended nothing
But sat there in a depressive daze.
"At the beginning I thought it would be us
    growing old together for a hundred years.
I never thought he wouldn't finish what he started.
The heartless will be revealed by Heaven—
Revealed by Heaven.

If what Zheng Heng says is true,
    then the student did not stint in his feelings for me before.
If what Zheng says is false, why have there been no letters?
So much! So much
I have suffered for him.
How could I know he would be this heartless?
It was my own mistake,
My own mistake!

Both doubting and regretting. In a word, it is resentment.

Coda
"When he was a poor student, he had me fill the role of 'Mrs. Zhang,'
And for no reason, once he's rich and noble, he calls someone else
    'Lady of the County.'
I can't bear being this upset. . . ."
And with a long moan, she slumped to the floor.

Slanderous words should be feared;
People may completely disbelieve, but doubt will surely come
    later.
Human anger is easily incited;
The breath fails, and sometimes it's deadly.

---

53 This phrase probably also carries the overtone of the more common phrase, "accounts will be totaled up after the fall harvest" 秋後必算帳; that is "he'll get his."

左右侍兒皆救，多時方蘇。

夫人泣曰「皆汝之不幸也。」密囑紅娘曰「姐姐萬一不快，必不赦汝。」

恆潛見夫人曰「珙與恆執親。況珙有新配，恆約在先，當以故相姑夫為念。」

夫人不獲已，陰許恆擇日成禮。議論間。

iv.25/vii.11 雙調（文如錦）

好心斜。

見鄭恆終是他親熱。

囑付紅娘，

「你管取您姐姐。

是他命裏

　　十分拙。

休教覓生覓死，

　　自推自擅。

有些兒好弱，

　　你根的不捨。」

鄭恆又譖言道，

「您姐姐休呆。

我比張郎，

　　是不好門地，

　　　　不好家業。

不是自家自賣弄，

　　我一般女婿，

　　　　也要人迭。

外貌即不中，

骨氣較別。

身分即村，

　　衣服兒忒撚。

The servants rushed to save her, and after a long time, she was revived.

Madam Cui wept, "All of this is your misfortune!" And she told Crimson in private, "If Oriole falls ill, I will not pardon you."

Heng secretly visited Madam Cui and said, "Who is closer in kinship, Gong or me? Moreover, Gong has a new fiancée, my marriage pact was prior to his, and we should take the wishes of my deceased uncle into consideration."

Madam Cui had no other choice. She granted Heng's wish and picked out a propitious day to complete the marriage rituals. And just as they were discussing everything. . . .

iv.25/vii.11 Shuang Diao Mode

Patterned Like Embroidery
She was too partial,
And viewed Zheng Heng as the closer to her.
She instructed Crimson,
        "You take care of your elder sister—
Her fate
        is just bad luck.
Don't let her think about suicide
        or hurt herself.
No matter what,
        don't let her out of your sight."
Then Zheng Heng, uninvited, weighed in,
"Your sister should stop being foolish.
        Is my pedigree worse than Zhang's?
                Have I less property?

I'm not just selling myself here,
        but a son-in-law like me
                is a great catch for anyone.
I may be hard to look at on the outside
        but my comport[54] is different than others.
My body might be ugly,
        but my clothes patch over what's missing.

---

54 Literally, "bone aura," most often meaning to have backbone; here, it likely means "I get what I want."

頭風即是有，
　頭巾兒蔚帖。
文章全不會後，
　《玉篇》都記徹。
張郎是及第，
　我承內祗，
子是爭得些些。
他別求了婦，
　你只管裏守志吵，
當甚貞烈。」

（尾）

言未訖簾前忽聽得人應喏，
已道「鄭衙內且休胡說，
兀的門外張郎來也。」

不意相逢，如
何措手。

鄭恆手足無所措。珙已至簾下，拜畢夫人。

夫人曰「喜學士別繼良姻。」

珙驚曰「誰言之。」

曰「都下人來，稔聞是說。今鶯已從前約。」

鄭恆以此言，使張君瑞添一段風流煩惱，增十般稔膩憂
愁。

夫人且將實言，唬君瑞面顏如土。

夫人道甚來。

仙呂（香山會）
　那君瑞聞道，

Indeed, I have scabies on my head,
    but my kerchief is nicely ironed.
True enough I cannot write fine literature,
    but I've fully memorized the *Jade Book*.[55]
Esquire Zhang has passed the Advanced Scholar Examination
    but I'm an Inner Intendant,[56]
        which is just about the same.
He's found another wife
    and you only care about remaining true—
        what's the point of holding on to your chaste name?"

Coda
He hadn't even finished speaking when the sound of greeting was heard
And someone said, "Palace Guard Zheng,[57] stop your foolishness,
It's Esquire Zhang right outside the door!"

*He never thought
what he would do,
should they meet.*

Zheng Heng didn't know what to do. Gong had already reached the curtain and finished his obeisances to Madam Cui.

Madam Cui said, "Congratulations, Academician, on finding an excellent second wife."

Astonished, Gong replied, "Who told you that?"

"Someone from the capital came who'd heard this old news. So, now Oriole will abide by the previous marriage pact."

Zheng Heng had told her this, and Zhang Junrui felt a flash of fear over his romantic relationship, increasing his anxieties tenfold in his mind.

Madam Cui told him the whole truth, and it scared him so much his face turned the color of loess.

And what did she say?

iv.26/vii.12 Xianlü Diao Mode

Meeting on Incense Peak
When Junrui heard the news,

55 The first character dictionary ever made.
56 A designation for low-ranking palace intendants, a far cry from Zhang's high position.
57 This is a term used to designate the offspring of high officials.

撲然倒地。
只鼻內似有游氣。
曲匝了半晌，
　收身強起。
傷自家來得較遲。

「誰曾受捉。
那說來的畜生在那裏。
喚取來夫人面前詰對。」
旁邊鄭衙內，
怎生坐地。
忍不定連打唏。

諧趣。

夫人曰「學士息怒。其事已然，如之奈何。」

生思之。鄭公，賢相也，稍蒙見知。吾與其子爭一婦人，
似涉非禮。

夫人令恆拜珙曰「此鶯兄也。」

珙視之。覷衙內結束模樣，越添煩惱。

iv.27/vii.13 中呂調（牧羊關）
張生早是心羞慘。
那堪見女婿來參。
不稔色村沙叚。
鶻鴒乾澹。
向日頭玃兒般眼。
吃蝨子猴猻兒般臉。
皂條攔胸系，
　羅巾腦後擔。

鬢邊蟣蝨渾如糝。
你尋思大小大俺嚕。
口呶似貓坑，
　咽喉似潑懺。

he passed out and fell to the floor.
Only a bit of breath circulated in his nose.
He rolled around a bit
    and then, recovering, forced himself to rise.
He was stricken that he'd arrived too late.

"Who said I was never taken into the family?
Where's the beast who said it?
Call him out here in front of Madam Cui so I can confront him!"
Palace Guard Zheng, there to one side
    and unable to sit still,   *Comic interest.*
Began to sneeze uncontrollably.

Madam Cui said, "Cease your anger, Academician, it's already been settled. There's nothing you can do."

The student thought about it. "The noble elder Zheng is a virtuous prime minister who knows me slightly. It would be a violation of etiquette should I contest with his son for a woman."

Madam Cui had Heng make obeisance to Gong, saying, "This is Oriole's older brother."

Gong looked at him, and seeing how he was decked out, was even more annoyed.

iv.27/vii.13 Zhong Diao Mode

Shepherd's Pass
Student Zhang was already abashed and downtrodden,
How could he stand watching the obeisance of this new son-in-
    law?
He was ugly, he was coarse,
His eyes were as dry and dull
As the orbs of a badger looking at the sun.
With a face like a monkey eating lice,
A black belt was stretched across his chest,
    and a silk handkerchief hung from the back of his head.

At his temples, nits and lice were just like like grain,
You can imagine just how filthy he was—
Breath from his mouth was like a cesspit,
    and his throat sounds like garbled incantations.

詐又不當個詐，
　　諂又不當個諂。
早是轆軸來粗細腰，
　　穿領布袋來寬布衫。

（尾）
　　莫難道詩骨瘦嵓岩。
　　掂詳了這廝趨蹌身分。
　　便活脫下鍾馗一二三。

生謂夫人曰「鶯既適人，兄妹之禮，不可廢也。」

夫人召鶯，久之方出。

iv.28/vii.14 仙呂調（點絳唇纏令）
　　百媚鶯鶯，
　　　見人無語空低首。
　　淚盈巾袖。
　　兩葉眉兒皺。

　　擷損金蓮，
　　　搓損蔥枝手。
　　從別後。
　　臉兒清秀。
　　比是年時瘦。

（天下樂）
　　拜了人前強問候。
　　做為兒嬌更柔。
　　料來他家不自由。
　　眉尖有無限愁。

　　「無狀的匹夫怎消受。
　　與做眷屬，
　　俺來得只爭個先後。
　　是自家錯也。
　　已裝不卸，

He could boast, but not really;
    could fawn, but there was nothing to praise.
He had a waist as thick as a stone grain-roller
    in a cotton robe as big as a sack.

Coda
Can't it be said he's a poet of skin and bone,[58]
Taking measure of this guy's ugly, cringing body,
He talked like stringing two or three phrases of Zhong Kui
    together.[59]

The student told Madam Cui, "Since Oriole is to marry another, the ritual greetings between us as elder brother and younger sister cannot be done away with."

Madam Cui called Oriole, who took a long time to appear.

iv.28/vii.14 Xianlü Diao Mode

Dotting Crimson Lips: A Bound Suite
The beautiful Oriole
    dropped her head and was silent.
Tears saturated her handkerchief and sleeves,
And the two leaves of her eyebrows wrinkled.

Shifting feet injured her golden lotuses,
    and wringing harmed her onion-sprout hands.
Her face was even more delicate than
When they parted,
And she was thinner than last year.

Happiness Under Heaven
Bowing there in front of him, she forced a hello.
Her actions were charming yet more gentle.
He figured she was not free to act—
On the tips of her brows were infinite sorrows.

"How could that waste of a man appreciate her?

58 Emaciated from working constantly on his verse.
59 Zhong Kui is best known as an ugly and frightening "ghost catcher" and demon expeller.

潑水難收」。

（尾）

鶯鶯悄似章台柳。

縱使柔條依舊。

而今折在他人手。

一踢一跌，故
自入人。

鶯鶯坐夫人之側。

生問日「別來無恙否。」

鶯鶯不言而心會。

iv.29/vii.15 越調（上平西纏令）

自年前，

　長安去，

　　斷行雲。

追邈初別情境
亦肖。

常記得分飲離樽。

一聲長喟，

　兩行血痕落紛紛。

耳畔叮嚀，

　囑付情人。

腸斷消魂。

馬兒上，

　駸駸地，

　　眠樵館，

　　　宿漁村。

最怕的愁到黃昏。

孤燈一點，

　被兒冷落又難溫。

眼前不見意中人，

枕滿啼痕。

To be her husband
    was only a matter of who got here first.
It's all my fault—
    you can't unhitch a mule after the cart is packed,
        and spilled water is hard to gather back up."

Coda
Oriole is just like a willow on Zhangtai Road,[60]
Even if she is that pliant branch of old
She's been snapped by someone else's hand!

Oriole sat by her mother's side.

The student asked her, "Have you been well since we parted?"

Oriole was silent, but she understood what he meant.

Every stumble naturally keeps one absorbed in reading.

iv.29/vii.15 Yue Diao Mode

The Emperor Quells the West: A Bound Suite
"From this time last year
    when I went to Chang'an
        floating clouds were cut off.[61]
I often remember we drank those stirrup cups by turns.
Our long sighs joined as one,
    our cheeks stained by two tracks of blood from fallen tears.
You whispered to me,
    'I beg you, my love. . . .'
My heart broke, my soul disappeared.

His recollection of when they first parted is precise.

On horseback
    I galloped on and on,
        sleeping in woodcutters' lodgings
            and staying overnight in fishermen's villages.
What I feared most was the sorrow that came at dusk—
One dot of a single lamp,
    a cold and lonely quilt, so hard to warm.
The one in my thoughts absent before my eyes,
    my pillow was fully stained by traces of tears.

60 Ready to be snapped off by any passerby.
61 To be parted from a lover.

（鬥鵪鶉）

把個唧[20]溜龐兒，
　　為他瘦損。
減盡從來，
　　稔膩風韵。
自到長安，
　　身心用盡。
自及第，
　　受皇恩。
奈何病體
　　淹延在身。

前者才初，
　　得封書信。
告假馳驅，
　　遠來就親。
比及相逢，
　　幾多愁悶。
雨兒又急，
　　風兒又緊。
為他不避，
　　甘心受忍。

（青山口）

甫能到此甚歡忻，
　　見夫人先話論。
道俺娶妻在侯門。
把鶯鶯改婚姻。
教人情慘切，
　　對景轉傷神。
喚將到女婿，
　　各敍寒溫。
覷了他家舉止行為，
　　真個百種村。
行一似揀老，

Fighting Quail
"My healthy and handsome face
 grew gaunt because of her
And lost its earlier
 lustrous and healthy glow.
From the time I reached Chang'an,
 I exhausted body and mind
To pass the examinations,
 and was honored by the emperor.
But alas, some ailment
 lingered on in my body.

Just as my success happened,
 I received her sealed letter.
I asked for leave and spurred back
 from afar to see my love.
But before we even met
 came much sorrow and depression.
On the road the rains drove hard
 and the winds raged.
But, for her I
 willingly suffered it all.

Green Mountain Pass
"Overjoyed when I first arrived,
 I went directly to Madam Cui to discuss the matter.
But she said that I was marrying another minister's daughter
 and so she changed Oriole's marriage plans.
My feelings were rent
 and the scene I faced injured my soul.
She summoned the new son-in-law to be
 and we exchanged greetings.
I looked at how he conducted himself,
 and it was truly coarse in a hundred ways.
He ambled just like a camel,

坐一似猢猻。
甚娘身分。
駝腰與龜胸，
　　包牙缺上邊唇。
這般物類，
　　教我怎不陰唔，
　　　是閻王的愛民。

（雪裏梅花）
　　更口臭把人薰，
　　　想鶯鶯好緣分。
　　暗思向日，
　　　和他共鴛衾。
　　效學秦晉。

仍歸到鶯身上
去。

　　誰想有今辰。
　　共別的待展紋裀。
　　暗暗覷地，
　　　玉容如花，
　　不施朱粉。

　　然憔悴，
　　　尚天真。
　　纖腰細褪羅裙。
　　下得下²¹得，
　　　將人不偢不問。

　　佯把眉黛顰，
　　　金釵鬈墜烏雲。
　　　恨他恨他，
　　索甚言破
　　　是他須自隱。

（尾）
　　淚珠兒滴了又重搵。
　　滿腹相思難訴陳。

and sat just like a monkey.
And that detestable body!
A camel waist and tortoise chest,[62]
      buck teeth pushing against his upper lip—[63]
How can I not sneer in secret?
      Creatures of this category
      are the beloved of the King of Hell.

Plum Blossoms in the Snow
"The stench of his breath is knocks one over—
      what a terrible fate for Oriole!
I think back silently on days gone by
      when we shared a lovers' quilt,
Imitating Qin and Jin in perfect harmony.

Again, it returns to Oriole's body.

Who could imagine a day would come when
      she would unroll the patterned futon for another?
I gaze secretly
      at her flower-like face of jade,
Unadorned by rouge or powder.

Haggard, yes,
      but still a natural beauty.
From her tiny lithe waist falls a silken skirt—
Cold, hard-hearted,
      she does not ask about me.
She feigns furrowing her eyebrows' kohl,
      and her gold hairpin droops from a cloud of raven's black.
I hate her, hate her,
      what else can I say—
         it is she who deceives herself.

Coda
"Pearly tears drip, then wiped away, drip again,
A belly stuffed with a love so hard to explain.

62 A hunchback.
63 Seems to indicate he also had a cleft palate.

吃喜的冤家,
怎生安穩。
合着眼不辨[22]個深情,
　豈思舊恩。
我然是個官人,
　卻待叫兀誰做「縣君」。

君瑞與鶯,各目視而內心皆痛矣。

iv.30/vii.16 中呂調（古輪台）
　好心酸。
　寸腸千縷若刀剜。
　被那無徒漢。
　把夫妻拆散。
　合下尋思,
　　料他不違言。
　說盡虛脾,
　　使盡局段。
　把人贏勾欺謾。
　天須開眼。
　覷了俺學士哥哥,
　　少年登第,
　　　才貌過人,
　　　　文章超世,
　　　　　於人更美滿。
　卻教我,
　　與這匹夫做繾綣。

　所為身分,
　舉止得人嫌。
　　事事不通疏,
　沒些靈變。
　　曠腳駝腰,
　禿鬢黃牙烏眼。
　不怕今宵,
　　只愁明夜,

My hateful little enemy,
      how can you be so composed?
You just close your eyes, indifferent to my deep love.
      Don't you ever ponder my past acts of kindness?
I might be a new official now,
      but whom can I call my 'Lady of the County?'"

Junrui and Oriole spoke to each other with their eyes, and their hearts
were in pain.

iv.30/vii.16 Zhonglü Diao Mode

Old Bögör[64]
"How it pains the heart—
A thousand threads in every inch of innards are dug out with a knife.
Wife and husband have been broken apart
By that obnoxious good-for-nothing.
When I first thought about it,
I thought he made sense,
But after telling all his lies
And using all his ploys and tricks,
And leading us on to hoodwink us,
Heaven will now open its eyes.
When I look at my brother, Academician now,
    I see one who passed his examinations at a young age,
        whose talent and looks surpass all others
            whose literary compositions transcend this world,
                and who, as a person, is even more lovely and
                    considerate.
Yet I am forced
    to tie the knot with that lout.

And for his attitude—
    his whole manner is odious to me:
        he understands nothing
            and has not the slightest cleverness.
His feet are huge, his back is hunched,
    beardless, yellow-toothed, and crow-eyed.
This evening, I don't care,
    but I worry about tomorrow night

64 Sung by Oriole.

繡幃深處效鴛鴦，
爭似孤眠。
最難甘眼底相逢，
有情夫婿，
不得團圓。
好迷留沒亂，
教人怎捨扮。
孜孜地，
覷着卻渾似天遠。

（尾）
如今「方驗做人難」。
儘他家間當，
不能應當[23]，
正是「新官對舊官」。

張君瑞坐止不安，遽然而起。

法聰邀珙於客捨，方便着言勸誘曰「學士何娶不可。無以一婦人為念。」

珙曰「師言然善，奈處凡浮，遭此屈辱，不能無恨。」

聰與珙抵足。珙披衣，取鶯鶯書及所賜之物，愈添沾灑矣。

iv.31/viii.1 黃鐘宮調 （間花啄木兒第一）
「黃昏後，
守僧捨。
那堪暮秋時節。
窗外琅玕弄翠影，
見西風飄敗葉。

---

65 According to a Tang short story, because they would soon be separated due to war, Xu Deyan 徐德言 broke a mirror and gave half to his wife, the Princess of Lechang 樂昌公主, to keep. She was captured by the next (Sui) dynasty, and entered the household of Yang Su, where she was highly valued. Later, when Xu visited Yang, she was overcome by tears and could not eat. Yang was so touched, he returned

when we will be like mating ducks deep within the bed
    curtains.
I would rather sleep alone.
What's harder to stand—having the husband I desire in front of
    my eyes
    or being unable to complete our union?
How can I forsake him?
Intently
    I look at him, but he seems a million miles away.

Coda
"Now I have proven that 'to be a good person is hard.'
Even should I prompt him to ask,
    I could not respond.
'The new official faces the old,' is true."[65]

Zhang Junrui sat uneasily in his seat, then quickly stood up.

Dharma Wit invited Zhang Gong back to his room and when the opportunity presented itself, he tried to encourage him, saying, "You can
have your pick of wives. Don't concern yourself over just one woman."

Gong replied, "What you say is right, Teacher, but I live in the imper-
manent world of the ordinary. I cannot help but get angry, meeting
such humiliation."

Dharma Wit slept toe to toe that night with Gong. Gong threw on a
robe and took out Oriole's letter and gifts, which only made his tears
more copious.

iv.31/viii.1 Zhonglü Diao Mode

Woodpecker in the Flowers: *First*
"I'll keep to the monk's lodgings
    until dusk is gone.
How can I bear the season of late spring?
Outside the window, fine bamboos sway their fresh green—
    and I see the wind toss fallen leaves.

her to Xu Deyan. She wrote the following poem in response: "How has this day
changed? / The new official faces the old; / I neither dare to laugh or cry, / I've just
had proof that it is hard to be a perfect person." The two were eventually reunited,
and the broken mirror became a common metaphor for a joyous reunion. See Luo
Ye 2015, 139–140.

煎煎地耳畔蚤吟切。

啾啾唧唧聲相接。

俺道了不恁恓惶,

　心腸除是鐵。

（整乾坤）

　「牽情惹恨,

　　幾時捱徹。

　聽戍樓,

　　角奏《梅花》,

　　　聲嗚咽。

　畫壁間一盞惱人燈,

　　碧熒熒半明不滅。

（第二）

　「思量俺,

　　好命劣。

　怎着恁惡緣惡業。

　幸自夫妻恁美滿,

　　被傍人廝間諜。

　兩口兒合是成間別。

　天教受此恓惶苦,

　　想舊日雨蹤雲跡,

　　　枉教做話說。

（雙聲疊韻）

　「玉漏遲,

　　鴛被冷,

　　　愁對如年夜。

　寶獸煙,

　　縈斷縷,

　　　裊裊噴龍麝。

　暫合眼,

　　強睡些。

　便會聖,

Distressing, crickets rasp at my ears,
Their buzzing turns to whirring and back again.
I say, 'Not too distressing—
        if your insides are made of iron.'

Setting the Cosmos Right
"Being pulled along by passion stirs such rancor.
        When will it come an end?
I listen for the guard tower
        where the horn plays 'Plum Blossoms'
                and its sad sound of weeping.
One solitary lamp between painted walls
        flickers blue, half bright, half dying away.

[Woodpecker in the Flowers:] Second
"I reflect upon my
        star-crossed fate—
How did I earn such ghastly karma?
In the beginning, we were so happy as husband and wife,
        and then were split apart by another—
Our fates seem destined for separation.
*Heaven has bestowed this grievous pain and
        our bouts of lovemaking back then
                will end up nothing but a story to tell.*

Alliteration and Rhyming
"The water clock drips slowly,
        the mandarin-duck quilt is cold
                as I sadly face this year-long night.
Smoke from the incense beast
        twines its broken threads,
                drifting in puffs of ambergris and musk.
I shut my eyes a moment
        to force myself to sleep,
But unless I were a divine one

怎寧貼。
　床兒上自推自搣。

（第三）
　「鎮思向日，
　　空教人氣快微憋。[24]
　小亭那畔，
　　撚吟鬚步廊月。
　朱扉半揿，
　　驀觀伊向西廂下，
　　　漸漸至空階側畔，
　　　　倚湖山，
　　　　　春困歇。

恬惶無寐，將
從前情事節節
提起，節節傷
懷。

（刮地風）
　「手把白團輕扇撚，
　有出塵容冶。
　　腰肢嫋娜纖如束，
　舉止殊絕。
　　柳眉星眼，
　杏腮桃頰，
　口兒小，
　　腳兒弓，
　　　扮得蔚貼。
　一時間，
　　暫相見，
　　　不能舍。

（第四）
　「兩情暗許，
　　着新詩意中寫。
　正相眷戀，
　　見紅娘把繡簾揭。
　低聲報道
　　『夫人使妾來喚，』

how could I settle comfortably?
I pound the bed and kick my feet.

[Woodpecker in the Flowers:] Third
"I focus on days past
 and I feel my breath quicken and a slight suffocation—
There, by the little pavilion,
 I twirled my poet's beard as I trod in the corridor's moonlight.
Vermillion gates of the compound only half shut,
 suddenly I spied her moving toward the western wing:
  gradually she reached the side of the empty steps,
  leaned against the rock mountain,
   and rested from her springtime ennui.

Sad and distressed and unable to sleep, he rehearses every event of the former love affair, and every event causes him emotional pain.

A Ground-Scraping Wind
"Her hands twirled a white, light round fan
 and her face was otherworldly gorgeous.
Her waist was lithe and willowy, as tiny as if bound,
 and every single movement was perfect.
Willow-leaf eyebrows, starry eyes,
 apricot cheeks, peach chin,
  small mouth,
   arched feet—
    and she was perfectly dressed.
We saw each other only for a moment,
 a blink in time,
  but I could never again rid her from my mind.

[Woodpecker in the Flowers:] Fourth
"Our emotions secretly acknowledged,
 I expressed them in a poem.
Right in that first flush of love,
 I saw Crimson raise the embroidered curtain
And whisper in low voice
 'Madam Cui has sent me to summon you,'

步促金蓮歸去，
　飄飄香暗惹。

（柳葉兒）

着情着情，訡
訡。

　「教人半晌如呆，
　　回來卻入書捨。
　後來更不相逢，
　　十分捨了休也。

（第五）

　「不幸蒲州
　　軍亂，
　　　把良民盡虜劫。
　一部直
　　臨此寺，
　　　周圍盡擺列。
　高聲喝叫，
　　　『得鶯鶯便把殘生怯。
　若是些小遲然，
　　都教化脣[25]血。』

（賽兒令）

　「騁些。
　英烈。
　被俺咱都盡除滅。
　滿門家眷得寧貼。
　那老婆，
　　把恩輕絕，
　　　是俺弄巧翻成拙。

（第六）

　「後來，
　　暗約。
　向羅幃鎮歡悅。
　夜來曉去，
　　約未近數月。

and back you trod on your little golden lotuses,
  leaving only a whiff of perfume to secretly stir me.

Willow Leaves
"*It dazed me for a moment and, addled,*
  I went back to the study.
We didn't meet again,
  and ended it with complete separation.

Struck with passion, he goes on and on.

[Woodpecker in the Flowers:] Fifth
"*Then misfortune happened as the Puzhou*
  army rebelled,
    plundering all the good people.
A squadron of them approached this monastery
  and formed up on all four sides.
Then they loudly shouted,
'*Give us Oriole and we'll spare your lives,*
  but hesitate even for a moment
    and you'll be turned to fat and blood.'

Song of the Passes
"*I gave full rein*
  to my bravery,
And all the rebels were destroyed by me alone.
All her family were safe
But that old woman
  just dismissed my act of benevolence—
    I made myself a fool trying to be clever.

[Woodpecker in the Flowers:] Sixth
"*After that*
  we had secret trysts
To claim our pleasure and joy within silken bed curtains.
For a mere few months
  she came at night and left at dawn.

不因敗漏，
才時許我為姻眷。
奈何名利拘人，
夫妻容易別。

（神仗兒）

「得臨帝闕。
帝闕。
蟾宮桂枝獨折。
名標金甲。
俺咱恁時，
準備了娶他來也。
不幸病纏惹。

（第七）

「想太君，
情性劣。
往日誇侈共撇。
陡恁地不調貼。
把恩不顧，
信無徒漢子他方說。
便把美滿夫妻，
恩情都斷絕。

說到此際，真
亦無可奈何。
不自禁其氣之
憤懣而詞之煩
復矣。

（四門子）

「這些兒事體難分別。
如今也。
待怎者。
鶯鶯情性那裏每也。
俏無了貞共烈。
你好毒，
你好呆。
恰才那裏相見些。

Only when our secret was leaked
      did Madam Cui temporarily give me her hand in marriage.
But, alas, a man is bound by need for fame and advantage,
      and husband and wife are all too easily separated.

A Guard of Spirits
"And when I got to go to the Imperial City,
That Imperial City,
I alone snapped the cassia branch in the Palace of the Toad.
My name was written on the golden Plaque of Firsts
And then
      I prepared to come back to marry her.
But a stubborn illness delayed me.

[Woodpecker in the Flowers:] Seventh
Thinking about that Grand Lady—
      her basic nature is awfully flawed.
Before it was all about ritual
Then suddenly she was dead set against our union.[65]
She paid no attention to my act of grace,
      and believed only what the good-for-nothing said,
Then completely cut off all the love and affection
      that made our union beautifully complete.

The Four Disciples
"This whole affair is hard to figure out.
And as it stands,
What should I do?
And what of Oriole's nature?
It's as if she has no desire to be a martyr for her chastity.
You were cruel,
      you were foolish.
When we met just now,

At this point in his speech, he is truly at a dead end. He can't control the indignation and anger, so the language becomes repetitive.

---

65 I am uncertain about these lines. They are left blank in the translation in DJY, 395;
    I here follow DJY07, 319.

你好羞，
　你好呆。
虧殺人也姐姐。

（第八）

「從來呵，
　慣受磨滅。
他家今日心已邪。
虧人問當不應對，
　虧人不怕神天折。
惱得人頭百裂。
便假饒
天下雪。
解不得我這腹熱。
一封小簡，
分明都是伊家寫。
只被你逗人來，
　一星星都碎擤百裂。

餘音嫋嫋。

（尾）

「斑管雖圓被風裂。
玉簪更堅也掂折。
似琴上斷弦難再接。」

聰見珙不快，起而勉之曰「足下聰明者也。以一婦人，惑至於此，吾與子不復友矣。」

珙曰「男女佳配，不易得也。加以情思，積有日矣。一旦被讒，反為路人，所以痛予心也。」

聰曰「足下儻得鶯，痛可已乎。」

珙曰「何計得之。」

聰曰「吾為子謀之。」

You were so shy,
  so foolish,
You really did me in, sister!

[Woodpecker in the Flowers:] Eighth
"Up to this point,
  I was used to being cheated.
But her heart has gone astray today.
Even if I questioned her, she wouldn't answer,
  how fortunate that she fears no punishment from Heaven.
She riles me so much my head is going to shatter.
Even if I could have
  the heavens snow on me
It could never extinguish this fire in my gut.
That single letter
  was clearly written by her.
Oh, I've been led on by you—
  I'll rip it a hundred times and tear it to tiny pieces.

Coda
"Though the writing brush handle is round, it is cracked by the
  wind;
The jade hairpin, though solid, is broken in half.
Now, like a broken string on the gem-set zither, we will never be
  joined again."

The lingering tone goes on and on.

Seeing that Gong was unhappy, Dharma Wit got up and pressured him:
"You're an intelligent person. If you're going to be so confounded by a
single woman, you and I will be friends no longer."

Gong replied, "My heart is pained by this: a perfect match between a
man and woman is hard to find, and on top of that, we have long loved
each other. Yet one morning I was suddenly slandered, and I became
a stranger to her."

Dharma Wit said, "Would this pain stop if you got Oriole?"

"I have no way to get her," replied Gong.

Dharma Wit said, "Let me figure out a plan for you."

iv.32/viii.2 中呂調 （碧牡丹）

「不須長嘆息。
便不失了咱丈夫的綱紀。
若人恥笑，
怎共貧僧做相識。
可惜了你才學，
枉了你擢高第。
莫憂煎，
休埋怨，
放心地。」

猛然離坐起。
壁中間取下戒刀三尺。
「兀的二更方盡，
不到三更已外。
比及這蠟燭燒殘，
教你知消息。
我去後必定有官防，
君莫怕，
我待做頭抵。」

侠士風概。

（尾）

「把忘恩的老婆梟了首級。
把反間的畜生教屍粉碎。
把百媚的鶯鶯分付與你。」

法聰言未已，隔窗聞[26]人笑曰「爾等行凶，豈不累我。」
言者是誰。是誰。

iv.33/viii.3 大石調 （玉翼蟬）

把窗間紙，
微潤開，
君瑞偷睛覷。
半夜三更，
不知是甚人，

iv.32/viii.2 Zhonglü Diao Mode

Blue-Green Peony
"No need to sigh longingly,
And lose your mettle as a man.
If people sneered at you,
    could you still be a friend of mine?
How unfortunate that your talented learning
    does little justice to the rank you achieved!
Don't simmer and stew—
    stop being resentful
        and give your mind some ease!"

He swiftly rose from his seat,
And took down the three-foot ordination knife from the wall,
"The second watch has just ended,
    and before the end of the third,
By the time the light of this candle is gone
    I'll give you some news.
There's sure to be a court case after I leave,
    but don't be afraid,
        because I want to be his enemy.[66]

Strong tenor of the knight-errant.

Coda
"I'll cut off the head of that ungrateful old lady,
Hack that beastly interloper's body into tiny bits,
And turn over the lovely Oriole to you."

Before Dharma Wit finished speaking, they heard someone laugh outside the window say, "Won't your violent actions also implicate me?"
    Who was it who spoke? Who?[67]

iv.33/viii.3 Dashi Diao Mode

A Jade-Winged Cicada
"Poking a hole in the window paper
    with a wet finger,
        Junrui stole a look.
Who could it be,
    coming especially to this place

---

66 And thus take all the blame.
67 Suspense point 12.

特來到於此處。

移時節，
　方認得，
　　是兩個如花女。
一個是鶯鶯騃騃步月來，
　紅娘向後面相逐。

開門相見，
　不問個東西便抱住。
可憎問當，
　「別來安否。」
也無閑話，
　只辦得燈前魆魆地哭。
猶疑夢寐之間，
　頻掐肌膚。
淚點兒盈盈如雨。
止約不住。
料想當日別離，
　不恁的苦。

（尾）

驟相見，悲喜
倉卒，無暇他
及。神情如
是。

比及夫妻每重相遇。
各自準備下萬言千語。
及至相逢卻沒一句。

多時，鶯語郎曰「學士淹留京國，至有今日，奈何。奈
何。」

iv.34/viii.4 中呂調（安公子賺）

拭卻淚點，從
頭告訴退想。
正在此際，白
中「多時」二
字大有關目。

女孩兒低聲道，
　道「別來安樂麼張學士。
憶自伊家赴上都，
　日許多時。
夜夜魂勞夢役。
愁何似。
似一川煙草黃梅雨，

at midnight?
A while passed
   before he recognized
      two women as beautiful as flowers.
One was Oriole, hastening through the moonlight,
   urged on by Crimson right behind her.

He opened the door to greet her
   and, without even a by-your-leave, he embraced her tightly.
That hateful little thing asked,
   "Have you been well since we parted?"
They said nothing else to each other,
   managing only to weep silently by the lamp.
Still suspicious it might be a dream,
   Zhang kept pinching himself.
Teardrops fell as full as rain,
And just as unstoppable.
It was even more painful
   than on the day they parted.

Coda
Each had prepared a thousand things to say
When husband and wife could meet again,
But not a sentence was uttered when they finally met.

> *Seeing each other so suddenly, pressured by both grief and happiness, they had no time for anything else. Such was their manner.*

After a long time, Oriole spoke to the young esquire, "You tarried so long in the capital, Academician, and it's caused our current problem. What should we do?"

iv.34/viii.4 Zhonglü Diao Mode

Master An: Beguiling Mode
The girl said in a low voice,
   "Have things been happy and peaceful since you left,
      Academician Zhang?
I remember when you went to the capital,
   a long time ago.
Night after night my soul was wearied by its flight in dreams,
And what was my sorrow like?
Like misty grasses along a river in springtime drizzle,

> *After wiping away her tears, she told him everything she had imagined from the beginning. It is right at this juncture that the two words, "long time," carry a lot of meaning.*

悶似長江，
　　攬得個相思擔兒。

遠別春三月，
　　恁時方有音書至。
火急開緘仔細讀，
　　元來是一首新詩。
披味那其間意思。
知你獲青紫。
滿宅家眷喜不喜。
以『縣君』呼之。
不枉了俺從前實志。」

（賺）

「誰知後來，
　　更何曾夢見個人傳示。
時暮秋，
　　令人特地傳錦字。
連衣袂。

玉簪斑管與絲桐，
　　一星星比喻着心間事。
臨去也，
　　囑付了千回萬次。
　　　　『早離京師。』

誰知鄭家那廝，
　　新來先自長安至。
誰曾問着，
　　從頭說一段希奇事。
道京師裏。

衛尚書家女孩兒，
　　新來招得個風流婿。
道是及第官，

三「誰知」大
有味。況前兩
「誰知」不無
埋怨，謂音書
不頻，離京不
早也。後「誰
知鰥居獨自」
則不勝憐之。

my depression, too, was endless as the Yangtze—
    such was the heavy burden of my love's longing.

And it was a full three months after you left
    before any missive arrived.
I opened it in a flash and carefully read it,
    and it turned out to be a new poem.
I perused the intent of it,
And learned you had obtained the colored ribbons of high office.
My whole family was happy
And called me 'Lady of the County.'
I fulfilled my prior true desire.

Beguiling Song
"Who could have known that, after that,
    no one brought a missive, not even in my dreams.
The season was late autumn
    and I had someone deliver my letter to you
Together with some clothes.

The jade hairpin, tear-stained brush, and zither:
    every iota was meant to represent feelings in my heart.
As the courier was about to leave
    I told him a thousand times
'Tell him to leave the capital soon.'

Who could have known that rascal from the Zheng family
    would arrive from Chang'an first?
Who invited him?
    But from the start he told a strange story
About something that happened in the capital.

The daughter of Secretary Wei
    had just taken in a sophisticated husband.
He said it was a new official, fresh from the examinations

The three repetitions of "who could know" carry a lot of flavor. But the first two are full of resentment, complaining about the infrequency of letters and his not leaving the capital earlier. The last "who could know. . .that you're living alone as a bachelor" shows endless pity for him.

雁序排連第三，
年紀二十六七。」

（渠神令）

「道是『洛京人氏。
先來曾蒲州居止。
見今編修國史。
莫比洛陽才子。』
夫人一向信浮詞。
不問是那不是。

許了姑舅做親，
擇下吉日良時。
誰知今日見伊。
尚兀子鰥居獨自。
又沒個婦兒妻子。
心上有如刀刺。
假如活得又何為。
枉惹萬人嗤。」

兒女至情。　　　鶯解裙帶擲於梁。

（尾）

「譬如往日害相思，
爭如今夜懸梁自盡，
也勝他時憔悴死。」

珙曰「生不同偕，死當一處。」

iv.35/viii.5 黃鐘宮（黃鶯兒）
憋噪。
憋噪。
似此活得，
也惹人恥笑。
把皂絛兒搭在梁間，
雙雙自吊。

ranked third highest on the final list,
About twenty-five or twenty-six years old.

Song of the Canal Spirit
"He said, 'It was someone from Luoyang,
Who had first stayed in Puzhou
And who was now an Editor in the Bureau of History—
Doesn't this match the genius of Luoyang, Zhang Gong?'
Now, my mother believes every fatuous story,
And never asks if it's right or not.

She gave my cousin permission to marry me,
*   and picked out an auspicious day.*
Who could know that today I would realize
You're still living alone as a bachelor,
And have no wife.
My heart feels as if it's been stabbed by a knife.
Even if I carry on living, what's the point?
It would only be to stir up sneers from countless others.

Oriole undid the belt of her skirt and tossed it over the rafter.

The perfect passion of a man and a woman.

Coda
"Better I hang myself tonight from this rafter
Than to suffer love's longing like I did in the past—
And so much better than fatally wasting away later."

"If we're unable to be together in life," said Gong, "better we die as one."

iv.35/viii.5 Huangzhong Gong Mode

Yellow Oriole
Such frustration!
Such shame!
To live on like this
    would only stir up the sneers of others.
He fixed his black belt to the rafters
    and the two hanged themselves together.

> 唬得紅娘，
> 忙扯着道。
> 　「休廝合造。
> 您兩個死後不爭，
> 　怎結末這禿屌。」

紅娘抱鶯。

聰止君瑞，曰「先生之惑愈甚矣。幸得續弦，死而何益。」

珙曰「鶯已適人，不死何待。」

聰曰「吾有一策，使鶯不適人，與子百年偕老。」

珙曰「策將安出。」

聰曰「吾不能矣。子謁一故人，事可濟矣。」

iv.36/viii.6 般涉調（哨遍纏令）

> 　君瑞懸梁，
> 　　鶯鶯覓死，
> 　　　法聰連忙救。
> 　「您死後教人打官防，
> 　　我尋思着甚來由。
> 好出醜。
> 夫妻大小大
> 　不會尋思，
> 　　笑破貧僧口。
> 人死後渾如悠悠地逝水，
> 　厭厭地不斷東流。
> 榮華富貴盡都休。
> 精爽冥寞葬荒丘。
> 一失人身，
> 　萬劫不復，
> 　　再難能觳。

解勸法大是貿
景，大是真
色。

Scared to death, Crimson
    grabbed them and said,
"Don't be so stupid—
After you two die, then what?
    How will this bald prick end up?

Crimson took hold of Oriole.

Dharma Wit stopped Junrui and said, "You're even more deluded! Now that you're fortunate enough to mend the string, what's the benefit of dying?"

Gong replied, "Oriole is already promised to another, what's the point of not dying?"

"I have a plan," said Dharma Wit, "to make it so Oriole is not betrothed, and can grow old with you for the next hundred years."

"Where will this plan come from?" said Gong.

"Not from me," said Dharma Wit, "but a formal call on an old friend can salvage the situation."

iv.36/viii.6 Huangzhong Gong Mode

Whistling Song: A Bound Suite
Junrui hung from the rafter,
    Oriole wanted to die,
        and Dharma Wit rushed to save them.
"After you die, I'll surely be charged in court,
        and what could I come up with to defend myself?
You two really make a humiliating spectacle of yourselves.
You're a husband and wife
    who can't think their way out of anything—
        it makes me split my sides laughing.
After a person dies, it's like water disappearing in the distance,
    relentlessly flowing eastward and
Fame, fortune, and status all vanish with it—
Your souls in dark nothingness, you are buried in wild hills.
And once you lose human form
    you will not have another for countless kalpas—
        a second recurrence is nearly impossible.

The method Wit uses to ultimately persuade him really changes the imagined scene and has a natural truth.

欲不分離，
　把似投托個知心友。
不索打官防，
　教您夫妻盡百年歡偶。
快準備，
　車乘鞍馬，
　　主僕行李，
　　　一發離門走。
投托的親知，
　不須遠覓，
　　而今只在蒲州。
昔年也是一儒流。
壯歲登科不到數餘秋。
方今是一路諸侯。

指次如面話。

（長壽仙衰）
　「初典郡城，
　　更牢獄無囚。
　後臨邊郡，
　　滅盡草賊猾寇。
　坐籌帷幄，
　　馳馬臨軍挑鬥。
　十場鎮贏八九。
　天下有底英雄漢，
　　聞名難措手。

先形容後出姓
名，董詞慣家
數。

　這個官人，
　　不枉食君祿。
　扶社稷安天下，
　　兼文銳武，
　　　古今未嘗曾有。

（急曲子）
　「也不愛耽花戀酒。
　也不愛打桃射柳。
　也不愛放馬走狗。

If you don't want to be apart,
>   better you rely on a good friend.
There's no need for a court case
>   to ensure you will live in happiness the rest of your lives.
Prepare now—
>   get the cart ready, saddle the horses,
>>   pack the baggage of master and servants
>>>   and set off at once from this place.

For a very close friend to rely on,
> *you needn't look far,*
>> *for right now he's in Puzhou.*

Previously a Confucian Scholar in his own right who
Not many autumns ago passed the examinations in his maturity,
To become a liege lord for the whole circuit.

Pointed out as if he were looking right at him.

Long-Life Immortals Tremolo
"He first governed a prefectural walled city,
>   and the prisons were empty and unneeded.
Then he approached bordering prefectures
>   to exterminate bandits and wily thieves.
He determined plans in curtained rooms,[68]
>   and approached armies with his four-horse team to stir them
>>   to battle.
He won eight or nine of every ten engagements.
None of the heroic braves in this world
>   found it easy to act after they heard his name.
This official
>   did not feast on his lord's pay for naught—
He supported the altars of earth and grain, stabilized the world,
>   and combined civil arts with military keenness;
>>   he stands unmatched in past and present.

First describing him and then producing the name. This is a common technique in Dong's lyrics.

An Accelerando Song
"He showed no love for seduction or wine,
No love for polo or archery,
No love for racing horses or hunting dogs,

68 The headquarters.

也不愛射生獵獸。
去年曾斬逆臣頭。
腰間劍是帝王親授。」

（尾）
「是百年萬軍都領袖。
天來大名姓傳宇宙。
便是斬砍自由的杜太守。」

生曰「杜太守謂誰。」

聰復言之。

iv.37/viii.7 高平調（于飛樂）
「告吾師，
　杜太守，
　　端的是何人。
與自家是舊友關親。」
法聰聞得道，
好口角。
　「君瑞休勞問。
果貴人多忘，
　早不記得賊黨臨門。

這官人。
與足下非戚非親。
您兩個舊友忘形。
與夫人連大眾，
真如面話。
　都有深恩。
太守謂誰，
　是去年白馬將軍。」

生曰「杜將軍驟拜太守也，以何故。」

聰曰「以威攝賊軍，亂清蒲右，蒙天子重知，數月前，特
授鎮西將軍、蒲州太守，兼關右兵馬處置使。」

No love for hunting and killing beasts.
Last year he cut off the head of that recalcitrant official.[69]
The sword at his waist is imperially bestowed.

Coda
"The Grand Commander of a myriad armies for a hundred years,
A reputation as big as the heavens is known throughout the cosmos—
He's that Grand Protector Du, who is free to decapitate anyone."[70]

"Who is Grand Protector Du?" asked the student.

Dharma Wit repeated his words.

iv.37/viii.7 Gaoping Diao Mode

A Perfect Marriage
"I'll ask you again, Dharma Wit,
        just who
            is Grand Protector Du?
Is he an old friend? A relative?"
As soon as a Dharma Wit heard this, he said,
        "Junrui, you don't need to ask,   *A fine way of*
People in high places really are forgetful,   *expressing it.*
        don't you remember when those bandits approached our gates?
This official
Is neither a relative nor your kin—   *Truly like speaking*
The two of you are fast friends,   *face to face.*
*Someone who performed a profound act of grace
        for Madam Cui and the whole congregation.*
Who is this Grand Protector?
        He's the White Horse General of yesteryear.

"Why was General Du suddenly appointed Grand Protector?" asked
the student.

"Because he overpowered that bandit army," said Dharma Wit, "and
brought order to the area of Western Pu. He has been made known
several times to the emperor who, just a few months ago, made special
appointments, and named him General for Suppression of the West,
Grand Protector of Puzhou, and concurrently, Military Supervisory
Commissioner for the Area West of the Hangu Pass."

69 Flying Tiger Sun.
70 The plaque of authority for such figures reads, "Bears the authority to behead before notifying the emperor."

珙喜謝曰「非吾師指迷，實不悟此。」

生攜鶯宵奔蒲州，時二更左右。

iv.38/viii.8 大石調（洞仙歌）
　　　收拾行李，
　　　　一步地都行上。
　　　兩口兒眉頭暫開放。
　　　望秋天即漸，
　　　　月澹星稀東方朗。
　　　隱隱城頭鼓響。

　　　抵曉[27]入城，
　　　　直至衙門旁。
　　　不及殷勤展參榜。閑綴
　　　門人通報，
　　　　太守出廳相見，
　　　　　未及把行藏問當。

淡寫如畫。

　　　太守道「君瑞喜登科。」
　　　君瑞道「哥哥
　　　　自別無恙。」

太守邀生入偏廳。

生曰「門外拙妻，參拜兄嫂子個。」

太守令夫人請鶯。客禮畢，夫人請鶯至後閤。珙與太守酌酒道舊。可謂
　　　　　青山牽夢寐，
　　　　　白髮喜交親。

Delighted, Gong thanked him: "If you hadn't clarified this puzzle, I never would have known it!"

The student and Oriole fled to Puzhou in the night, around the second watch.

iv.38/viii.8 Dashi Diao Mode

Song of Immortals in a Cavern
They got their baggage in order
    and set out together on the road.
The two of them could relax a bit now.
They watched the autumn day come on—
    the moon grew pale and fewer stars dotted the eastern glow
And then, barely perceptibly, the first drum marker of the day
    echoed in the city.

They entered the city gates at dawn
    and went straightway to wait beside the yamen gates.
It took no time to diligently present a writ for audience, *so*
    leisurely stitched together
And the guard quickly relayed his report,
    the Grand Protector came out of the courtroom to greet them.
        Before they could exchange pleasantries
The Grand Protector said, "Junrui, I am delighted you passed
    the examinations,"
And Junrui said, "Brother,
    have you been well since we parted?"

As meticulously portrayed as if it were a painting.

General Du welcomed the student into a side room.

The student said, "My humble wife is outside the door and should come and formally greet you, my brother and sister-in-law."

Du ordered someone to fetch Madam Du, and after the obligatory rites, Madam Du invited Oriole to the rear chambers.

Gong shared a few cups of wine with the Grand Protector, talking about the old days. Truly, it can be said,

    The green hills of future meetings are found only in dreams,
    The white hair of old age finds delight in friends and kin.

iv.39/viii.9 越調（上平西纏令）

杜將軍，
　張君瑞。
話別離。
至坐上各序尊卑。
別來經歲。
故人青眼喜重期。
兩情談論正投機。
一笑開眉。

情相慕，
　心相得。
重相見，
　舊相知。
便暢飲彼此無疑。
風流太守，
　請生滿滿金杯。
「喜君仙府探花歸。
高步雲梯。」

（鬥鵪鶉）

君瑞聞言，
　欠身避席。
飲罷躬身，
　向前施禮。
道「多謝哥哥，
　此般厚意。
據自家，
　寡才藝。
盡都是父母
陰功所得。

幸得今朝，
　弟兄面會。
敢煩將軍，

iv.39/viii.9 Yue Diao Mode

The Emperor Quells the West: A Bound Suite
General Du
    and Zhang Junrui
Spoke of their separation,
    as they seated themselves as the rules of hierarchy
        prescribe.
Years had passed since their parting
And it was a pleasure meeting as old friends again.
Their sentiments as they discussed were in perfect accord,

And they were happy.
Each admired the other,
    and their perceptions were shared equally.
They met again,
    these old friends
And drank happily, without diffidence.
The gallant Grand Protector
    invited the student to fill his golden cup again and again:
"I am so happy you plucked the flower in the capital
    and now climb high on the ladder to the clouds."

Fighting Quail
Hearing these words Junrui,
    rose slightly from his seat in respect and then stood.
He finished his cup and bowed deeply
    to perform a formal ritual of gratitude,
Saying, "Thank you very much, brother,
    for your kindness.
But if you consider my
    meager talents,
It was in every way the hidden merit of my parents
    that allowed me to achieve this.

"It is due to fortune today
    that we brothers have met again. . . .
Dare I trouble you, General—

　　萬千休罪。
小子特來，
　　有些事體。
記去年，
　　離上國。
訪諸先覺，
　　遊學到這裏。

董詞最善敍
述，如「鎮思
想日」套，述
法渾象暗地思
怨。此一套述
法渾象當面告
訴。

（看花回）

　　「普救院，
　　權居止。
詩書諳[28]理。
卻不幸，
　　蒲州元帥渾公逝。
亂軍起。
無人統，
　　殘郡邑。
害良民蒲州裏。
滿城鐵騎。

神鬼哭，
　　生靈死。
哀聲振地。
至普救，
　　諸多僧行難隄備。
關閉得。
　　山門着，
　　　怎當眾軍卒，
群刀手砍，
　　是鐵門也粉碎。」

（青山口）

　　「眾僧欲走又不及。
須識前朝崔相國。
那家女孩兒叫鶯鶯，

and please don't be offended—
The special reason I am here
is that I have a problem.
Remember last year
when I left Luoyang
To visit enlightened teachers,
and my travels to study brought me here?

Coming Back from Looking at Flowers
"I stayed for a while
in Puzhou Monastery,
Where I reviewed the classics.
Unfortunately,
the Grand Marshal of Puzhou, the Noble Hun, passed away,
And a rebellious army arose.
No one to lead them,
they laid waste to prefectural towns
And savaged people inside the walls of Puzhou.
The whole city was filled with heavy cavalry.

Ghosts and divinities wept
as good souls perished,
Sounds of mourning shook the earth.
And when they reached Puzou Monastery
it was nigh on impossible for monks and laymen to prepare,
So they tightly sealed it up.
But the main gate
could not withstand the host of troops,
and their hacking blades—
even a gate of iron would have turned to powder.

Green Mountain Pass
Every monk wanted to flee but time ran out.
You must know Minister of State Cui from the prior reign,
And his family's daughter, called Oriole,

The very best of Dong's lyrics are like the suite "I focus on days past" where the narrative technique perfectly conveys a subtle thinking about rancor, and this one, in which the narrative technique perfectly conveys a personally delivered report.

當時未及笄歲。
群賊門外逼。
道『得鶯後便西歸。』
相國老夫人，
　聽得悲泣。
不奈之何，
故諉微生，
　願求脫命計。
特仗法聰，
　曾把書寄。
太守既到那裏。
飛虎唬來癡。
群賊倒槍旗。
退卻亂軍，
　免卻生離，
　都是哥哥虎威。」

（渤海令）
　「那夫人，
　　感恩義。
許鶯鶯與俺為妻。
幸天子開賢路，
　因而赴帝裏。
也已高攀月中桂。
不幸染沉疾。
風散難醫治。
淹延近一歲。

誰知個，
　鄭衙內。
與鶯鶯舊關親戚。
恐嚇使為妻室。
不念鶯鶯是妹妹。
夫人不敢大喘氣。
連忙揀下吉日。

Who had yet to come of age.[71]
Outside the gates that army of rebels pressed,
Shouting 'Give us Oriole and we'll head back west.'
The aged wife of Minister Cui heard this
    and began weeping grievously.
Out of ideas,
    they called on me, this insignificant little student,
        seeking a plan to help them escape with their lives.
I relied on Dharma Wit
    to deliver a missive to you.
And as soon as you reached the monastery
Flying Tiger was scared witless.
All the rebels turned their spears and flags upside down,
And the rebellious army was forced to withdraw,
    sparing all our lives.
All this was due to your awesome might, brother.

Song of Bohai
"Oriole's mother
    was moved by gratitude,
And promised that Oriole would be my wife.
And then the emperor opened a path for the worthy,
    and I went off to the capital.
Alas, I climbed to that cassia tree in the moon,
But came down with a serious illness
That, despite treatment, was hard to cure
And dragged on for nearly a year.

Who knew about a certain
    Zheng Heng,
A long time relative of Oriole's,
Who would intimidate her and force her to be his wife?
He never considered the fact Oriole was a younger cousin,
And Madam Cui dared not take even a deep breath
Before she hastily picked a date for the marriage.

71 This would be fifteen *sui*, or fourteen years old; according to her mother, Oriole is seventeen *sui*.

只爭一腳地。
大分與那畜生效了連理。」

（尾）

「是他的親姑舅要做夫妻。
倚仗是宰臣家有勢力。
不辨個清濁沒道理。
托付你個慷慨的相識。
別辨個是非。
與俺做些兒主意。
看那骨脹的哥哥近俺甚的。」

太守曰「吾弟放心。不為則已，爭則吾必斬恆。少待，公退間話。」

iv.40/viii.10 大石調（還京樂）

驀觀儀門開處，
　兩廊下俏不聞鴉。
鼕鼕地皷響
　正廳上，太守升衙。
堦前軍吏
　誰敢鬧嘈雜。
大案前行本把。
五日三朝家。
沒紙兒文字，
　官清法正無差。
大牢虞候羊兒般善，
　　是有大人彈壓。
有子有牢房地匣。
有子有欄軍夾畫。
有子有鐵裏榆枷。
更年沒罪人，
　戴他犯他。
獄門前草長，

If I hadn't stepped in at the last minute
Oriole would have found herself that beast's wife.

Coda
It was Oriole's own cousin who wanted the match,
Relying on the prestige of being son of a Prime Minister—
He lacked any scruples, could not see the right thing to do.
I rely on you, my generous and forthright friend,
To make this distinction between right and wrong
And set things right on my behalf.
Judge how that gag-inducing brother compares to me."

Du said, "Rest easy, brother. If Zheng Heng does nothing, then it's over. If he fights it, I'll decapitate him. Just wait a bit, when official duties are finished, we can chat then."

iv.40/viii.10 Dashi Diao Mode

Happiness of Returning to the Capital: A Bound Suite
The student quickly looked as the second door opened on the
    hall—
       the two facing corridors were so quiet not a raven was
         heard.[72]
The sound of drums boomed and
       in the main hall, the Grand Protector ascended the dais.
Army runners in front of the steps
       dared not make a noise.
Office clerks approached the great desk
But for the last several days
There had been no writs of accusation,
       as happens when officials are pure, and the law is upright.
Inside the jails, wardens were gentle as lambs,
       because of the watchful control of the great one.
They had prisons cells and prisoner pits,
Stockades and finger presses,
And iron-wrapped cangues of elm.
But for many years there had been no prisoners,
       no one to wear them or bear their brunt.
Grass grew long in front of the jailhouse gate,

---

72 Everyone was standing at attention.

有誰曾蹉。
有刑罰徒流絞斬，
　吊拷絣把。
設而不用，
　束杖理民寬雅。
地方千里，
威教有法。
治也不愛
侵官弄法。

善為政威而不猛，
寬而有勇，
　一方人喚做「菩薩」。
　但曾坐處，
絕了群盜，
　縱有敢活拏。
　正不怕明廉暗察。
信不讓春秋裏季札。
　治不讓潁川黃霸。
　　蒲州裏大小六十萬家。
人人欽仰，
　悄如爹媽。

（尾）
　虎符金牌腰間掛。
　英雄鎮着普天之下。

73　Usually then hung upside down from a wall.
74　Overseers of provincial judicial offices.
75　Ji Zha 季札 (BCE 576–485) was a brilliant politician who urged leaders of states that he visited to take action to correct problems in their state. When he visited the state of Lu 魯, he gave an appreciation of their music and dance and how it

for no one trod there.
The punishments of exile, and death by strangling or beheading,
    being strung up and flogged, or stripped and trussed up[73]
Were all available, but unused.
    Staves and clubs were bundled up, and he governed with
        tolerant measure.
For a thousand miles around
    his powerful instructions were principled by law.
Nor did his under-officials love either
    bribery or documentary malfeasance.
Highly skilled in governance, he exuded power but was not fierce;
    tolerant yet brave,
        the people of his district called him the "benevolent
            bodhisattva."
Wherever his seat of government had been,
    he had cleared out gangs of brigands
        and should there be any who remained, they were taken
            alive.
He didn't fear the investigations of the Surveillance
    Commissioners.[74]
His trustworthiness was no less than Ji Zha of the Springs and
    Autumns era;[75]
His administrative skill no less than Huang Ba in Yingchuan.
Six hundred households of Puzhou, large and small
Look up to him with reverence
    just as if he were their parent.

Coda
The Tiger-Headed Golden Plaque hangs from his waist,
And his manly bravery keeps the world tranquil,
While recalcitrant sons and thieving officials tremble at his
**   approach.**

expressed conditions within the state. He was a loyal minister who several times rejected overtures to take over the reins of the state of Wu, instead continuing in loyal service to the ruler. Huang Ba 黃霸(BCE 130–51), known as an incorruptible official for several consecutive emperors of the Han, in part earned his reputation through his tenure in Ying Prefecture (Yingzhou 穎州) where his concern for his junior officials and the people they were in charge of led to Ying becoming the most populous prefecture during his years of leadership.

唬得逆子賊臣望風的怕。

　　分符守郡，

　　昔年楊震不清白。

　　迪簡在廷，

　　曩日比干非骨鯁。

太守公坐之次，鄭恆鞭馬叩門，遽然而下。

iv.41/viii.11

中呂調（古輪台）

　　鄭衙內，

　　　當時休道不心嗔。

　　侍候的每怎遮攔，

　　　大走入衙門。

　　直上廳來，

　　　悄不顧白馬將軍。

　　氣莽聲高，

　　　叫呼對人。

　　騁盡百般村。

　　　都說元因。

　　道「化了的相國姑夫，

　　　在時曾許

　　　　聘與鶯鶯。

　　不幸身死，

　　　因此上未就親。

　　如今服闋也，

　　　卻序舊婚姻。

　　許多財禮，

　　　一划是好金銀。

　　十萬貫餘錢，

　　　首飾皆新。

　　百件衣服，

Bestowed the office of Protector of the Commandery,
Yang Zhen[76] of old would be considered impure by comparison.
To be selected for the court of the King—
Bi Gan of old would not seem as steely and upright.[77]

Just as the Grand Protector was taking his seat, Zheng Heng whipped
his mount to the door, knocked, and then swiftly dismounted.

iv.41/viii.11 Zhonglü Diao Mode

Old Bögör
Official Zheng
    was destined to be unhappy that day, one might say:
With no way for the gate guards to block him,
    he raced straight through the yamen door
And came directly into the court,
    paying not the slightest heed to the White Horse General.
Rude in manner, loud in voice,
    he yelled at those in court
In a most obscene, offensive, and crude way.
He explained his reasons,
Saying, "When that long departed uncle of mine, Minister Cui,
    was still around,
        he promised Oriole to me.
But unfortunately, he died
    and because of that, we didn't see it through.
Now that the mourning rites are over,
    the precedence of the betrothal rites can be restored.
To Oriole's family, I gave so many gifts
    of the finest silver and gold,
Ten thousand strings of cash or more—
    hair ornaments that are all brand new,
A hundred sets of clothes,
    with capes of sunset's glow and long skirts on top of that!

76 Yang Zhen 楊震 (54–124; byname Boqi 伯起), Eastern Han official noted for his incorruptibility.
77 Bi Gan (obit. 1047 BCE) is a figure of the classical and historical tradition who was put to death by his nephew, the licentious king Zhou (紂王) of the Shang dynasty, because of his continual remonstrations about the king's bad behavior. He once refused to leave court for three days, staying to remonstrate with his nephew. Zhou finally said, "I've heard that the human heart has seven apertures," and cut open Bi Gan's heart. Bi was nicknamed "the fishbone" because the emperor could not pull the "bone" of remonstrance out of his throat.

更兼霞帔長裙。

準備了筵席，

造下食飯，

杯盤水陸地鋪袇。

今日是良辰。

去昨宵半夜已來，

四更前後，

不覺鶯鶯。

隨人私走，

教人怎不忿。

我尋思，

那張珙哥哥好沒人情。」

（尾）

「鶯鶯那裏怎安穩。

覷着自家般丈夫

下得隨人逃走，

短命的那孩兒沒眼睛[29]。」

參差。。。。   太守怒曰「子欺我乎。公廳對官無禮，私下怎話。」

iv.42/viii.12 雙調（文如錦）

那將軍，

見鄭恆分辯後衝衝地怒。

道「打脊匹，

夫怎敢唬吾。

當日個，

孫飛虎。

因亡了元帥，

奪人妻女。

鶯鶯在普救，

參差被虜。

若非君瑞，

以書求救，

怎地支吾。

I'd already laid out the banquet mat
    and had the food prepared:
        cups and plates for viands from land and sea, with
           cushions set out on the floor.
Today was the propitious day.
But sometime after midnight last night
    around the fourth watch,
        I had no idea that Oriole
Was eloping with someone.
    How can I not be angry?
I've thought about it, and
    Brother Zhang Gong really has no human feelings.

Coda
"How can Oriole act so calm?
Seeing a man like me,
And suddenly running off with another,
    that silly child has no eyes at all."

The Grand Protector said angrily, "You think you can put one over on
me? And be disrespectful to officers in this court of law! You think you   [Unreadable
can say whatever you want?   comment.]

iv.42/viii.12 Shuang Diao Mode

Patterned Like Embroidery
After listening to Zheng Heng's
    disputation, the general was irate
And said, "You fit for a flogging good-for-nothing!
    How dare you try to intimidate me!
Back then,
    Flying Tiger Sun
Had lost his commander,
    and seized any woman or girl he wanted.
Oriole was in Universal Salvation
    and was nearly captured.
If it weren't for Junrui
    seeking my help via a letter
        how could they have held out?

怕賢不信，
　試問普救裏僧行、
　我手下兵卒。」

因此上夫人把親許。
不望你中間，
　　說他方言語。
今日他來，
　先曾告訴。
君瑞待把
　鶯鶯娶。
你甚倚強壓弱，
　廝欺廝負。
把官司誆諕。
全無畏懼。
你可三思，
　婚姻良賤，
　　明存着法律。
莫粗疏。
姑舅做親，
　便不敗壞風俗。

（尾）
　「平白地混賴他人婦。
　若不看您朝廷裏的慈父。
　打一頓教牒將家去。」

鄭恆對眾官，但稱。「死罪。非君瑞之愆。」又曰「我之
過矣。倘見親知，有何面目。」

iv.43/viii.13 大石調（伊州袞）
　添煩惱。
　情懷似刀攪。
　「都是自家錯。
　花枝般媳婦，
　　又被別人將了。

And lest you, my fine gentleman, don't believe me,
    just ask the monks and laypeople in Puzhou Monastery
      and all the soldiers under my command.

Because of this, Madam Cui assented to the marriage.
Now suddenly you interpose yourself
    and fabricate a different claim.
But he's already been here today
    and told me about what has gone on.
Junrui is going to marry Oriole.
You're using your power to oppress the weak
    and take advantage of him.
In this court you prevaricate and make threats
Without the slightest concern.
Think carefully—
    for marriages between both the good and the base,
      there are clearly written laws.
Don't be careless now.
Your uncle's promise of a marriage
    would certainly contravene custom, wouldn't it?

Coda
"Baselessly, you claim another's wife as your own.
If I didn't care about your compassionate father, who serves the
    imperial court,
I'd flog you soundly and send you home with a writ of censure."

Zheng Heng faced the assembled officials, and could only confess,
"There's been no wrong by Junrui." Then he said, "It is definitely my
transgression. How can I face my relatives or friends now?"

iv.43/viii.13 Dashi Diao Mode

Yizhou Tremolo
Zheng Heng grew more vexed,
And his emotions seem twisted around a blade.
"It's all my own fault.
A woman like a flowering sprig
    has been taken by another.

我還歸去，
　若見鄉裏親知，
　　甚臉道。
待別娶個人家，
　覷了我行為肯嫁的少。」
怎禁當，

衙門外，
　打牙打令譁，
　　匹似閑唬哨。
等着衙內，
　待替君瑞着言攢槊。
鄭恆打慘
　道「把如吃恁摧殘，
　　廝合燥。
不出衙門，
　覓個身亡卻是了。」

（尾）
　覷着一丈來高石階級搴衣跳。
　衙內每又沒半個人扯着。
　頭扎番身吃一個大碑落。

　浣紗節婦，
　　昔年抱石身亡。
　好色窮人，
　　今日投階而死。

太守令手下拽屍於門外，退廳張宴。

iv.44/viii.14 南呂宮（瑤台月）
　從今至古，
　　自是佳人，
　　　合配才子。
　鶯鶯已是縣君，
　　君瑞是玉堂學士。

If I go home now
    and am seen by my friends in town,
        how can I face them?
And should I seek a wife from a different family,
    few will be willing after seeing what I've done.

Outside this yamen door
    how will I bear
        the locals' whispered judgments and derisive jokes,
            their gratuitous cat calls and teasing whistles?
They are waiting for me, a son of a minister,
    so that they can rain down curses in Junrui's stead."
Zheng Heng thought hard, then said,
    "Rather than suffer this kind of ruin
        and feel their scorn,
Better not to depart through the yamen gate,
    but find a way to die and be done with it."

Coda

He looked at the ten-foot-tall flight of stone steps, gathered up his
    robe, and jumped.
No one from the yamen even tried to stop him.
Somersaulting headlong, he fell smack onto his back.

    In days of old a virtuous woman, a washer of silk,
    clutched a stone to drown;
    today a man with nothing, a lecher,
    threw himself on the steps and died.

    The Grand Protector had his underlings drag the corpse outside the
    door, withdrew from the hall, and started a banquet.

iv.44/viii.14 Nanlü Gong Mode

Moon on the Jasper Terrace
From now to the distant past,
    It has always been a fact: beauties
        should be matched with talented men.
Oriole is now Lady of the County
    and Junrui an Academician of the Jade Hall.

一個文章天下無雙，
　一個稔色寰中無二。
似合歡帶，
　連理枝。
題彩扇，
　寫新詩。
從此。
趁了文君深願，
　酬了相如素志。

將軍滿滿勸金巵。
道「今日極醉休辭。」
歡喜煞[30]這兩個也，
　乾撞殺鄭恆那村廝。
牙關緊氣堵了咽喉，
　腦袋裂血污了階址。
後門外，
　橫着死屍。
牌寫着，
　數行字。
出示。
「這廝一生愛女，
　今番入死。」

（尾）
　會見乾堆每強相思。
　從前已往有浮浪兒。
　誰似這廝般少年花下死。

　君瑞鶯鶯，美滿團圓，還都上任。

　鄭恆衙內，自恥懷羞，投階而死。

　　　　　方表才子施恩，
　　　　　足見佳人報德。

One's writing has no parallel in the world,
 the other's beauty is unmatched in the realm.
They are like a lover's knot
 or branches intertwined.
Inscribing colored fans,
 they write new poems.
From now on
The deep desire of Wenjun has been won
 and the long-held wish of Xiangru granted.

The general pressed full gold goblets on them
Saying, "Today is a day to get drunk. Don't beg off!"
The two were overjoyed with happiness.
 And that clod Zheng Heng was dead for nothing,
His teeth tightly clenched, his breath blocked in his throat,
 his skull split, and blood stains on the foot of the stairs.
Outside the rear gates
 his corpse was displayed
With a placard, a few lines
To serve as a warning:
"Here lies a guy who coveted women his whole life,
 but today the last has led him to his death."

Coda
Every time he encountered a dry pile of wood, he would think of
 love.
There have always been frivolous and dissipated lads,
But none like this youngster, who died for a flower.

Junrui and Oriole, having had a beautiful reunion, returned to the capital so he could take his position.

Zheng Heng, the official's son, ridden with shame and embarrassment, threw himself down the steps to die.

 And so were displayed the talented one's acts of grace;
 So was revealed the beauty's repayment for virtue.

怎見得有此事來。蓬萊劉汭題詩曰

> 蒲東佳遇古無多，
> 鏤板將令鏡不磨。
> 若使微之見新調，
> 不教專美伯勞歌。

How do we know this happened? Liu Rui of Penglai inscribed a poem that reads:

> In Pudong a beautiful encounter was seldom seen of old;
> The blocks upon which the story is carved will leave mirrors unpolished.
> If Yuan Zhen could be made to see these songs,
> He would find it impossible to praise only the one about the shrike.

Endnotes

1 Reading 渌 for 漂.
2 Reading 比似 for 比時.
3 Replacing 緣 with 綠.
4 Reading 挹 for 抑.
5 Replacing 風合合 with 香風合.
6 Removing 猬 (猿).
7 Replacing 令纏 with 纏令.
8 Replacing 揚 with 楊.
9 Replacing 緣 with 綠.
10 Replacing 稍 with 梢.
11 Reading 嗤嗤 as 抽抽.
12 Reading 門 for 悶.
13 Reading 寄語 for 寄與; if the latter, "I send this to share. . . ."
14 Reading 斑管 for 班管.
15 Reading 深 for 探.
16 Reading 黯 for 點.
17 Reading 雉 for 稚.
18 Reading 三 for 玉.
19 Reading 嘸 for 輒.
20 Reading 唧 for 湢.
21 Reading 下 for 得.
22 Reading 辨 for 辯.
23 Following original text and reading 當 for 對, which restores the *-an/-ang* rhyme of the suite.
24 Reading 撇 as 憋.
25 Reading 臀 for 臀.
26 Reading 聞 for 間.
27 Reading 曉 for 關.
28 Reading 譜 for 暗.
29 Reading 睛 for 斤.
30 Replacing 教 with 煞.

附錄一

趙令時鼓子詞

《元微之崔鶯鶯商調蝶戀花詞》

夫傳奇者，唐元微之所述也。以不載於本集而出於小說，或疑其非是。今觀其詞，自非大手筆孰能與於此。至今士大夫極談幽玄，訪奇述異，無不舉此以為美話。至於娼優女子，皆能調說大略。惜乎不被之以音律，故不能播之聲樂，形之管弦。好事君子極飲肆歡之際，願欲一聽其說，或舉其末而忘其本，或紀其略而不及終其篇，此吾曹之所共恨者也。

今於暇日，詳觀其文，略其煩褻，分之為十章。每章之下，屬之以詞。或全摭其文，或止取其意。又別為一曲，載之傳前，先敘前篇之義。調曰商調，曲名蝶戀花。句句言情，篇篇見意。

奉勞歌伴，先定格調，後聽蕪詞。

> 麗質仙娥生月殿。
> 謫向人間，
> 　　未免凡情亂。
> 宋玉牆東流美盼。
> 亂花深處曾相見。
> 密意濃歡方有便。
> 不奈浮名，
> 　　旋遣輕分散。
> 最恨多才情太淺。
> 等閒不念離人怨。

Appendix One
Zhao Lingzhi's Drum-Song Version of
"The Tale of Oriole" with Inserted *Song* Lyrics

Now, this tale was told by Yuan Zhen of the Tang dynasty, although that is sometimes doubted because it was not in his collected works and appeared as a fictional tale. But, observing his words now, we find that only a great writer could have been involved. Up to the present day, men of worth love to talk about abstruse mysteries, and seek out the strange or narrate otherness. All of them take this as an example of a beautiful tale. Even courtesan entertainers can narrate the general gist of the story. But alas, it has never been set to a song pattern, so it cannot be conveyed via music or given shape by instruments. Gentlemen seeking something new when drinking and pursuing pleasure desire to hear the whole thing. Sometimes entertainers will give the ending but forget how it originates or outline the plot but not finish it—this is something people of my ilk hate.

In my spare time I have carefully investigated the text, excised its confusing and impertinent parts, and divided it into ten sections. I have added a lyric poem at the end of each section that either discusses a whole section or simply seizes directly on its import. I have also created a separate song and put it at the head the story to explain the significance of the first section. The mode is *Shangdiao*, the formula of the song is *Butterflies Love Flowers*; every line speaks of passion and every verse reveals its meaning. Let me now trouble my singing companions, and ask that they first set the mode, and then let us hear my crazy verses.

> The beautiful essence of a Chang'e born in the palace of the moon
> Was banished to the mortal realm,
> > unable to avoid being confused.
> Song Yu let his beautiful gaze wander to the eastern wall,
> Where once he saw her, deep in the riotous thicket of flowers.

> Intimate affection and deep pleasure had just found a way
> When, alas, his desire to make a name
> > sent him quickly on his way; he parted from her lightly.
> The most hateful thing is a talented man whose passions are
> > too shallow
> > > and too dismissive of the complaints of the one left behind.

傳曰：余所善張君，性溫茂，美丰儀，寓於蒲之普救寺。適有崔氏孀婦，將歸長安，路出於蒲，亦止茲寺。崔氏婦鄭女也。張出於鄭，緒其親，乃異派之從母。

是歲，丁文雅不善於軍，軍人因喪而擾，大掠蒲人。崔氏之家，財產甚厚，多奴僕。旅寓惶駭，不知所措。先是張與蒲將之黨有善，請吏護之，遂不及於難。

鄭厚張之德甚，因飾饌以命張，中堂宴之。復謂張曰：「姨之孤嫠未亡，提攜幼稚。不幸屬師徒大潰，實不保其身。弱子幼女，猶君之所生也，豈可比常恩哉。今俾以仁兄之禮奉見，冀所以報恩也。」乃命其子曰歡郎，可十餘歲，容甚溫美。次命女曰：「鶯鶯，出拜爾兄。爾兄活爾。」久之，辭疾。鄭怒曰：「張兄保爾之命。不然，爾且虜矣，能復遠嫌乎？」又久之，乃至常服睟容，不加新飾。垂鬟淺黛，雙臉斷紅而已。顏色艷異，光輝動人。張驚，為之禮。因坐鄭旁，凝睇怨絕，若不勝其體。張問其年歲。鄭曰：「十七歲矣。」張生稍以詞導之，不對，終席而罷。

奉勞歌伴，再和前聲。

The tale says: our good Sir Zhang was mild-mannered and handsome. He was lodging in the Universal Salvation Monastery in the district of Pu. It just so happened that the widow Madam Cui, who was heading back to Chang'an, was also staying there since it was on the way. Madam Cui was born into the Zheng family. Zhang came from the Xu line of the Zheng lineage, so she was a maternal aunt of a different family in the same lineage.

That year, Ding Wenya was unable to control his troops, and the soldiers created a huge disturbance and plundered the people of Puzhou. The Cui family was well propertied and rich, and had many slaves and servants, so Madam Zheng was frightened there in her lodgings, and did not know what to do. Zhang had a longtime friendship with the circle around the general at Puzhou, and he requested that one of the underlings protect her, so she was kept from any trouble.

Madam Zheng was deeply impressed by the extent of Zhang's virtue and so laid on a banquet and invited him to the central hall. She told him, "Our period of mourning as widow and orphans has yet to end, and I have been traveling with my children. Unfortunately, the troops attached to the army rose up and caused trouble, and I was unable to protect our lives. My young son and daughter owe their lives to you—how could this be considered an ordinary kindness? Now I would like you to be served with the rituals appropriate to an elder brother and so hope to repay your help." First, she summoned her son, Happy, who was a little older than nine and was gentle and handsome. Then she summoned her daughter and told her, "Oriole, come out and pay obeisance to your elder brother. He saved your life." For a long time, Oriole begged off, saying she was ill. Madam Zheng said angrily, "Brother Zhang protected your life. You would have been taken prisoner otherwise. How can you keep your distance now?" Another long period passed, and then Oriole presented herself.

Her face was kind, and she was in ordinary daily dress, with no new adornments. Her hair hung in coils, and she had applied only light shadow to her eyebrows. Only her face showed a peachy red. She was gorgeous and startlingly radiant. Zhang was shocked but greeted her with proper ritual. Since she was seated beside Madam Zheng, she stared resentfully, as though not in control of her body. Zhang asked how old she was, and Madam Zheng said, "She's just turned sixteen." Student Zhang tried to engage her in conversation, but she refused to respond all throughout the banquet.

May I trouble my singing companions to again match the previous sounds?

錦額重簾深幾許。
繡履彎彎，
　　未省離朱戶。
強出嬌羞都不語。
絳綃頻掩酥胸素。

黛淺愁紅妝淡佇。
怨絕情凝，
　　不肯聊回顧。
媚臉未勻新淚污。
梅英猶帶春朝露。

張生自是惑之，願致其情，無由得也。崔之婢曰紅娘，生私為之
禮者數四，乘間遂道其衷。

翌日復至，曰：「郎之言，所不敢言，亦不敢洩。然而崔之族
姻，君所詳也，何不因其媒而求娶焉！」

張曰：「予始自孩提時，性不苟合。昨日一席間，幾不自持。數
日來，行忘止，食忘飯，恐不能逾旦暮。若因媒氏而娶，納採問
名，則三數月間，索我於枯魚之肆矣。」婢曰：「崔之貞順自
保，雖所尊不可以非語犯之。然而善屬文，往往沈吟章句，怨慕
者久之。君試為諭情詩以亂之。不然，無由得也。」張大喜，立
綴春詞二首以授之。

奉勞歌伴，再和前聲。

Damask valances and doubled curtains, how hidden is she?
In embroidered shoes with curved arches,
    she has never left the vermillion doors.
Forced to be charming and bashful, she never spoke,
But kept covering her bosom as white as curds with her
    crimson silks.

With faint eyebrow shadow and a sad red face, she stood in
    her light makeup.
Extremely resentful, with her emotions concentrated,
    she refused to pay him any attention.
Her charming face was mottled, soiled by the stains of new
    tears—
A plum blossom still carrying the dew of a spring morn.

Student Zhang was infatuated from that moment on. He wanted to express his feelings but had no way to do it. Oriole's maidservant was called Crimson, and the student secretly treated her with great courtesy on several occasions, and taking advantage of an opening, he fully expressed what lay in his heart.

Crimson came back the next day and said, "I dare not forget what you told me, and I dare not reveal it either. But you, sir, are quite knowledgeable about the Cui clan, why not get a matchmaker and try to make her your wife?"

Zhang replied, "From the time I was a child, it hasn't been in my nature to make improper connections, but yesterday at that feast I nearly lost my self-control. For the past few days, I've walked without knowing where I was going and eaten without noticing the food. I fear I won't last much longer. If I rely on a matchmaker for the ritual exchanging betrothal gifts and requesting her name and birthdate, then after the three months that will take, you'll find me in the dried fish market." The maid said, "With Oriole's chaste compliance and self-control, even those she respects can't cross her with an inappropriate word. However, she is skilled at writing. She is often lost in chanting verse and chapter, feeling the effects of the rancor or yearning for a long time afterward. You will have to write her a poem clearly expressing your passion to seduce her. I'm afraid that's the only way." Zhang was delighted and immediately wrote two "Spring Lyrics" to send to her.

May I trouble my singing companions to kindly match the previous sounds again?

懊惱嬌痴情未慣。
不道看看，
　　役得人腸斷。
萬語千言都不管。
蘭房跬步如天遠。

廢寢忘餐思想遍。
賴有青鸞，
　　不必憑魚雁。
密寫香箋論繾綣。
春詞一紙芳心亂。

是夕，紅娘復至，執彩箋以授張曰：「明月三五夜。」其詞曰：

待月西廂下，
迎風戶半開。
拂牆花影動，
疑是玉人來。

奉勞歌伴，再和前聲。

庭院黃昏春雨霽。
一縷深心，
　　百種成牽系。
青翼驀然來報喜。
魚箋微諭相容意。

待月西廂人不寐。
簾影搖光，
　　朱戶猶慵閉。
花動拂牆紅萼墜。
分明疑是情人至。

張亦微諭其旨。是夕，歲二月旬又四日矣。崔之東牆有杏花一
樹，攀援可逾。既望之夕，張因梯樹而逾焉。達於西廂則戶半開

He was vexed by her guilelessness, not yet accustomed to passion.
Don't say, "Just a look,"
     since it brought a broken heart.
Not heeding ten thousand words, a thousand phrases—
The half step to her orchid chamber was as distant as the heavens.

Abandoning sleep, forgetting meals, he was full of thoughts.
There was a blue simurgh on which he could rely,
     and he needed no fish or goose.
Writing densely on fragrant stationary, he discussed deep
     emotions.
Those "Spring Lyrics" on a single page seduced her fragrant heart.

Crimson returned that night, bringing a colorful note to give to Zhang
with a poem titled "The Bright Moon on the Night of the Fifteenth."
It read,

     Waiting for the moon by the western wing,
     Greeting the breeze, the gate half opened.
     Brushing the wall, flowers' shadows move,
     Could it be the Jade One coming?

May I trouble my singing companions to again match the previous sounds?

Dusk in the courtyard of the compound as spring rains clear away.
A single strand of thought in a deep heart
     multiplied by a hundred becomes a constant obsession.
Those blue wings suddenly come to report happiness.
Fish-roe textured paper clearly reveals an openness to accept.

"Waiting for the moon by the western wing"—she's not asleep.
Curtain's shadows shimmer with light,
     the vermillion doors closed as always.
Flowers move, brushing the wall, and red calyces fall,
Clearly, she suspects it is a lover arriving.

Zhang had a subtle understanding of the import of her poem. This was
already the evening of the fourteenth of the second month. There was an
apricot tree in flower at the east wall of the Cui compound, by which he
could get over the wall. On the night of the fifteenth, Zhang used the tree

矣。無幾紅娘復來，連曰：「至矣，至矣。」張生且喜且駭，謂
必獲濟。

及女至，則端服儼容，大數張曰：「兄之恩，活我家厚矣，由是
慈母以弱子幼女見倚。奈何因不令之婢，致淫佚之詞。始以護人
之亂為義，而終掠亂而求之。是以亂易亂，其去幾何。誠欲寢其
詞，則保人之奸不義；明之母，則背人之惠不祥；將寄於婢妾，
又恐不得發其真誠。是用托於短章，願自陳啓。猶懼兄之見難，
是用鄙靡之詞以求必至。非禮之動，能不愧心。特願以禮自持，
毋及於亂。」言畢，翻然而逝。

張自失者久之，復逾而出，由是絕望矣。

奉勞歌伴，再和前聲。

> 屈指幽期惟恐誤。
> 恰到春宵，
> 　明月當三五。
> 紅影壓牆花密處。
> 花陰便是桃源路。
>
> 不謂蘭誠金石固。
> 斂袂怡聲，
> 　恣把多才數。
> 惆悵空回誰共語。
> 只應化作朝雲去。

後數夕，張君臨軒獨寢，忽有人驚至。驚而起，則紅娘斂衾攜枕

as a ladder and jumped over. He reached the western wing, and the door was indeed half open. Crimson arrived in a moment and kept repeating, "She's coming, she's coming." Student Zhang was both delighted and trepidatious but convinced he would be successful.

When she arrived, however, she was in formal dress and regarded Zhang sternly. She scolded, "Your grace in saving our family is truly profound, brother. Because of this, my compassionate mother has entrusted me and my brother to you. So why would you have this worthless maid deliver such a lascivious poem to me? At first, you thought it righteous to rescue me from rape, but then you ended up wanting to seduce me. Substituting seduction for rape, how much difference is there? I wanted to bury these words, but it would be wrong to cover up your act of seduction. I wanted to reveal it to my mother, but it's inauspicious to turn one's back on acts of kindness. I was going to avail myself of my maidservant, but I feared she couldn't express my true feelings. So, I put it into a short passage, hoping to explain myself fully. I didn't want to put you in a bad situation, so I used vulgar words to make sure you came. How can you not feel shame for these improper actions? I hope you exercise self-restraint and do not continue such seductions." Finished, she turned and left.

Feeling an emptiness that would last for a long time, Zhang climbed back over the wall and left. From that point on, he was completely without hope.

May I trouble my singing companions to again match the previous sounds?

With the crook of a finger, the tryst turned to a troubling mistake.
Just reaching spring evenings
    when the moon was round and full.
Red shadows weighed on the wall where flowers were dense,
Flowers' shadows that were the pathway to the Peach-Spring
    Fount.
Don't say that thoroughwort is truly solid as iron and stone.
Gathering her sleeves, in a gentle voice
    she let fly her criticism of that talented man.
Distressed, he returned alone, with no one to talk to—
It'd be best if he could transform into a morning cloud.

Several nights later, Zhang was sleeping alone near the porch when suddenly someone woke him, and he got up, startled. Crimson brought

而至。撫張曰：「至矣，至矣，睡何為哉？」並枕重衾而去。張
生拭目危坐久之，猶疑夢寐。

俄而紅娘捧崔而至，則嬌羞融冶，力不能運支體。曩時之端莊，
不復同矣。是夕，旬有八日，斜月晶熒，幽輝半床。張生飄飄
然，且疑神仙之徒，不謂從人間至也。有頃，寺鐘鳴曉。紅娘促
去。崔氏嬌啼宛轉，紅娘又捧而去。終夕無一言。張生辨色而
興，自疑曰：「豈其夢耶？」所可明者，妝在臂，香在衣，淚光
熒熒然，猶瑩於茵席而已。

奉勞歌伴，同和前聲。

> 數夕孤眠如度歲。
> 將謂今生，
> 　會合終無計。
> 正是斷腸凝望際。
> 雲心捧得嫦娥至。
>
> 玉困花柔羞抆淚。
> 端麗妖嬈，
> 　不與前時比。
> 人去月斜疑夢寐。
> 衣香猶在妝留臂。

是後又十數日，杳不復知。張生賦《會真》詩三十韻，未畢，紅
娘適至，因授之以貽崔氏，自是復容之。朝隱而出，暮隱而入，
同安於曩所謂西廂者，幾一月矣。張生將之長安，先以情諭之。

a quilt and pillow, and said consolingly to Zhang, "She'll come, she'll come. Why are you sleeping?" Then, she put the pillows side by side, doubled the quilt and left. Zhang rubbed his eyes and sat bolt upright. After a while, he thought that it had all been a dream.

In no time at all, Crimson came with Oriole, who was charming, bashful, and pliant, powerless to even move her limbs. She was totally different than her former stern self. This was the night of the eighteenth, and the falling moon glistened like crystal, making the bed half-light, half-dark. Zhang felt as if he were floating, suspecting she was a divine transcendent and not from the human world.

After a while, the morning monastery bell rang, and Crimson urged her to leave. Oriole wept in a charming way as she turned to go. Crimson hurried her off. She had been silent the whole night. Student Zhang got up as soon as he discerned light, and said doubtfully, "Wasn't it a dream?" The only evidence was makeup on his arm, perfume on his clothes, and sparkling radiance of tears still visible on his bed.

May I trouble my singing companions to again match the previous sounds?

> For several nights he slept alone, each night as long as a year.
> Who would say that in this life
>   there was no way to be together.
> Just as the broken-hearted man was staring vacantly,
> The heart of the clouds had offered up Chang'e herself.
>
> The jade languorous and her flower soft, she bashfully wiped away
>   tears.
> Properly beautiful, full of charm,
>   there was no comparison to before.
> She left as the moon declined, and he suspected it was a dream,
> With perfume still on his clothes and makeup still smudged on his
>   arm.

For ten-plus days after this, there was no news. Student Zhang composed a poem, "Thirty Rhymes on Encountering a Perfected One," and had yet to finish it when Crimson suddenly showed up, so he gave the poem to Crimson to present to Oriole. From that time on, she accepted him, leaving secretly in the morning and coming back secretly at night. They found peace for almost a month in the western wing where they had met.

Student Zhang was about to go to Chang'an, and he first expressed his feelings for her. Oriole said nothing unpleasant about it, but her sad,

崔氏宛無難詞，然愁怨之容動人矣。欲行之再夕，不復可見，而張生遂西。

奉勞歌伴，再和前聲。

> 一夢行雲還暫阻。
> 盡把深誠，
> 　綴作新詩句。
> 幸有青鸞堪密付。
> 良宵從此無虛度。
>
> 兩意相歡朝又暮。
> 爭奈郎鞭，
> 　暫指長安路。
> 最是動人愁怨處。
> 離情盈抱終無語。

不數月，張生復游於蒲，捨於崔氏者又累月。張雅知崔氏善屬文，求索再三，終不可見。雖待張之意甚厚，然未嘗以詞繼之。

異時，獨夜操琴，愁弄悽惻。張竊聽之，求之，則不復鼓矣。以是愈惑之。張生俄以文調及期，又當西去。

當去之夕，崔恭貌怡聲，徐謂張曰：「始亂之，今棄之，固其宜矣，愚不敢恨。必也君始之，君終之，君之惠也。則沒身之誓，有其終矣，又何必深憾於此行。然而君既不懌，無以奉寧。君嘗謂我善鼓琴，今且往矣。既達君此誠。」

因命拂琴，鼓霓裳羽衣序，不數聲，哀音怨亂，不復知其是曲也。左右皆欷歔，張說遽止之。崔投琴擁面，泣下流漣，趣歸鄭

resentful face was poignant. On the eve of his departure, he was unable to see her, and the next day he headed west.

May I trouble my singing companions to again match the previous sounds?

> A whole dream of traveling clouds returned and was suddenly
>   blocked.
> All his deep sincerity
>   was stitched into new poetic lines.
> Fortunately, a blue simurgh was willing to relay them in secret,
> And their pleasant nights afterward were not spent alone.
>
> Mornings and nights, their two desires found delight in each other.
> But alas the gentleman's horsewhip
>   pointed temporarily toward the road to Chang'an.
> The truly touching part was the sadness and resentment;
> In their passions of parting and full embraces, she said not a word.

Some months later, Student Zhang once more traveled in Pu District, and lodged at the Cui compound for a period of months. Zhang knew that Oriole was excellent at writing, and he requested letters over and over, but they never appeared. Although she wanted Zhang's thoughts, she never followed up by writing. At another time, she had sorrowfully played heartbreaking tunes on the zither alone at night. Zhang listened to her secretly, but when he asked her to play more, she refused. He became even more infatuated because of this. Then suddenly, because the examination period was upon him, he had to go back west.

On the night before he left, Oriole spoke to Zhang respectfully in a slow, pleasant voice: "To have seduced me in the beginning and cast me away now is appropriate, and I don't dare feel angry about it. You began it, you finished it—that was to your favor; but our oath to live together forever is no more, so why should we regret this parting? Still, you're unhappy, and I have no way to bring you peace. You once said that I play the zither well. Since you're about to depart, let me play to express my sincerity."

So, she played the "Prelude to Rainbow Skirts and Feathered Chemise" on the zither, but after only a few notes, the sounds of grief and resentment made the song unrecognizable. Those around her began to sob with their faces hidden, and Zhang quickly stopped her. Oriole threw

所遂不復至。

奉勞歌伴，再和前聲。

> 碧沼鴛鴦交頸舞。
> 正恁雙棲，
> 　又遣分飛去。
> 灑翰贈言終不許。
> 援琴請盡始衷素。
>
> 曲未成聲先怨慕。
> 忍淚凝情，
> 　強作霓裳序。
> 彈到離愁淒咽處。
> 弦腸俱斷梨花雨。

詰旦，張生遂行。明年，文戰不利，遂止於京。因貽書於崔，以廣其意。崔氏緘報之詞，粗載於此，曰：

捧覽來問，撫愛過深。兒女之情，悲喜交集。兼惠花勝一合，口脂五寸。致耀首膏脣之飾，雖荷多惠，誰復為容。睹物增懷，但積悲嘆耳。伏承便於京中就業，於進修之道，固在便安。但恨鄙陋之人，永以遐棄。命也如此，知復何言！

自去秋以來，嘗忽忽如有所失。於喧譁之下，或勉為笑語。閒宵自處，無不淚零。乃夢寐之間，亦多紛感咽離憂之思。綢繆繾綣，暫若尋常，幽會未終，驚魂已斷。雖半衾如暖，而思之甚遙。

down the zither and covered her face, her tears flowing without cease. She went back to the Zheng compound and did not show herself again.

May I trouble my singing companions to again match the previous sounds?

> On azure ponds mandarin ducks dance with necks entwined.
> Just as they were roosting as a pair,
>   they were dispatched to fly apart again.
> Brandishing the brush to offer her words was never allowed.
> Holding the zither, she asked to exhaust her true feelings.
> But before one note was struck, the song was already full of
>   remorse and yearning.
> She bore her tears and concentrated feelings,
>   forcing herself to play the "Prelude to Rainbow Skirts."
> She played until she sobbed with the heartbreak of parting;
> Her heart and the zither strings broke amid rain on the pear
>   blossoms.

The next morning Student Zhang left. Unsuccessful in his battle to pass the examinations, the next year he remained in the capital, but sent a message to Oriole to console her. Her reply was roughly as follows:

> I read your letter, and its sentiments were perhaps excessively deep. The passions of a young man and young woman are a mix of grief and joy. You sent me hair adornments and five inches of lip rouge, to make my head sparkle and keep my lips glossy. It's a great favor, but for whom should I wear it all? Looking at them only increases my cares, and all I can do is accumulate sad sighs. You say that it is better for you to stay in the capital and work on the examination curriculum, and of course it is more convenient that way. I just hate that I, a simple ordinary person, am always to be cast aside. Well, that is my fate, and there is nothing else to say.
>   Ever since last autumn, I seem to have been in a daze, as though I had lost something of myself. On boisterous occasions, I can sometimes make myself join in the laughter and conversation. But every evening alone I weep, and even sleeping I often rehearse my thoughts about the sadness of separation. And when, for a while, our lovemaking seems like it was before our secret tryst has reached completion, I am startled awake, and it ends. Although half the quilt is still warm, I think of how far away you are.

一昨拜辭，倐逾舊歲。長安行樂之地，觸緒牽情。何幸不忘幽微，眷念無。鄙薄之志，無以奉酬。至於終始之盟，則固不忒。鄙昔中表相因，或同宴處；婢僕見誘，遂致私誠。兒女之情，不能自固。君子有援琴之挑，鄙人無投梭之拒。及薦枕席，義盛恩深。愚幼之情，永謂終托。豈期既見君子，不能以禮定情，致有自獻之羞，不復明侍巾櫛。沒身永恨，含嘆何言，儻若仁人用心，俯遂幽劣，雖死之日，猶生之年。

如或達士略情，捨小從大，以先配為醜行，謂要盟之可欺，則當骨化形銷，丹忱不泯，因風委露，猶托清塵。存歿之誠，言盡於此。臨紙嗚咽，情不能申，千萬珍重。

奉勞歌伴，再和前聲。

> 別後相思心目亂。
> 不謂芳音，
> 　忽寄南來雁。
> 卻寫花箋和淚卷。
> 細書方寸教伊看。
>
> 獨寐良宵無計遣。

Another year has passed since you left. Chang'an is a land of pleasure, with attractions to lure the passions. How fortunate that you have not forgotten the faded fragrance of our trysts and have not grown tired of me. What shallow intentions I might have are unworthy of yours. As for our vow to be together always, it remains solid and unchanging. I first met you at a banquet, where we met as cousins. My maid was enticed to reveal your feelings to me, and I was unable to keep my own heart in check. You played the zither like Sima Xiangru to arouse me, but I did not reject you by throwing a shuttle. And when I offered a pillow and mat for your bed, you graciously did right by me. In my childish passion, I would have said I could rely on you for a lifetime. How could I expect that once I had seen my gentleman, he could not offer betrothal presents as ritual dictates. Judging our relationship then as enduring as pine or cypress, I suffered the embarrassment of offering myself to you. I cannot openly serve you with comb and cloth as a proper wife, a regret I will carry to the end of my life. But I will swallow my sighs—what is there to say? If, as a good person, you should give your heart to this unworthy one, were that the day I died, it would be as the year of my birth.

If, as an accomplished man, you consider these emotions trivial, then cast aside the minor feelings to follow the greater things. If you take your first match as misconduct, and say that this important covenant can be abused, then though my bones may decay and my form disappear, my vermilion heart will never vanish. Riding on the wind and transported by the dew, it will always be there, in the clear dust behind your tread.

My sincerity in life or death can never be questioned. I face the paper and sob, unable to express my feelings. Take care of yourself.

May I trouble my singing companions to again match the previous sounds?

Thoughts of love after parting disordered his very heart.
It could not be called the fragrant sounds of poetry,
　　but it was given to a southward flying goose.
It may have been written on flowered paper, and rolled up along
　　with tears,
Her heart written out in tiny characters for him to read.

She slept alone on fine nights, with no way to send it on.
The vagueness of dreams

夢里依稀，
　暫若尋常見。
幽會未終魂已斷。
半衾如暖人猶遠。

玉環一枚，是兒嬰年所弄，寄充君子下體之佩。玉取其
堅潔不渝，環取其終始不絕。兼致彩絲一絇，文竹茶合
碾子一枚。此數物不足見珍，意者欲君子如玉之潔，鄙
志如環不解。淚痕在竹，愁緒縈絲。因物達誠，永以為
好耳。心邇身遐，拜會無期。幽憤所鍾，千里神合。千
萬珍重。春風多厲，強飯為佳。慎言自保，毋以鄙為深
念也。

奉勞歌伴，再和前聲。

尺素重重封錦字。
未盡幽閨，
　別後心中事。
佩玉彩絲文竹器。
願君一見知深意。

環玉長圓絲萬系。
竹上斕斑，
　總是相思淚。
物會見郎人永棄。
心馳魂去神千里。

張之友聞之，莫不聳異。而張之志固絕之矣。歲余，崔已委

    at times seemed like ordinary meetings.
Their clandestine tryst not yet ended; her dream soul was already
    sundered.
Half of the quilt seemed warm, but the other person was still far
    away.

I am sending a jade bracelet that I used to play with as a toddler, to be
hung from the waist as a pendant. Jade signifies a firmness and purity
that does not change; the bracelet signifies that there is no beginning or
end—one is the other. This is sent with a skein of colored thread, a tea
roller of mottled bamboo, and a tea box. None of these things is worth
valuing, but they are meant to say that I hope you will be as clean as
the jade, since my own intentions, like the bracelet, cannot be undone.
There are tear marks on the bamboo, and my sorrowful thoughts are as
tangled as the skein of silk. I express my sincerity through these things,
tokens of my timeless love and nothing more. Our hearts may be close,
but our bodies are distant, and there is no set time for our reunion. When
repressed anger is concentrated, souls can merge a thousand miles away.
Be sure to take care of yourself. Spring winds are often harsh, and you
should make yourself eat. Be circumspect in your speech and protect
yourself. And don't think too deeply about me!

May I trouble my singing companions to again match the previous
sounds?

    A foot of silk folded over and over sealed her writing.
    After their parting, the affairs of her heart
        Did not end in her secluded boudoir.
    Jade pendant, colored silk, mottled bamboo tools—
    "I hope when you see them you will understand their deep
        significance."

    The jade of the oval-shaped bracelet, and the strands of silk
        knotted ten thousand times,
    The mottling on the bamboo
        that will forever show the tears of love—
    These things may be discarded forever by the young gentleman,
    But her heart spurred her soul to a thousand miles away.

When Zhang's friends heard about this, they were all amazed, yet Zhang's
desire put a firm end to it. In another year or so, Oriole was betrothed
to another, and Zhang had taken a wife. He once passed by where she

身於人，張亦有所娶。適經其所居，乃因其夫言於崔，以外
兄見。夫已諾之，而崔終不為出。張怨念之誠，動於顏色。
崔知之，潛賦一詩寄張曰：

> 自從消瘦減容光。
> 萬轉千回懶下床。
> 不為旁人羞不起，
> 為郎憔悴卻羞郎。

竟不之見。後數日張君將行，崔又賦一詩以謝絕之。詞曰：

> 棄置今何道，
> 當時且自親。
> 還將舊來意，
> 憐取眼前人。

奉勞歌伴，再和前聲。

> 夢覺高唐雲雨散。
> 十二巫峰，
> 　隔斷相思眼。
> 不為旁人移步懶。
> 為郎憔悴羞郎見。
>
> 青翼不來孤鳳怨。
> 路失桃源，
> 　再會終無便。
> 舊恨新愁無計遣，
> 情深何似情俱淺。

逍遙子曰：「樂天謂微之能道人意中語。僕於是益知樂天之言為
當也。何者？夫崔之才華婉美，詞彩艷麗，則於所載緘書詩章盡
之矣。如其都愉淫冶之態，則不可得而見。及觀其文，飄飄然彷

lived and sent word through her husband that he would like to meet her as a distant cousin. The husband assented, but in the end, Oriole never came out. An honest look of remorse passed across Zhang's face. When Oriole found out, she secretly sent him a poem:

> I grew thin and my face lost all luster;
> I tossed and turned and tossed again, languidly lying abed.
> It's not because of others that I'm too embarrassed to rise;
> I grew haggard because of you and am embarrassed for you to see.

In the end he never saw her. But as he was about to leave several days later, she sent another poem refusing him. It read:

> Rejected, cast aside, what is there to say?
> We were close for a while.
> You can still take those old feelings you had for me
> And take pity on the one who will be in front of you.

May I trouble my singing companions to again match the previous sounds?

> Awaking from a dream, the clouds and rain on Gaotang disperse,
> And the twelve peaks of Mount Shamanka
>   obstruct eyes pining for love.
> It's not because of others that she wearily shuffles her feet.
> "I grew haggard because of you and am embarrassed for you to see."
>
> No blue wings come now; the orphaned phoenix is resentful.
> The road to the Peach Spring Fount is lost,
>   with no possibility of meeting again.
> Old rancor, new sorrow, and no way to get rid of it—
> How can deep feelings compare to those that are shallow?

Mister Free Wanderer said, "Bai Juyi once said that Yuan Zhen could really speak in the voice of others. Now I know even more that Bai Juyi's words were correct. And why is that? Oriole was gifted and beautiful, and the literary quality of her work was gorgeous, fully displayed in her letters and poetic compositions. But one cannot see her playful or lascivious attitudes at all. Yet when one looks at her writing, she seems

彿出於人目前。雖丹青摹寫其形狀，未知能如是工且至否？僕嘗採撤其意，撰成鼓子詞十一章，示余友何東白先生。」

先生曰：「文則美矣，意猶有不盡者，胡不復為一章於其後，具道張之於崔，既不能以理定其情，又不能合之於義。始相遇也，如是之篤；終相失也，如是之遽。必及於此，則完矣。」

余應之曰：「先生真為文者也。言必欲有終箴戒而後已。大抵鄙靡之詞，止歌其事之可歌，不必如是之備。若夫聚散離合，亦人之常情，古今所共惜也。又況崔之始相得而終至相失，豈得已哉。如崔已他適，而張詭計以求見；崔知張之意，而潛賦詩以謝之，其情蓋有未能忘者矣。樂天曰：「天長地久有時盡，此恨綿綿無盡期」，豈獨在彼者耶？予因命此意，復成一曲，綴於傳末云。

　　　　鏡破人離何處問。
　　　　路隔銀河，
　　　　　歲會知猶近。
　　　　只道新來消瘦損。
　　　　玉容不見空傳信。

to float right before the eyes; I'm not sure that even a fine painter could paint her form in such a skillful and perfect way. I once wrote ten lyric stanzas based on using or concealing her meaning. I showed them to my friend Mister Bai of the Hedong area.

He said, "The writing is beautiful, but the meaning itself is sometimes not all brought out. Why don't you write one more stanza at the end and explain why Zhang and Oriole could neither pledge their love according to principle nor reconcile it with righteousness. When they first met, it seemed so solid, but in the end, when they were lost to each other, it fell apart so abruptly. You have to tackle that and then it will be complete."

I responded, "You really are a writer! In a text, you must seek to have a beginning and an end, stopping only after you have admonished people and put them on their guard. Generally, coarse and trivial lyrics only express the singable parts of an affair, and they need not be as exhaustive as you would like. As for meetings and separations, they produce constant emotions in people's lives and have always elicited sympathy. What's more, how can his first getting Oriole but then losing her be something that suddenly comes to an end? For instance, she is already married to someone else, but Zhang devises a crafty plan to be able to see her. She understands what he means and secretly sends him a poem to refuse him—but there is something in her passion she still cannot forget. Bai Juyi wrote, 'Heaven is forever and earth is eternal, but both will end sometime; / This rancor goes on and on, never in time will it stop.' How can that refer only to his own poem?"

Thus, I have created one more song along those lines, which I have stitched on to the end of the story:

The mirror is broken, the people parted; where can we ask for
        news of them?
The road is cut off at the Milky Way,
        but they know their annual meeting is soon.[1]
She simply says she's "grown thin of late."
Her jade face unseen, her words were sent in vain.

1   In legend, magpies fly up to Heaven and form a bridge across the Milky Way. From the story of lovers who inhabit the constellations Altair and Vega, and who are allowed to meet only once a year, on the seventh day of the seventh month, when magpies form a bridge for them to cross the Heavenly River (known in the West as the Milky Way) to meet..

棄擲前歡俱未忍。
豈料盟言，
　陡頓無憑准。
地久天長終有盡，
綿綿不似無窮恨。

Neither can bear to cast away their former pleasure.
How could they expect the words of their covenant
    to suddenly lack all basis?
    Earth is eternal, heaven is forever, but in time they will end,
But neither can match love's endless rancor.

附錄二

《都城紀勝》節選

嘌唱：謂上鼓面唱令曲、小詞，驅駕虛聲縱

弄宮調，與叫果子、唱耍曲兒為一體本。只街市，今宅院往往有之。

叫聲：自京師起撰，因市井諸色歌吟賣物之聲，採合宮調而成也。若加以嘌唱為引子次用四句就入者謂之下影帶。無影帶者名散叫。若不上鼓面祇敲盞者謂之打拍

唱賺：在京師 有纏令，纏達。有引子，尾聲為纏令；引子後，只以兩腔遞且循環間用者為纏達。中興後，張五牛大夫，因聽動鼓板中又有四片太平令或賺鼓板—即今拍板大篩揚處是也—遂撰為賺。賺者，悞賺之義也。令人正堪美聽，不覺已至尾聲。是不宜為片序也。今又有覆賺又且變花前月下之情及鐵騎之類。凡賺最難，以其兼慢曲、曲破、大曲、嘌唱、耍令、番曲、叫聲諸家腔譜也。

Appendix Two

Excerpt from *A Record of the Splendors of the Metrocapital*[2]

For singing beguiling style music (*zhuan* 賺), in the capital city[3] there were only the *bound suite* and the *bound repetition*. If there were both an introduction and a coda it was a *bound suite*; if there were only two songs repeating themselves in order, then it was a *bound repetition*.

After the Middle Revival,[4] the talented Zhang Five Oxen was listening to a drum and clapper performance, in which there was either the "Song of Great Peace" or a beguiling drum and clapper—*what is now the major clapper section of the exuberant performance.* The word *zhuan* means to put something over on someone. It makes listeners enjoy its beautiful sounds and come to the coda before they even realize it. So, it is not suited to a partial presentation of its full gamut. Nowadays there is also the "repetitive beguiling song" that has adapted sentiments of romantic love or the category of battles between armies.

Of all the songs, the beguiling song is the most difficult because it combines the musical performance formulas of slow tempo, breakdown, major songs, quick songs, playful songs, foreign songs, and songs of fruit peddlers.

---

2   Guanpu naide weng 1885, 10a–b.
3   The former capital of Bianliang.
4   The revival of the Southern Song after 1126. This is a way to tactfully address the fact that the government was content to exercise its control over only a part of their former empire.

附錄三

《新編纂圖增類羣書類要事林廣記》節選

夫唱賺一家，古謂之「道賺。」腔必真，字必正，欲有墩亢擊拽之殊。字有唇喉齒舌之異。抑分輕清重濁之聲，必別合口半合口之字‧更忌馬嚚口子，俗語鄉談，如對聖案‧但唱樂道、山居、水居、清雅之詞‧切不可以風情花柳艷冶之曲；如此則為瀆聖。社條不賽‧筵會吉席‧上壽慶賀‧不在此限‧假如未唱之初‧執拍當胸‧不可高過鼻‧須假鼓板攄掇，三拍起引子，唱頭一句。又三拍至兩片結尾，三拍煞入序。尾三拍巾斗煞。入賺，頭一字當一拍，第一片三拍，後做此。出賺三拍，出聲巾斗，又三拍煞尾聲。總十二拍‧第一句四拍‧第二句五拍‧第三句三拍煞‧此一定不踰之法‧

Appendix Three

Excerpt from *The Expanded Record of a Forest of Affairs,
A Categorization of Important Information from Collected
Texts, Newly Compiled, Complete with Pictures, and with
Added Categories* [5]

That school of singing the "beguiling song" was once called "speaking a
beguiling song." The tune must be authentic, the words must be correct,
and there must be a difference between a quick-upward and drawn-out
vocalization. Words are distinguished by labial, velar, dental, and alveolar
consonants. There is a distinction between light-voiceless and heavy-
voiced sounds as well as fully- and half-rounded vowels that must also be
kept distinct. One must also avoid military language, common language,
dialect, and regionalisms—just as if one were facing a table of ancestral
spirit tablets. Simply sing elegant and refined poems about "delighting in
the Way," "living in the mountains," or "living on the waters." You simply
cannot do songs about love affairs, brothel quarters, or the gorgeous and
indecent. If you sing tunes like this then it disparages the Sage. [6]

According to the rules of our club we do not engage in competition,
but exceptions are made for marriage banquets, formal feasts, birthday
celebrations, and congratulatory events.

Before one begins singing, hold the clappers level with the chest, and
by no means raise them higher than the nose. One must avail oneself
of the quick tempo of the drum and clapper, strike the clappers three
times to begin the introduction and sing the first line. Then there are
three more clapper strikes to begin the concluding coda after the two
stanzas of the lyric, three sounds to enter the introduction, and three
strikes for the quick-tempo ending of the coda.

When beginning the beguiling song, there is one clapper beat on
the very first word and three beats for the first stanza, and then carry
on as such. When leaving the beguiling song, there are three clapper
beats—the exiting sounds must be in quick tempo—then three more
beats until ending in the coda. There are altogether twelve beats: four
on the first line, five on the second, and finish the beats with three on
the third. This is a set rule that cannot be violated. [7]

---

5 Chen Yuanjing 1993, 7.6b.
6 Confucius.
7 See Yu Yunfei 2015 and 2009.

附錄四

《張協狀元》諸宮調

> 張秀才應舉往長安
> 王貧女古廟受飢寒
> 呆小二村　調風月
> 莽強人大鬧五雞山

末白【水調歌頭】

> 韶華催白髮，
> 　光影改朱容。
> 人生浮世，
> 　渾如萍梗逐西東。
> 　陌上爭紅紫，
> 窗外鶯啼燕語，
> 　花落滿庭空。
> 世態只如此，
> 　何用苦匆匆。
>
> 但咱們，
> 　雖宦裔，
> 　　摠皆通。
> 彈絲品竹，
> 　那堪詠月與嘲風。
> 苦會插科使砌，
> 　何吝搽灰抹土，
> 　　歌笑滿堂中。
> 一似長江千尺浪，
> 　別是一家風。

再白【滿庭芳】

> 暫息喧嘩，
> 　略停笑語，

---

8 This is an old lyric (*Shuidiao getou* 水調歌頭), a "water tune" sung by workers in the Sui Dynasty ditching the Bian River from Kaifeng south. It was used as a text, either chanted or sung, to introduce the intricate Grand Songs (*daqu* 大曲) of the Tang court. Likewise,

Appendix Four

Top Graduate Zhang Xie, All-Modes Excerpt

Young Scholar Zhang goes to Chang'an to Sit for the Examinations.
Poor Lass Wang Suffers Cold and Hunger in an Old Temple.
Silly Xiao'er Makes a Crude Try at Romance.
A Violent Man Raises Hell at Mount Five Jetties.

The OPENING MALE *(**mo** 末) opens in plain language*: To the *Ci* Lyric
Pattern *Song Leader of the Water Melody*[8]

The splendor of youth urges on white hair;
>light and shadow change our ruddy complexions.
A human life floats through time
>like a duckweed stem pushed in every direction.
Red and purple contest on paths through the paddies—
>orioles call and swallows chatter outside the window
>>as flowers fall to fill the empty courtyard.
If this is just the way the world is,
>what is the point of suffering?

But we,
>the offspring of officials,
>>always know it all:
Plucking the strings, playing the bamboo,
>all to sing of the moon and mock the breeze.
We know when to inject interludes and employ the props,
>and we're never stingy patting on the ash or rubbing on
>>grime—
>>song and laughter fill the room—
And like towering waves of the Yangtze,
>we are a tradition unto ourselves.

OPENING MALE *speaks a second time in plain language*
A Fragrance That Fills the Courtyard
Cease your hubbub for now,
>stop your laughing banter,

---

one can notice here that although all arias sung below have a single lyric stanza, *"Water
Tune"* and the next poem, "Fragrance Fills the Courtyard" have the usual two stanzas
of a regular performative lyric.

　　　試看別樣門庭。
　教坊格範
　　　緋綠可仝聲。
　酬酢詞源諢砌，
　　聽談論
　　　　四座皆驚。
　渾不比，
　　乍生後學，
　　　謾自逞虛名。

　《狀元張協傳》，
　　前回曾演，
　　　汝輩搬成。
　這番書會，
　　要奪魁名。
　佔斷東甌盛事，
　　諸宮調
　　　唱出來因。
　廝羅響，
　　賢門雅靜，
　　　仔細說教聽。

【鳳時春】
　張協詩書遍歷。
　困故鄉功名未遂。
　欲佔春闈登科舉，
　　暫別爹娘，
　　　獨自離鄉里。

白：看的，
　　　　世上萬般俱下品，
　　　　思量惟有讀書高。

若論張葉，家住西川成都府，兀誰不識此人，兀誰不敬重此人。

and take a gander at our special way of performing:
The standard forms of the Music Bureau
    and sounds that match the Crimson and Green.[9]
We'll treat you to tunes galore and jokes and props,
    and when you listen to what we discuss
        the whole place will be astounded!
It's so unlike
    upstarts and amateurs,
        who uselessly vaunt their empty fame.

"The Story of Top Graduate Zhang Xie"
    was just elaborated in the previous session—
        and those fellows did a splendid job.
This time our writing club
    wants to snatch away first prize.
For this great affair, which has captured the whole of Eastern Ou,
    an all-modes ballad
        will spin out its causes in song.
Sound the gong!
    Silence please, worthy patrons.
        Listen now as I speak in detail.

Spring in the Windy Season
Zhang Xie had made it through all the Odes and the Documents,
But was troubled that neither fame nor merit came at home.
He wanted to dominate the examination field and win a degree,
    so, he left his parents a while
        and parted from his home alone.

In plain language: My fine members of the audience,

    Everything in the world is of lesser value;
When you think of it, only reading books is worthwhile.

Should we discuss Zhang Xie, then his home was in Chengdu Superior
Prefecture in Sichuan, where he was known to all. Truly, this fellow

---

9 A famous troupe of dramatic performers in Lin'an (modern Hangzhou), the temporary
    capital of the Southern Song. The full name of the group was "The Society of Pure
    Sounds of the Playboys in Crimson and Green"(子弟緋綠清音社).

真個此人：
朝經暮史，
晝覽夜習，
口不絕吟，
手不停披。

正是：

煉藥爐中無宿火，
讀書窗下有殘燈。

忽一日，堂前啟覆爹媽：「今年大比之年，你兒欲待上朝應舉。覓些盤費之資，前路支用」。

爹娘不聽這句話，萬事俱休；才聽此一句話，托地兩行淚下。

。孩兒道：「十載學成文武藝，今年貨與帝王家。欲改換門閭，報答雙親，何須下淚！」

唱

【小重山】
前時一夢斷人腸。
教我暗思量。
平日不曾為宦旅，
憂患怎生當？

白：孩兒覆爹媽：「自古道：一更思，二更想，三更是夢。大凡情性不拘，夢幻非實；大抵死生由命，富貴在天；何苦憂慮！」

爹娘見兒苦苦要去，不免與他數兩金銀，以作盤費。再三叮囑孩兒道：「未晚先投宿，雞鳴始過關。逢橋須下馬，有渡莫爭先。孩兒領爹娘慈旨，目即離去。

Read classics in the morning and history at dusk-light,
  Perusing during the day to review at night;
    His mouth never ceased chanting,
  His hand never stopped leafing through books.

Truly it was thus:

In the furnace where drugs are refined, there is no overnight fire;
  By the window where books are read, there will be a guttering lamp.

Out of the blue one day, he informed his parents, "This is the year of the great competition, and I want to go to court and sit for the examinations. I'm looking for a little travel money to sustain myself on the road ahead."

Now, if his parents had not listened to these words, everything would have been fine. But hearing just the first phrase, their tears began to fall.

Their son said, "'Ten years of study have turned to arts both civil and martial, / This year I want to sell them to the house of emperors and kings.' I want to raise our household status and repay you. Why cry?"

Sings:

Little Mountain upon Little Mountains
A single dream broke my heart before,
And made me silently consider:
I've never tried an official career
    and I worry and fret, wondering how I'll manage.

In plain language: The son told his parents, "From long in the past it has been said, 'What you ponder at the first watch and contemplate at the second turns into a dream in the third.' In most cases though, feelings and nature become unharnessed, and the illusions of a dream are not real. In general, life and death are preordained, and wealth and nobility are Heaven's choice. Why worry so much!"

Seeing that their son had made up his mind to leave, the parents had no choice but to shell out a few taels of gold and silver for travel expenses. Repeatedly, they enjoined him: "You must find a place to rest before it gets dark and wait till the crow of the cock to pass the fortress. Whenever there is a bridge, get off your horse, and don't try to be first at the ferrying dock." The son obediently accepted the loving admonitions from his parents. Promptly he bid farewell and left.

唱　　　【浪淘沙】
　　　　迤邐離鄉關。
　　　　回首望家山。
　　　　白雲直下把淚偷彈。
　　　　極目荒郊無旅店，
　　　　只聽得流水潺潺。

白話：休絮煩。那一日正行之次，自覺心兒裏悶。在家春不知
耕，秋不知收，真個嬌妳妳也。每日詩書為伴侶，筆硯作生
涯。在路平地尚可，那堪頓著一座高山，名做五磯山。怎見得
山高？

　　　　巍巍侵碧漢，
　　　　　　望望入青天。
　　　　鴻鵠飛不過，
　　　　　　猿穴怕扳緣。
　　　　稜稜層層，
　　　　奈休行鳥道。
　　　　齁齁齁齁，
　　　　　　為藤挂須尖。
　　　　人皆平地上，
　　　　　　我獨出雲顛。
　　　　雖然未赴瑤池宴，
　　　　　　也教人道散神仙。
　　　　野猿啼子
　　　　遠聞得咽咽嗚嗚。
　　　　落葉辭柯
　　　　　　近睹得撲撲簌簌。

　　　　　　　　　　　前無旅店，
　　　　　　　　　　　後無人家。

　　　　【犯思園】
　　　　刮地朔風留思飄。

Sings:

> **Waves Scour the Sand**
> At a leisurely pace, he left his district's gates,
> Turning his head to gaze at home,
> And, directly under the clouds, he secretly flicked away a tear.
> As far as he could see were desolate fallows, and no inn to be
>   found—
> All he could hear was the trickling of flowing water.

In plain language: Well, let's not go on and on. Throughout that day traveling, he felt quite depressed. At home, in the spring he knew nothing of plowing, and in the fall, nothing of harvesting—truly he was spoiled! The *Odes* and *Documents* were his daily companions, and brush and inkstone his only life. He could manage on level roads, but suddenly there it was, a tall mountain, known as Mount Five Jetties. How can we get a sense of the mountain's height?

> Towering up, it encroached on the Milky Way.
> Seen from afar, it penetrated the blue heavens.
> Wild swans could not fly over it,
> gibbons showed fear clambering up to their niches.
> Jutting and dangerous, layer rose upon layer—
> alas! Do not travel on paths meant only for birds!
> He was puffing and panting, snorting, and gasping—
> all because rattan hung down like whisker ends.
> "Everyone else is on level land,
> I alone emerge above the clouds."
> He might not have made it to the feast at Jasper Pond,
> but one would say he's an immortal on the loose.
> Gibbons in the wild cry for their offspring—
> far off one can hear their muted sobbing, muted sighs.
> Falling leaves leave their branches—
> close at hand one can see the piles rustling and whispering.

> > No inn ahead,
> > No private homes behind.

[*Sings:*]
> **Garden of Wrong Thoughts**
> A boreal wind scrapes the ground as willow-floss snowflakes
>   fly;

山高無旅店，
　景蕭條。
跨跕何處過今宵？
思量只恁地，
　路迢遙。

白：道猶未了，
　只見
　　怪風淅淅，
　　蘆葉飄飄；
　　野鳥驚呼，
　　山猿爭叫。
　只見
　　一個猛獸，
　　金睛閃閃，
　尤如
　　兩顆銅鈴；
　　錦體斑斕，
　　好若半團霞綺。
　　一副牙如排利刃，
　　十雙爪密布鋼鉤。
　　跳出林浪之中，
　　直奔草徑之上。
　號得張協
　　三魂不附體，
　　七魄漸離身，
　　僕然倒地。

霎時間只聽得鞋履響，腳步鳴。張協抬頭一看，不是猛獸，是個人。如何打扮？

　　虎皮磕腦皮袍，
　　兩眼光輝志氣豪。

The mountain is high and there are no inns,
    the whole scene nothing but desolation.
I curl up my limbs. Where shall I spend the night—
All I can think of is this:
    the road trailing off in the distance."

In plain language:

    All he saw
before he finished speaking,
was a strange wind's whispering rustle,
leaves of rushes flitting and flying
the startled call of birds in the wild
and mountain gibbons outdoing each other's cries.
    He was only aware of
a ferocious beast
with golden pupils glimmering in its eyes
    precisely like
two copper bells.
Its brocade form
was striped and mottled
like half a roll of auric silk.
A pair of canine teeth were like keen blades put in a row
and ten claws like steel hooks tightly arrayed.
Out it leapt from forest depths
to race straight along the grassy path.
    It so scared Zhang Xie
that his three cloud souls no longer occupied his form
and his seven earth souls dispersed slowly from his body—
he fell with a thump upon the ground

In that moment, he heard only the slap of sandals along with the sound of footsteps. Zhang Xie lifted his head to look. It was no ferocious beast; it was a man. And how was he costumed?

    A tiger skin scarf and a tiger skin cloak,
    Two eyes of luminous rays and a brave spirit!

「使留下來金珠饒你命，你還不肯不相饒。」
末介唱

【繞池游】
張協拜啓。
"念是讀書輩。
往長安擬欲應舉。
些少裹足。
路途里欲得支費。
望周全不須劫去。"

白強人不管他說。

怒從心上起，
惡向膽邊生。
左手捽住張協頭稍，
右手扯住一把光霍霍冷搜搜鼠尾樣刀，
番過刀背，
去張協
左肋上劈，
右肋上打。
打得它大痛無聲，
奪去查果金珠。
那張協性分如何。
慈鴉共喜鵲同枝，
吉凶事全然未保。

似恁唱說諸宮調，何如把此話文敷演。後行腳色，力齊鼓兒，
饒個攛掇，末泥色饒個踏場。

"If you leave your gold and jewels behind, I'll spare your life. If you insist on keeping them, I'll spare you not!"

Sings:

Ramble Around the Pond
Zhang Xie introduced himself respectfully.
"Consider, sir, that I am a student
On my way to Chang'an to take the examinations.
What small amount of money I possess
I need for expenses on the road.
I hope you'll be so kind as to not steal it!"

He explained this to the bandit, who paid him no attention.

Rather, anger issued from his heart,
and evil sprang from his gall.
His left hand grabbed the top of Zhang Xie's head,
And his right tightly held a glimmering rat-tail knife, fresh from the
    whetstone and cold as hell.
He flipped the knife over
and lunged at Zhang Xie,
striking his left ribcage
and then pounding his right.
He beat Zhang until he was breathless with pain,
and took away all his gold and gems.
And what of Zhang Xie's life then?
Crows of compassion sat on the same branch as the magpie of
    happiness—
neither fortune nor misfortune was fully guaranteed.

We've laid it all out like this in our all-modes performance, so how about we dramatize this story? All you actors in the rear ranks, drum away together, play the music, and let's have the main actor take a turn on the stage.[10]

---

10 Jiushan shuhui 1522–1572, 13b–14b; see also Hu Xuegang 2006, 1–11; and Llamas 2021, 89–94.

Appendix Five
List of Songs by Translated and Chinese Titles

A. Songs by Translated Title

An Accelerando Song	*Ji quzi*	急曲子
Adjusting a Ritual Cap of Gold	*Zheng jinguan*	整金冠
Alliteration and Rhyming	*Shuangsheng dieyun*	雙生疊韻
Approaching the River Sylph	*Lin jiangxian*	臨江仙
Arranging the Flowered Hat	*Zheng huaguan*	整花冠
Auspicious Lotus Song	*Ruilian'er*	瑞蓮兒
Bean Leaves Yellow	*Dou ye huang*	豆葉黃
Beauty Within Beauty	*Meizhong mei*	美中美
Beguiling Song	*Zhuan*	賺
A Big Forkload	*Yihu cha*	一斛叉
Blue-Green Peony	*Bi mudan*	碧牡丹
A Bound Suite	*chan, chanling*	纏、纏令
Boundless Sorrow	*Zhuozhuo qi*	倬倬戚
Celebrating the Xuanhe Reign	*Qing Xuanhe*	慶宣和
Cherishing My Love's Beauty	*Xi nu jiao*	惜奴嬌
Cherishing the Chrysanthemum	*Xi huanghua*	惜黃花
Chinese-Mulberry Branch Song	*Zhezhi ling*	柘枝令
Clever Harmonizing	*Qiao hesheng*	喬和聲
Coda	*Wei*	尾
Comically Catching a Snake	*Qiao zhuo she*	喬捉蛇
Coming Back from Looking at Flowers	*Kanhua hui*	看花回
Delight in Springtime Anew	*Xi xinchun*	喜新春
Delighting in Orioles Aflight	*Xi qian ying*	喜遷鶯
Descending Yellow Dragon, Tremolo	*Jiang huanglong gun*	降黃龍袞
Doffing the Cotton Shirt	*Tuo bushan*	脫布衫

Dotting Crimson Lips	*Dian jiangchun*	點絳唇
Dragon that Muddies the River (Dredge)	*Hun jiang long*	混江龍
Dried Licorice Root	*Gancaozi*	甘草子
Drunk and Down on My Luck	*Zui luopo*	醉落魄
Drunken Mama Xi	*Zui Xi po*	醉奚婆
The Embroidered Belt	*Xiu dai'er*	繡帶兒
The Emperor Quells the West	*Shang Pingxi*	上平西
Enlightened at the Meeting on Incense Peak	*Tihu Xiangshan hui*	醍醐香山會
Fighting Quail	*Dou anchun*	鬥鵪鶉
Fisherman's Haughtiness	*Yujia ao*	漁家傲
The Flower's Heart Trembles	*Huaxin dong*	花心動
Flowers on the Wall	*Qiangtou hua*	牆頭花
The Four Disciples	*Si Menzi*	四門子
Fragrant Winds Converge	*Xiangfeng he*	香風合
Frost That Fills the Courtyard	*Man ting shuang*	滿庭霜
Golden Lad Minding Incense	*Shixiang jintong*	侍香金童
Great Peace Beguiling Style	*Taiping zhuan*	太平賺
Green Mountain Pass	*Qingshan kou*	青山口
A Ground-Scraping Wind	*Guadi feng*	刮地風
A Guard of Spirits	*Shen zhang'er*	神仗兒
Guffawing Song	*Haha ling*	哈哈令
Happiness of Returning to the Capital	*Huan jing le*	還京樂
Happiness Under Heaven	*Tianxia le*	天下樂
Happy As Can Be	*Yiyi ling*	台台令
The Hawk Takes the Hare	*Hu da tu*	鶻打兔
Jade Enwraps the Stomach	*Yu bao du*	玉抱肚
A Jade-Winged Cicada	*Yuyi chan*	玉翼蟬
Jolly Child (or *Joyfulness*)	*Kuaihuo'er*	快活兒
Jumping Across a Mountain Stream	*Mu shanxi*	驀山溪

Laughing Song	*Haihai ling*	哈哈令
Leaves of Lotus and Water Caltrop are Fragrant	*Jihe xiang*	芰荷香
Liang Prefecture	*Liangzhou*	梁州
Liang Prefecture Song	*Liangzhou ling*	梁州令
Liang Prefecture: Three Terraces	*Liangzhou santai*	梁州三臺
Long-Life Immortals Tremolo	*Changshou xian gun*	長壽仙滾
Love Rendezvous	*Xiangsi hui*	相思會
Magnolia Blossoms	*Mulan hua*	木蘭花
Master An	*An gongzi*	安公子
Master Wen Xu	*Wen Xu zi*	文序子
Meeting on Incense Peak	*Xiangshan hui*	香山會
Minor Sixth Accelerando	*Liu(Lu)yao shicui*	六幺實催
Moon on the Jasper Terrace	*Yaotai yue*	瑤台月
Moonlight Climbs up the Crabapple	*Yue shang haitang*	月上海棠
Moved by the Emperor's Grace	*Gan huang'en*	感皇恩
Music of the Great Sage	*Da sheng yue*	大聖樂
Old Bögör	*Gu Luntai*	古輪台
One Minor Sixth Section of the Great Song	*Liuyao bian*	六幺遍
Parting Cranes	*Li he cao*	離鶴操
Patterned Like Embroidery	*Wen ru jin*	文如錦
A Perfect Marriage	*Yu feile*	于飛樂
Persian Sprinkling Dance	*Sumuzhe (samāche?)*	蘇幕遮
A Platform of Gold	*Huangjin tai*	黃金臺
Playing the Child	*Shua hai'er*	耍孩兒
Pleasing the Spirits	*Le shen ling*	樂神令
Plum Blossoms in the Snow	*Xueli meihua*	雪裏梅花
A Plum in the Snow	*Xueli mei*	雪裏梅
Pockmarked Crone	*Ma pozi*	麻婆子
Powdery Butterfly	*Fen die'er*	粉蝶兒

Puppets	*Kuilei*	傀儡
Quilt with the Fragrance of Love	*Lian xiang qin*	戀香衾
Raising the Alms Bowl	*Jie bozi*	揭鉢子
Red Silk Padded Jacket	*Hong luo ao*	紅羅襖
Responding to Lengthening Days	*Ying tian chang*	應天長
Return to the Green Mountains	*Zhuan qingshan*	轉青山
A River Running Red	*Man jiang hong*	滿江紅
Roaming at Night in the Palace	*Ye you gong*	夜遊宮
Sculling a Solitary Boat	*Zhuo gu zhou*	棹孤舟
Sending Out the Dance Troupe	*Chu duizi*	出隊子
Setting the Cosmos Right	*Zheng qiankun*	整乾坤
Settling Windblown Waves	*Ding feng bo*	定風波
Shepherd's Pass	*Muyang guan*	牧羊關
Someone Leaning on the Rail	*Pinglan ren*	憑欄人
Song of a Green Waist	*Luyao/Lüyao ling*	六幺令、綠腰令
Song of Bohai	*Bohai ling*	渤海令
Song of Immortals in a Cavern	*Dongxian ge*	洞仙隔
Song of the Canal Spirit	*Qushen ling*	渠神令
Song of Lots of Sugar	*Tang duo ling*	糖多令
Song of the Passes	*Sai'er ling*	塞兒令
Song of Treading the Sedge	*Tasuo xing*	踏莎行
Sounds of Wu	*Wu yinzi*	吳音字
Spread by the River Song	*Hechuan ling*	河傳令
A Sprig of Flowers	*Yizhi hua*	一枝花
Spring in the Princess's Garden	*Qinyuan chun*	沁園春
Tang Xuanzong's Birthday Song	*Qianqiu jie*	千秋節
The Case of Unblemished Jade	*Qing yu an*	清玉案
The Moon on Branch Tips of a Plum Tree	*Meixiao yue*	梅稍月
The Winning Gourd	*Sheng hulu*	勝葫蘆
Three Terraces	*Santai*	三臺
Time to Enjoy the Flowers	*Shanghua shi*	賞花時
Treading the Imperial Path	*Yujie xing*	御街行

Trimming the Silver Lamp	Ti yindeng	剔銀燈
Tuning the Strings	Jiao zhengpa	攪箏琶
Untying the Red	Jie hong	解紅
Water Dragon Chant	Shuilong yin	水龍吟
Welcoming the Immortal One	Ying xianke	迎仙客
Whistling Song	Shaobian	哨遍
Willow at the Front of the Courtyard	Ting qian liu	廳前柳
Willow Leaves	Liu ye'er	柳葉兒
Wind Blows the Lotus Leaves	Fengchui lianye	風吹蓮葉

B. Songs by Romanized Chinese Title

An gongzi	安公子	Master An
Bi mudan	碧牡丹	Blue-Green Peony
Bohai ling	渤海令	Song of Bohai
chan, chanling	纒、纏令	A Bound Suite
Changshou xian gun	長壽仙滾	Long-Life Immortals Tremolo
Chu duizi	出隊子	Sending Out the Dance Troupe
Da sheng yue	大聖樂	Music of the Great Sage
Dian jiangchun	點絳唇	Dotting Crimson Lips
Ding feng bo	定風波	Settling Windblown Waves
Dongxian ge	洞仙隔	Song of Immortals in a Cavern
Dou anchun	鬥鵪鶉	Fighting Quail
Dou ye huang	豆葉黃	Bean Leaves Yellow
Fen die'er	粉蝶兒	Powdery Butterfly
Fengchui lianye	風吹蓮葉	Wind Blows the Lotus Leaves
Gan huang'en	感皇恩	Moved by the Emperor's Grace
Gancaozi	甘草子	Dried Licorice Root
Gu Luntai	古輪台	Old Bögör

Guadi feng	刮地風	A Ground-Scraping Wind
Haha ling	哈哈令	Guffawing Song
Haihai ling	咍咍令	Laughing Song
Hechuan ling	河傳令	Spread by the River Song
Hong luo ao	紅羅襖	Red Silk Padded Jacket
Hu da tu	鶻打兔	The Hawk Takes the Hare
Huan jing le	還京樂	Happiness of Returning to the Capital
Huangjin tai	黃金臺	A Platform of Gold
Huaxin dong	花心動	The Flower's Heart Trembles
Hun jiang long	混江龍	Dragon that Muddies the River (Dredge)
Ji quzi	急曲子	An Accelerando Song
Jiang huanglong gun	降黃龍袞	Descending Yellow Dragon, Tremolo
Jiao zhengpa	攪箏琶	Tuning the Strings
Jie bozi	揭鉢子	Raising the Alms Bowl
Jie hong	解紅	Untying the Red
Jihe xiang	芰荷香	Leaves of Lotus and Water Caltrop are Fragrant
Kanhua hui	看花回	Coming Back from Looking at Flowers
Kuaihuo'er	快活兒	Jolly Child (or Joyfulness)
Kuilei	傀儡	Puppets
Le shen ling	樂神令	Pleasing the Spirits
Li he cao	離鶴操	Parting Cranes
Lian xiang qin	戀香衾	Quilt with the Fragrance of Love
Liangzhou	梁州	Liang Prefecture
Liangzhou ling	梁州令	Liang Prefecture Song
Liangzhou santai	梁州三臺	Liang Prefecture: Three Terraces
Lin jiangxian	臨江仙	Approaching the River Sylph
Liu ye'er	柳葉兒	Willow Leaves
Liu(Lu)yao shicui	六幺實催	Minor Sixth Accelerando

Liuyao bian	六幺遍	One Minor Sixth Section of the Great Song
Luyao/Lüyao ling	六幺令、綠腰令	Song of a Green Waist
Ma pozi	麻婆子	Pockmarked Crone
Man jiang hong	滿江紅	A River Running Red
Man ting shuang	滿庭霜	Frost That Fills the Courtyard
Meixiao yue	梅稍月	The Moon on Branch Tips of a Plum Tree
Meizhong mei	美中美	Beauty Within Beauty
Mu shanxi	驀山溪	Jumping Across a Mountain Stream
Mulan hua	木蘭花	Magnolia Blossoms
Muyang guan	牧羊關	Shepherd's Pass
Pinglan ren	憑欄人	Someone Leaning on the Rail
Qiangtou hua	牆頭花	Flowers on the Wall
Qianqiu jie	千秋節	Tang Xuanzong's Birthday Song
Qiao hesheng	喬和聲	Clever Harmonizing
Qiao zhuo she	喬捉蛇	Comically Catching a Snake
Qing Xuanhe	慶宣和	Celebrating the Xuanhe Reign
Qing yu an	清玉案	The Case of Unblemished Jade
Qingshan kou	青山口	Green Mountain Pass
Qinyuan chun	沁園春	Spring in the Princess's Garden
Qushen ling	渠神令	Song of the Canal Spirit
Ruilian'er	瑞蓮兒	Auspicious Lotus Song
Sai'er ling	塞兒令	Song of the Passes
Santai	三臺	Three Terraces
Shang Pingxi	上平西	The Emperor Quells the West
Shanghua shi	賞花時	Time to Enjoy the Flowers
Shaobian	哨遍	Whistling Song
Shen zhang'er	神仗兒	A Guard of Spirits
Sheng hulu	勝葫蘆	The Winning Gourd
Shixiang jintong	侍香金童	Golden Lad Minding Incense

Shua hai'er	耍孩兒	*Playing the Child*
Shuangsheng dieyun	雙生疊韻	*Alliteration and Rhyming*
Shuilong yin	水龍吟	*Water Dragon Chant*
Si Menzi	四門子	*The Four Disciples*
Sumuzhe (*samāche?*)	蘇幕遮	*Persian Sprinkling Dance*
Taiping zhuan	太平賺	*Great Peace Beguiling Style*
Tang duo ling	糖多令	*Song of Lots of Sugar*
Tasuo xing	踏莎行	*Song of Treading the Sedge*
Ti yindeng	剔銀燈	*Trimming the Silver Lamp*
Tianxia le	天下樂	*Happiness Under Heaven*
Tihu Xiangshan hui	醍醐香山會	*Enlightened at the Meeting on Incense Peak*
Ting qian liu	廳前柳	*Willow at the Front of the Courtyard*
Tuo bushan	脫布衫	*Doffing the Cotton Shirt*
Wei	尾	*Coda*
Wen ru jin	文如錦	*Patterned Like Embroidery*
Wen Xu zi	文序子	*Master Wen Xu*
Wu yinzi	吳音字	*Sounds of Wu*
Xi huanghua	惜黃花	*Cherishing the Chrysanthemum*
Xi nu jiao	惜奴嬌	*Cherishing My Love's Beauty*
Xi qian ying	喜遷鶯	*Delighting in Orioles Aflight*
Xi xinchun	喜新春	*Delight in Springtime Anew*
Xiangfeng he	香風合	*Fragrant Winds Converge*
Xiangshan hui	香山會	*Meeting on Incense Peak*
Xiangsi hui	相思會	*Love Rendezvous*
Xiu dai'er	繡帶兒	*The Embroidered Belt*
Xueli mei	雪裏梅	*A Plum in the Snow*
Xueli meihua	雪裏梅花	*Plum Blossoms in the Snow*
Yaotai yue	瑤台月	*Moon on the Jasper Terrace*
Ye you gong	夜遊宮	*Roaming at Night in the Palace*
Yihu cha	一斛叉	*A Big Forkload*
Ying tian chang	應天長	*Responding to Lengthening Days*
Ying xianke	迎仙客	*Welcoming the Immortal One*

Yiyi ling	台台令	*Happy As Can Be*
Yizhi hua	一枝花	*A Sprig of Flowers*
Yu bao du	玉抱肚	*Jade Enwraps the Stomach*
Yu feile	于飛樂	*A Perfect Marriage*
Yue shang haitang	月上海棠	*Moonlight Climbs up the Crabapple*
Yujia ao	漁家傲	*Fisherman's Haughtiness*
Yujie xing	御街行	*Treading the Imperial Path*
Yuyi chan	玉翼蟬	*A Jade-Winged Cicada*
Zheng huaguan	整花冠	*Arranging the Flowered Hat*
Zheng jinguan	整金冠	*Adjusting a Ritual Cap of Gold*
Zheng qiankun	整乾坤	*Setting the Cosmos Right*
Zhezhi ling	柘枝令	*Chinese-Mulberry Branch Song*
Zhuan	賺	*Beguiling Song*
Zhuan qingshan	轉青山	*Return to the Green Mountains*
Zhuo gu zhou	棹孤舟	*Sculling a Solitary Boat*
Zhuozhuo qi	倬倬戚	*Boundless Sorrow*
Zui luopo	醉落魄	*Drunk and Down on My Luck*
Zui Xi po	醉奚婆	*Drunken Mama Xi*

Editions Used of *Laureate Dong's All-Keys-and-Modes Story of the Western Wing*

DJY: Kin Bunkyō et al. 金文京 (ほか) 共者代. 1998 *A Study of Master Dong's Story of the Western Wing in All Modes*. (Tō kaigen Seishōki kyūchō *kenkyū* 董解元西廂記諸宮調研究). Kyūkoshoin.

DJY01: The Free and Unrestrained One of Piney Creeks in the Yan Mountains (Yanshan songxi fengyi ren 燕山松溪風逸人), coll., 2011. *An Old Edition of Master Dong's Story of the Western Wing*. (*Guben Dong Jieyuan Xixiang ji* 古本董解元西廂記). Eight chapters. Preface by Man of Yellow Crane Mountain, Zhang Yu (黃鵠山人張羽, byname Xiongfei 雄飛) dated the eighth month of the thirty-sixth year of Jiajing reign period of the Ming dynasty (明嘉靖丁巳秋八月, 1557.08.24–09.22). Includes postscript by Yang Xunji 楊循吉 (1456–1544). Photoreprinted in 1963 by Zhonghua shuju, and fair copy photoreprint in 2011 by National Library of China in *Collection of Fine Editions of Story of the Western Wing in the National Library of China* (*Guojia tushuguan cang Xixiang ji shanben congkan* 家圖書館藏西廂記善本叢刊).

DJY02: *An Old Edition of Master Dong's Story of the Western Wing*. (*Guben Dong Jieyuan Xixiang ji* 古本董解元西廂記) 2020. Reprint of DJY 01, with second collation by Master Happy-Go-Lucky, Free and Unrestrained Useless One of Haiyang 海陽風逸散人適適子. National Central Library of China edition. Reprinted in 1957 by Gudian wenxue chubanshe, in 1984 by Shanghai guji chubanshe, and in 2020 in *Recut Editions of Chinese Rare Books* (Zhonghua zaizao shanben congshu 中華再造善本叢書) by National Central Library Press.

DJY03: *Master Dong's Western Wing. Dong Jieyuan Xixiang* 董解元西廂 1937. Four chapters. Annotated by Tang Xianzu (Yireng) of Linchuan (Linchuan Tang Xianzu, Yireng fu ping 臨川湯顯祖義仍甫評). Published by the Ling Family of Wuxing between 1615–1644 天啟崇禎間吳興凌氏刊). Reprint, Commercial Press.

DJY04: *Master Dong's Western Wing (Dong Jieyuan Xixiang* 董解元西廂) Four Chapters. Recutting and printing of the Corrected Definitive Four-chapter Edition of DJY 03, original draft set by Woodcutter of Mount Guzhu (Guzhu shan qiao 孤注山樵) Zang Maoxun 臧懋循 (1550–1620, byname Jinshu 晉叔). Published by the Min Family of Wucheng 烏程 under the auspices of Min Sheng 閔聲 (1590–1680,

bynames Xiangzi 襄子, Yifu 毅夫/甫) and Min Yingzhang 閔暎
張 (ca. 1600). Red and black edition held by the National Central
Library, Taipei, Taiwan. Accessed at: https://rbook.ncl.edu.tw/

DJY05:   Collated and revised version of DJY 04, by Liu Shiheng 劉世珩
(1874/5–1926, bynames Congshi 蔥石 and Jizhi 季芰) of Guichi
貴池, published as the first exempla of *The Collected Woodblock
editions of* Zaju *and* Chuanqi *Drama* (Zaju chuanqi huike 雜劇傳
奇彙刻), 1917. Collated in 1915 by Wu Mei 吳梅 (1884–1939) and
published by the Nuanhong House (Nuanhong shi 暖紅室) as a
single volume.

DJY06:   *Master Dong's Western Wing. Dong Jieyuan Xixiang.* 1962. Eight
chapters. Annotations by Ling Jingyan 凌景埏Renmin wenxue
chubanshe.

DJY07:   *Annotated and Translated Edition of the Story of the Western Wing
in All Modes.* 1982. (*Xixiang ji zhugongdiao zhuyi* 西廂記諸宮調
注譯) in *The Complete All-Keys-and-Modes* (Quan zhugongdiao
全諸宮調) 49–174. Annotation and translation by Zhu Pingchu
朱平楚. Lanzhou: Gansu renmin chubanshe.

DJY08:   *Master Tung's Western Chamber Romance* (*Tung Hsi-hsiang
chu-kung-tiao*): *A Chinese Chantefable.* 1976. Translated from
the Chinese with an introduction by Li-Li Ch'en. Cambridge
University Press.

DJY09:   Mijnheer Dong. *Het verhaal van de westerkamers in alle toonaarden.*
Uit het Chinees vertaald en engeleid door W. L. Idema. 1984.
Muelenhoff.

Sources Cited and Consulted

Anon. 1960. *Duanju shisanjing jingwen* 斷句十三經經文 [*Text of the Thirteen Classics with Sentence Breaks*]. Kaiming shudian.

Anon. 2005. *Liu Zhiyuan zhugongdiao* 劉知遠諸宮調 [*Liu Zhiyuan All-Keys-and-Modes*]. In *Zhonghua zaizao shanben* 中華再造善本 [*Redone Rare Books of China*], vol. 754. Beijing Tushuguan chubanshe.

Berthel, Ken. 2016. "How did Zhong Ziqi Understand Bo Ya's Heart-mind? Hetero-Referential Aspects of Early Chinese Music Theory." *Philosophy East and West* 66 (1): 259–270.

Burkus-Chasson, Anne. 2010. *Through a Forest of Chancellors: Fugitive Histories in Liu Yuan's Lingyan ge, an Illustrated Book from Seventeenth-century Suzhou*. Harvard University Press.

Cao Cao 曹操. 1959. *Cao Cao ji* 曹操集 [*Cao Cao's Collected Works*]. Zhonghua shuju.

Cao Zhi and Robert Cutter, trans. 2021. *The Poetry of Cao Zhi. Library of Chinese Humanities*. De Gruyter Mouton.

CBETA. Chinese Buddhist Electronic Text Association. 2021. Dianzi Fodian jicheng 電子佛典集成, edited by CBETA. Taipei, Taiwan: CBETA.

Chen Anmei 陳安梅. 2021. "*Liu Zhiyuan zhugongdiao* zai Riben" 《劉知遠諸宮調》在日本 [The 'Liu Zhiyuan All-Modes' in Japan]. *Wenjiao ziliao* 文教資料 (7): 43–45.

Chen, Fan Ben. 1990–1992. "Yang Kuei-fei in 'Tales from the T'ien-pao Era: A *chu-kung-diao* Narrative.'" *Journal of Song-Yuan Studies* 22: 1–22.

Chen, Fan Ben. 2006. "Translations from Wang Bocheng's *Tales of the Tianbao Era* (Tianbao yishi): Genre and Eroticism in the *Zhugongdiao*." *CHINOPERL Papers* 25: 35–85.

Ch'en, Li-li. 1972. "Outer and Inner Forms of Chu-kung-tiao, With Reference to Pien-wen, Tz'u and Vernacular Fiction." *Harvard Journal of Asiatic Studies* 32: 124–149.

Chen Ruizan 陳瑞贊. 2020. "Shilun Nanxi 'yanduan' *Zhang Xie zhugongdiao*" 試論南戲'豔段'《張協諸宮調》 [On the 'Yanduan' in Southern Drama and the *Zhang Xie All Modes*]. *Wenzhou daxue xuebao* 溫州大學學報 33 (5): 39–46.

Chen Yuanjing 陳元靚. 1993. Chunzhuang shuyuan 椿莊書院, ed. *Xinbian zuantu cenglei qunshu leiyao Shilin guangji* 新編纂圖增類羣書類要事林廣記 [*The Expanded Record of a Forest of Affairs: A Categorization of Important*

Information from Collected Texts, Newly Compiled, Complete with Pictures, and with Added Categories]. Zhonghua shuju.

Cheng Pei-kai鄭培凱. 1995. *Tang Xianzu yu wan Ming wen hua* 湯顯祖與晚明文化 [*Tang Xianzu and Late Ming Culture*]. Yunchen wenhua shiye gufen youxian gongsi.

Cheng Pei-kai鄭培凱. 2016. "Tang Xianzu and Chinese Culture." In "2016 Hong Kong Chinese Opera Festival." Chinese Opera Festival.

Cutter, Robert Joe. 2003. "On the Authenticity of the 'Poem in Seven Paces.'" In *Studies in Early Medieval Chinese Literature and Cultural History, Dedicated to Donald Holzman and Richard B. Mather,* edited by Paul W. Kroll and David R. Knechtges, 1–26. T'ang Studies Society.

Davis, Edward L. 2001. *Society and the Supernatural in Song China.* Honolulu: University of Hawai'i Press.

Denecke, Wiebke. 2023. "The-Politics of (Dis)similarity: New Tools to Understand the Emergence of Modern Literary Historiography in East Asia." In *Ähnlichkeit in Lyrik und Poetik der Gegenwart,* edited by Nikolas Immer, Frank Kraushaar, and Henrieke Stahl. Peter Lang.

Dolby, William. 1997. "'Tea-Trading Ship' and the Tale of Shuang Chien and Su Little Lady." *Bulletin of the School of Oriental and African Studies, University of London* 60 (1): 47–63.

Doleželová-Velingerová, Milena and J. I. Crump, trans. 1971. *Ballad of the Hidden Dragon.* Clarendon Press.

Dong Jieyuan 董解元 and Ling Jingyan 凌景埏. 1962. *Dong Jieyuan Xixiang ji* 董解元西廂記 [*Laureate Dong's Western Wing*]. 1st. ed. Renmin wenxue chubanshe.

Dong Jieyuan 董解元. Zhang Yu 張羽, ed. 1963. *Ming Jiajing ben "Dong Jieyuan Xixiang ji" zhugongdiao* 明嘉靖本董解元西廂記諸宮調 [*Ming Jiajing edition of Laureate Dong's "Western Chamber in All-Keys-and- Modes"*]. 8 vols. Vol. 2. Zhonghua shuju.

Du Fu杜甫. Qiu Zhao'ao 仇兆鰲, ann. 1979. *Du shi xiangjie* 杜詩詳解 [*Detailed Explanations of Du Fu's Poetry*]. Vol. 4. Zhonghua shuju.

Durrant, Stephen, Wai-yee Li, and David Schaberg, trans. 2017. *Zuo Tradition / Zuozhuan / Commentary on the Spring and Autumn Annals.* 3 vols. Vol. 1. *Classics of Chinese Thought.* Seattle: University of Washington Press.

Ebrey, Patricia Buckley, 1999. *The Cambridge Illustrated History of China.* Cambridge University Press.

Fu Xuanzong 傅璇琮 et al., ed. 1991. *Quan Song shi* 全宋詩 [*Complete Song Poems*]. Vol. 1. Beijing daxue chubanshe.

Gao Bing 高冰 and Wang Dingyong 王定勇. 2015. "Tu Long, Tang Xianzu Suichang huiyu xinzheng—jianyu Wu Xinmiao boshi shangque" 屠隆、湯顯祖遂昌會晤新證—兼與吳新苗博士商榷 [New Evidence for Tu Long and Tang Xianzu's Meeting in Suichang—Including a Counter Discussion with Dr. Wu Xinmiao]. *Lishui xueyuan xuebao* 麗水學院學報 37 (1):7–11.

Gao Ming and Jean Mulligan, trans. 1980. *The Lute: Kao Ming's P'i-P'a Chi.* Columbia University Press.

Goh, Meow Hui. 2009. "Knowing Sound: Poetry and "Refinement" in Early Medieval China." *Chinese Literature: Essays, Articles, Reviews (CLEAR)* 31: 45–69.

Gong Yanming 龔延明. 1997. *Song dai guan zhi ci dian* 宋代官職辭典 [*Dictionary of Song Dynasty Official Titles*]. 1st. ed. Zhonghua shuju.

Gu Xuejie 顧學頡, ed. 1979. *Bai Juyi ji* 白居易集 [*Bai Juyi's Collected Works*]. Zhonghua shuju.

Guanpu naide weng 灌圃耐得翁. 1885. *Ducheng jisheng* 都城紀勝 [*A Record of the Splendors of the Metrocapital*]. Jiahuitang.

Guo Maoqian 郭茂倩. 1979. *Yuefu shiji* 樂府詩集 [*Collection of Yuefu Poems*]. Zhonghua shuju.

Hamid Ahap (?) (Amiti Ahafu 哈米提·阿哈甫). 2013. "Damo zhong aiqingde gushi—Qiemoxian faxian de Yuan 'Xixiang ji' chaoben canye" 大漠中愛情的故事—且末縣發現的元《西廂記》抄本殘葉 [A Love Story in the Desert: Remnant Pages from a Yuan Dynasty Handwritten Copy of the 'Record of the Western Chamber' Discovered in Qiemo District]. Dongfang shoucang 東方收藏 (1): 118–119.

Hightower, James R. 1973. "Yuan Chen and 'The Story of Ying-ying.'" *Harvard Journal of Asiatic Studies* 33: 90–123.

Hong Jinfu 洪金富, ed. 2016. *Hong Jinfu jiaoding Yuan dianzhang* 洪金富校定本元典章 [*Hong Jinfu's Set Text of the Yuan Law Codes*]. Vol. 1. Zhongyang yanjiuyuan lishi yuyan yanjiusuo.

Hong Mai 洪邁 and He Zhuo 何卓. 1981. *Yi Jian zhi* 夷堅志 [*Record of the Listener*]. Vol. 2. Zhonghua shuju.

Hong Sheng. Trans. Yang Xianyi and Gladys Yang. 1983. *Palace of Eternal Youth.* Waiwen chubanshe.

Hong Sheng 洪昇. Ann. Xu Shuofang 徐朔方. 1975. *Changsheng dian* 長生殿 [*Palace of Long Life*]. Renmin wenxue chubanshe.

Hong Sheng. Trans. Xu Yuanzhong and Xu Ming. 2012. *Love in Long Life Hall.* Wuzhou chuanbuo chubanshe.

Hsia, C. T. 1968. "A Critical Introduction." In *The Romance of the Western Wing*, xi–xxxii. Columbia University Press.

Hsia, C.T., Wai-yee Li, George Kao, eds. 2014. *The Columbia Anthology of Yuan Drama.* Columbia University Press.

Hsieh, Daniel. 2008. *Love and Women in Early Chinese Literature.* Chinese University of Hong Kong.

Hu Ji 胡忌. 2008. *Song Jin zaju kao* 宋金雜劇考 [*A Study of the Song and Jin Variety Play*]. Rev. ed. Zhonghua shuju.

Hu Xuegang 胡雪岡. 2006. *Zhang Xie zhuangyuan jiaoshi* 張協狀元校釋 [*Emendation and Notation to Top Scholar Zhang Xie*]. Shanghai shehui kexueyuan.

Huan Kuan 桓寬. Wang Liqi 王利器, ed. 1992. *Yantie lun jiaozhu* 鹽鐵論校注 [*Annotations to the "Discourse on Salt and Iron"*]. Vol. 1. Zhonghua shuju.

Huang Dongbo 黃冬柏. 1995. "Sōdai Seishō monogatari to So Shoku : Chō Reisho 'Shōchō chōrenka' o megutte" 宋代西廂故事と蘇軾：趙令時「商調蝶戀花」をめぐって" [Su Shi and the *Story of the Western Wing*: Concerning Zhao Lingshi's Tune 'Butterflies Love Flowers' in the Shang Mode]. *Kyūshū daigaku daigakuen hakasei kōki katei* 九州大學大學院博士後期課程 (24): 47–64.

Huang Dongbo 黃冬柏. 2020. "Seishōki hensen shi kenkyū" 西廂記變遷史 [Evolution of the *Story of the Western Wing*]." Ph.D., Graduate School of Humanities, Kyushu University (文博乙第0212号).

Huang, Tingjian 黃庭堅. 2001. *Huang Tingjian quanji* 黃庭堅全集 [*Collected Works of Huang Tingjian*]. Vol. 1. Sichuan daxue chubanshe.

Idema, Wilt L. 1978. "Master Tung's Western Chamber Romance (Tung Hsi-hsiang chu-kung-tiao), a Chinese Chantefable by Li-li Chen." *T'oung Pao* 64 (1/3): 132–144.

Idema, Wilt L. 1981. "The 'Wen-ching yüan-yang hui' and the 'chia-men' of Yüan-Ming 'ch'uan-ch'i'." *T'oung Pao* 67 (1/2): 91–106.

Idema, Wilt L. 1984. "The Story of Ssu-ma Hsiang-ru and Cho Wen-chün in Vernacular Literature of the Yüan and Early Ming Dynasties." *T'oung Pao* 70 (1/3): 60–109.

Idema, Wilt L. 1993. "'Chu-kung-tiao'": A Reassessment of Conflicting Opinions." *T'oung Pao* 79 (1/3): 69–112.

Idema, Wilt L., and Haiyan Lee. 2008. *Meng Jiangnü Brings Down the Great Wall: Ten Versions of a Chinese Legend*. University of Washington Press.

Idema, Wilt L. and Stephen H. West, eds. and trans. 2012. *Battles, Betrayals, and Brotherhood: Early Chinese Plays on the Three Kingdoms*. Hackett Publishing.

Idema, Wilt L. and Stephen H. West, eds. and trans. 2016. *Records of the Three Kingdoms*. Hackett Publishing.

Jiao Xun 焦循. 1959. *Jushuo* 劇說 [*On Drama*]. Zhonghua xiju chubanshe.

Jin Shengtan 金聖嘆 and Lu Lin 陸林, anns. and eds. 2016. *Baihua xiaoshuo juan (xia)* 白話小說卷 （下) [*Part Two of the Sections on Colloquial Literature*]. Vol. 4. *Jin Shengtan quanji* 金聖嘆全集 [*Collected Works of Jin Shengtan*]. Fenghuan chubanshe.

Jiushan shuhui 九山書會 [Book Club of Jiushan]. 1522–1572. *Zhang Xie zhuangyuan* 張協狀元 [*Head of the List Zhang Xie*.] Yongle dadian 永樂大典 [Grand Compendium of the Yongle Reign]. Ming inner court.

Josephs, Hillary K. 1976. "The Chanda: A Sung Dynasty Entertainment." *T'oung Pao* 62 (4/5): 167–198.

Kim Bunkyō 金文京 et al. 1998. *Tō kaigen Seishōki shokyūchō kenkyū* 董解元西廂記諸宮調研究 [*Studies on Dong Jieyuan's Story of the Western Wing*]. Kyūko shōen.

Kuang Zhouyi 況周頤. Tang Guizhang 唐圭璋, ed. 1926. *Huifeng cihua* 惠風詞話 [*Talks on Ci Lyrics from the Hall of Gentle Breezes*]. Hu shi Tongjian tang.

Lan Hui 蘭慧. 2017. "Zhao Linghzhi de yu yu hui jiqi cide jieshou wenti" 趙令時的譽與毀及其詞的接受問題 [The Praise and Slander of Zhao Lingzhi and the Problem of the Reception of his Ci Lyric]. *Duanpian xiaoshuo* 短篇小說 (29):44–46.

Legge, James. 1876. *The She King; or, The Book of Ancient Poetry, Translated in English Verse, with Essays and Notes*. Trübner & Co.

Li Diankui 李殿魁. 1989. *Shuang Jian Su Qing gushi kao* 雙漸蘇卿故事考 [*Investigations of the Story of Shuang Jian and Su Qing*]. Wenshizhe chubanshe.

Li Fang 李昉. 1986. *Taiping guangji* 太平廣記 [*Expansive Records of an Era of Peace*]. Vol. 5. Zhonghua shuju.

Li Han 李瀚. 1987. *Mengqiu ji zhu* 蒙求集註 [*Collected Commentary on a Student Primer*]. Vol. 892. *Siku quanshu* 四庫全書 [*Complete Texts of the Four Bibliographic Categories*], edited and annoted by Xu Ziguang 徐子光. Shangwu yinshuguan.

Li Han 李瀚. Xu Ziguang 徐子光, ann. 2004. *Buzhu Mengqiu* 補注蒙求 [*Supplementary Notation to Seeking Help to Understand*]. Beijing tushuguan chubanshe.

Li Jie 李誡. 1989. *Yingzao fashi* 營造法式 [*Codes and Rules for Construction*]. Zhongguo shudian.

Li Shen 李紳 and Wang Xuanbo 王旋伯, ann. and comp. 1985. *Li Shen shiji* 李紳詩集 [*Poetic Works of Li Shen*]. Shanghai guji chubanshe.

Li, Wai-yee. 2022. *The Promise and Peril of Things*. Columbia University Press.

Li Xiusheng 李修生. 1994. "Yuan sanqu tonglun xu" 元散曲通論序 [Preface to a Comprehensive Study of Yuan Popular Songs]. *Sichuan shifan xueyuan xuebao* 四川師範學院學報 (1): 70–73.

Liu Xiao 劉曉 and Shang Yongliang 尚永亮. 2017. "Baqiao fengxue luzi bei: yige jingdian yixiang de duoyuan shanbian yu shi, hua jiedu" 灞橋風雪驢子背：一個經典意象的多元嬗變與詩、畫解讀.[On the Back of a Donkey in the Snow and Wind on Ba Bridge: Multiple Changes in Traditional Images and the Analysis of Poetry and Painting.] *Wenyi yanjiu* 文藝研究 (1): 111–127.

Liu Xiaomei 劉小梅. 2018. "Lun kouyu wenhua shijiaoxia zhugongdiao wenhua xingtai de yanjin" 論口語文化視角下諸宮調文化形態的演進 [On the Evolution of the Cultural Morphology of the All-Modes from the Perspective of Oral Culture]. *Minzu yixue yanjiu* 民族藝術研究 (4): 69–76.

Liu Xuwu 劉敘武. 2021. "Lianxiang banyan xinzheng" 連廂搬演新證 [New Evidence on the Performance of Variety Shows]. *Wenhua yichan* 文化遺產 (3): 71–78.

Liu, Yiqing 2002. Richard Mather, ed. and trans. *Shih-shuo hsin-yü: A New Account of Tales of the World*. Michigan Center for Chinese Studies.

Llamas, Regina S., trans. 2021. *Top Graduate Zhang Xie: The Earliest Extant Chinese Southern Play*. Columbia University Press.

Long Jianguo 龍建國. 2003a. "Guanyu ershishiji zhugongdiao de zhengli yu yanjiu" 關於二十世紀諸宮調的整理與研究 [On the Study and Reorganization of the All-Modes in the Twentieth Century]. *Wenxue pinglun* 文學評論 (6): 43–51.

Long Jianguo 龍建國. 2003b. *Zhugongdiao yanjiu* 諸宮調研究 [*A Study of the All-Modes Ballad*]. Jiangxi renmin chubanshe.

Lu Shihua 盧世華. 2009. *Yuandai pinghua yanjiu—Yuanshengtai de tongsu xiaoshuo* 元代平話研究——原生態的通俗小說 [*Studies in Yuan Dynasty Plain Tales: Popular Novels in their Original Form*]. Zhonghua shuju.

Lü, Buwei. 2000. John Knoblauch and Jeffery Riegel, eds. and trans. *The Annals of Lu Buwei: A Complete Translation and Study*. Stanford University Press.

Luo Xiaoqian 駱曉倩. 2008. "Xixiang gushi liubiande jinliang: lun Zhao Lingzhi guzi ci 'Dielian hua'" 西廂故事流變的津梁;論趙令時鼓子詞「商調蝶戀花」. [A Bridge in Changes to the Storycycle of the Western Chamber: On the Shangdiao Mode 'Butterflies Love Flowers' Ci Lyrics of Zhao Lingzhi's Drum Song]. *Xiju wenxue* 戲劇文學 (5):57–60

Luo Ye 羅燁. 1957. *Zui weng tan lu* 醉翁談錄 [*Drunken Man's Talk*]. Gudian wenxue chubanshe.

Luo, Ye. 1981. Gabriele Foccardi, ed. and trans. *The Tales of an Old Drunkard*. Harrasowitz.

Luo, Ye. 2015. Alister David Inglis, ed. and trans. *The Drunken Man's Talk: Tales from Medieval China*. University of Washington Press.

Ma, Rongqian. 2014. "Cui Hu's Mural Poem and Its Resonance in the Story of 'Renmian taohua': A Dialogic Analysis." MA, Dietrich School of Arts and Sciences, Universty of Pittsburgh.

Mather, Richard. 1988. *The Poet Shen Yueh (441–513): The Reticent Marquis*. Princeton University Press.

Meng Yuanlao 孟元老 et al. 1956. *Dongjing meng Hua lu wai sizhong* 東京夢華錄外四種 [*Dreaming of Splendors Past in the Eastern Capital and Four Other Texts*]. Gudian wenxue chubanshe.

Meng Yuanlao 孟元老. 1941. *Yuanben Youlan jushi Dongjing meng Hua lu* 元本幽蘭居士東京夢華錄 [Dreaming of Splendors Past in the Eastern Capital; Original Edition by the Lay Hermit of Hidden Thoroughwort]. Seikaidō bunko.

Muller, Charles, ed. 2012. *Digital Dictionary of Buddhism*. http://www.buddhism-dict.net/ddb: Charles Muller.

Mulligan, Jean, trans. 1980. *The Lute: Kao Ming's P'i-p'a ji. (Translations from the Asian Classics)*. Columbia University Press.

Nienhauser, William, trans. 1986. "Miss Jen." In *Traditional Chinese Stories: Themes and Variations*, edited by Joseph S. M. Lau and Yau-Woon Ma, 339–345. Columbia University Press.

Nienhauser, WIlliam H., Jr., ed. 2016. *Tang Dynasty Tales: A Guided Reader*. World Scientific.

Owen, Stephen. 1992. "The Great Preface." In *Readings in Chinese Literary Thought*, 37–56. Harvard University Asia Center.

Owen, Stephen. 1995. *Anthology of Chinese Literature: Beginnings to 1911*. W. W. Norton.

Peng Dingqiu 彭定求1960. *Quan Tang shi* 全唐詩 [*Complete Tang Poems*]. 12 Vols. Zhonghua shuju.

Pregadio, Fabrizio, ed. 2008. *Encyclopedia of Taoism*. 2 vols. Routledge.

Qi Xiaofeng 齊曉鳳. 1988. *Shuang Jian yu Su Xiaoqing yanjiu* 雙漸與蘇小卿研究 [*Studies of the Story of Shuang Jian and Su Xiaoqing*]. Wenshi zhe.

Qian Zhonglian 錢仲聯, ed. 1984. *Han Changli shi xinian jishi* 韓昌黎詩繫年集釋 [*A Chronological Arrangement of Gathered Explications of Han Yu's Poetry*]. Vol. 2. Shanghai guji chubanshe.

Qin Guan 秦觀. 1985. Xu Peijun 徐培勻, ann. *Huaihai jushi changduan ju* 淮海居士長短句 [*The Ci Lyrics of the Layman Hermit of Huai Hai*]. Shanghai guji chubanshe.

Qin Guan 秦觀. 2003. Luo Ligang 羅立剛and Xu Peijun 徐培勻, anns. 2006. *Qin Guan ci xinshi jiping* 秦觀詞新釋輯評 [*New Explanations and Collated Critical Comments on the Ci Poetry of Qin Guan*]. Zhonghua shuju.

Qiu Shaohua 邱少華. 2001. *Ouyang Xiu ci xinshi jiping* 歐陽修詞新釋輯評 [*New Explanations of Ouyang Xiu's Ci Lyric Songs with Collected Comments*]. Zhongguo shudian.

Qu Wanli 屈萬里. 1984. *Shangshu jinzhu jinyi* 尚書今註今譯 [*Modern Commentary and Modern Translation of the Classic of Documents*]. Taiwan Shangwu yinshuguan.

Reiter, Florian C. 2010. "Taoist Thunder Magic (五雷法), Illustrated with the Example of the Divine Protector Chao Kung-ming 趙公明." *Zeitschrift der Deutschen Morgenländischen Gesellschaft* 160 (1): 121–154.

Reiter, Florian C. 2011. "Taoist Transcendence and Thunder Magic, As Seen in the Great Rituals of Heavenly Ting of Metal and Fire in the Divine Empyrean (神霄金火天丁大法)." *Zeitschrift der Deutschen Morgenländischen Gesellschaft* 161 (2): 415–444.

Roy, David T. 1977. "*Master Tung's Western Chamber Romance* (Tung Hsi-hsiang chu-kung-tiao) by Li-li Ch'en." *Harvard Journal of Asiatic Studies* 37 (1): 207–222.

Ruan Yuan 阮元, ed. 1965. *Liji zhushu* 禮記注疏 [*Commentary and Sub-commentary on the Record of Rites*] Comm., Kong Yingda 孔穎達 and Zheng

Xuan 鄭玄, subcomm. Vol. 6 *Chongkan Songben Shisan jing zhushu fu jiaokan ji* 重刊宋本十三經注疏附校勘記 [I]. Yiwen yinshuguan.

Shang Zhongxian. David Hawkes, ed. and trans. 2003. *Liu Yi and the Dragon Princess: A Thirteenth-Century Zaju Play by Shang Zhongxian*. Chinese University of Hong Kong.

Shen Yifu 沈義父. 1981. "Yuefu zhimi jianshi" 樂府指迷箋釋 [Explanations of *Clearing up Doubtful Points about Musical Poetry*]. In *Ci yuan zhu; Yuefu zhimi jianshi* 詞源注；樂府指迷箋釋 [*Notes to the Origin of Lyric Poetry; Explanatory Notes to Pointing Out Confusing Points in Yuefu*] 33–88. Renmin wenxue chubanshe.

Shen Yifu 沈義父. 1986. "Yuefu zhimi" 樂府指迷 [Pointing Out Confusing Points in Yuefu]. In *Cihua congbian* 詞話叢編 [*Collected Discussions on Lyric Poetry*], edited by Tang Guizhang 唐圭璋, 275–286. Zhonghua shuju.

Sima Qian. Burton Watson, ed. and trans. 1971. *Records of the Grand Historian of China*. 2 vols. Columbia University Press.

Slingerland, Edward. 2003. *Confucius Analects: With Selections from Traditional Commentaries*. Hackett Publishing.

Song Tianzheng 宋天正, ann. 1977. *Zhongyong jinzhu jinyi* 中庸今註今譯 [*New Annotations to and New Translation of the "Doctrine of the Mean"*]. Shangwu yinshuguan.

Strassberg, Richard, trans. 2002. *A Chinese Bestiary: Strange Creatures from the Guideways Through Mountains and Seas*. University of California Press.

Strickmann, Michel. 2002. *Chinese Magical Medicine*. Stanford University Press.

Sturman, Peter. 1995. "The Donkey Rider as Icon: Li Cheng and Early Chinese Landscape Painting." *Artibus Asiae* 56, no. 1/2: 43–97.

Su Shi 蘇軾. Wang Wengao 王文誥 and Kong Fanli 孔凡, eds. 1982. *Su Shi shiji* 蘇軾詩集 [*The Poetry of Shu Shi*]. Vol. 2. Zhonghua shuju

Su Shi 蘇軾. Zhang Zhilie 張志烈, Ma Defu 馬德福 and Zhou Yukai 周裕鍇, eds. 2010. *Su Shi quanji jiaozhu* 蘇軾全集校注 [*A Collated and Annotated Edition of Su Shi's Complete Works*]. Vol. 7. Hebei renming chubanshe.

Sui Shusen 隋樹森. 1964. *Quan Yuan sanqu* 全元散曲 [*Complete Popular Songs of the Yuan*]. 2 vols. Zhonghua shuju.

Sun Kaidi 孫楷第. 1981. *Yuanqu jia kaolüe* 元曲家考略 [*Brief Studies of Writers of Yuan Popular Songs*]. Shanghai guji chubanshe.

Sun Kaidi 孫楷第. 1985. "Dong Jieyuan xiansuo Xixiang ji zhong de liangge diangu" 董解元弦索西廂記的兩個典故 [On Two Allusions in Laureate Dong's String-Accompanied *Story of the Western Wing*]. In *Cangzhou houji* 滄州後記 [*Later Record of Cangzhou*]. Zhonghua shuju.

Sun Yingkui 孫映逵. 1983. "Dong Jieyuan shi Nan Song ren ma" 董解元是南宋人嗎 [Is Laureate Dong a Person from the Southern Song?]. *Jiangsu shifan daxue xuebao* 江蘇師範大學學報 (3): 34–35.

Tang Guizhang 唐圭璋, ed. 1979. *Quan Jin Yuan ci* 全金元詞 [*The Complete Jin and Yuan Ci Lyrics*]. Vol. 1. Zhonghua shuju.

Tang Guizhang 唐圭璋, ed. 1986. *Cihua congbian* 詞話叢編 [*Collected Talks on the Ci Lyric*]. Vol. 5. Zhonghua shuju.

Tang Xianzu 湯顯祖. Xu Shuofang 徐朔方, ed. 1998. *Tang Xianzu quanji* 湯顯祖全集 [*The Complete Works of Tang Xianzu*]. Vol. 3. Beijing guji chubanshe.

Tao Zongyi 陶宗儀. 1958. *Nancun Chuogeng lu* 南村輟耕錄 [*Nancun's Records from A Break in Plowing*]. Zhonghua shuju.

Tsai Meng-Chen 蔡孟珍. 1994. "Tang Xianzu 'aozhe tianxiaren sangzi' zhiyi—jiantan *Mudanting de qiangdiao wenti*" 湯顯祖「拗折天下人嗓子」質疑- 兼談《牡丹亭》的腔調問題 [Doubts about Tang Xianzu's Statement, 'I'll wrench the throat of everyone under Heaven'—And a Discussion of the Metrical Pattern of Song in *The Peony Pavilion*.] *Jiaoxue yu yanjiu* 教學與研究 (16): 83–97.

Tseng Yong-yih 曾永義. 1971. "Xi Shi gushi zhiyi" 西施故事質疑 [Doubts about the Story of Xi Shi]. *Xiandai wenxue* 現代文學 (44):84–90.

Tseng Yong-yih 曾永義. 2003. "Xi Shi gushi" 西施故事 [The Story of Xi Shi]. In *Su wenxue gailun* 俗文學概論 [*An Introduction to Popular Literature*], edited by Zeng Yongyi. Sanmin shuju.

Tuotuo (Toqto) 脫脫, et al. 1975. *Jinshi* 金史 [*History of the Jin Dynasty*] 6 Vols. Zhonghua shuju

Wang Bocheng 王伯成. Zhu Xi 朱禧, ann. 1986. *Tianbao yishi zhugongdiao* 天寶遺事諸宮調 [*The All-Modes on Old Affairs from the Tianbao Reign*]. Tianjin guji chubanshe.

Wang Gang 王鋼. 1991. *Jiaoding "Lugui bu" sanzhong* 校訂《錄鬼簿》三種 [*Collating and Correcting Three Editions of the "Register of Ghosts"*]. Zhongzhou guji chubanshe.

Wang Guowei 王國維. 1915. *Song Yuan xiqu shi* 宋元戲曲史 [*History of the Music Drama in the Song and Yuan Dynasties*]. Shangwu yinshuguan.

Wang Jide 王冀德. 1614. *Xin jiaozhu guben* Xixiangji 新校注古本西廂記 [*New Corrections and Notes to the Old Edition of the "Story of the Western Wing"*]. Wangshi Xiangxue ju.

Wang Rubi 王汝弼, ed. 1980. *Bai Juyi xuanji* 白居易選集 [*A Selection of Bai Juyi's Writing*]. Shanghai guji chubanshe.

Wang Shifu 王實甫. Ming, Hongzhi 1499 ed. Printed by Yue Family of Jintai, ed. 2006. *Xinkan dazi kuiben quanxiang canzeng qimiao zhushi Xixiang ji* 新刊大字魁本全相參增奇妙註釋西廂記 [*Newly Published Large Character Fine Edition of the "Story of the Western Wing" with Full Illustrations and Remarkable Added Notes*]. 2 vols. Hebei jiaoyu chubanshe.

Wang, Shifu. Stephen H. West and Wilt L. Idema, eds. and trans. 1995. *Story of the Western Wing*. University of California Press.

Wang Yong 王栐1981. *Yanyi yimou lu* 燕翼詒謀錄 [*A Record of Giving Benefits to Descendants*]. Zhonghua shuju.

Wang, Yuanfei. 2021. "What Hangs on a Hairpin: Inalienable Possession and Language Exchange in Two Marriage Romances." *Ming Studies* 2021: 3–21.

Wang Zhihan 王之涵. 2015. "Song guanben zaju duanshu yanjiu" 宋官本雜劇段數研究 [Studies of the List of Official Variety Plays.] Ph. D., Shanghai shifan daxue 上海師範大學 (112100017).

Wang Zhuo 王灼 and Yue Zhen 岳珍, ann. 2000. *Biji manzhi jiaozheng* 碧雞漫志校正 [*Collation and Correction of the "Record of the Ward of the Azure Cock"*]. Ba Shu shushe.

Wang Zuoliang 王作良. 2004. "Zhao Lingzhi guzici 'Shangdiao Die lian hua' jianlun" 趙令畤鼓子詞 《商調蝶戀花》 簡論 [A Brief Discussion of Zhao Lingzhi's Drum Song 'Shangdiao mode Die lian hua']. *Xi'an Jianzhu keji daxue xuebao* 西安建築科技大學學報23:11–13.

Wei Qingzhi 魏慶之. 2007. *Shiren yuxie* 詩人玉屑 [*Jade Chips from Poets*]. Vol. 1. Zhonghua shuju.

West, Stephen H. 2021. "Autumn Thoughts: Shared Images, Shifting Phrases, and Promiscuous Poetics." *Early Medieval China* 27: 101–120.

West, Stephen H. and Wilt L. Idema. 2010. *Monks, Bandits, Lovers and Immortals: Eleven Early Chinese Plays*. Hackett Publishing.

West, Stephen H. and Wilt L. Idema. 2025. *Winners and Losers in the World of Dust*. Brill Publishing.

Wu Runting 武潤婷. 2023. *Tianbao yishi zhugongdiao jilu jiaozhu* 天寶遺事諸宮調輯錄校注 [*Compiled and Annotated Edition of the All-Keys-and-Modes of the Tianbao Years*]. Renmin wenxue chubanshe.

Wu Xinmiao 吳新苗. 2005. "*Yuming tang piding Dong Xixiang* wei Tang Xianzu zuo kaolun" 《玉茗堂批订董西厢》 為湯顯祖作考論" [Considering Whether the *Dong Western Wing from the Studio of the Jade Camelia* Was Composed by Tang Xianzu]. *Nanchang daxue xuebao* 南昌大學學報36 (6): 131–133.

Wu Zimu 吳自牧. Fu Linxiang 傅林祥, ann. 2000. *Mengliang lu* 夢粱錄, in *Mengliang lu, Wulin jiushi* 夢粱錄，武林舊事 [*A Record of a Dream that Passed While a Pot of Millet Cooked* and *Old Affairs of Wulin*]. Shandong youyi chubanshe.

Wu, Yenna. 1995. *The Chinese Virago*. Harvard-Yenching Institute.

Xia Xinyan 夏心言. 2017. "*Dong Jieyuan Xixiang ji* banben de liubian" 《董解元西廂記》 版本的流變 [On the Dispersal of Editions of *Laureate Dong's Story of the Western Wing*. *Wenxian shuangyue kan* 文獻雙月刊1: 82–90.

Xiao, Tong and David R. Knechtges, trans. 1982. *Wen xuan or Selections of Refined Literature, Volume One: Rhapsodies on Metropolises and Capitals*. Princeton University Press.

Xiao, Tong and David R. Knechtges, trans. 1996. *Wen xuan or Selections of Refined Literature, Volume Two: Rhapsodies on Natural Phenomena, Birds and Animals, Aspirations and Feelings, Sorrowful Laments, Literature, Music, and Passions*. Princeton University Press.

Xu Dajun 徐大軍. 2023. "Yi shi chuan wen: jingshiyanyi yu Song Yuan tongsu ciqu xushi xingtai" 以詩傳文：經史演義與宋元通俗詞曲敍事形態 [Transmitting Prose Text by Poetry: Romances on the Classics and History and the Narrative Forms of Popular Ci Lyrics]. *Wenxue yichan* 文學遺產 (5):139–149.

Xu Shuofang 徐朔方. 1984. "*Yuming tang piding Dong Xixiang* bianwei" 《玉茗堂批订董西厢》辨伪 [On the Fake *Laureate Dong's Western Chamber from the Studio of the Jade Camelia*]. *Shehui kexue zhanxian* 社會科學戰線 (2): 328–329.

Xu Yaozuo. Richard Lynn, trans. 2020. "The Tale of Miss Liu." In *Anthology of Tang and Song Tales: The Tang Song chuanqi ji of Lu Xun*, ed. by Lu Xun and Victor Mair, 84–92. World Scientific.

Xue Mingzhen 薛明貞. 2016. "Zhang Dafu de jibing xushi yanjiu" 張打復的疾病敍事研究 [Studies on the Narratives of Zhang Dafu's Illness]. MA, National Zhengzhi University.

Yang Wanli 楊萬里. 2007. "Chengzhai Guiqulaixi yin" 誠齋歸去來兮引 [Chengzhai's Introduction to *Songs of Returning*]. In *Yang Wanli ji jianjiao* 楊萬里集箋校, edited by Xin Gengru 辛更儒. Zhonghua shuju.

Yang, Xiaoshan. 2022. "Dream, Memory, and Reflection: Transfigurations of Su Shi's Qiuchi Rock in Song Poetry." *Journal of Chinese Humanities* 7, no. 3: 310–341. https://doi.org/ https://doi.org/10.1163/23521341-12340119.

Yang Yu 楊瑀. *Shanju xinhua* 山居新話 [*New Talks from Dwelling in the Mountains*]. In *Siku quanshu* [*Complete Texts of the Four Bibliographic Categories*]. Ai'ersheng Center for the Study of Digitalization. http://server. wenzibase.com.libproxy.berkeley.edu.

Yang Zhaoying 楊朝英. 1958. *Chaoye xinsheng Taiping yuefu* 朝野新聲太平樂府 [*New Musical Songs of an Era of Peace at Court and Abroad*]. Zhonghua shuju.

Yu Han 于涵. 2019. "Qian xi *Guben Dong Jieyuan Xixiang ji* zhugongdiao zhong de huanjing miaoxie" 浅析《古本董解元西厢记》诸宫调中的环境描写 [A Cursory Analysis of the Depicted Environment in *The Old Edition of Laureate Dong's Western Chamber*]. *Mingzuo xinshang* 名作欣賞 (6): 151–153.

Yu Tianchi 于天池. 1999. "Songdai wenren shuochang jiyi guzici" 宋代文人說唱伎藝鼓子詞 [Song Literati Prosimetric Arts: Drum Songs]. *Beijing shifan daxue xuebao* 北京師範大學學報 (5):86–90.

Yu Yunfei 于韻菲. 2009. "*Shilin guangji* zhi *Yuan chengshuang shuangshengzi ji* yijie" 《事林廣記》之《願成雙·雙勝子急》譯解 [An Explanatory Note on the *Shuangsheng zi ji* from the Suite *Yuan chengshuang* in the *Extensive Record of a Forest of Affairs*]. *Wenhua yishu yanjiu* 文化藝術研究2 (6): 181–185.

Yu Yunfei 于韻菲. 2015. "Songdai chang zhuan *Yuan chengshuang* pu xinyi' chuyi" 宋代唱賺「願成雙」譜新譯芻議 [My humble opinion on a new translation of *Yuanchengshuang* formulary and singing the *zhuan* in the Song]." *Zhongguo yinyue xue* 中國音樂學 (3): 12–18.

Yu Zhenrong 余崢嶸. 2014. "Chuancheng yu ronghe—zhugongdiao yu nanxi ji liyuanxi de guanxi" 傳承與融合—諸宮調與南戲及梨園戲的關係 [Receiving and Melding: The Relationship between the All-Modes and the Pear Garden Plays]. *Taiyuan chengshi zhiye jishu xueyuan xuebao* 太原城市職業技術學院學報12 (161): 195–197.

Yuan Ke 袁珂. 1983. *Shanhai jing jiaozhu* 山海經校注 [*Annotated Edition of the Classic of Mountains and Seas*]. Shanghai guji chubanshe.

Zeng Gongliang et al. 1988. *Wujing zongyao* 武經總要 [*General Principles of Military Classics*]. In *Zhongguo bingshu jicheng* 中國兵書集成 [*Compilation of Chinese Books on Warfare*]. Liao Shen shushe.

Zhang Dafu 張大復. 1986. *Meihua caotang ji* 梅花草堂集 [*Pen Notes from the Grass Hut of Beautiful Flowers*]. In *Xuxiu siku chuanshu* 續修四庫全書 [*Supplement to the Complete Library of the Four Classes*], vol. 1380. Shanghai guji chubanshe.

Zhang Haimei 張海媚. 2014. *Jindai zhugongdiao cihui yanjiu* 金代諸宮調詞滙研究 [*Studies in the Lexicon of All-Keys-and-Modes from the Jin*]. Nanjing daxue chubanshe.

Zhang Hua 張華. Fan Ning 范寧, ed. 1980. *Bowu zhi jiaozheng* 博物志校證 [*Corrected Version of the "Record of Wide Learning"*]. Zhonghua shuju.

Zhang Xuehuan 張雪歡. 2020. "Zai yi zhugongdiao zhi yun yu gongdiao" 再議諸宮調之韻與宮調 [A Second Discussion of the Rhymes and Modes of All-Keys-and-Modes]. *Tianjin yinyue xueyuan xuebao* 天津音樂學院學報 4.48–53, 63.

Zhang Yan 張炎. 1981. "Ci yuan zhu" 詞源注 [Notes to The Font of Ci]. In *Ci yuan zhu; Yuefu zhimi jianshi* 詞源注；樂府指迷箋釋, edited by Xia Chengtao 夏承燾. In *Zhongguo gudian wenxue lilun piping zhuanzhu xuanji* 中國古典文學理論批評專著選輯, 1–33. Renmin wenxue chubanshe.

Zhang Yan 張炎. 1986. "Ci yuan" 詞源 [The Font of Ci]. In *Cihua congbian* 詞話叢編 [*Collection of Literary Discussions of Ci*], edited by Tang Guizhang 唐圭璋, 235–272. Zhonghua shuju.

Zhang Yu 張羽. 2014. *Shi ben shi* 詩本事 [*Affairs Turned to Poetry*]. In *Congshu jicheng chubian* 叢書集成初編 [*First Compilation of the Collection of Series of Texts*], edited by Wang Rizhuo 王日卓, Zhang Chao 張朝. Shanghai shudian.

Zhang Yuchu 張宇初, Shao Yizheng 邵以正 and Zhang Guoxiang 張國祥, eds. 1985. "Shangqing yufu Wulei dafa yuqu lingwen-Jilüling dashen" 上清玉府五雷大法玉樞靈文——祭律令大神 [Noumenal Script from the Jade Pivot of the Great Method of the Five Thunder Gods in the Jade Precincts of Upper Clarity]. In *Daofa huiyuan* 道法會元 [*Corpus of Daoist Ritual*]. In *Zhengtong Daozang* 正統道藏 [*Daoist Corpus of the Zhengtong Reign*], 128a–b. Hsin wenfeng chuban

Zhang Yue 張說1937. *Zhang Yangong ji* 張燕公集 [*Collected Works of Zhang Yue*]. Vol. 1846. *Congshu jicheng chubian* 叢書集成初編 [*First Compilation of the Collection of Series of Texts*]. Shangwu yinshuguan.

Zhang, Zhenjun, trans. 2010. "Huo Xiaoyu zhuan" 霍小玉傳 [The Tale of Huo Shaoyu]. In *Tang Dynasty Tales: A Guided Reader*, edited by William Nienhauser, 189–232. World Scientific.

Zhao Jingshen 趙景深. 1940. "Tianbao yishi zhugongdiao jiyi" 天寶遺事諸宮調輯逸 [Edited Remains of the All-Modes on Old Affairs from the Tianbao Reign]. *Xueshu* 學術 3: 123–56.

Zhao Lingzhi 趙令時. 2000. "Yuan Weizhi 'Cui Yingying' Shang diao Dielian hua ci" 元微之「崔鶯鶯」商調《蝶戀花》詞 [The Ci Lyric to the Shang mode and formula "Butterflies Love Flowers" of Yuan Zhen's "Story of Oriole Cui"]. In *Houqing lu, Moke huixi, Xu Moke huixi* 侯鯖錄 [*A Record of Tasty Feasts*], 墨客揮犀 [A Literary Man Shaking his Fly-Whisk],續墨客揮犀[*Continuation of A Literary Man Shaking his Fly-Whisk*], edited by Kong Fanli, 135–143. Zhonghua shuju.

Zhao Ye 趙曄. Huang Rensheng 黃仁生, ann. and trans.Li Zhenxing 李振興, coll. 2009. *Xinyi Wu Yue chunqiu* 新譯吳越春秋 [*A New Translation of the Spring and Autumn Annals of the States of Wu and Yue*]. Sanmin shuju.

Zheng Sixiao 鄭思肖.1991. *Zheng Sixiao wenji* 鄭思肖文集 [*Collected Writings of Zhen Sixiao*]. Shanghai guji chubanshe.

Zheng, Guangzu. 2010. "Dazed Behind the Green Ring Lattice, Qiannü's Soul Leaves Her Body." In *Monks, Bandits, Lovers, and Immortals: Eleven Early Chinese Plays*, edited and translated by Stephen H. West and Wilt L. Idema, 195–235. Hackett Publishing.

Zhou Mi 周密. Li Xiaolong 李小龍 and Zhao Rui 趙銳, eds. 2007. *Chatu ben Wulin jiushi* 插圖本武林舊事 [*"Old Affairs of Wulin" with Pictures*]. Zhonghua shuju.

Zhou Qi 周琪. 2023. *Yuan jue jing* 圓覺經 [*Sutra of Perfect Enlightenment*]. CBETA X0253.

Zhu Decai 朱德才, ed. 1997. *Zeng ding zhushi Quan Song ci* 增訂注釋全宋詞 [*Enlarged Version of the Complete Song Ci Lyrics with Explanatory Notes*]. Vol. 4. Wenhua yishu chubanshe.

Zhu Hong 朱鴻. 2005. "Zhugongdiao de zuojia yu zuopin" 諸宮調的作家與作品 [The Works and Authors of All-Keys-and-Modes] *Huanghe keji daxue xuebao* 黃河科技大學學報 7 (4): 69–71.

Zhu Xi 朱熹. 1958. *Shi ji zhuan* 詩集傳 [Notes on the *Classic of Poetry*]. Zhonghua shuju.

Zhu Xi 朱熹. 1983. *Sishu zhangju jizhu* 四書章句集注 [*Collected Comments on each Section of the "Four Books"*]. Zhonghua shuju.

Zhu Yixuan 朱一玄. 1997. *Ming chenghua shuochang cihua congkan* 明成化說唱詞話叢刊 [*Collected Printing of the Ci Lyric Tale Prosimetric from the Chenghua Reign of the Ming*]. Zhengzhou guji chubanshe.

Zhu Youdun 朱有敦, Liao Ben 廖奔, and Liao Li 廖立, ann. 2017. *Zhu Youdun zaju ji jiaozhu* 朱有敦雜劇集校注 [*Collation and Notes to the Zaju Collection of Zhu Youdun*]. Vol 2. Huangshan shushe.

Zhuang Yifu 莊一拂. 1982. *Gudian xiqu cunmu huikao* 古典戲曲存目彙考 [*Comprehensive Investigation of the Extant Titles of Traditional Drama*]. Vol. 1. Shanghai guji chubanshe.

Wind Enters the Pines	風入松	*Feng ru song*
Wooden Fish-Sounding Board	木魚兒	*Muyu'er*
Woodpecker in the Flowers	間花啄木兒	*Jianhua zhuomu'er*
Worried About Seeing the Emperor	朝天急	*Chaotian ji*
Yellow Oriole	黃鶯兒	*Huang ying'er*
Yizhou Tremolo	伊州袞	*Yizhou gun*

A. Songs by Chinese Titles

An gongzi	安公子	*Master An*
Bi mudan	碧牡丹	*Blue-Green Peony*
Bohai ling	渤海令	*Song of Bohai*
chan, chanling	纏令、纏	*A Bound Suite*
Changshou xian gun	長壽仙滾	*Long-Life Immortals Tremolo*
Chaotian ji	朝天急	*Worried About Seeing the Emperor*
Chu duizi	出隊子	*Sending Out the Dance Troupe*
Da sheng yue	大聖樂	*Music of the Great Sage*
Dian jiangchun	點絳唇	*Dotting Crimson Lips*
Ding feng bo	定風波	*Settling Windblown Waves*
Dongxian ge	洞仙隔	*Song of Immortals in a Cavern*
Dou anchun	鬥鵪鶉	*Fighting Quail*
Dou ye huang	豆葉黃	*Bean Leaves Yellow*
Fen die'er	粉蝶兒	*Powdery Butterfly*
Feng ru song	風入松	*Wind Enters the Pines*
Fengchui lianye	風吹蓮葉	*Wind Blows the Lotus Leaves*
Gan huang'en	感皇恩	*Moved by the Emperor's Grace*
Gancaozi	甘草子	*Dried Licorice Root*
Gu Luntai	古輪台	*Old Bögör*
Guadi feng	刮地風	*A Ground-Scraping Wind*
Haha ling	哈哈令	*Guffawing Song*
Haihai ling	哈哈令	*Laughing Song*
Hechuan ling	河傳令	*Spread by the River Song*
Hong luo ao	紅羅襖	*Red Silk Padded Jacket*
Hu da tu	鶻打兔	*The Hawk Takes the Hare*

Huan jing le	還京樂	*Happiness of Returning to the Capital*
Huang ying'er	黃鶯兒	*Yellow Oriole*
Huangjin tai	黃金臺	*A Platform of Gold*
Huaxin dong	花心動	*The Flower's Heart Trembles*
Hun jiang long	混江龍	*Dragon that Muddies the River (Dredge)*
Ji quzi	急曲子	*An Accelerando Song*
Jiang huanglong gun	降黃龍袞	*Descending Yellow Dragon, Tremolo*
Jianhua zhuomu'er	間花啄木兒	*Woodpecker in the Flowers*
Jiao zhengpa	攪箏琶	*Tuning the Strings*
Jie bozi	揭鉢子	*Raising the Alms Bowl*
Jie hong	解紅	*Untying the Red*
Jihe xiang	芰荷香	*Leaves of Lotus and Water Caltrop are Fragrant*
Kanhua hui	看花回	*Coming Back from Looking at Flowers*
Kuaihuo'er	快活兒	*Jolly Child* (or *Joyfulness*)
Kuilei	傀儡	*Puppets*
Le shen ling	樂神令	*Pleasing the Spirits*
Li he cao	離鶴操	*Parting Cranes*
Lian xiang qin	戀香衾	*Quilt with the Fragrance of Love*
Liangzhou	梁州	*Liang Prefecture*
Liangzhou ling	梁州令	*Liang Prefecture Song*
Liangzhou santai	梁州三臺	*Liang Prefecture: Three Terraces*
Lin jiangxian	臨江仙	*Approaching the River Sylph*
Liu ye'er	柳葉兒	*Willow Leaves*
Liu(Lu)yao shicui	六幺實催	*Minor Sixth Accelerando*
Liuyao bian	六幺遍	*One Minor Sixth Section of the Great Song*
Luyao/Lüyao ling	六幺令、綠腰令	*Song of a Green Waist*
Ma pozi	麻婆子	*Pockmarked Crone*
Man jiang hong	滿江紅	*A River Running Red*
Man ting shuang	滿庭霜	*Frost That Fills the Courtyard*

Meixiao yue	梅稍月	The Moon on Branch Tips of a Plum Tree
Meizhong mei	美中美	Beauty Within Beauty
Mu shanxi	驀山溪	Jumping Across a Mountain Stream
Mulan hua	木蘭花	Magnolia Blossoms
Muyang guan	牧羊關	Shepherd's Pass
Muyu'er	木魚兒	A Wooden Fish Sounding Board
Pinglan ren	憑欄人	Someone Leaning on the Rail
Qiangtou hua	牆頭花	Flowers on the Wall
Qianqiu jie	千秋節	Tang Xuanzong's Birthday Song
Qiao hesheng	喬和聲	Clever Harmonizing
Qiao zhuo she	喬捉蛇	Comically Catching a Snake
Qing Xuanhe	慶宣和	Celebrating the Xuanhe Reign
Qingshan kou	青山口	Green Mountain Pass
Qing yu an	清玉案	The Case of Unblemished Jade
Qinyuan chun	沁園春	Spring in the Princess's Garden
Qushen ling	渠神令	Song of the Canal Spirit
Ruilian'er	瑞蓮兒	Auspicious Lotus Song
Sai'er ling	塞兒令	Song of the Passes
Santai	三臺	Three Terraces
Shang Pingxi	上平西	The Emperor Quells the West
Shanghua shi	賞花時	The Season to Appreciate Flowers
Shaobian	哨遍	Whistling Song
Shen zhang'er	神仗兒	A Guard of Spirits
Sheng hulu	勝葫蘆	The Winning Gourd
Shixiang jintong	侍香金童	Golden Lad Minding Incense
Shua hai'er	耍孩兒	Playing the Child
Shuangsheng dieyun	雙生疊韻	Alliteration and Rhyming
Shuilong yin	水龍吟	Water Dragon Chant
Si menzi	四門子	The Four Disciples

Sumuzhe (samāche?)	蘇幕遮	*Persian Sprinkling Dance*
Taiping zhuan	太平賺	*Great Peace Beguiling Style*
Tang duo ling	糖多令	*Song of Lots of Sugar*
Tasuo xing	踏莎行	*Song of Treading the Sedge*
Ti yindeng	剔銀燈	*Trimming the Silver Lamp*
Tianxia le	天下樂	*Happiness Under Heaven*
Tihu Xiangshan hui	醍醐香山會	*Enlightened at the Meeting on Incense Peak*
Ting qian liu	廳前柳	*Willow at the Front of the Courtyard*
Tuo bushan	脫布衫	*Doffing the Cotton Shirt*
Wei	尾	*Coda*
Wen ru jin	文如錦	*Patterned Like Embroidery*
Wen Xu zi	文序子	*Master Wen Xu*
Wu yinzi	吳音字	*Sounds of Wu*
Xi huanghua	惜黃花	*Cherishing the Chrysanthemum*
Xi nu jiao	惜奴嬌	*Cherishing My Love's Beauty*
Xi qian ying	喜遷鶯	*Delighting in Orioles Aflight*
Xi xinchun	喜新春	*Delight in Springtime Anew*
Xiangfeng he	香風合	*Fragrant Winds Converge*
Xiangshan hui	香山會	*Meeting on Incense Peak*
Xiangsi hui	相思會	*Love Rendezvous*
Xiu dai'er	繡帶兒	*The Embroidered Belt*
Xueli mei	雪裏梅	*A Plum in the Snow*
Xueli meihua	雪裏梅	*Plum Blossoms in the Snow*
Yaotai yue	瑤台月	*Moon on the Jasper Terrace*
Ye you gong	夜遊宮	*Roaming at Night in the Palace*
Yihu cha	一斛叉	*A Big Forkload*
Ying tian chang	應天長	*Responding to Lengthening Days*
Ying xianke	迎仙客	*Welcoming the Immortal One*
Yiyi ling	台台令	*Happy As Can Be*

Yizhi hua	一枝花	A Sprig of Flowers
Yizhou gun	伊州衮	Yizhou Tremolo
Yu bao du	玉抱肚	Jade Enwraps the Stomach
Yu feile	于飛樂	A Perfect Marriage
Yue shang haitang	月上海棠	Moonlight Climbs up the Crabapple
Yujia ao	漁家傲	Fisherman's Haughtiness
Yujie xing	御街行	Treading the Imperial Avenue
Yuyi chan	玉翼蟬	A Jade-Winged Cicada
Zheng huaguan	整花冠	Arranging the Flowered Hat
Zheng jinguan	整金冠	Adjusting a Ritual Cap of Gold
Zheng qiankun	整乾坤	Setting the Cosmos Right
Zhezhi ling	柘枝令	Melonberry Branch Song
Zhuan	賺	Beguiling Song
Zhuan qingshan	轉青山	Return to the Green Mountains
Zhuo gu zhou	棹孤舟	Sculling a Solitary Boat
Zhuozhuo qi	倬倬戚	Boundless Sorrow
Zui luopo	醉落魄	Drunk and Down on My Luck
Zui Xi po	醉奚婆	Drunken Mama Xi

Text-Critical Endnotes

Endnotes to Book 1

i. From a story first found in *The Record of Wide Learning* (*Bowu zhi* 博物志), in which a man who dwells by the sea sees a raft float by every year in the eighth month. One year, he prepares clothing and supplies and boards it. After a long period of travel, he arrives at a city with walls and residences, where he sees a woman weaving at a loom and meets a man leading an ox to drink in the river. When he asks where he is, he is told to wait until he has reached Shu (the area of modern Sichuan) on his return voyage and there to question a certain Yan Zun 嚴遵 (byname Junping 君平), a famous astrologer. He does as he is instructed, and Yan informs him that "on a certain day of a certain month a transient star encroached on the Islet of the Ox"—on a constellation in the Milky Way, that is. It is then that he realizes that he has floated beyond the confluence of the Yellow River and the Milky Way and out onto the Silver River itself: the man and woman he encountered were the Herdboy (Niulang 牛郎) and the Weaving Girl (Zhinü織女), both also Chinese names for constellations roughly around the stars Altair and Vega. These were two lovers separated by the Milky Way and allowed to meet only once a year, on the seventh day of the seventh month, when magpies fly up from earth to form a bridge for them to cross. In later times the traveler on the raft became associated with Zhang Qian 張騫 (d. 114 BCE, byname Ziwen 子文), a famous explorer of the Han period who traveled extensively in Central Asia. Bearing the same surname as student Zhang, this explorer of wild and uncharted waters is an apt allusion to the young student and the adventure on which he is about to embark. See also Zhang Hua 1980, 111.

ii. Reading *matou* 馬頭 as a phonetic equivalent of *matou* 碼頭.

iii. The texts of *Laureate Dong's All-Keys-and-Modes of the Western Chamber* all write this name as Feng Zhi 封陟 but most of the annotators replace it with封騭, a man who refused four marriage proposals from a goddess. See Li Fang 1986, 424–426.

iv. I am following DJY, 106, in understanding the line as a metaphor. DJY08, 59 and DJY09, 36 both understand the line as referring to the basin of an actual water clock.

Endnotes to Book 2

i. DJY, 118 provides variants *tangyi* 猱夷、唐衣 and *tangni* 猱猊, noting the first appearance of the word in the *Spring and Autumn Annals of the States of Wu and Yue*; see Zhao Ye 2009, 364. DJY08, 42 translates this as "Two suits of lion-hide armor." According to Huang Rensheng's notes on the *Spring and Autumn* passage (Zhao Ye 2009, 366, n. 7), this is a homophonic transliteration for the term *tangyi* 棠鋏, which is a general term for armor.

ii. Following DJY, 121 in understanding *bu fangfu* 不彷彿 as an error (or unknown usage) for the more common *bu tibei* 不隄備.

iii. As DJY, 130 notes, this phrase (胯大臀腰) is either comparative, as it is translated here, or 腰 is a mistranscription for something else.

iv. This line calls for a rhyme in the category of *xiaohao* 蕭豪 (-au) which does not occur here. I am, however, counting it as the end of a rhymed line.

v. This line also calls for a rhyme; in this and the case above, the phrase *dudang* 睹當, to "withstand" or "defend," takes the place of a rhyming phrase, accentuating the phrase.

vi. These two lines once again call for a rhyme in the category of *xiaohao* 蕭豪 (-au); in both cases the phrase *dudang* 睹當, to "withstand" or "defend," takes the place of a rhyming phrase, accentuating the need to defend the monastery.

vii. Tentative translation for the phrase *ye ma yiyi* 也麼台台.

viii. This passage of parallel prose is found in the earliest printing of the work but is deleted in this edition. I have restored it for the reader, uncertain if the deletion was accidental or on purpose.

ix. From the opening chapter of the *Zuo Commentary* to the *Spring and Autumn Annals*. Duan was the favorite son of Madam Jiang, the wife of the late Duke of the state of Zheng. Her older son, Duke Zhuang, was the first born but was a breech birth delivery and was thought unlucky by his mother, who fought to have Duan placed in the line of succession. Following his mother's wishes to some extent, Duke Zhuang placed his younger brother as head of the fief of Jing. Duan built a power base there and Duke Zhuang was warned by his ministers to attack Duan. Zhuang insisted that Duan would cause his own downfall and that he would strike when the time was right. He finally attacked Duan, who had fomented a coup with his mother's aid. The fief of Jing rebelled against Duan during the attack and Duan fled to the fief of Gong, where he was finally crushed (his full historical name is Gong shu Duan: literally, Duan the younger from the Fief of Gong). While the *Zuo Commentary* accuses Duan of being unfilial to his brother, it also levies a criticism against Duke Zhuang for "failing his teaching" by acceding to his mother's private wishes to install Duan rather than fulfilling what the rites called for. Thus, the author of the *Zuo* gives Zhuang a historical name (Zheng bo 鄭伯), Earl of Zheng, the second of five feudal ranks, rather than the title Duke of Zheng, which would be the normal designation for rulers of large states. See Durrant, Li, and Schaberg 2017, vol. 1, 9–13.

x. Reading *Xueli mei* 雪裏梅 for *Xue'er mei* 雪兒梅.

xi. DJY04, 56b gives a longer marginal note here that is missing in the text used here for the translation: "This has a far deeper flavor than the passages like, 'spring-like face' and 'being suitable for anger or joy'" 較宜嗔、宜喜、春風面等語，味深多矣. It is unclear if this note is copied from a different edition of the Tang Xianzu text, or if it was added to clarify the meaning of the marginal text to which it referred.

xii. The literate reader would recognize this as a line cobbled together from two lyric poems, one by Fan Zhongyan 范仲淹 (989–1015), and the other by Ouyang Xiu 歐陽修 (1007–1072). From Fan's poem, titled "Embosoming the Past" 懷舊, to the lyric pattern *Sumuzhe* 蘇幕遮,:

酒入愁腸, / 化作相思淚<u>Wine enters my grieving bowels</u>, / transforming into tears of love's longing.

From Ouyang's poem, to the lyric pattern *Ding fengbo* 定風波:

把酒花前欲問他，/ 對花何吝<u>醉顏酡</u>。Holding wine before the flowers, I want to ask him, / Facing these flowers, why begrudge your <u>drunken face turning red</u>?

This is an excellent example of how "catchy" phrases in the literary canon were appropriated into the world of colloquial literature.

Endnotes to Book 3

i. Based on the first stanza of Wu Ji's 吳激 (1090–1142) lyric poem to the formula (*cipai* 詞牌) "Spring Comes from Heaven" 春從天上來. See Tang Guizhang 1979, vol. 1, 6.

ii. A difficult line to interpret. DJY08, 108 has it as: "Mother's principal objection / Is that Brother Chang hasn't yet distinguished himself." DJY07, 167 reads: "The important circumstance here, / is that Student Zhang is still unclear about things." DJY, 231 reads: "The problem is that brother has not looked carefully into the situation." DJY, 230 remarks, "The idea here is that Student Zhang has still not clearly investigated secrets I have that are hard for me to speak of, so he teases me." .

iii. DJY01 has the phrase 云云 here. This probably designates a point in the story where the performer has freedom to improvise an *ad libitum*. As the introduction points out, since these phrases occur at suspenseful moments, they may have been used to solicit money from the audience. The editor of this text, however, reads it here in its more common use as a marker for the repetition of a prior phrase.

iv. Following DJY, 264 and identifying this as an independent suite since it belongs to the *Zhonglü diao* mode and not to the *Gaoping diao* mode, which never takes a coda.

v. Following the notes of DJY, 271, which translates the term *shenjiao* 神腳 as "blockhead" (*baka no* 馬鹿め). However, the same note also suggests that this term could refer to the role-type that plays a ghost or spirit on stage or at court. This would fit with the scene, where Student Zhang's body wobbling along appears to be acting out the movements a spirit might make on stage. The allusion to role types and acting also reveals the dramatized and staged nature of Zhang's illness.

vi. It is unclear to whom the pronoun "I" refers. DJY06, 222 takes it to refer to Oriole; DJY07, 148 to Student Zhang; DJY, 293 and DJY08, 268 leave it ambiguous.

vii. The use of the word *xian* 險 here offers two possible interpretations: "I consider that the offense I have committed makes it dangerous for me to go now and have drinks," or "My own role in this offense is insidious and not clearly out in the open; it is something I brought on myself."

Endnotes to Book 4

i. This entire aria is a reworking of a long lyric poem by Liu Yong, the celebrated poet and lover of the Song dynasty.
See Zhu Decai 1997, vol. 1, 88.

ii. This edition writes the two characters 云云 as 云ﾉ, and places them before the full stop (○). In the earliest edition the text is unpunctuated so the same phrase 云ﾉ could also mean, "improvise" or "*ad libitum*" at this point.

iii. This may also be understood as "removes the heart" greens. It is not *ipomoea aquatica,* the "empty-heart green" or "water spinach" (*kongxin cai* 空心菜) known in the West by its Cantonese name, Ongchoi (蕹菜), but refers to crow-dipper (*pinellia ternata*), called "heartless greens" (*wuxin cai* 無心菜). Here the citation refers to the fictional account of the Shang minister Bi Gan 比干 in the novel *Investiture of the Gods* (封神演義), who is forced to cut out his own heart. After leaving the capital, he runs into a woman selling "no heart greens," who tells him a person without a heart would soon die. Bi Gan immediately dies.

iv. The term 捻 (here pronounced *nie*) has several meanings, one of which is to "patch up a hole or a crack." DJY07, 304 simply says, "my clothes are beautiful." DJY09, 329 says, "my clothes are particularly nice." DJY08, 206 says, "my clothes are impeccably tailored," which comes closer to the idea of smoothing out his form by adding material to take away the ugly posture.

v. DJY, 402 reads *buzheng* 不爭 as *naihe* 奈何; DJY07, 327 translates as "It's of no consequence if you die, but...."(你兩個死了不大緊). DJY08, 222 translates as "It's fine for you to die."

vi. There is a great deal of discussion of this term, *guzhang* 骨脹, in DJY, 410; DJY07, 336; and DJY06, 168. The term frequently occurs for obstruction of the throat caused by swelling or material obstruction, particularly in veterinary texts. This is extended to mean: "to rely on one's power," "to obstruct or get in the way," "to be an obstacle to another." Since the symptoms seem to occur in tandem with the release of pus through the nose and the inability to breathe freely, it does not conjure pleasant images.

vii. This line is unclear. I have followed DJY07, 169's understanding of the term *lanjun* 欄軍; a survey of the use of *jiahua* 夾畫 in fifty-two texts from the tenth to the seventeenth century indicates that the term is always the first two characters in a verb-adjective-noun formation, in which something is flanked by a colored object (boats, wheels, walls, etc.). This suggests some sort of painted device that might be squeezed (*jia* 挾) on a prisoner's body part to elicit a confession.

viii. "Landing smack on his back" is my translation for the phrase 吃一個大 碑落, which I understand is to suffer a fall as loud and hard as a stone stele falling.